Contemporary Perspectives on Social Learning in Early Childhood Education

A volume in
Contemporary Perspectives in Early Childhood Education
Series Editors: Olivia N. Saracho and Bernard Spodek

Contemporary Perspectives in Early Childhood Education

Series Editors:
Olivia N. Saracho, *University of Maryland,*
Bernard Spodek, *University of Illinois*

Contemporary Perspectives on Social Learning in Early Childhood Education

Edited by

Olivia N. Saracho
and
Bernard Spodek

INFORMATION AGE
PUBLISHING

Charlotte, NC • www.infoagepub.com

Library of Congress Cataloging-in-Publication Data

Contemporary perspectives on social learning in early childhood education /
edited by Olivia N. Saracho and Bernard Spodek.
    p. cm. – (Contemporary perspectives in early childhood education)
  Includes bibliographical references.
  ISBN 978-1-59311-742-9 (pbk.) – ISBN 978-1-59311-743-6 (hardcover)
  1. Social learning. 2. Early childhood education–Social aspects. 3.
Child development. I. Saracho, Olivia N. II. Spodek, Bernard.
LC192.4.C665 2007
303.3'2–dc22

                                         2007009428

Printed in the United States of America

CONSULTING EDITORS

CONTENTS

INTRODUCTION

SOCIAL LEARNING IN THE EARLY CHILDHOOD YEARS

Olivia N. Saracho and Bernard Spodek

INTRODUCTION

Social learning relates to both a content area and a set of skills, knowledge, and values that pervade all the activities in an early childhood classroom. Over the years, early childhood educators have been primarily concerned with three areas of personal social learning:

1. Social competence, including social skills that are necessary to interact appropriately with others;
2. A sense of morality and values; and
3. An understanding of roles and rules within a community.

Children need to learn how to live and work together with others within small and large communities, starting with the family, and the classroom. Additionally, they need to develop an understanding of the concepts that underlie the scholarly areas of the social sciences at a level that is developmentally appropriate. These, then, become the basis of the social pedagogy that has developed in early childhood education.

Contemporary Perspectives on Social Learning in Early Childhood Education, pages ix–xx

COMPONENTS OF A SOCIAL PEDAGOGY

Social learning is especially important for children to function within a democratic society. Social learning promotes children's emotional and practical competence, their perception of themselves, and acceptance of others regardless of their competencies and limitations. According to National Council for the Social Studies (1984), a social learning program helps young children understand and function in their personal and social worlds. Young children are active, curious, and want to learn social learning skills consisting of socialization, social values, and self awareness.

Socialization is the process by which children learn to interact with and respond to the expectations and responsibilities of different groups. In an early childhood program, young children need to learn their role in the school or center, rules of behavior, what is expected of them, society's way of life, and the important social values. They also learn the need for sharing and appropriate ways of interacting with others, including family members, peers, and teachers. Young children learn behaviors that are in harmony with the standards of a particular society.

Socialization is a particularly important role for early childhood education. The children need to move beyond the family as a social group and the early childhood class is their entrance into the larger society. They have to learn a new role within a new social institution. They have to build relationships with a wide range of individuals—adults and other children. They must learn school appropriate behavior and become competent in serving their own needs and in interacting with others. Personal competence within a social context becomes an important goal of social learning in the early childhood years.

Social Values that are essential to convey to children include concern for the worth of the individual, concepts of freedom and responsibility, the importance of democratic decision making, and care for the safety of persons and property. Children develop appropriate social values when they experience a wide array of opportunities for individual selection of goals and activities and consider the alternatives and possible consequences of their actions and of their own feelings. Young children learn social values through role playing, creative dramatics, literature, and art experiences. They also pick up the values of those around them whom they consider important, including parents and teachers.

Children's values are related to their concept of morality—what they consider to be just and right. Psychologists such as Kohlberg (Tureil, 1973) and others have identified stages of moral development in young children. The values and moral reasoning that children acquire are part of children's developmental processes. Teachers should be concerned that children do not just learn a set of moral rules or values by rote, but understand the moral judgments they can make at their own level.

Self-Awareness focuses on the young children's affective development. Children learn to explore their self-concepts, cope with feelings about themselves and others, and use appropriate ways to express themselves and interact with others. They need to learn how to cope with their emotions and become aware of themselves. Young children learn self-awareness through discussions, role playing, storytelling, and other opportunities where young children are motivated to convey their feelings or concerns with the teacher; alone or in a group. (NCSS, 1984)

Young children develop knowledge and skills that they need to function in their everyday life. They learn directly about the physical world through their senses: seeing, touching, and listening to physical things. They learn about the social world through interactions with individuals and learning to understand that their behavior is important. Recently, studies have provided evidence on the nature of young children's learning processes and on using their personal experiences as the basis for constructing knowledge and creating meaning. Thus, it is important that children be provided with immediate, first hand experiences as the basis for them to learn.

SOCIAL STUDIES PROGRAM

A social studies program can assume an important role in assisting young children to identify their responsibilities in the larger community and understand the organization of their society. They need to learn their society's values, rituals, symbols, and myths. A social studies program can include the celebration of holidays, listening to stories about historic figures and heroes, and singing traditional songs to help young children understand the organization of society and their expected roles and behaviors.

Some of the pioneers in early childhood education developed approaches to social studies that were innovative and meaningful to young children. Patty Smith Hill, a follower of John Dewey, suggested that children's social experiences are the basis for knowledge and that teachers could use the themes they develop in their dramatic play activities to learn about the world. Children play out what they know and what they experience with family, friends, and community. These can be replicated, refined, and understood (Hill, 1913).

Lucy Sprague Mitchell (1967) designed a program that helped young children use their experiences in their personal environment to learn basic concepts about geography. Abstract ideas can be illustrated with concrete materials to allow them to gain access to sophisticated knowledge. Maria Montessori (1964) also was interested in helping children see abstract ideas through concrete activities. She literally created time lines with children so they could see the relationship of historical events within a temporal framework, symbolizing time through distance on a rope so that children could begin to understand the relationship between events within the framework of historical time. Similarly, she used map puzzles to give children a sense of geography.

Traditionally, early childhood social studies programs have had a limited number of topics. Young children's experiences are with things and events that are close to them in time and space. For young children themes relate to home and family, the school (including the classroom), the neighborhood (stores, supermarkets, filling stations), and the local community (community services, agencies, and workers), as well as transportation and communication. As the children grew older, the scope of their social studies program became wider and allowed them to deal with things that were more remote in time and space. Comparative studies have also been implemented so that children could see similarities and differences among communities, such as the urban community versus the rural or suburban community.

Recently, social studies programs have widened topics for study by young children, such as family life in other countries, a broader comparative community study, and concepts from the social sciences. These include the relationship between consumers and producers from the field of economics or an understanding of actions and interactions among people from the field of sociology. In addition, social studies programs have included the following:

1. *Teaching History.* Young children can understand time concepts and history if concepts are presented at the children's developmental level. Young children are able to differentiate between past and present by age 4 and understand the cyclical and sequential nature of events by age 5 or 6. Time concepts can be taught in relation to history. When young children are introduced to historical events and ideas, they can develop an understanding of important time concepts. According to Vygotsky, this type of education can have an important effect on young children's intellectual development.

2. *Teaching Geography.* Studies on young children's understanding of space indicate that they can develop concepts of topological space (e.g., proximity, enclosure, continuity, separation, order). When young children begin to understand how things relate to each other in space, they are developing a beginning of geographic (Sunal, 1993). Young children are able to learn about their surroundings as they interpret simple maps. According to Lucy Sprague Mitchell (1967), the world is a laboratory that assists young children to develop geographic understandings.

3. *Political Socialization.* Research provides evidence that young children are intuitive political thinkers (Sunal, 1993). Presently, they understand the electoral process, the voting process, and the qualifications of the local and national candidates. An early childhood education social studies program can help them become politically socialized by taking advantage of these events. During elections, children can discuss the offices and candidates. They can also hold mock elections for the candidates or can have an election of class officers. Acting out the electoral process can assist young children to understand it.

4. *Economics.* Studies indicate that children as young as 5 can learn economic concepts and use them to make decisions. At a very early age, young children acquire economic knowledge including economic attitudes, through unprocessed direct experiences, and cognitive capacities. Young children experience economic processes daily when they go with their parents to stores and purchase commodities. They observe transactions and understand that each item has a price and can be obtained with money. When children engage in dramatic play, they can act out these roles.

Over the years, the social studies program has been organized around the young children's basic human needs. They learned how these needs are met in their home, community, the wider society, and communities more remote in time and space. The social studies program usually has themes that include the school and family, the neighborhood, and the municipality. Young children may take field trips into the community such as the bakery where they can observe how customers select and pay for bread. Later in school, they can use dramatic play to act out their interpretations of the field trip to make sense of their interpretations. Instruction in a social studies program needs to consider the children's learning abilities.

SOCIAL LEARNING AND OTHER AREAS OF KNOWLEDGE

Social learning is usually integrated with other areas of knowledge in the curriculum. According to Charlesworth (1988), preschool children can learn math and science concepts through a social studies unit. During block play, children build with blocks, act out social roles, and look at pictures. Children can create models or dioramas as part of a unit. They can also work on arts and crafts activities and develop expressive skills. Young children can use paintings, drawings, and constructions as nondiscursive ways to communicate what they have learned.

The music and literature of a culture can help young children understand its symbol system and values. Ethnic music, songs, stories, and poetry provide an important contribution to children's social learning. Good children's literature helps them to acquire insight into people, institutions, and social relationships that are difficult to describe in direct exposition. Children can sympathize with individuals when they share their feelings before they can intellectually understand them. Basic concepts of topological geometry help young children understand geography and maps. In map reading, young children can find places and determine proximity and separation.

Language and literacy are excellent resources to facilitate young children's social learning. Children create dramatic presentations or puppet shows in relation to social events. They can read about these events in books and write their own story. In dramatic play young children act out roles and relationships. They can tell or write stories that communicate their understanding of these relationships. They also need to develop language skills to effectively collect information and share their learning with others.

An integrated curricula cutting across many areas of knowledge was supported in a position paper that was developed by the Consortium for Interdisciplinary Teaching and Learning (1994) which included the major national subject-matter organizations (e.g., National Council of Teachers of Mathematics, the National Council of Teachers of English, the International Reading Association, the National Science Teachers Association, the National Council for the Social Studies, the Speech Communication Association, and the Council for Elementary Science International). Their joint position paper addressed the need for curricula to focus on conceptual learning that is integrated across traditional subject areas from Preschool to Grade 4. The participating organizations contended that young children's educational experiences need to stimulate their natural curiosity and their drive to create meaning. An emphasis on relationships across disciplines can contribute to creative problem solving and decision making. This relationship gives children the opportunity to view the perspectives, knowledge, and data-gathering skills of all the disciplines. It would also prompt young children to interact with others in a learning community where diversity in cultures is valued.

ABOUT THE BOOK

Social epistemology is a broad set of approaches to the study of knowledge and ways to gain information about the social dimensions. This intellectual movement of wide cross-disciplinary sources reconstructs the problems of epistemology when knowledge is considered to be intrinsically social. In the first chapter, "Social Epistemology and Social Learning," Olivia Saracho and Bernard Spodek discuss the social and historical contexts in which different forms of knowledge are formulated based on the perspective of social epistemology. They also discuss the emergence of social epistemology, which guides researchers to investigate social phenomena in laboratory and field settings. Social factors "external" to the appropriate business of science have a major impact in the social studies researchers' historical case studies. Thus, social studies researchers may be considered social epistemologists, because (a) they focus on knowledge of social influences and (b) they infer epistemologically significant conclusions from their sociological or anthropological research. In addition, analyses indicate that studies of scientific paradigms are basically a struggle for political power rather than reflecting reliable epistemic merit. Social studies researchers focus on knowledge of social influences on knowledge, which is analogous to the knowledge of the social epistemologists. They also use their sociological or anthropological research to infer epistemologically significant conclusions.

During the early years, a primary developmental task for children is to coordinate the social rules, beliefs, and values that they learn from adults with their own individual social insights and their interaction with peers. Teachers have considerable influence on the social beliefs of children in the early childhood years and on the social dynamics of the classroom. They are able to promote social competence and adjustment by creating contexts that are supportive of the behavioral and social needs of their students. Teachers scaffold and guide children in new interactions and relationships in ways that foster productive social roles and while preventing problematic social behavior. In the second chapter titled, "Social Dynamics of Early Childhood Classrooms: Considerations and Implications for Teachers," Kathleen Cranley Gallagher, Kimberly Dadisman, Thomas W. Farmer, Laura Huss, and Bryan C. Hutchins consider how social interchanges and classroom social dynamics contribute to children's early school adaptation.

In the next chapter titled, "The Development of Social Identity and Intergroup Attitudes in Young Children," Kurt Kowalski notes how the individual's social identity is considered as that part of the self that we have in common with others and that is derived from our membership in groups. This identity has important implications for both personal well-being and social behavior. This chapter examines how children's developing awareness of social group membership (e.g., gender, race, and ethnicity) supports this identity development and influences how they see themselves and others. Previous research in this area is reviewed and discussed in the context of new developments in the application of social identity and self-categorization theory to children's social development. Special attention is given to how social categories like gender and ethnicity function in young children's day-to-day social interactions as suggested by the results of a recent naturalistic study in this area conducted in kindergarten. Important implications for practice that stem from this work, and the other research reviewed, are discussed.

Early childhood is a critical time for children to develop the social, self-regulatory, and academic skills that are important for a successful transition to formal schooling. While many navigate this transition well, it can be difficult for children who have not achieved those skills needed to do well in school. The chapter, "Executive Function, Self-Regulation, and Social-Emotional Competence: Links to School Readiness" by Megan M. McClelland, Claire E. Cameron, Shannon B. Wanless, and Amy Murray, focuses on the importance of children's learning-related skills for early school success. The chapter begins with a brief outline of child and family influences on social and academic development. Then the authors define three areas of learning-related skills (including executive function, behavioral self-regulation, and social-emotional competence) and describe how they relate to early academic achievement. They also examine evidence for the assertion that these areas form a broad learning-related skill construct. Finally, they focus on teaching factors as an important influence in children's learning-related skills and achievement, and provide practical implications for improving learning-related skills and school success.

The human, financial, and social capital that children access both through their homes and through their schools is influential in promoting child well-being. In the chapter, "Capital at Home and at School as Determinants of Child Social Adjustment," Toby L. Parcel argues that child social adjustment is important in its own right and as a determinant of academic performance. She pays particular attention to the role of social capital at home and at school. Her review suggests that social capital at home is influential, while findings are less abundant and conclusive regarding the role of social capital at school. Findings are also unclear regarding the context from which capital is more important, the home or the school, although studies point to capital at home being especially influential.

The next four chapters focus on the relationship between the home environment and the school environment. In "Parenting and Schooling Influences on Early Self-Regulation Development," Abigail M. Jewkes and Frederick J. Morrison discuss two important influences on early self-regulation development: parenting and schooling. They review research studies in these two domains across the early childhood period (birth through age 8), including findings from large nationally-representative research studies and recent research conducted as part of their longitudinal study of young children's literacy development. Parenting and schooling impact children's self-regulation in unique and specific ways. They conclude with intriguing cross-cultural research between the United States and Asian countries that may help illuminate our understandings of young children's self-regulation development.

For most young children, primary caregivers, including parents, provide scaffolding, prompting, and other bridges to learning. These processes function most effectively when a positive parent–child relationship is present. In some families, however, poor parent–child relationships may blunt the effectiveness of the parent as a model or the parent may lack the critical skills to support their child's development, often as a result of their own difficult early histories. The provision of supports to parents through the establishment of a positive parent–provider relationship is frequently an important component of early intervention and care giving programs. In "Positive Parent–Provider Relationships: A Key to Healthy Parent–Child Relationships," Angela M. Tomlin uses constructs from attachment and social learning theories to offer a perspective on the many ways in which providers from a variety of early childhood programs use relationship-based approaches to both enhance parent–child relationships and support child development outcomes.

Foster children are often at risk for poor school outcomes. Given the possible experiences of early stress and maltreatment, these children might have particular vulnerabilities that decrease the likelihood of a successful transition to elementary school. They are likely to have difficulties with self-regulation, which might interfere with their abilities to relate to peers, to maintain focused attention, to follow directions, and to acquire academic skills. Foster children might also be at a disadvantage in terms of caregiver involvement in school, an important predictor of early school success. In "Promoting School Readiness in Foster Children," Katherine C. Pears, Philip A. Fisher, Cynthia V. Heywood, and Kimberly D. Bronz review a number of preventive intervention programs designed for at-risk children, including one targeted specifically at foster children. The success of these programs in preparing children for school and the long-term benefits of such programs suggest that interventions targeting school readiness in foster children might help to deflect these children from trajectories of school failure.

Social learning is usually integrated with other disciplines. The next three chapters review studies on the children's social learning and a discipline, such as history, social studies, and literacy. In "Growing Up With a Past: Teaching History to Young Children," Gary Fertig begins with a review of research on the nature and significance of relationships between children's developing understanding of time and their ability to learn history. Findings indicate that students as young as 5 years of age possess a working knowledge of social history which they can use as a basis for making temporal distinctions in organizing and understanding the past in meaningful ways. Rather than viewing children's intuitive ways of knowing as impediments to learning history, research suggest that prior knowledge and experience be used as a foundation for scaffolding formal instruction. History as an academic discipline is discussed in terms of an integrated approach to teaching and learning social studies, followed by a consideration of cultural universals as appropriate content for young children. Suggestions for teaching cultural universals using classroom time lines and historical biography are presented as a means for connecting with and building on children's knowledge of chronology and social history. Investigating cultural universals within the context of compelling stories that feature interesting people and their social interactions encourage children to put a human face on the past by evoking effective responses as well as intellectual associations that make learning social studies a more meaningful and memorable experience.

Working from a perspective that understands literacy as a social practice, in "Play as Group Improvisation: A Social Semiotic, Multimodal Perspective on Play and Literacy," Stacy L. DeZutter argues that because children's pretend play involves group improvisation, play provides an important context for the development of early literacy. Children's play is open-ended and collaborative. It requires ongoing explicit and implicit negotiations both about the content of the play and about how that content will be represented. Pretend play provides a setting for children to engage in the kind of socially shared symbolic activity that is the basis for the many kinds of literacy in which young children will participate throughout their lives. DeZutter introduces the chapter by reviewing early approaches to researching the connections between play and literacy. She then discusses how new ways of thinking about literacy require researchers to focus on the improvisational aspects of play, and how doing so can help us understand the group semiotic processes involved. Finally, she considers the implications of this discussion for researchers and educators.

In "Language, Literacy, and Social Experiences in Early Childhood: Progress, Problems, and Interventions," Adriana G. Bus, Maria T. de Jong, and Marinus H. van IJzendoorn suggest that when adult caregivers read books to children, they enter into a cognitive apprenticeship that scaffolds or supports youngsters' literacy learning. Social interaction serves as a major force in the growth of children's literacy competence. As a result, becoming literate is deeply rooted in social interactions. Adult–child interaction enables children to come into contact with a particular type of (written) language which serves as a precursor to literacy. A negative history of parent–child interactive experiences might inhibit adult-led book encounters resulting in a considerably higher risk of developing reading problems later at school. It is often considered an alarming development that stories on television, Internet sites, videotapes, and DVDs are increasingly replacing book sharing. The authors shed light here on the potential positive dimension of multimedia.

The next two chapters focus on social (e.g., ethnicity, race, home language) and moral issues in preschool classrooms. In their chapter titled, "If You're Not Like Me, Can We Play? Peer Groups in Preschool," Carollee Howes and Linda Lee discuss different play groups to understand how play groups and playing are organized in preschool classrooms including who plays with whom; who gets to play, and who does not play. They particularly focus on classrooms in which children do not share an ethnic/racial heritage and/or home language. To address this question they used a theoretical framework that integrates constructs of cultural community drawn from Rogoff (2003) with constructs drawn from attachment theory and applied to preschool contexts (Howes & Ritchie, 2002). They suggest that both home practices brought into the classroom and the everyday practices of classrooms influence the development of peer group organization. They show that friendships and play groups are organized around shared race, ethnicity, and home language; that in some cases children who are different on these dimensions may be excluded from play and friendship; and that the consequences of exclusion may be maladaptive peer relations.

In "Social Life of Young Children: Coconstruction of Shared Meanings and Togetherness, Humor, and Conflicts in Child Care Centers," Elly Singer and Dorian de Haan review the research on early social and moral learning. They discuss the social life of infants and toddlers in child care centers such as how young children make contact and create togetherness; how they make fun and jokes together, and how they deal with peer conflicts and coconstruct social and moral rules. They briefly discuss the educational consequences, how teachers can support social life in the peer group. Their focus is on studies of peer interactions from a socioconstructivist theoretical approach. First they focus on the sense of togetherness in young children. What are the psychological skills and mechanisms in young children that enable them to communicate and to coconstruct a sense of togetherness and shared reality? Imitation, recurrent actions and routines, relational language, and humor appear to be important means in peer relationships of young children. Secondly, they review studies on peer conflicts and reconciliation, and on how children learn and construct rules in peer conflicts. Finally they briefly discuss the teachers' role in creating positive peers relationships.

In the final chapter, Social Learning as the Basis for Early Childhood Education, Olivia N. Saracho and Bernard Spodek review the role of social learning in early childhood education. They identify principles of learning related to young children. They also share themes of content in social learning derived form the National Council of the Social Studies position statements. Finally, they note that children's social behavior must be understood in the contexts in which that behavior is evidenced.

SUMMARY

Young children's social learning should help young children to understand social processes and develop their skills for social inquiry. Through social learning, young children acquire a better understanding of themselves in relation to their social world. They learn to understand and appreciate individuals from different backgrounds and cultures who differ from their own. An understanding and knowledge of the physical world, assists young children to make reasonable decisions about their situations.

REFERENCES

Charlesworth, R. (1988). Integrating math with science and social studies: A unit example. *Day Care and Early Education, 15*(4), 28–31.

Consortium for Interdisciplinary Teaching and Learning & Endorsed by the National Council for the Social Studies (1994). *Interdisciplinary learning, Pre-K–Grade 4.* Retrieved August 24, 2006, from http://www.socialstudies.org/positions/interdisciplinary/.

Hill, P. S. (1913). Second report in committee of nineteen. *The Kindergarten.* Boston: International Kindergarten Union.

Howes, C., & Ritchie, S. (2002). *A matter of trust: Connecting teachers and learners in the early childhood classroom.* New York: Teachers College Press.

Mitchell, L. S. (1967). *Young Geographers.* New York: Basic Books.

Montessori, M. (1964). *The Montessori method.* New York: Schocken.

National Council for the Social Studies. (1984). *Social studies for young children.* Prepared by the National Council for the Social Studies Elementary/Early Childhood Education Committee. Retrieved August 23, 2006, from http://www.socialstudies.org/positions/children/.

Rogoff, B. (2003). *The cultural nature of human development.* New York: Oxford University Press.

Sunal, C. S. (1993). Social studies in early childhood education. In B. Spodek (Ed.), *Handbook of research on the education of young children.* New York: Macmillan.

Tureil, E. (1973). Stage transition in moral development. In R. M. W. Travers (Ed.), *Second handbook of research in teaching* (pp. 732–758). Chicago: Rand McNally & Company.

CHAPTER 1

SOCIAL EPISTEMOLOGY AND SOCIAL LEARNING

Olivia N. Saracho and Bernard Spodek

INTRODUCTION

Social learning refers to the acquisition of social knowledge and social skills. Social knowledge is usually obtained by communicating with members of a society (Fallis, 2002). Theories of knowledge can help explain the nature of social knowledge and social learning. Thus, they can be used as the basis for research about social learning and social education.

Social epistemology is an intellectual movement based on a wide set of cross-disciplinary sources that makes an effort to reconstruct the problems of epistemology when knowledge is considered to be intrinsically social (Fuller, n.d.). It reflects a broad set of approaches to the study of knowledge and efforts to gain information about the social dimensions. Although there is disagreement on the definition of "knowledge," the scope of "social," and the purposes of the studies, some philosophers believe that social epistemology should serve the same purpose as classical epistemology (Goldman, 2006). Other philosophers hold that social epistemology is radically different from classical epistemology, but it could replace the epistemology that was traditionally conceptualized.

Contemporary Perspectives on Social Learning in Early Childhood Education, pages 1–16
Copyright © 2007 by Information Age Publishing

The classical approach to social epistemology can focus on the traditional epistemic goal of acquiring true beliefs. Social practices can be studied in relation to the truth-values of an individual's beliefs. A different interpretation of classical epistemology could focus on the epistemic goal of developing confirmed or logical beliefs. In addressing the social realm, it can focus on a cognitive mediator in accepting the statements and opinions. The social dimensions of knowledge are the context, the culture, or the community's understanding and beliefs. These identify the social forces and influences that contribute to the development of knowledge. The major role that social epistemology assumes in the process of developing knowledge makes it theoretically important to society. In addition, its role in the redesign of information-related social institutions makes social epistemology important in practice.

The explosive amount of information related to the acquisition of knowledge was difficult to record and manage. In 1952, two information scientists, Margaret Egan and Jesse Shera, suggested that a new discipline needed to be created to effectively provide a theoretical framework to effectively study the complex problem of the intellectual processes in society. They called this new discipline *social epistemology* (Fallis, 2002). The term "social epistemology" first appeared in an article written by Margaret Egan and Jesse Shera (1952), although Shera has been the one who has been credited with the concept. They related social epistemology to economics, sociology, and psychology, as well as to traditional epistemology (Furner, 2004). Egan and Shera (1952) consider social epistemology to provide a theoretical framework to study the production, distribution, and utilization of intellectual products. They also seem to be influenced by Talcott Parson's (1951) structural functionalist analysis (Furner, 2004; Gingrich,1999) that includes a range of theoretical perspectives within anthropology and sociology concerning the relationship between social activity and an overall social system. Edgar (2006) used structural functionalist analysis to explain societies and provide a method to investigate the social sciences that was modeled after biological research. Structural functionalism compounds the characteristics of social foundations and behaviors that affect the stability and structure within society (Wikipedia Encyclopedia, 2006a).

Talcott Parson (1951) developed a refined interpretation of structural functionalism in terms of culture and the structure and function of society. Later, Habermas (1987b) used Parson's work in his volume entitled, *The theory of communicative action.* Egan and Shera (1952) built upon Parson's (1951) structural functionalist analysis of individual action in terms of three "modes of orientation": the cognitive, the goal directed, and the affective. They state that (a) sociologists investigate goal directed and affective behavior at the social level, (b) psychologists investigate goal-directed and affective behavior at the individual level, (c) traditional epistemologists investigate cognitive behavior at the individual level, but (d) in all fields, scholars have neglected to investigate cognitive behavior at the social level, despite the primary importance of the cognitive mode in determining the structure of society (Egan & Shera, 1952).

Research into the cognitive mode consists of examining the process of the actor's efforts in learning (Furner, 2004; Gingrich, 1999) or, as Egan and Shera (1952) would interpret, in becoming involved in a relationship of "knowing" in a specific situation where the action occurs. Their definition of social epistemology is "the study of those processes by which society *as a whole* seeks to achieve a perceptive understanding in relation to the total environment" (p. 132). According to Furner (2004), Egan and Shera (1952) identified three issues of inquiry to meet their goal.

1. *Information needs.* Referred to as "situation analysis" which methodologists use for classifications based on the information needs that individuals display in those situations.

2. *Knowledge organization.* Referred to as the "analysis of information unit" where methodologies are used for classification based on the content.

3. *Methods of measurement.* Acknowledged that the analysis of the results is essential for the selection of statistical procedures.

Egan (1951) assumed that communication has social value when it stimulates behavior that has a social effect. According to Shera (1970), "Social epistemology is the study of knowledge in society. The focus of this discipline should be upon the production, flow, integration, and consumption of all forms of communicated thought throughout the entire social fabric" (p. 86). Shera (1970) was particularly interested in the affinity between social epistemology and librarianship. The way that knowledge is organized could be translated into how libraries could be organized. Other social epistemologists are concerned with the disciplines of the humanities and social sciences, particularly philosophy and sociology. In addition, social epistemologists work in the interdisciplinary field of Science and Technology Studies (Wikipedia, 2006a).

In 1987, Alvin Goldman and Steve Fuller edited a special issue of the philosophical journal, *Synthese,* on social epistemology. These two philosophers have continued their work in social epistemology, but they have deviated in the most characteristically divergent paths. In 1987 Fuller established a quarterly journal, *Social Epistemology* (published by Taylor and Francis since 1987), which focuses on knowledge, culture, and policy. Shortly after, Fuller (1988) published his first book, *Social Epistemology;* Goldman (1999) also published a book titled, *Knowledge in a Social World.*

In 2004, Goldman became the editor of the journal *Episteme* (published by the Edinburgh University Press since 2004), which is a journal of social epistemology. In many respects the aims and scope of *Social Epistemology* and *Episteme* overlap, but *Social Epistemology* usually focuses more on scientific studies rather than on philosophy. In contrast, *Episteme* does not publish straightforward empirical studies or qualitative studies, which they often refer to as case studies. Rather, it focuses on analytical philosophy, although different rigorous approaches are accepted if they are of interest to an interdisciplinary audience. *Episteme* publishes articles on the social dimensions of knowledge from the perspective of philosophical epistemology and related social sciences (e.g., economics, political theory, information science). Both journals, for example, welcome papers that include a policy dimension. More practical applications of social epistemology can be found in the areas of library science, academic publishing, and knowledge about policy. (Wikipedia Encyclopedia, 2006a)

The concept of social epistemology is described in detail in Goldman's (1999) book, *Knowledge in a Social World.* He argues that in everyday life and in special areas (e.g., science, law, education), there is a definite value in true beliefs rather than false beliefs or no opinion (uncertainty). He devotes the rest of the book to discussing the types of social practices (e.g., speech practices of reporting and arguing) that contribute to this value. Kitcher (1993) credits the development of social practice to individual practices that relate to the individuals' beliefs, credible informants, and acceptable methodology of scientific reasoning. A "core" consensus practice involves the components of individual practices that all members of the community share. Presently, all types of social epistemology are fully "academic" or "theoretical" which focus on the social significance of knowledge and the cultural value of social epistemology (Wikipedia Encyclopedia, 2006a).

Studying Social Epistemology

Researchers depend on theories to generate hypotheses about natural or social phenomena that are tested in laboratories or field settings. A theory related to human interests developed by Jürgen Habermas (1968a, 1968b, 1979, 1987a) has been used as an example of contemporary theory representing processes of social knowledge construction, which dynamically focuses on a broad range of issues and uses a wide variety of traditions and methods. The continuous reconstruction of this theoretical framework can enrich an inflexible tradition and simultaneously challenge its epistemological and methodological assumptions. Habermas considered rationality to be a multidimensional process that continuously interacts with these interests. Such processes are aimed toward specific purposes that focus on interests, which are initially cognitive interests that develop the individual's thoughts. They may convey those interests that guide the individual's actions and communication to form social relations (Popkewitz & Maurice, 1991). The close relationship between knowledge and human interests created the groundwork of Habermas' (1972) theory of cognitive interests, which encompasses the following processes of inquiry.

1. In *natural sciences and social sciences*, Habermas considers that empirical-analytic sciences focus on the achievement of nomological knowledge.

2. In *humanities and historical and social sciences*, Habermas believes they represent the historical-hermeneutic sciences that focus on the achievement of an interpretive understanding of human communicative interaction.

3. In *critically oriented sciences*, Habermas classifies psychoanalysis, critical social theory, and philosophy to be a reflective and critical discipline.

Habermas assumes that each process of inquiry integrates a specific cognitive interest and attests, "The approach of the empirical-analytic sciences incorporates a *technical* cognitive interest; that of the historical-hermeneutic sciences incorporates a *practical* one; and the approach of critically oriented sciences incorporates the *emancipatory* cognitive interest" (1972, p. 308). Habermas assigns a different conceptual level to each of these cognitive interests. Some interests depend on other interests. The technical cognitive interests describe the orientation of the sciences and technologies, where individuals relate to nature as an instrumental action. An equivalent conceptual dependence relationship exists between the empirical-analytic and historical-hermeneutic sciences as well as the critically oriented sciences. This methodological framework supports Habermas' complete hierarchy of knowledge and interests (Cummings, 2002).

Theoretically, Habermas (1968a, 1968b, 1979, 1987a) classifies knowledge and communication into three types of interest: *instrumental, interpretive,* or *critical-emancipator.* This rigid classification scheme can be confusing because any social science theory or research program uses a variety of ways of to understand and interpret social phenomena (Popkewitz & Maurice, 1991). According to Habermas (1968a, 1968b, 1979, 1987a), scientific rationality is a broad term where socially constructed indices provide the frameworks to identify social patterns and processes as rational interactions based on cognitive and communicative interests. Social science theory helps to understand and interpret social phenomena (Tabachnick, 1981), but it may be more important to expand and communicate this type of knowledge that reflects the situations under which they occur. Therefore, in relation to using traditional and critical approaches to theory, Habermas (1966/1988) submits that

> The traditional idea of theory is abstracted from scientific activity as it is carried on within the division of labor at a particular stage of the latter's development. It corresponds to the activity of the scholar which takes place alongside all other activities of a society, but in no immediately clear connection with them. In this view of theory, therefore, the real function of science is not made manifest; it conveys not what theory means in human life, but only what it means in the isolated sphere, in which, for historical reasons, it comes into existence. As opposed to this, critical theory is to become conscious of its calling; it knows that in and through the very act of knowing it belongs to the objective context of life that it strives to grasp. The context of its emergence does not remain to the theory; rather the theory takes this reflective up into itself. (p. 401)

Habermas (1966/1988) perceives theories to be highly claimed communication acts that are found in specified settings as researchers pose competing questions about possibilities to establish techniques, mediate meanings, and create changes. This approach requires that researchers select acts of "reconstruction" and articulate and criticize political or cultural consequences of theoretical statements (Popkewitz & Maurice, 1991).

According to Habermas (1979), the researchers in the social and natural sciences have different approaches to social epistemology. Social science researchers explore a more symbolically structured reality; whereas natural scientists are mainly empirical. They make theoretical statements that "develop nomological hypotheses about domains of observable events" (Habermas, 1979, p. 9). Although such theories are incessantly examined and modified, social scientists use theoretical statements to distinguish between observation and understanding. Observation is a characteristic of nomological hypothesis testing, while understanding is more characteristic of reconstructive science. Hypotheses testing relates to the researchers' expected variations or consistencies in phenomena, while reconstructed theories related to unexpected new concepts that develop into new patterns in different social contexts.

Research procedures (e.g., research questions or hypotheses testing, experimental methods) influence the conclusions based on the premises of inquiry. Theories are reconstructed as part of a series of research studies related to a set of research questions within specific epistemological traditions and social instructional situations (Cummings, 2002). According to Habermas (1972), the theory of knowledge put into effect the identification of science. Habermas states:

For the philosophy of science that has emerged since the mid-nineteenth century as the heir of the theory of knowledge is methodology pursued with a scientistic self-understanding of the sciences. *Scientism* means science's belief in itself; that is, the conviction that we can no longer understand science as *one* possible form of knowledge, but rather must identify knowledge with science. (p. 4)

Habermas (1968a, 1968b, 1979, 1987a) believes that researchers need to critically analyze incongruent theories and practices and pose scientific questions to examine the nature or society. Habermas (1968a, 1968b, 1979, 1987a) expects for researchers to acknowledge that their work requires continuous and complex symbolic transactions and use theories as tentative acts of communication that are modified in different contexts and for different reasons. Educational research is used to understand communicative action, particularly in reconstructing theories. Researchers examine the practitioner's speech, acts, and contexts with a guiding purpose. Habermas (1968a, 1968b, 1979, 1987a) affirms that knowledge and truth are problematic in all social situations (Popkewitz & Maurice, 1991).

The conceptualization of an obsolete social epistemology surfaced in Alvin Goldman's work that was published from the late 1970s through the mid-1980s (Goldman 1978, 1986, 1987). In order to study knowledge and how individuals process it, Goldman believes that epistemology needs to be separated into two entities: (a) individual epistemology and (b) social epistemology (or "epistemics") in the use of logic, philosophy, psychology, and linguistics. Both entities need to assess their contributions to identify and evaluate processes, methods, or practices in the production of true belief. Individual epistemology identifies and assesses the epistemic subject's psychological processes; whereas social epistemology identifies and assesses the social processes that epistemic subjects use to interact with other agents who influence their beliefs. On the other hand, Habermas (1968a, 1968b, 1987a) believes that social epistemology is defined in broader terms than individual consciousness; because socially constructed rules offer the frameworks upon which principles of validity are developed. Social systems are complex, but they have precise and rigorous hallmarks of reason. Habermas (1968a, 1968b, 1987a) contends that social patterns and processes can be studied as rational interactions based on cognitive and communicative interests (Habermas, 1968a, 1968b, 1987a).

Scholars differ in their conceptions of social epistemology in studying group knowledge in whole or in part. Pettit (2003) presents the view that groups are subjects of propositional attitudes, which can be considered when they exhibit a certain kind of rational unity. Their intentional attitudes and their response to those attitudes need to be continuously displayed to maintain a pattern of rational unity. Pettit (2003) then rationalizes that some groups, which he labels "social integrates," exhibit rational unity. Since collective judgments and intentions may always supervene on the attitudes and relations among their members, they fail to represent an ontologically emergent domain (Pettit, 2003). Group-oriented social epistemologists realize that groups specify their beliefs voluntarily, which may be incompatible with positive epistemic properties like knowledge or justification. The point is that groups tend to accept views for nonepistemic reasons regardless of whether their views represent the truth. Wray (2003) and McMahon (2003) contend that groups rely on their goals to justify their true positions. For example, tobacco companies adopt the position that smoking does not cause cancer, although their executives may not actually believe this. On the other hand, Mathiesen (2006) disagrees that all group beliefs are intentionally selected. In addition, List (2005) maintains that individuals within the group differ in their levels of expertise on different propositions. He suggests that groups be divided into subgroups, where members of each subgroup specialize on an area. Each subgroup collectively judges its assigned area and uses the collective judgment on the different areas for the group's conclusions. List (2005) believes that this "distributed" procedure outperforms the traditional nondistributed (premise-based) procedure. Hongladarom (2002) rationalizes that each culture differs in their epistemic objectives. He describes how the Thai culture values continuity over truth. He suggests that his diversity of epistemic objectives needs to guide scholars to use cross-cultural epistemic practices. In order for social epistemology to make active group belief and group knowledge, it needs to consider the differences in the groups and many conceptualizations of group belief and knowledge. According to Goldman (2004), one size does not fit all.

In social epistemology the other agents and the institutional structures' communicational acts are major examples of social-epistemic practices that need to be investigated. Social epistemology can be studied descriptively or normatively. A descriptive project explains whether a social isolate (like Robinson Crusoe) can have knowledge. On the other hand, a normative project identifies how groups should be organized for them to produce reliable and effective knowledge (Kusch, 1998).

Another conventional epistemological matter emerges in *descriptive research*, which is usually referred to as "atheoretical" (Toulmin, 1972; Popkewitz, & Maurice, 1991; Wartofsky, 1997). Researchers often select specific methods to obtain information on social phenomena. They plainly expose them without bias. For example, researchers using survey methods (e.g., Smith, 1986) collect data that can be classified in several categories of multiple variables. Researchers cluster the data in what they refer to as "cross-sections" to represent a complex and fleeting phenomena like classroom life. Popkewitz and Maurice (1991) use the term "dustbowl" empiricism to refer to data that are aggregated without explicit theoretical statements, because researchers expect that all potential groups can be analyzed using large scale statistical techniques.

Some qualitative or naturalistic case studies become authentic through accurate portrayals of educational phenomena rather than through survey research; the field studies are viewed as documentation of the individual's natural speech and actions. For epistemological studies, data are gathered for the purpose of descriptive research and are somehow separated from processes of theoretical speculation. Popkewitz and Maurice (1991) use the study by Shermis and Washburn (1986) as an example where they use a survey of social studies teachers to collect data about the teachers' backgrounds, career patterns, political opinions, professional perspectives, and beliefs concerning the social studies curricular material. Shermis and Washburn (1986) refer to their study as descriptive and nontheoretical, although they organize their data into categories (e.g., career patterns, definition of reading as a school skill) and use these terms to make imposed categories (e.g., decision making, empowerment, cognition) as theoretical constructs with distinctive historical and philosophical characteristics (Popkewitz & Maurice, 1991).

Apparently atheoretical data are products of the structures, norms, and standards that are the result of the researchers' intellectual traditions and social situations. In social epistemology, any factual statement must consider the presenter's embedded beliefs and the language's structural inferences. Facts (regardless of the number and accuracy) and large sets of data represent a blend of interpretations. As a matter of fact, dynamic and reciprocal relationships between theory and data are correspondingly multiplied as the data set increases (Popkewitz, & Maurice, 1991).

Moral Reasoning

Valid scientific knowledge concepts in contemporary social contexts are interpreted to explain particular theoretical statements based on both general rules of validity and practical situations. Habermas (1968a, 1968b, 1979, 1987a) created a theory of interests to represent the processes of social knowledge development. He provides many of his own ideas, actions, and examples of rational reconstruction. For example, he criticizes Kohlberg's theory of moral development as it has widely influenced social studies education. According to Habermas (1983), Kohlberg's concept of moral development needs to be empirically tested to be interpreted as a self-referential process that is analogous to a hermeneutic circle. Habermas (1983) proposes that "...empirical theory proposes the normative validity of reconstruction by which it is informed, yet this validity becomes doubtful as soon as the reconstruction does not work empirically" (p. 269). Kohlberg disagrees; his purpose was to identify the individual's stages of moral development. Under logical interpretation, these stages can be applied repeatedly as a communicative interest that is particularly related to interpretive styles of knowing and communicating. In framing his philosophy, Habermas (1983), believes that

> Both the psychologist's subjects and the moral philosopher adopt the same performance attitude of a participant in practical discourse. In both cases, the outcome of moral reasoning, whether it is an expression of the layperson's moral intuition or the expert's reconstruction of it, is evaluated in the light of claims to normative rightness. (pp. 265–266)

Habermas (1983) equates the cognitive and communicative interests of both experts and lay individuals. When theories are under development, knowledge that is learned is conveyed, explored, and verified. A reconstructive strategy needs to relate theoretical knowledge and communication to practical situations. Habermas (1983) affirms that theories similar to Kohlberg's are provisional forms of knowledge and communication that are frequently dependent on the situations. Thus, differentiations (a) between cognition and communication, and (b) among technical, interpretive, and critical types of interests, are more like connections than restrictions. Conflicting types of knowledge, communication, and behaving may be analytically separate; but these interact in precise modes within certain social fields. The technical-analytic interests in a theory of moral development are consolidated with interpretive-hermeneutic interests when hypotheses are clearly stated and developed based on critical emancipatory interests; while researchers, subjects, and their audiences (both lay persons and experts) communicate.

Another philosopher, Stephen Edelston Toulmin, also focuses his work on the analysis of moral reasoning. Toulmin (1972) seeks to explore the way individuals reason about both ethical and moral issues. In his work, he attempts to develop practical arguments to effectively assess the ethics behind moral issues. In his writings, he develops practical arguments to effectively assess the ethics behind moral issues. Most of his writings are based in the field of rhetoric where he analyzes rhetorical arguments (Toulmin, 1972; Wikipedia, 2006b; Wartofsky, 1997). However, he uses this process to analyze moral reasoning. This work helped Toulmin to enter a field that motivated him to consider the problems of formal logic as both a descriptive and a prescriptive argumentation tool, which became a critical concept in his later works. For example, in 1958, Stephen Toulmin (1958/2003) published *The Uses of Argument*, which is the most cited work in rhetoric, particularly his model of argumentation. In this book he introduces the

Toulmin model of argumentation, which describes the components of his model, and provides practical implications of his model. It is a diagram that has six interrelated components used for analyzing arguments. This model is considered his most influential work, especially in the fields of rhetoric and communication as well as computer science. Toulmin's new model of argument deviates from former, more traditional models. He uses this model to analyze moral reasoning and ethical issues. He forms a resolution concerning the problematic of conceptual change (Wartofsky, 1997).

The management of theory in social education research may be similar to that of text that is being analyzed and interpreted just like new generations of responsive readers are constantly reconstructing the meaning of literary works (such as Shakespeare's *Othello*) or historical documents (such as the United States Constitution's Bill of Rights). Advocates of moral-stage theories in social studies generally initiate their communicative interactions by wondering, "What do these theories say about moral development?" Habermas believes that they would wonder, "What are the conditions in which particular representations of moral considerations may occur?" Kohlberg or Habermas are scholars who are associated with concepts and discourses that have diversified cognitive and communicative interests (Popkewitz, & Maurice, 1991).

THEORY DEVELOPMENT IN SOCIAL STUDIES

Social epistemology provides the basis for theories in the social sciences. It also provides the basis for theories in social studies education. Theory development in social studies education focuses on scientific knowledge that is socially constructed and institutionally grounded. Contemporary educational researchers depend on certain assumptions to select concepts, variables, and methods that help interpret school phenomena. Researchers consider questions concerning social studies teaching and learning that are related to social epistemology. Many believe that Habermas' work (1968a, 1968b, 1979, 1987a) provides a theory that represents the processes of social knowledge construction. He views rationality as continuously interacting with the multidimensional processes, which are the individuals' cognitive interests, thoughts, and actions that become linguistic terms and processes in social relationships. Habermas (1968a, 1968b, 1979, 1987a) believes that scientific rationality must extend beyond individual consciousness, because socially constructed labels build the frameworks' validity and assure that the complex social systems are precise and rigorous hallmarks of reason. He assumes that social patterns and processes can be studied as rational interactions based on cognitive and communicative interests. Social science theory includes different forms of understanding and interpreting social phenomena (Tabachnick, 1981). It is more relevant to examining how the different forms of knowing and communicating reflect the situations that are being studied.

A conflicting revelation on social science was Kuhn's (1962/1970, 1996) *Structure of Scientific Revolutions* and its impact on the development of the social studies of science. Kuhn (1962/1970, 1996) rejects rules as a basis to determine scientific outcomes and allows other factors that are external to science to explain scientific judgments. However, a stabilized paradigm restricts these judgments, which can be influenced by facts about an individual's life history, personality, nationality, or reputation. Kuhn (1977) shows how social and political factors that are extrinsic to science have an impact on scientific arguments. Kuhn (1977) identifies values that can guide the researcher's judgment. He also acknowledges the possibility that scientists may have to use other values, as other scholars have demanded (Bird, 2004; Longino, 2006).

Several social studies researchers who focus on social knowledge reject or ignore the classical concerns of epistemology as truth, justification, and rationality. They believe that such concepts lack legitimacy or usefulness for their own aims. They prefer to assume the role of anthropologists who describe the norms or mores of a culture. Thus, these social studies researchers describe and understand a selected community's norms of rationality; but they refute the existence of any universal or "objective" norms of rationality, or criteria of truth. As Barnes and Bloor (1982) state, "there are no context-free or supercultural norms of rationality" (p. 27). Since they assume that certain practices are more rational or more truth-conducive than others, they refuse to judge the epistemic attributes of any belief-forming practices; because they believe that these judgments lack the culture-free basis or foundation. Therefore, they prefer belief-forming practices (Goldman, 2006).

Since social studies researchers focus on knowledge of social influences on social education, they may be considered social epistemologists. These researchers are considered social epistemologists, because they infer epistemologically significant conclusions from their sociological or anthropological research. Social factors "external" to the appropriate business of science have a major impact in the social studies researchers' historical case studies. In addition, social analyses of science indicate that their studies of scientific persuasion are basically a struggle for political power rather than reliable epistemic merit. Several sociologists contend that scientific "facts" may be false. For example, data on independent human social interactions are mainly mere "fabrication" outcomes from those social interactions. Such epistemological thesis may be of some philosophical significance as some of these researchers may have philosophical motivation rather than social science motivation (Goldman, 2006).

Some social studies researchers who are considered to be social epistemologists expand the description and explanation of science. Fuller
(1987, 1988, 1999), a well known scholar in social epistemology, perceives
the endeavor as normative. He believes that knowledge is a matter of
empirical discovery, which raises the questions: How can science be investigated? If science has a variety of outcomes, which are the ones to be
accepted? Helen Longino (1990, 2002), a social studies scholar, focuses
on the normative. She (2002) suggests that the social does not pervert the
normative, or justificatory, dimension of science. In contrast, she
attributes justificatory reasoning to be part of a social practice that is challenging and responsive.

Historically, research in social studies education, and social sciences are
interrelated. Although there might be a lack of histories of epistemology in
social studies research practices, some histories in social science may lead
to those theoretical constructions within social studies. For example, the
major research journal, *Theory and Research in Social Education*, which is published by the National Council of Social Studies, includes articles whose
topics and interests associated with social studies; but these publications
are founded on general theories and methodological procedures from
other such disciplines as sociology, anthropology, phenomenology, socialization, and others (Popkewitz, & Maurice, 1991). These theories provide
structures for the foundation of research paradigms; but the concepts,
methods, and analyses in the cognitive and behavioral psychologies, political socialization, sociology, and anthropology are the driving forces in conducting research in social studies education.

Social studies research takes place among intersecting institutional
developments. The changeable institutional character of theories is
neglected in contemporary scientific discussions, which often focus on
individuals, innovators, creators, and sometimes geniuses who add to the
corpus of knowledge. Thus, biographical or intellectual histories of social
studies educators are written to illustrate the growth of the field. Although
the scientists and practitioners intend to assume important roles in processes of change, their knowledge is nonetheless socially constructed.
Statements by the individual scholars or professionals exist in an historical
context. The rules of language and logic that govern scientific inquiry are
contingent upon the values of particular communities in specific circumstances. Epistemological assumptions manifest the implicit social rules
about research practice and communication. Those practices are modified
and can be challenged, but all researchers' thinking and communication
hold on to residual forms, unquestioned and untested elements (Popkewitz, & Maurice, 1991).

SUMMARY

Contemporary theorists and researchers of social studies education have inherited structures and practices from the late 19th and early 20th century during the Progressive Era of reforms and social engineering. These provide analogies to the present procedures and influence the course of disciplined research. Regardless of the influence of the progressive reforms that are targeted at attaining a stable and remain ambiguous goals. As we look at the future, social education has to contend with ethical moral problems as did their precursor, in a world that seems to be more detrimental than the contexts in which progressive reformers originally made their idealist assertions (Popkewitz, & Maurice, 1991).

Social epistemology is a continuing process. The theoretician's major goal to develop a foundation for theory is to select the valid types of knowledge and develop cognitive and communicative interests as social conditions change in space and time. It also includes a continuous inquiry into the past and present theories of science and education. It is important to know the continuous inquiry of social situations that contribute to the theoretical statements for future research.

Social studies research is a search for truth and relationships. Social epistemology informs theory as related different human interests. It identifies whose truth is being sought as well as the means and goals of inquiry. Theories provide evidence about the world, practical applications for establishing and maintaining social relations, and controlling human life through the norms of possibility and admissibility (Popkewitz & Maurice, 1991).

REFERENCES

Barnes, B., & Bloor, D. (1982). Relativism, rationalism, and the sociology of knowledge. In M. Hollis & S. Lukes (Eds.), *Rationality and relativism* (pp. 21–47). Cambridge, MA: MIT Press.

Bird, A. (2004). Thomas Kuhn. In *The Stanford encyclopedia.* Retrieved September 17, 2006, from http://plato.stanford.edu/entries/thomas-kuhn/#6.3.

Cartwright, N., Cat, J., Fleck, L., & Uebel, T. E. (1996). *Otto Neurath: Philosophy between science and politics.* New York: Cambridge University Press.

Cummings, L. (2002). Why we need to avoid theorizing about rationality: A Putnamian criticism of Habermas's epistemology. *Social Epistemology, 16*(2), 117–131.

Edgar, A. (2006). *Habermas: The key concepts.* New York: Routledge.

Egan, M. E. (1951). Synthesis and summary. In J. H. Shera & M. E. Egan (Eds.), *Bibliographic organization: Papers presented before the fifteenth annual conference of the Graduate Library School, July 24–29, 1950* (pp. 253–265). Chicago: University of Chicago Press.

Egan, M. E., & Shera, J. (1952). Foundation of theory in bibliotherapy. *Library Quarterly, 22*(2), 125–137.

Fallis, D. (2002). Introduction: Social epistemology and information science. *Social Epistemology, 16*(1), 1–4.

Fuller, S. (1987). On regulating what is known: A way to social epistemology. *Synthese, 73,* 145–183.

Fuller, S. (1988). *Social epistemology.* Bloomington, IN: Indiana University Press.

Fuller, S. (1999). *The governance of science: Ideology and the future of the open society.* London: Open University Press.

Fuller, S. (n.d.). *What is social epistemology?* Retrieved September 17, 2006, from http://www.warwick.ac.uk/~sysdt/socialepist.html.

Furner, J. (2004). "A brilliant mind": Margaret Egan and social epistemology. *Library Trends, 52*(4), 792–809. Also online at http://polaris.gseis.ucla.edu/jfurner/05libtrends-compact.pdf.

Gingrich, P. (1999). *Functionalism and Parsons.* Retrieved September 17, 2006, from http://uregina.ca/~gingrich/n2f99.htm.

Goldman, A. I. (1978). Epistemics: The regulative theory of cognition. *Journal of Philosophy, 75,* 509–523.

Goldman, A. I. (1986). *Epistemology and cognition.* Cambridge, MA: Harvard University Press.

Goldman, A. I. (1987). Foundations of social epistemics. *Synthese, 73,* 109–144.

Goldman, A. I. (1999). *Knowledge in a social world.* Oxford, UK: Oxford University Press.

Goldman, A. I. (2004). Group knowledge versus group rationality: Two approaches to social epistemology. *Episteme: Journal of Social Epistemology, 1*(1), 11–22.

Goldman, A. I. (2006). Social epistemology. In *The Stanford encyclopedia of philosophy.* Retrieved September 17, 2006, from http://plato.stanford.edu/entries/epistemology-social/.

Habermas, J. (1966/1988). *On the logic of the social sciences* (S. W. Nicholson & J. Stark, Trans.). Cambridge, MA: Harvard University Press. (Original work published in 1966.)

Habermas, J. (1968a). The idea of the theory of knowledge as social theory. Retrieved September 17, 2006, fromhttp://www.marxists.org/reference/archive/habermas/1968/theory-knowledge.htm.

Habermas, J. (1968b). *Knowledge & human interest.* Boston: Beacon Press.

Habermas, J. (1979). *Communication and the evolution of society.* Boston: Beacon Press.

Habermas, J. (1983). Interpretive social science vs. hermeneutics. In. N. Haan (Ed.), *Social science as moral inquiry* (pp. 251–269). New York: Columbia University Press.

Habermas, J. (1987a). *Knowledge & human interest.* Boston: Polity Press.

Habermas, J. (1987b). *The theory of communicative action: Vol. 2. Lifeword and system: A critique of functionalist reason.* Boston: Polity Press.

Hongladarom, S. (2002). Cross-cultural epistemic practices. *Social Epistemology, 16*(1), 83–92.

Kitcher, P. (1993). *The advancement of science.* New York: Oxford University Press.

Kuhn, T. S. (1962/1970, 1996). *The structure of scientific revolutions.* Chicago: University of Chicago Press.

Kuhn, T. S. (1977). Objectivity, value judgment, and theory choice. In *The essential tension: Selected studies in scientific tradition and change* (pp. 320–239). Chicago: University of Chicago Press.

Kusch, M. (1998). *Social epistemology*. Department of History and Philosophy of Science. Cambridge, UK: University of Cambridge. Retrieved September 17, 2006, from http://www.hps.cam.ac.uk/research/se.html.

List, C. (2005). Group knowledge and group rationality: A judgment aggregation perspective, *Episteme: A Journal of Social Epistemology, 2*(1), 25–38.

Longino, H. (1990). *Science as social knowledge*. Princeton, NJ: Princeton University Press.

Longino, H. (2002). *The fate of knowledge*. Princeton, NJ: Princeton University Press.

Longino, H. (2006). The social dimensions of scientific knowledge. In *Stanford encyclopedia of philosophy*. Retrieved September 17, 2006, from http://plato.stanford.edu/entries/scientific-knowledge-social/.

Mathiesen, K. (2006). The epistemic features of group belief. *Episteme: A Journal of Social Epistemology, 2*(3),161–175.

McMahon, C. (2003). Two modes of collective belief. *Protosociology, 18/19,* 347–362.

Parsons, T. (1951). *The social system*. New York: Free Press.

Pettit, P. (2003). Groups with minds of their own. In F. Schmitt (Ed.), *Socializing metaphysics*. Lanham, MD: Rowman & Littlefield.

Popkewitz, T. S., & Maurice, H. S. (1991). Social studies education and theory: Science, knowledge, and history. In J. P. Shaver (Ed.), *Handbook of research in social studies teaching and learning* (pp. 27–40). New York: Macmillan.

Shera, J. (1970). *Sociological foundations of librarianship*. New York: Asia Publishing House.

Shermis, S., & Washburn, D. (1986). Social studies educators and their beliefs: Preliminary data from Indiana colleges and Universities. *Theory and Research in Social Education, 14*(4), 3321–340.

Smith, L. (1986). *Behaviorism and logical positivism: A reassessment of the alliance*. Stanford, CA: Stanford University Press.

Tabachnick, B. R. (1981). Teacher education as a set of dynamic social events. In B. R. Tabachnick, T. S. Popkewitz, & B. B. Szekely (Eds.), *Studying teaching and learning: Trends in Soviet and American research* (pp. 76–86). New York: Praeger.

Toulmin, S. E. (1958/2003). *The uses of argument*. Cambridge, UK: Cambridge University Press.

Toulmin, S. E. (1972). *Human understanding: The collective use and evolution of concepts*. Princeton, NJ: Princeton University Press.

Wartofsky, Marx W. (1997). Stephen Toulmin: An intellectual odyssey. *Humanities, 18*(2), 8- 13.

Wikipedia Encyclopedia. (2006a). *Social epistemology*. Retrieved September 17, 2006, from http://en.wikipedia.org/wiki/Social_epistemology.

Wikipedia Encyclopedia. (2006b). *Structural functionalism*. Retrieved September 17, 2006, from http://en.wikipedia.org/wiki/Structural_functionalism.

Wray, K. B. (2003). What really divides Gilbert and the rejectionists. *Protosociology, 18/19,* 363–376.

CHAPTER 2

SOCIAL DYNAMICS OF EARLY CHILDHOOD CLASSROOMS

Considerations and Implications for Teachers[1]

Kathleen Cranley Gallagher, Kimberly Dadisman, Thomas W. Farmer, Laura Huss, and Bryan C. Hutchins

> Children come to see themselves as being able to construct order in society either through adults or with peers. Not knowing what the rules of order are, children focus on interactions and construct out of them patterns which connect their actions with the actions of others. The result is a discovery of two relationships within which persons can arrive at order. (Youniss, 1980, p. 21)

Beginning as early as the preschool years, classroom social dynamics impact children's behavioral adjustment and interpersonal adaptation. When children are grouped together in classrooms during early childhood, they typically form social structures and a peer culture that both reflects and influences their interpersonal characteristics and behavior patterns (Corsaro & Eder, 1990; Estell, Farmer, Cairns, & Cairns, 2002; Strayer & Santos, 1996). As suggested by the quote above, the classroom societies that children construct involve distinct interchanges with adults and peers and are the product of the interactions that they experience within these two different forms of social relationships (Cairns, 1979). As teachers work

Contemporary Perspectives on Social Learning in Early Childhood Education, pages 17–48
Copyright © 2007 by Information Age Publishing
All rights of reproduction in any form reserved.

to support students during the early school years, it is important to understand the two social worlds of children and to scaffold between the interpersonal rules and expectations they learn from adults in the home and the interactional contexts they coconstruct with peers in school. Accordingly, the goal of this chapter is to consider how social interchanges and classroom social dynamics contribute to children's early school adaptation, particularly in contemporary classroom contexts with children from diverse backgrounds, cultures, and abilities.

Toward this goal, we will review literature on early childhood social development with a focus on the role of social synchrony in the establishment, maintenance, and change of students' social cognitions and patterns of interpersonal behavior. This discussion will examine how the behavior of parents, teachers, and peers may elicit, reinforce, and modify the thoughts, beliefs, and behavior of young children. Next, we will consider how children's individual characteristics impact their social relationships. This will include a focus on temperament and emotional regulation, patterns of behavior and social roles, and the social opportunities and needs of children from different backgrounds, cultural and ethnic groups, ability levels, and gender. This discussion will be followed by a review of the literature on classroom social structures and peer group processes, focusing on selective affiliation and homophily (i.e., the tendency to associate with similar peers), the formation and functions of social dominance hierarchies in early childhood classrooms, and the peer group boundaries and social roles.

Next, we will consider the implications of this literature for teachers' classroom practices. Teachers serve as a bridge between the social rules children learn from their parents and caregivers and the social structure that they coconstruct with peers in the classroom. To effectively support students' school adjustment, it is helpful for teachers to be aware of the classroom social dynamics and to serve as an "invisible hand" (Cairns & Cairns, 1994; Farmer, 2000). In this role, teachers can scaffold and guide children in new interactions and relationships in ways that unobtrusively foster productive relationships and social roles while preventing bullying, victimization, and other problematic patterns of social behavior.

This chapter will conclude with a focus on new directions in early childhood social development research. At this point, much is known about how children's characteristics, skills, and abilities contribute to their social relationships. There is also considerable information on the role of parents and family processes in children's social development and there is a growing body of literature on social structures and peer group processes in early childhood classrooms. However, in terms of methodology and focus, more work is needed with regard to situating the individual within the context of peer groups and classroom social structures and understanding the interrelated patterns of development of these three foci across time. In particular, there is a need to develop strategies to examine how children's conceptions of classroom peer relations and peer group dynamics are related to their social behavior and classroom adjustment. As a corresponding focus, there is a need to examine the naturalistic supports that teachers provide for children who are experiencing difficulties or who have diverse backgrounds and perspectives from those of students who make up the majority culture of the classroom. Possible approaches to address these issues will be considered.

SOCIAL DEVELOPMENT IN EARLY CHILDHOOD

The interpretive view structure is seen as both constraining and enabling. The process is interpretive in the sense that children do not merely individually internalize the external adult culture. Rather, children become a part of adult culture and contribute to its reproduction through their negotiations with adults and their creative production of a series of peer cultures with other children. (Corsaro & Eder, 1990, p. 201)

Children aged three to eight years old are ready, by all accounts, to participate in the social world outside of the family circle. Multiple developmental achievements during this period prepare a child for the social challenges of preschool and early elementary school, interacting with peers and teachers (Berk, 2005). Children's cognitive and language skills develop rapidly during this time. Their developing theory of mind allows children to assume others' perspectives, and to hold multiple perspectives in consideration. Simultaneously, children's expressive language skills blossom, and children can more accurately describe their emotions, desires, and goals. They can more skillfully "use their words" to attain what they want and need, and later, to negotiate. After three years old, children's ability to understand emotions and regulate their own emotions increases. Children learn that some circumstances warrant expressing emotion, while others require they hide how they feel (Denham, Zoller, & Couchoud, 1994). Over the early education years, children's ability to regulate emotion and behavior increases, and emerging self-care skills provides children with a sense of independence from the physical care of caregivers. The combined effect of these developmental achievements renders children "ready" for expanded opportunities for interacting with peers and adults in classroom settings. It is the role of adults in the environment to support these early interactions, and ensure a safe, secure environment for children's ongoing development and social competence.

During the early school years, a primary developmental task for children is to coordinate the social rules, beliefs, and values that they learn from significant adults in their lives with their own individual social perspectives as they enter novel situations in daily interactions with peers. At one level, interchanges with peers can be viewed in terms of social learning properties (i.e., evocation, recurrence, consolidation, differentiation, generalization) (Cairns, 1979; Patterson, 1980; Snyder et al., 2005). At a second level, peer interactions involve a range of cognitive processes (i.e., assimilation, accommodation, coconstruction, mutuality) that they apply to their relationships (Piaget, 1965; Sullivan, 1953; Youniss, 1980). The interplay between behavioral, and cognitive components of social interchange is important for clarifying the distinct roles parents, peers, and teachers occupy in the course of early childhood social development. To understand these different roles, it is necessary to consider the concept of social synchrony.

Social Synchrony

Social interaction involves the interchange of behavior between two persons. When individuals are grouped together in a social unit such as a family or classroom, there is a tendency for organization and exchange (Cairns, 1986; Patterson & Reid, 1984). Over time, interactions become coordinated and evolve into distinct patterns of behavior and sustained social relationships (Farmer, Xie, Cairns, & Hutchins, in press). Hence, the term *social synchrony* refers to social interchanges in which the behaviors of two individuals are mutually coordinated and dependent such that the actions of each support and are necessary for the expression of the actions of the other (Cairns, Cairns, Neckerman, Ferguson, & Gariepy, 1989).

There are two forms of social synchrony that reflect distinct types of social relationships: complementarity and reciprocity (Cairns, 1979). In *complementary* social interchanges, the two individuals have different behavioral roles and the behavior of each person is dependent upon the behavior of the other (follower–leader, teacher–student, bully–victim). In complementary relationships the individuals have unequal social status, but each role requires the other. Therefore, while the actions of the two individuals are different, the meaning or impact of the behavior is not realized without the behavior of the other. In contrast, in *reciprocal* social relationships the two persons tend to be of equal status and their actions are not bound by their social roles. Therefore, in reciprocal interchanges there is a tendency to behave similarly and to support patterns of behavior that are similar across each of the individuals.

To this point, social synchrony has been described in behavior and social interaction terms. However, there is also a cognitive and constructive component of synchronized social actions. In the two social worlds of children, complementary (i.e., those with adults and higher status peers) and reciprocal (i.e., those with equal status peers) relationships provide different opportunities for learning the social rules and principles (Youniss, 1980). In complementary relationships, children seek order and adults assume the authority role to teach children social expectations and rules.

> In this (complementary) relationship, children's participation is restricted. Rather than asserting initiatives freely or inserting reactions with the aim of directing interactions, children produce initiatives and reactions which meet the directives offered by adults. When they do initiate actions, they look to adults to tell them if those actions are appropriate or acceptable. (Youniss, 1980, p. 25)

In contrast, in reciprocal relationships, two children come to the relationship with equal status, each expecting that they understand the universal rules that govern social interaction. However, they quickly learn that there is not a shared view of order and that it is necessary to mutually construct rules to govern their actions. With the potential for unresolvable disputes in reciprocal interchanges, children discover that they can cooperate.

> Instead of allowing disputes to keep peers at loggerheads, children learn how to deal with differences of opinion. Specifically, they construct procedures of *discussion, debate, argument, negotiation,* and *compromise.* In each of these procedures, children learn how to present an opinion, listen to another's opinion, and adjust their own opinion in light of the other's view. (Youniss, 1980, p. 32)

The Role of Parents

As described by Youniss (1980), parents and other adults interact socially with children to promote the child's adaptation or adjustment to living in society. Parents have rules and values that they believe are critical to social order and they impart these views to the child by endorsing social behavior or by stopping the interaction and requiring changes. In this way, the parent and the child engage in interactions with different social-cognitive perspectives. The parent knows what is expected and accepted in a particular social interchange without direct knowledge of the child's perspective. Conversely, the child does not comprehend the social expectations but has a particular interest or viewpoint. Therefore, while the child is obliged to learn social rules from adults, they can also construct their own perspective.

Parents also provide the emotional support children need for coping with challenges outside of the family environment. When children's needs for comfort and support are met by parents, their expectations of relationships as positive, reciprocal interchanges is fostered (Sroufe, 2000). Generally, children with close emotional ties to parents interact more confidently and positively with adults and peers in school, and children with less close parental relationships are more prone to conflicted relationships with adults and peers in school (Howes, Matheson, & Hamilton, 1994; Pianta, Nimetz, & Bennett, 1997).

While the role of parent–child interactions in social development has been described to this point as one-sided transmissions of social cognitions flowing from the adult to the child, a different viewpoint emerges when adult–child interchanges are considered from a social learning perspective (Cairns, 1979; Patterson & Reid, 1984). As parents and children interact with each other, their behavior patterns become synchronized so that the behavior of each reinforces the behavior of the other. While such processes can promote positive social adjustment, parent–child interchanges can also support negative social patterns. Describing the child as both victim and architect of a maladaptive social system, Patterson (1982) suggests that coercive family processes may emerge as parents respond to a child's social behavior in ways that model, evoke, and reinforce patterns of problem behavior. Thus, while parent–child interchanges can be a means of teaching social rules and values, they can also become a channel for the development and expression of antisocial behavior.

The Role of Peers

When children begin to interact with peers in group settings such as day care, preschool, and kindergarten, they enter these interchanges with the sense that they understand the social order as taught to them by adults (Youniss, 1980). However, rules and social expectations learned at home may not apply in the new setting. Therefore, as children interact with peers whom they view as being of equal status, they learn to coconstruct new rules through cooperative activities with the peer. In the absence of such cooperation, children learn that their social interests and needs are likely to go unmet if they are not able to establish and support shared viewpoints, values, and expectations. This viewpoint presupposes that the relationship is reciprocal and that each is free to respond to the other in a similar manner.

However, children may sometimes interact with others who do not share their interests or may have unequal status. In such situations, the children may terminate the interaction, and perhaps the relationship. In the case of unequal status, a complementary relationship may be established (Cairns, 1979; Farmer et al., in press). Therefore, rather than coconstructing new rules and perspectives, the higher status child may make demands to which the lower-status child complies, and adds to her or his behavioral repertoire (Youniss, 1980; Farmer et al., in press).

Corsaro and Eder (1990) identified three themes of peer culture that emerged from their study of preschoolers' peer interactions. In their ongoing play interactions, children negotiated (a) sharing and friendship, (b) control and autonomy, and (c) conflict and social differentiation. Children balanced their interest in prosocial sharing and affiliation with the need to feel control and status. Over time, these negotiations, many characterized by conflict, resulted in a gradual differentiation of roles and status among the children.

The Role of Teachers

Teachers take on a special role in the social development of children. Like parents and other adults, teachers act as authority figures, imparting knowledge about social rules and expectations. Yet, beyond this complementary adult–child relationship, teachers supervise the social interactions and relationships of classrooms of children across several days, weeks, and months. In this role, teachers may serve both as the leader of a social group and as an unobtrusive "invisible hand." Teachers may facilitate social opportunities, allowing children to construct and develop their own peer culture, including establishing rules for interpersonal activities and development of friendships, peer cliques, and social structures (Cairns & Cairns, 1994; Holmberg, 1980).

In this position of adult authority and classroom leader, teachers have considerable influence on children's social views and beliefs and on the social dynamics of the classroom (Farmer, 2000; Van Acker & Wehby, 2000). While teachers may behave in ways that enhance children's interpersonal and social development, the way they manage the classroom and respond to individual students can contribute to patterns of problem behavior and social adjustment difficulties (Baker, 1999; Kellam, Ling, Merisca, Brown, & Ialongo, 1998; Sutherland & Oswald, 2005). Likewise, teachers' views and relationships with children may impact students' school adjustment and their relationships with peers. For example, Head Start teachers' views of children's abilities may contribute to their subsequent adaptation as they transition to public school (Skinner, Bryant, Coffman, & Campbell, 1998) and teachers' support for ethnically diverse and academically at-risk first graders is related to their peer acceptance (Hughes & Kwok, 2006). Thus, while teachers work to foster productive and well-behaved classroom contexts, they must be aware that their views about specific children and their actions toward them not only impact the child but also how classmates view and relate to the child. This is particularly true for children who have diverse needs and characteristics that are distinctively different from the majority of children in the classroom.

The relationships teachers form with children are influential in peer relations and peer culture. Generally, preschool children who have closer relationships with their teachers demonstrate better social competence with peers and are rated as more desirable playmates by their peers (Howes, Matheson & Hamilton, 1994), and poorer teacher–child relationships are associated with more peer aggression (Howes, 2000). The quality of teachers' interactions with students is associated with how peers view each other socially. When teachers used frequent negative feedback in their interactions with particular students, children in the classroom were more likely to rate these students lower in social competence (Wentzel, 2002). Studies reveal that students are attuned to aspects of their peers' relationships with teachers, and these relationship features are associated with their assessment of peers' competence in the classroom (Hughes, Cavell, & Willson, 2001).

SOCIAL CHARACTERISTICS AND DIVERSITY IN SOCIAL DEVELOPMENT

As each child begins life's journey, she is given a dozen or so pigments, a few brushes, a canvas, and instructions to paint as lovely a scene as she is able. There is no need to feel a blue mood of failure if a carefully painted sunrise is a little less than perfect because a needed pigment was not originally put in the kit. It is the effort that deserves the dignity we award one another as each of us works, sometimes painstakingly, on our mural. (Kagan, 1994, p. xxiii)

Children bring a variety of individual characteristics to their relations with adults and peers, and they influence these social relations by contributing to and drawing from interactions in a dynamic developmental process (Bronfenbrenner & Morris, 1998; Lerner, 1988; Magnusson & Stattin, 1998). Children's competence with peers emerges from these daily reciprocal processes, creating a unique, socializing peer culture in the classroom. The following section highlights aspects of children's individual contributions to peer relations in the classroom. Temperament, emotion regulation, and disability status are reviewed as characteristics the child brings to social interactions. In addition, gender and ethnicity of the individual child elicit cultural socialization that may frame their importance in a more pervasive way. Finally, the social roles children assume and their developmental significance for peer relationships and adjustment is considered.

Temperament, Emotional Regulation, and Peer Relations

Thomas and Chess (1977) determined that children who were temperamentally less regulated, highly emotionally reactive and negative, and fearful were difficult for parents to socialize, giving rise to the concept of *difficult temperament*. However, Thomas and Chess (1977) were clear in their assertion that temperament characteristics were not negative or positive, but that their "goodness of fit" with the social environment indicated their value for adjustment. Children of different temperament characteristics elicit different socializing behavior from parents, teachers, and peers. Contemporary research confirms that characteristics of temperament, such as effortful control, negative emotionality, and fearfulness, are related to children's initiating and responding to social interactions, and are associated with developing peer relations in ways that are adaptive and maladaptive (Rothbart & Putnam, 2002; Rothbart & Bates, 1998; Sanson, Hemphill & Smart, 2004).

Children high in *effortful control* attend and switch attention easily, regulate emotional expression, and modulate responsive impulses (Rothbart, 1988; Rothbart & Bates, 1998); therefore, better effortful control may allow children to participate more effectively in processes of social interaction (Sanson, Hemphill, & Smart, 2004). In several studies, children low in effortful control were more likely to experience difficulty interacting with peers and were rated lower in social competence by teachers (Eisenberg et al., 2001; Eisenberg et al., 2003; Smart & Sanson, 2001). Children who express frequent and intense *negative emotionality* may have difficulty engaging in interpersonal activities, elicit negative reactions from others, or simply miss opportunities to engage in beneficial proximal processes. Children high in negative emotionality sometimes demonstrate poorer social skills (Eisenberg et al., 1993) but may more likely take a leadership role in some play interactions (Dunn & Cutting, 1999). Negative emotionality may be most associated with difficult peer relations when combined with poor emotion regulation (Eisenberg et al., 1993). Finally, children high in *fearful inhibition* are prone toward shyness or social withdrawal in classroom settings (Rubin, Burgess, & Hastings, 2002), but they may also demonstrate self control and less aggression in times of conflict (Rothbart & Putnam, 2002).

Temperament may influence children's social skills directly, but increasing evidence suggests that temperament characteristics influence children's developing social skills indirectly, via social interaction processes (Bronfenbrenner & Morris, 1998; Bates, Pettit, Dodge, & Ridge, 1998; Gallagher, 2002; Rubin, Burgess, & Hastings, 2002). However, children with certain temperament characteristics are at risk for negative socialization. For these children, early socialization efforts on the part of parents and teachers may modify the negative and support children's positive behavior, such that children will be less likely to exhibit difficult temperament, and risk of poor social treatment is decreased.

Children's Emotion, Regulation, and Social Dynamics with Peers

Children's emotional competence, incorporating ability to send, receive, interpret, and experience emotional content of interpersonal interactions (Halberstadt, Denham & Dunsmore, 2001), contributes to peer competence. Younger children's limited experience with emotional events and language may interfere with their ability to properly interpret and send emotional messages. Older children and those with higher cognitive-language abilities are better able to identify emotional expression and situations (Denham, Zoller, & Couchoud, 1994).

While knowledge of emotions is helpful for children's competent interactions with peers, the ability to regulate emotion and attention may be particularly important for children's social relationships in the classroom. Emotion regulation consists of physiological, behavioral, and cognitive abilities that help the individual to manage their emotional experience and expressiveness in pursuit of a specific goal (Bridges, Denham, Ganiban, 2004). Unregulated expression of negative emotion causes difficulty in social situations, anger escalates conflict, anxiety and fear undermine a child's power in a social situation, and sadness creates discomfort in the other children. It is therefore helpful to use emotion regulation strategies to control the expression of negative emotion—anger, sadness, or fear—that may make social partners uncomfortable. Children who regulate emotional expression effectively demonstrate more cooperative play skills (Fantuzzo, Sekino, & Cohen, 2004; Spinrad et al., 2004), and children with less-skilled emotion regulation are more likely to be the victims of bullies (Mahady Wilton, Craig, Pepler, 2000).

Temperamental emotion expression and regulation influence children's behavior in the context of social interaction and relationships. However, only in the context of these relationships and the school environment are negative characteristics problematic. Alone, children's emotional reactivity may not be maladaptive, but in some contexts certain predispositions toward behavior present risk for poor peer relations. Rather than frame this risk from a child-based deficit perspective, however, it is valuable to consider each of these overlapping domains from a "goodness-of-fit" perspective (Thomas and Chess, 1977). School environments, and more importantly, teachers, can structure the classroom environment such that positive peer interactions are supported. Ideally, these positive interactions can inform children's developing social-emotional style, and support positive regulation in the school setting. Research on the transition to kindergarten and first grade verifies the importance of emotion regulation, attention, and motivation for success in school (Pianta & Cox, 1999). However, regulatory capacities continue to develop over the early school years, and the school setting should help the child to process, interpret, and respond to challenging interactions.

The Role of Gender in Peer Relations

Gender plays a critical role in children's early peer socialization. Boys and girls act as gender-specific socialization guides for peer relations, such that Maccoby (1990) suggested boys and girls develop in "separate subcultures." Children's preference for same-sex peer play is reflected in their beliefs (Martin, Fabes, Evans, & Wyman, 1999) and their actual play (Martin & Fabes, 2001; Fabes, Martin, & Hanish, 2003). Boys' play, compared to girls', is more active, physical, and stereotyped, and often takes place outside of adults' supervision (Fabes, Martin, & Hanish, 2003). Boys create their own rules in play activities; girls are more likely to play by adult-created conventions (Fabes, Martin, & Hanish, 2004). Through preschool and the elementary years, same-sex peer play increases, and one study reported that more play with same-sex partners in preschool resulted in greater sex-role differentiation in elementary school play (Fabes, Martin, & Hanish, 2003). While young children choose same-sex play most often when choosing their own play, mixed-sex play offers opportunities that same-sex play does not. For example, boys are less physical and active when playing in a mixed-sex group, and girls are more active and less stereotyped in their mixed-sex play (Fabes, Martin, & Hanish, 2003).

Both boys and girls engage in social aggression, but boys are more likely to be physical in their aggression, and girls engage more in social alienation and gossiping (Cairns, Cairns, et al., 1989; Crick, Ostrov, Appleyard, Jansen, & Casas, 2004). Parents and teachers typically rate girls as more socially competent than boys (Eisenberg et al., 2003); however, this difference in adult report may be related to girls' tendency to play closer to adults and to integrate more adult rules into their play interactions (Leaper, 1994). Factors facilitating the development of these gender differences in social interactions are controversial; however, research suggests that differences can be attributed to socialization differences from infancy (Brooks-Gunn & Warren, 1989).

Children With Disabilities and Peer Relationships

Children's language and cognitive abilities are associated with the quality of their peer relationships (Denham et al., 1994; Wiener, 2004). Children with disabilities, who often have difficulty communicating and interpreting social cues, experience challenges in developing peer relationships, particularly in complex group settings. Despite difficulties with being excluded in social interactions, children with disabilities desire peer contact (Wolfberg et al., 1999). Young children with disabilities fare better when they are able to pursue social relationships with typically developing children, as well as with other children with disabilities (Odom & Diamond, 1998).

Friendships may serve as protective mechanisms for children (Ladd, 1999) and may be particularly important for children with disabilities. Children with disabilities benefit from friendships in similar ways as typically developing children; children with friendships demonstrate more positive and less negative behaviors, and are more prosocial in their interactions with peers (Field, 1984; Guralnick & Groom, 1988; Buysse, 1993; Wiener, 2004). Unfortunately, in studies comparing peer relations of children with and without disabilities, children with disabilities had fewer friends, and were more likely to have no friends, according to teachers' reports (Buysse, Goldman, & Skinner, 2002). Observational studies confirm teachers' reports. Young children with disabilities have fewer friends (Guralnick, Gottman, & Hammond, 1996) and fewer interactions with peers than their typically developing classmates (Harper & McCluskey, 2003), and have difficulty maintaining friendships over long periods of time compared to their nondisabled peers (Buysse, 1993; Howes, 1983; Lederberg, Rosenblatt, Vandell, & Chapin, 1987).

When teachers facilitate peer relations and friendship development among children with disabilities and typically developing children, all children benefit. For example, when teachers used structured play groups in an inclusive preschool, peer ratings of children with disabilities improved (Odom et al., 1999). In the same study, when teachers facilitated peer-mediation or directly taught social skills, frequency and quality of peer social interaction increased for children with disabilities. While some children with disabilities require more intensive support from teachers (Odom, 2002), children with disabilities benefit from and contribute to meaningful, positive relationships with peers. Typically developing children are more accepting of children with disabilities when they have frequent, supported opportunities to interact in preschool settings (Diamond, 2001).

Ethnicity, Culture, and Peer Relations

Social dynamics in early childhood are embedded in the context of culture, though research has much to learn regarding how children's culture operates in classroom dynamics. Schools reflect a dominant culture, and the teacher and children bring their own understanding of culture to the classroom. Cultures even differ in the degree to which they promote developing long-term relationships outside of family relationships (Edwards, Knoche, Aukrust, Kumru, & Kim, 2006). Key in this cultural dance in the classroom are participants' expectations of the role of independence versus interdependence in relationships (Greenfield, Keller, Fuligni, & Maynard, 2003). Teachers communicate a set of cultural messages about expected social dynamics that may or may not be consistent with children's previous experience in the family and community. Children may have very different expectations about what to expect in relationships with peers.

Cross-cultural studies of Asian and Western preschoolers indicate that there are ethnic differences among children in emotion understanding (Wang, 2003), internalization of rules (Hadley, 2003), and parenting styles that support social development (Greenfield et al., 2003; Pearson & Rao, 2003). Some cross-ethnic research suggests that young children prefer to play with same-ethnicity peers (Finkelstein & Haskins, 1983; Lederberg, Chapin, Rosenblatt, & Vandell, 1986), though at least one study suggests that this preference is stronger for Euro-American children than for other groups (Howes & Wu, 1990). Comparative literature documenting children's play with peers cites more similarities than differences among cultures (Corsaro, Molinari, Hadley, & Sugioka, 2003, Farver, Kim, & Lee-Shin, 2000). For example, Corsaro and colleagues (2003) documented increases in same-sex play over the preschool years in their observations of Italian and U.S. preschoolers, noting that certain contexts of school culture seemed to support mixed-gender play more than others.

In addition to cross-cultural differences, it is important to consider differences among children developing in their family's national culture versus a different culture. In one study, Asian Indian children living in the United States had poorer perceived peer acceptance than Asian-Indian children living in India (Jambunathan & Counselman, 2004). Teachers should consider that children's difficulties with peers may arise from difficulty reconciling social messages from families and peers, particularly when the culture of family differs from that of the classroom.

Social Roles

Within social contexts such as early childhood classrooms, social hierarchies are established and individual children tend to develop social roles and relationship patterns that contribute to and help sustain social behavior (Corsaro & Eder, 1990; Farmer, 2000; Hanish, Ryan, Martin, & Fabes, 2005). Children adopt social roles that either put them at risk for sustained behavior problems or support positive developmental paths. Perhaps the most commonly identified set of social roles are those of bully, victim, and bully-victim (Perren & Alsaker, 2006; Kochenderfer & Ladd, 2001). Bullies tend to be physically and verbally aggressive, especially against their weaker peers (Pellegrini, 1998); socially active; part of large social clusters or networks; have well-developed leadership skills; and popular with peers (Estell, Farmer, & Cairns, in press; Perren & Alsaker, 2006; Hawley & Vaughn, 2003; Xie, Swift, Cairns, & Cairns, 2002). While there are specific social patterns of bullies, bullying is an interactive pattern that occurs within a social context (Pepler, Craig, & O'Connell, 1999), and is associated with social, behavioral, and academic outcomes.

The social behavior patterns of victims look quite different than those of bullies. Victims are more submissive, have poor leadership skills, are withdrawn, have few playmates, yet can also be cooperative and prosocial (Perren & Alsaker, 2006; Kochenderfer-Ladd, 2004). Peer victimization has been associated with academic, social, emotional, and psychological maladjustment including academic difficulties, less peer acceptance and fewer friendships (Hanish et al., 2005), lower self-esteem, generalized social anxiety (Kochenderfer-Ladd, 2004), and loneliness (Perren & Alsaker, 2006). There is also evidence to suggest that not all children are impacted in the same manner, and that individual differences in children's coping strategies may account for these variations (Kochenderfer-Ladd, 2004; Kochenderfer-Ladd & Ladd, 2001). Being liked by peers and having friends can act as a buffer, thus reducing the negative effects of victimization on children's developmental outcomes (Hanish et al., 2005). The social behavior pattern of bully-victims is mixed (Perren & Alsaker, 2006); bully-victims tend to be rejected by their peers, are less cooperative and less social, and are aggressive. Bully-victims are reactive in their aggression, acting defensively, whereas bullies are proactive in their aggression, acting offensively (Perrin & Alsaker, 2006; Crick & Dodge, 1996).

Socially withdrawn children develop social behavior patterns that put them at risk for maladaptive outcomes across the life span (Rubin & Coplan, 2004). Socially withdrawn children exhibit more anxiety, problems adjusting to school, low self-esteem, restricted verbal communication, and academic difficulties while experiencing peer rejection, social isolation, loneliness, and depression (Rubin & Coplan, 2004; Schneider, 1999; George & Hartmann, 1996). However, research has also found socially withdrawn children to have friendships (Schneider, 1999; Parker & Asher, 1993). In a classroom context, friendships may be a protective factor for withdrawn children by providing them with companionship and support, and lessoning the discomfort they feel in large group contexts (Rubin & Coplan, 2004; Schneider, 1999).

Friendships make a unique and important contribution to young children's social and emotional development (Ladd, Kochenderfer, & Coleman, 1996), and serve as a special context in which young children practice and refine social behaviors (Vaughn, Colvin, Azria, Caya, & Krzysik, 2001). Young children are identified as having quality friendships when they are socially competent and accepted by peers, exhibit prosocial behaviors, recognize the established norms and understand emotional situations in social contexts (Gagnon & Nagle, 2004; Keane & Calkins, 2004). Friendships can act as buffers against peer victimization and provide support to socially withdrawn children, as well as ease difficulties associated with the transition to school (Tomada, Schneider, de Domini, Greenman, & Fonzi, 2005). Tomada and colleagues (2005) found that even children as young as 7 years of age experienced changes in their attitudes towards school after the transition from an unstructured to the more formal, structured setting that occurred at the end of second grade. Children with close friendships experienced a more successful transition (Tomada et al., 2005).

The ability for young children to understand the social world of the early childhood classroom is dependent on their ability to understand and interpret social roles and relationships (Porath, 2003). The more experience children have in classroom contexts, the better able they are at analyzing and understanding the social dynamics, social roles, and social hierarchies of that context (Porath, 2003; Hawley & Little, 1999).

CLASSROOM SOCIAL STRUCTURES AND PEER GROUP PROCESSES

The emphasis of modern educational theory on the socioemotional aspects of human growth has imposed the necessity of developing techniques for evaluating the degree and character of social development. The problem has been complicated by the fact that social development applies not only to the individual but also to the social organization of which he is a part. Variations occur not only in the social status of a particular person within the group, but also in the structure of the group itself—that is, in the frequency, strength, pattern, and basis of the interrelationships which bind the group together and give it distinctive character. (Bronfenbrenner, 1943, p. 363)

Although Bronfenbrenner wrote this statement over sixty years ago, it continues to be highly relevant today. When considering classroom social dynamics, it is necessary to focus on both the individual and the social structure in which he or she is embedded. While there have been tremendous gains in methods for studying the social status of the individual (see Rubin, Bukowski, & Parker, 1998) and the emergence of a variety of methods for examining children's social networks and social structures (e.g., Adler & Adler, 1998; Bost, Vaughn, Boston, Kazura, & O'Neal, 2004; Cairns, Leung, Buchanan, & Cairns, 1995; Farver, 1996; Strayer & Santos, 1996), little research has examined the social status and peer affiliations of children across time in relation to the changing social dynamics of the classroom and the peer group. Therefore, while the current discussion will focus on peer group composition and social structures, the underlying dynamic processes that contribute to these structures will be considered in relation to the social characteristics of individual children.

Selective Affiliation, Homophily, and Complementarity

Following from the concept of social synchrony, as children are grouped in classroom settings, they begin to organize their interactions around smaller groups of peers. While preferences and choices may be somewhat temporary during the first days that children are placed together, patterns of interactions evolve into identifiable friendships. As children organize their friendships in relation to the friendships of their friends, distinct peer groups emerge. Such friendships and groups are not random but tend to reflect processes of selective affiliation. Typically, children affiliate with peers who are similar to them on key social characteristics. Known as homophily, this process is evident in both preschool and elementary classroom settings. Children form groups with peers who are similar to them in terms of aggression level (Estell, Cairns, Farmer, & Cairns, 2002; Farver, 1996; Snyder, West, Stockemer, Gibbons, & Almquist-Parks, 1996), academic achievement (Estell et al., 2002; Kindermann, 1993), and level of popularity (Bagwell, Coie, Terry, & Lochman, 2000; Farmer et al., 2002; Ladd, 1983). Through reciprocal interactions (i.e., social synchrony) children who affiliate with similar peers are likely to support and sustain each others' social behavior, whether positive or negative.

However, some peer groups appear to engage in complementary as well as reciprocal interactions and relationships. That is, some children may affiliate with peers who are similar to them on some characteristics but dissimilar on others. For example, in some elementary peer groups, boys may be dissimilar on levels of aggression but similar in terms of popularity or status in the social hierarchy (Adler, Kless, & Adler, 1992; Farmer et al., 2002; Farmer & Farmer, 1996). In essence, it appears that children's peer groups form around shared values, behaviors, and beliefs and around the degree to which the relationship helps to support and sustain the child's status or position in the classroom social structure (Farmer et al., in press).

Social Structures and Dominance Hierarchies

Children not only develop friendships and peer groups, they also establish dominance hierarchies and social networks. Within early childhood classrooms, children's ability to influence others and to control resources results in the emergence of dominance hierarchies (Charlesworth & LaFreniere, 1983; Hawley & Little, 1999; Strayer & Strayer, 1976). While such hierarchies may be viewed as the relative influence of an individual student on her or his peers in the classroom, it is also possible to identify levels of influence within peer groups or across peers (Strayer & Santos, 1996). Likewise, individual children and groups can be distinguished by their general level of prominence or centrality both within a peer group and in the general social structure of the classroom (Adler & Adler, 1998; Estell, Cairns, et al., 2002; Farmer & Rodkin, 1996).

Dominance hierarchies and hierarchical social structures can help to support and sustain social order in the classroom (Farmer et al., in press; Strayer & Trudel, 1984). Rather than having children repeatedly challenging each other for the control of resources, the emergence of a dominance hierarchy can help to reduce overall conflict and aggressive behavior in the classroom. As dominance hierarchies are established, children tend to synchronize their behavior to avoid direct confrontation. However, there can be a dark side to social hierarchies and social synchrony. In some instances, children may find themselves in relations (i.e., bullies, victims) that they cannot escape because of their patterns of affiliation, their social reputation, and their limited opportunities to establish new social roles (Cairns, Neckerman, & Cairns, 1989; Hymel, Wagner, & Butler, 1990). Thus, it is important for teachers to be aware of the classroom social hierarchy, children's roles within the hierarchy, and the general processes by which children maintain peer group membership and support their social roles.

The Maintenance of Peer Group Boundaries and Social Roles

As suggested in the quote by Bronfenbrenner (1943), peer groups and social roles are highly fluid in the early childhood years. In later childhood and early adolescence, studies have shown that children are constantly jockeying for social position and that they will use a variety of physical (i.e., displays of physical dominance, bullying) and social (i.e., rumors, gossiping, manipulating friendships) strategies to promote and sustain the boundaries of their peer group (i.e., protect the group from less popular peers or to keep more popular peers from taking away one's friends). While these strategies are generally considered the domain of adolescence, work on early elementary peer group affiliations, social competence, peer acceptance, social dominance, and resource control all suggest that the social dynamics in early childhood may be similar to that of later childhood (Estell, Farmer, et al., 2002; Hawley, 2003; Strayer & Santos 1996; Vaughn,

Vollenweider, Bost, Azria-Evans, and Snider, 2003). As methods to assess social dynamics in preschool and early elementary classrooms are developed, it is likely that new views will emerge regarding the relationship between children's behavior, their social relationships, and the broader social network.

CONSIDERATIONS AND IMPLICATIONS FOR TEACHERS

The classroom is a complex social setting requiring understanding of the expectations and roles of teachers and peers and adaptation to a particular set of social rules and responsibilities. Moreover, there are "contexts with context" in classrooms, as groups, friendship, and instructional situations evolve and change over time. Children who are able to understand and adjust to this complexity are more likely to experience academic success. (Porath, 2003, p. 471)

As the review to this point suggests, early childhood teachers encounter a variety of factors that influence the interpersonal relationships and social dynamics in the classroom. Social dynamics is defined here as the interpersonal characteristics, peer group processes, and social structural factors that evolve as children are grouped together and try to synchronize their behavior (Adler & Adler, 1998; Cairns, 1979; Farmer, 2000). But this doesn't mean that teachers are simply working with what they can see before them. On the contrary, children's interactions with their parents, the behaviors and values they learn from their family members, their cultural beliefs and norms, their general abilities and skills, and their past social development history all influence social dynamics in the classroom. This is further amplified when the classroom has many children who come from different backgrounds. Thus, at one level, managing classroom dynamics involves getting to know the children, their families, their cultural beliefs and values, and their views with regard to appropriate behaviors and relationships among children and between children and adults. However, a review of these factors is beyond the scope and aims of this chapter. Instead, these factors should be considered in relation to the interpersonal processes and social network factors that emerge in the classroom over time. Accordingly, this section focuses on scaffolding to support young children's interpersonal interactions, understanding classroom social processes and social structures, and strategies to prevent bullying and victimization.

Scaffolding to Support Young Children's Interpersonal Interactions

With very young children and toddlers, child-care teachers provide considerable guidance and support to children's social interactions. For example, in a study of 18 to 42 month old children, Holmberg (1980) found that in day care settings, adults paced the children, but the children's needs and skill levels determined the pace. For the youngest children, adults directly supported and monitored children's social interactions. For older children, adults provided relatively little direct support and only interceded in situations or circumstances that were clearly beyond the children's ability to successfully negotiate among themselves. Thus, in early childhood settings, adults simultaneously engage in complementary adult–child interaction and facilitate reciprocal child–child interchanges that promote children's cognitive and behavioral social competence.

Likewise, in preschool and early elementary classrooms, children's social competence is positively associated with teacher involvement (Baker, 1999; Bost et al., 2004; Howes, 1988; Kontos & Wilcox-Herzog, 1997). Adults scaffold competencies by making suggestions for behavior, asking questions, and offering physical assistance to children. Supporting social competence requires that adults adjust their involvement to meet the needs of the current functioning of the child, understanding that more socially competent children may need less teacher involvement (Kontos & Wilcox-Herzog; 1997). In contrast, students who have school adjustment difficulties are least likely to feel that they are being supported by adults even though they command significantly more adult time and direct involvement (Baker, 1999). Therefore, teachers must be able to "read" the level of support individual students need and proactively structure activities to provide a level of scaffolding that blends the level of direct guidance and independence that the child needs to function successfully in the classroom while providing opportunities to develop new levels of social competence.

Understanding Classroom Social Processes and Social Structures

To promote social contexts that enhance children's social development and reduce social adjustment problems, it is helpful for teachers to go beyond understanding the competence level and skill needs of individual students and to be aware of peer group processes and social structural factors that influence their behavioral patterns and social-cognitive exchange (Farmer, Pearl, & Van Acker, 1996; Rodkin & Hodges, 2003). This includes being aware of a variety of social factors including classroom peer groups, children's placement in the social structure, social dominance hierarchies, identification of children in key social roles (i.e., classroom leaders, popular children, children who are supportive of others, bullies, victims), identification of children who lack friends or group membership, synchronous relationships (both reciprocal and complementary) that contribute to problematic behavior patterns, issues of deviancy training (i.e., social reinforcement for problem behavior), and the general ebb and flow of relationships in the classrooms.

However, teachers must also be aware of how their behavior, values, and viewpoints can influence the classroom social dynamics. For example, while it is important for teachers to be aware of the social roles that children have in the social structure it is also important for teachers to not treat such roles as traits and to respond to children in ways that inadvertently support and sustain the role. Also, it is important for teachers to be aware that children they view as "good kids" can contribute to the problems of others and children who they perceive to be troubling can be viewed positively by their peers. Building from the concept of the two forms of social synchrony and the two social worlds of children (Youniss, 1980), teachers must establish clear ground rules and expectations that help make the classroom a comfortable and safe place for all children while simultaneously providing opportunities for children to collectively construct social rules and expectations that are meaningful for them and that facilitate cognitive linkages between the social importance of their behavior in terms of the relationships that they have with each other.

Strategies to Prevent Bullying and Victimization

To prevent bullying and victimization, it is helpful for teachers to be aware of which groups of children are most influential in the social structure. It is not uncommon for bullies to be children who are viewed by teachers and peers as being among the leaders in the classroom (Adler & Adler, 1998). In classrooms where children are jockeying for social power, students are more likely to engage in aggressive and bullying activities (Pellegrini, 1998; Strayer & Strayer, 1976). Further, bullying tends to involve others within the classroom community and in elementary classrooms it is not uncommon for classmates to help shield the bully from being detected by the teacher (Adler, Kless, & Adler, 1992; Atlas & Pepler, 1998). Therefore, it may be productive for teachers to identify ways for the classroom community to decide how they can collectively guard against bullying and to establish procedures for classmates to intervene or to seek the support of an adult. However, teachers should be careful not to support a specific child or group of children from being identified as "bullies." Instead, it may be more productive to have children focus on the behaviors that they feel comfortable trying to stop or to get assistance from an adult.

Because behaviors are synchronized, it is important to focus on the behavior of the bully, but also to address factors that support chronic victimization. On one hand, this may involve addressing the behaviors of the victim that makes her or him vulnerable to being bullied and picked-on by others. On the other hand, this may also require careful and unobtrusive efforts aimed at helping the child to gain a new social role and social reputation that reduces the likelihood that children would target the child for victimization. But again, it is important that teachers do not draw attention to the child's difficulties or inadvertently support the child's identity as a victim. Rather, such interventions should occur during normal daily activities and not be initiated in response to a specific incident or problem.

NEW DIRECTIONS IN EARLY CHILDHOOD SOCIAL DEVELOPMENT RESEARCH

By recognizing that some aggressive behavior serves an adaptive function, researchers can continue to more finely focus their efforts to identify the precise configurations of form and function that are associated with negative consequences and develop more targeted remediation efforts. At the same time, identifying the precise configurations of form and function that are associated with positive outcomes can help to derive the complicated calculus that balances individual and social needs and gives rise to socially competent aggressive individuals. (Hawley & Vaughn, 2003, p. 242)

There is much to be learned regarding the social dynamics in early childhood classrooms. First, building from work on peer group processes, resource control, and the relationship between aggression, popularity, and social competence, there is a need to clarify how children gain social influence and power in the classroom. As Hawley and Vaughn (2003) suggest, rather than simply viewing prosocial-aggressive leaders as a problem, we need to clarify whether the influence of such children can be channeled in ways that promote a supportive context without marginalizing some classmates. Second, as Bronfenbrenner (1943) suggests, new methods are needed that permit the investigation of the social development of individual children in relation to the dynamic change of the peer groups in which they are embedded. By developing methods that explore the relationship between children's development of social cognitive skills and behaviors in relation to their social interaction patterns and their peer group membership, it may be possible to clarify ways in which classroom social dynamics can be adapted to support the development of children's social competence. Third, as Porath (2003) suggests, teachers need strategies they can use to support children as they learn how to navigate the complexities of classroom social contexts. This includes helping children understand different relationships among peers (i.e., friendships, peer groups) and the social roles in the class. Such work should include a focus on determining whether children's ability to navigate classroom social dynamics enhances their peer relations, academic achievement, and engagement in classroom activities.

The Productive Expression of Aggression and Social Influence in the Classroom

As Kagan (1994) asserts, children come to each relationship with a set of experiences or skills that predisposes them to behave certain ways. As Corsaro and Eder (1990) observed, children seek affiliation, power, and autonomy in their peer cultures. It is the task of the teacher in the early childhood classroom to support children's individual differences in the context of the peer culture. For children prone to aggression, this may mean providing opportunities to experience leadership while learning benefits of sharing. Given a positive outlet, aggression may be reflected in leadership or achievement motivation (Hawley, 1999; Hawley & Vaughn, 2003). For children prone to withdrawal, or shyness, the teacher may need to provide opportunities by scaffolding challenges into small, achievable steps. In all cases, the teacher must recognize that children's expression of their social self has potential for positive and negative adaptation for the classroom peer culture.

Methods to Examine the Developmental Interplay Between Children and Their Peer Groups

In addition to studying mechanisms of children's peer development, new methods for studying children's peer cultures in context are needed. Most studies of peer relations rely on parent, teacher, and peer report using sociometric measures and ratings of "social competence." These, along with observation measures based on short periods of time and narrow behavioral descriptions, don't provide the rich understanding of peer cultures that is desirable. Research will benefit from moving beyond "liking," "popularity," and "social competence" to understanding of the quality of children's relationships, including mechanisms of peer support and conflict, communication of emotion content, shared affect, and comfort-seeking. Researchers need to find methodologies that measure the quality of children's relationships, and mechanisms that facilitate high quality relationships. Mixed methods, discourse analysis, and observation of children in context, observed over time and across contexts, could yield rich data for understanding the social dynamics of early childhood peer groups. Ethnographic approaches to the study of peer culture show promise, as in William Corsaro's studies of children's peer cultures in preschools in Italy and the United States (Corsaro et al., 2003; Corsaro & Nelson, 2003; Eder & Corsaro, 1999). Additional strategies are needed to understand the characteristics of children in relation to the characteristics of the peer group and the characteristics of the group in relation to the larger context (i.e., classroom, grade, and school). Also, more research is needed considering mechanisms associated with children's positive peer experiences, including more about gender preference in play, ethnic preferences, and peer relations that support children with disabilities.

Strategies to Enhance Children's Understanding of Classroom Social Dynamics

Much as parents coach children in their social interactions (Mize & Pettit, 1997), teachers can assist children in their understanding of classroom peer dynamics. Teachers need to create opportunities for positive interaction with all students and make these interactions explicit for other children. Serving as models for appropriate social behavior, teachers can encourage students to interact with one another despite differences in behavior or relational styles. Assisting children in their skills, emotion understanding (Denham et al., 1994), and communication provides opportunities for children to think explicitly about positive peer exchanges that may not come naturally.

CONCLUSION

Research of the last few decades has provided rich information about the social structures of children's peer relations and friendships from the perspectives of parents and teachers, and a smaller amount from children's perspectives. However, our view of the complex processes of children's peer cultures is challenged by the difficulty of studying child-in-context. Bronfenbrenner (1979) noted this difficulty when he described developmental psychology as "the science of the strange behavior of children in strange situations with strange adults for the briefest possible periods of time" (p. 513). Despite significant gains in this regard, the need remains for new methods and procedures to study children's perspectives of peer group processes. It is not sufficient to describe the peer cultures of the majority; rather, we also must examine peer processes for those children at the margins of the social structure. Similarly, focusing on the individual in exclusion of the group, or deficit in exclusion of strength, fails to capture the richness of the peer experience in children's development, and could also fail to provide guidance for informing practice in the classroom.

NOTE

1.   This chapter was supported by grant: H324C040230 from the Office of Special Education Programs and by grants: R305L030162 and R305A040056 from the Institute of Education Sciences to Thomas W. Farmer (Principal Investigator). The views expressed in this article are ours and do not represent the granting agencies.

REFERENCES

Adler, P. A., & Adler, P. (1998). *Peer power: Preadolescent culture and identity.* New Brunswick, NJ: Rutgers University Press.

Adler, P. A., Kless, S., & Adler, P. (1992). Socialization to gender roles: Popularity among elementary school boys and girls. *Sociology of Education, 65,* 169–187.

Atlas, R. S. & Pepler, J. (1998). Observation of bullying in the classroom. *The Journal of Educational Research, 92,* 86–99.

Bagwell, C. L., Coie, J. D., Terry, R. A., & Lochman, J. E. (2000). Peer clique participation and social status in preadolescence. *Merrill-Palmer Quarterly, 46,* 280–305.

Baker, J. A. (1999). Teacher–student interaction in urban at-risk classrooms: Differential behavior, relationship quality, and student satisfaction with school. *Elementary School Journal, 100,* 57–70.

Bates J. E., Pettit, G. S., Dodge, K. A., Ridge, B. (1998). Interaction of temperamental resistance to control and restrictive parenting in the development of externalizing behavior. *Developmental Psychology, 34*(5), 982–995.

Berk, L. E. (2005). *Child development.* Boston, MA: Pearson.

Bost, K. K., Vaughn, B. E., Boston, A. L, Kazura, K. L., & O'Neal, C. (2004). Social support networks of African-American children attending Head Start: A longitudinal investigation of structural and supportive network characteristics. *Social Development, 13,* 393–412.

Bridges, L. J., Denham, S. A., & Ganiban, J. M. (2004). Definitional issues in emotion regulation research. *Child Development, 75,* 340–345.

Bronfenbrenner, U. (1943). A constant frame of reference for sociometric research. *Sociometry, 6,* 363–397.

Bronfenbrenner, U. (1979). *The ecology of human development: Experiments by nature and design.* Cambridge, MA: Harvard University Press.

Bronfenbrenner, U., & Morris, P. (1998). The ecology of developmental processes. In R. M. Lerner (Ed.), *Theoretical models of human development* (pp. 993–1028). New York: Wiley.

Brooks-Gunn, J., & Warren, M. P. (1989). Biological and social contributions to negative affect in young adolescent girls. *Child Development, 60*, 40–55.

Buysse, V. (1993). Friendships of preschoolers with disabilities in community-based child care settings. *Journal of Early Intervention, 17*, 380–395.

Buysse, V., Goldman, B. D., & Skinner, M. L. (2002). Setting effects on friendship formation among young children with and without disabilities. *Exceptional Children, 68*, 503–517.

Cairns, R. B. (1979). *Social development: The origins and plasticity of interchanges.* San Francisco, CA: Freeman.

Cairns, R. B. (1986). Phenomena lost: Issues in the study of development. In Jaan Valsiner (Ed.), *The individual subject and scientific psychology* (pp. 97–111). New York: Plenum.

Cairns, R. B., & Cairns, B. D. (1994). *Lifelines and risks: Pathways of youth in our time.* New York: Harvester Wheatsheaf.

Cairns, R. B., Cairns, B. D., Neckerman, H. J., Ferguson, L. L., & Gariépy, J-L. (1989). Growth and aggression: Childhood to early adolescence. *Developmental Psychology, 25*, 320–330.

Cairns, R. B., Leung, M.-C., Buchanan, L., & Cairns, B. D. (1995). Friendships and social networks in childhood and adolescence: Fluidity, reliability, and interrelations. *Child Development, 66*, 1330–1345.

Cairns, R. B., Neckerman, H. J., & Cairns, B. D. (1989). Social networks and the shadows of synchrony. In G. R. Adams & R. Montemayor (Eds.), *Biology of adolescent behavior and development. Advances in adolescent development: Vol. 1. An annual book series* (pp. 275–305). Thousand Oaks, CA: Sage Publications, Inc.

Charlesworth, W. R., & LaFreniere, P. (1983). Dominance, friendship, and resource utilization in preschool childrens groups. *Ethology and Sociobiology, 4*, 175–186.

Corsaro, W. A. & Eder, D. (1990). Children's peer cultures. *Annual Review of Sociology, 16*, 197–220.

Corsaro, W. A., Molinari, L., Hadley, K. G., & Sugioka, H. (2003). Keeping and making friends: Italian children's transition from preschool to elementary school. *Social Psychology Quarterly, 66*, 272–292.

Corsaro, W. A., & Nelson, E. (2003). Children's collective activities and peer culture in early literacy in American and Italian preschools. *Sociology of Education, 76*, 209–227.

Crick, N. R., & Dodge, K. A. (1996). Social information-processing mechanisms on reactive and proactive aggression. *Child Development, 67*, 993–1002.

Crick, N. R., Ostrov, J. M., Appleyard, K., Jansen, E. A., Casas, J. F. (2004). Relational aggression in early childhood: "You can't come to my birthday party unless...". In M. Putallaz & K. Bierman (Eds.), *Aggression, antisocial behavior, and violence among girls: A developmental perspective* (pp.71–89). New York, NY: Guilford Publications, Inc.

Denham, S. A., Zoller, D., & Couchoud, E. A. (1994). Socialization of preschoolers' emotion understanding. *Developmental Psychology, 30*, 928–936.

Diamond, K. E. (2001). Relationships among young children's ideas, emotional understanding, and social contact with classmates with disabilities. *Topics in Early Childhood Special Education, 21*(2), 104–113.

Dunn, J., & Cutting, A. L. (1999). Understanding others, and individual differences in friendship interactions in young children. *Social Development, 8*, 201–219.

Eder, D., & Corsaro, W. A. (1999). Ethnographic studies of children and youth. *Journal of Contemporary Ethnography, 28*, 520–531.

Edwards, C. P., Knoche, L., Aukrust, V., Kumru, A., & Kim, M. (2006). Parental ethnotheories of child development: Looking beyond independence and individualism in American belief systems. In U. Kim, K-S Yang, & K-K Hwang (Eds.), *Indigenous and Cultural Psychology: Understanding people in context* (pp. 141–162). New York, NY: Springer Science + Business Media.

Eisenberg, N., Cumberland, A., Spinrad, T. L., Fabes, R. A., Shepard, S. A., & Reiser, M. M., et al. (2001). The relations of regulation and emotionality to children's externalizing and internalizing problem behavior. *Child Development, 72*(4), 1112–1134.

Eisenberg, N., & Fabes, R. A. (1992). Emotion, regulation, and the development of social competence. In M. Clark (Ed.), *Emotion and social behavior* (pp.119–150). Thousand Oaks, CA: Sage Publications, Inc.

Eisenberg, N., Fabes, R. A., Bernzweig, J., Karbon, M., Poulon, E., & Hanish, L. (1993). The relations of emotionality and regulation to preschoolers' social skills and sociometric status. *Child Development, 64*, 1418–1438.

Estell, D. B., Cairns, R. B., Farmer, T. W., & Cairns, B. D. (2002). Aggression in inner-city early elementary classrooms: Individual and peer-group configurations. *Merrill Palmer Quarterly, 48*, 52–76.

Estell, D. B., Farmer, T. W., & Cairns, B. D. (in press). Bullies and victims in rural African-American youth: Behavioral characteristics and social network placement. *Aggressive Behavior.*

Estell, D. B., Farmer T. W., Cairns R. B., & Cairns, B.D. (2002). Social relations and academic achievement in inner-city early elementary classrooms. *International Journal of Behavioral Development, 26*, 518–528.

Fabes, R. A., Martin, C. L., & Hanish, L. D. (2003). Young children's play qualities in same-, other-, and mixed-sex peer groups. *Child Development, 74*, 921–932.

Fabes, R. A., Martin, C. L., & Hanish, L. D. (2004). The next 50 years: Considering gender as a context for understanding young children's peer relationships. *Merrill-Palmer Quarterly, 50*, 260–273.

Fantuzzo, J., Sekino, Y., & Cohen, H. L. (2004). An examination of the contributions of interactive peer play to salient classroom competencies for urban Head Start children. *Psychology in the Schools, 41*, 323–336.

Farmer, T. W. (2000). The social dynamics of aggressive and disruptive behavior in school: Implications for behavior consultation. *Journal of Educational and Psychological Consultation, 11*, 299–321.

Farmer, T. W., & Farmer, E. M. (1996). The social relationships of students with exceptionalities in mainstream classrooms: Social network centrality and homophily. *Exceptional Children, 62*, 431–450.

Farmer, T. W., Leung, M-C., Pearl, R., Rodkin, P. C., Cadwallader, T. W., & Van Acker, R. (2002). Deviant or diverse groups? The peer affiliations of aggressive elementary students. *Journal of Educational Psychology, 94*, 611–620.

Farmer, T. W., Pearl, R., & Van Acker, R. M. (1996). Expanding the social skills deficit framework: A developmental synthesis perspective, classroom social networks, and implications for the social growth of students with disabilities. *The Journal of Special Education, 30,* 232–256.

Farmer, T. W., & Rodkin, P. C. (1996). Antisocial and prosocial correlates of classroom social positions: The social network centrality perspective. *Social Development, 5,* 176–190.

Farmer, T. W., Xie, H., Cairns, B. D., & Hutchins, B. C. (in press). Social synchrony, peer networks, and aggression in school. In P. Hawley et al. (Eds.), *Prosocial and antisocial functions of aggression.* Mahwah, NJ: Lawrence Erlbaum Associates.

Farver, J. A. (1996). Aggressive behavior in preschooler's social networks: Do birds of a feather flock together? *Early Childhood Research Quarterly, 11,* 333–350.

Farver, J. A., Kim, Y. K., & Lee-Shin, Y. (2000). Within cultural differences: Examining individual differences in Korean American and European American preschoolers' social pretend play. *Journal of Cross-Cultural Psychology, 31,* 583–602.

Field, T. M. (1984). Early interactions between infants and their postpartum depressed mothers. *Infant Behavior & Development, 7,* 517–522.

Finkelstein, N. W., & Haskins, R. (1983). Kindergarten children prefer same-color peers. *Child Development,* 54(2), pp. 502–508.

Gagnon, S. G., & Nagle, R. J. (2004). Relationships between peer interactive play and social competence in at-risk preschool children. *Psychology in the Schools, 41,* 173–189.

Gallagher, K. C. (2002). Does child temperament moderate the influence of parenting on adjustment? *Developmental Review, 22,* 623–643.

George, T. P., & Hartmann, D. P. (1996). Friendship networks of unpopular, average, and popular children. *Child Development, 67,* 2301–2316.

Greenfield, P. M., Keller, H., Fuligni, A., & Maynard, A. (2003). Cultural pathways through universal development. *Annual Review of Psychology, 54,* 461–490.

Guralnick, M. J., Gottman, J. M., & Hammond, M. A. (1996). Effects of social setting on the friendship formation of young children differing in developmental status. *Journal of Applied Developmental Psychology, 17,* 625–651.

Guralnick, M. J., & Groom, J. M. (1988). Friendships of preschool children in mainstreamed play groups. *Developmental Psychology, 24,* 595–604.

Hadley, K. G. (2003). Children's word play: Resisting and accommodating confucian values in a Taiwanese kindergarten classroom. *Sociology of Education,* 76(3), 193–208.

Halberstadt, A. G., Denham, S. A., & Dunsmore, J. C. (2001). Affective social competence. *Social Development, 10,* 79–119.

Hanish, L. D., Ryan, P., Martin, C. L., & Fabes, R. A. (2005). The social context of young childrens' peer victimization. *Social Development, 14,* 2–19.

Harper, L. V., & McCluskey, K. S. (2003). Teacher-child and child-child interactions in inclusive preschool settings: Do adults inhibit peer interactions? *Early Childhood Research Quarterly 18,* 163–184.

Hawley, P. H. (1999). The ontogenesis of social dominance: A strategy-based evolutionary perspective. *Developmental Review, 19,* 97–132.

Hawley, P. H. (2003). Prosocial and coercive configurations of resource control in early adolescence: A case for the well-adapted Machiavellian. *Merrill-Palmer Quarterly, 49,* 279–309.

Hawley, P. H., & Little, T. D. (1999). On winning some and losing some: A social relations approach to social dominance in toddlers. *Merrill-Palmer Quarterly, 45,* 185–214.

Hawley, P. H., & Vaughn, B. E. (2003). Aggression and adaptive functioning: The bright side of bad behavior. *Merrill-Palmer Quarterly, 49,* 239–242.

Holmberg, M. C. (1980). The development of social interchange patterns from 12 to 42 months. *Child Development, 51,* 448–456.

Howes, C. (1983). Patterns of friendship. *Child Development, 54,* 1041–1053.

Howes, C. (1988). Relations between early child care and schooling. *Developmental Psychology, 24,* 53–57.

Howes, C. (2000). Social-emotional classroom climate in child care, child–teacher relationships and children's second grade peer relations. *Social Development, 9,* 191–204.

Howes, C., Matheson, C. C., & Hamilton, C. E. (1994). Children's relationships with peers: Differential associations with aspects of the teacher–child relationship. *Child Development, 65,* 253–263.

Howes, C., & Wu, F., (1990). Peer interactions and friendships in an ethnically diverse school setting. *Child Development,* 61(2), 537–541.

Hughes, J. N., Cavell, T. A., & Willson, V. (2001). Further support for the developmental significance of the quality of the teacher–student relationship. *Journal of School Psychology, 39,* 289–301.

Hughes, J. N., & Kwok, O. M. (2006). Classroom engagement mediates the effect of teacher–student support on elementary students' peer acceptance: A prospective analysis. *Journal of School Psychology, 43,* 465–480.

Hymel, S., Wagner, E., & Butler, L. J. (1990). Reputational bias: View from the peer group. In S. Asher & J. Coie (Eds.), *Peer rejection in childhood* (pp. 120–129). Cambridge University Press.

Jambunathan, S., & Counselman, K. P. (2004). Perception of self-competence among Asian Indian preschoolers living in the USA and India. *International Journal of Early Years Education,* 12(1), 17–23.

Kagan, J. (1994). *Galen's prophecy: Temperament in human nature.* New York, NY: Basic Books Inc.

Keane, S. P., & Calkins, S. D. (2004). Predicting kindergarten peer social status from toddler and preschool problem behavior. *Journal of Abnormal Child Psychology, 32,* 409–423.

Kellam, S.G., Ling, X.G., Merisca, R., Brown, C. H., & Ialongo, N. (1998). The effect of the level of aggression in the first grade classroom on the course and malleability of aggressive behavior into middle school. *Development and Psychopathology, 10,* 165–185.

Kindermann, T. A. (1993). Natural peer groups as contexts for individual development: The case of children's motivation in school. *Developmental Psychology, 29,* 970–977.

Kochenderfer-Ladd, B. (2004). Peer victimization: The role of emotions in adaptive and maladaptive coping. *Social Development, 13,* 329–349.

Kochenderfer-Ladd, B., & Ladd, G. W. (2001). Variations in peer victimization: Relations to children's maladjustment. In J. Juvonen and S. Graham (Eds.),

Peer harassment in school: The plight of the vulnerable and victimized (pp. 25–48). New York: Guilford Press.

Kontos, S., & Wilcox-Herzog, A. (1997). Influences on children's competence in early childhood classrooms. *Early Childhood Research Quarterly, 12,* 247–262.

Ladd, G. (1983). Social networks of popular, average, and rejected children in school settings. *Merrill-Palmer Quarterly, 29,* 283–307.

Ladd, G. W. (1999). Peer relationships and social competence during early and middle childhood. *Annual Review of Psychology,* 50, 333–359.

Ladd, G. W., Kochenderfer, B. J., & Coleman, C. C. (1996). Friendship quality as a predictor of young children's early school adjustment. *Child Development, 67,* 1103–1118.

Leaper, C. (1994). Exploring the consequences of gender segregation on social relationships. In C. Leaper (Ed), *Childhood gender segregation: Causes and consequences* (pp. 67–86). San Francisco, CA: Jossey-Bass.

Lederberg, A. R., Chapin, S. L., Rosenblatt, V., & Vandell, D. L. (1986). Ethnic, gender, and age preferences among deaf and hearing preschool peers. *Child Development,* 57, 375–386.

Lederberg, A. R., Rosenblatt, V., Vandell, D. L., & Chapin, S. L. (1987). Temporary and long-term friendships in hearing and deaf preschoolers. *Merrill-Palmer Quarterly, 33,* 515–533.

Lerner, R. M. (1988). Developmental contextualism and person-context interaction in a life-span perspective. *Schweizerische Zeitschrift Fur Psychologie-Revue Suisse de Psychologie, 47,* 83–91.

Maccoby, E. E. (1990). Gender and relationships: A developmental account. *American Psychologist, 45,* 513–520.

Magnusson, D., & Stattin, H. (1998). Person-context interaction theories. In W. Damon & R. M. Lerner (Eds.), *Handbook of child psychology: Volume 1: Theoretical models of human development (5th ed.)* (p. 685–759). Hoboken, NJ: John Wiley & Sons, Inc.

Mahady Wilton, M., Craig, W. M., Pepler, D. J., (2000). Emotional regulation and display in classroom victims of bullying: Characteristic expressions of affect, coping styles, and relevant contextual factors. *Social Development,* 9(2), 226–245.

Martin, C. L., & Fabes, R. A. (2001). The stability and consequences of young children's same-sex peer interactions. *Developmental Psychology, 37,* 4311–4446.

Martin, C. L., Fabes, R. A., Evans, S. M., & Wyman, H. (1999). Social cognition on the playground: Children's beliefs about playing with girls versus boys and their relations to sex segregated play. *Journal of Social and Personal Relationships, 16,* 751–771.

Mize, J., & Pettit, G. S. (1997). Mother' social coaching, mother–child relationship style and children's peer competence: Is the medium the message? *Child Development, 68,* 312–332.

Odom, S. L. (2002). Narrowing the question: Social integration and characteristics of children with disabilities in inclusion settings. *Early Childhood Research Quarterly, 17*(2), 167–170.

Odom, S. L., & Diamond, K. E. (1998). Inclusion of young children with special needs in early childhood education: The research base. *Early Childhood Research Quarterly, 13*(1), 3–25.

Odom, S. L., McConnell, S. R., McEvoy, M. A., Peterson, C., Ostrosky, M., Chandler, L. K., et al. (1999). Relative effects of interventions supporting the social competence of young children with disabilities. *Topics in Early Childhood Special Education, 19*(2), 75–91.

Parker, J. G., & Asher, S. R. (1993). Friendship and friendship quality in middle childhood: Links with peer-group acceptance and feelings of loneliness and social dissatisfaction. *Developmental Psychology, 29*, 611–621.

Patterson, G. R. (1980). Mothers—The unacknowledged victims—Introduction. *Monographs of the Society for Research in Child Development, 45*, 1–64.

Patterson, G. R. (1982). *A social learning approach: Coercive family process.* Eugene, OR: Castilia.

Patterson, G. R., & Reid, J. B. (1984). Social interactional processes within the family: The study of moment by moment family transactions. *Journal of Applied Developmental Psychology, 5*, 237–262.

Pearson, E., & Rao, N. (2003). Socialization goals, parenting practices, and peer competence in Chinese and English preschoolers. *Early Child Development and Care, 173*(1), 131–146.

Pelligrini, A. D. (1998). Bullies and victims in school: A review and call for research. *Journal of Applied Developmental Psychology, 19*, 165–176.

Pepler, D., Craig, W. M., & O'Connell, P. (1999). Understanding bullying from a dynamic systems perspective. In A. Slater & D. Muir (Eds.), *Developmental psychology: An advanced reader* (pp. 440–451). Malden, MA: Blackwell Publishers.

Perren, S., & Alsaker, F. (2006). Social behavior and peer relationships of victims, bully-victims, and bullies in kindergarten. *Journal of Child Psychology and Psychiatry, 47*, 45–57.

Piaget, J. (1965). *The moral judgment of the child.* New York, NY: The Free Press.

Pianta, R., & Cox, M. (1999). *The transition to kindergarten.* Baltimore, MD: Brookes-Cole.

Pianta, R. C., Nimetz, S. L., & Bennett, E. (1997). Mother–child relationships, teacher–child relationships, and school outcomes in preschool and kindergarten. *Early Childhood Research Quarterly, 12*, 263–280.

Porath, M. (2003). Social understanding in the first years of school. *Early Childhood Research Quarterly, 18*, 468–484.

Rodkin, P. C., & Hodges, E. V. E. (2003). Bullies and victims in the peer ecology: Four questions for psychologists. *School Psychology Review, 32*(3), 384–400.

Rothbart, M. K. (1988). Temperament and the development of inhibited approach. *Child Development, 59*, 1241–1250.

Rothbart, M. K., & Bates, J. E. (1998). Temperament. In W. Damon & N. Eisenberg (Eds.), *Handbook of child psychology, 5th ed.: Vol 3. Social, emotional, and personality development* (pp. 105–176). Hoboken, NJ: John Wiley & Sons, Inc.

Rothbart, M. K., & Putnam, S. P. (2002). Temperament and socialization. In L. Pulkinnen, & A. Caspi (Eds.), *Paths to successful development: Personality in the life course* (pp. 19–45). Cambridge, UK: Cambridge University Press.

Rubin, K. H., Bukowski, W., & Parker, J. (1998). Peer interactions, relationships, and groups. In N. Eisenberg (Ed.), *Handbook of child psychology, 5th ed.: Social, emotional, and personality development* (pp. 619–700). New York: Wiley.

Rubin, K. H., Burgess, K. B., & Hastings, P. D. (2002). Stability and social-behavioral consequences of toddlers' inhibited temperament and parenting behaviors. *Child Development, 73, 483–495*.

Rubin, K. H., & Coplan, R. J. (2004). Paying attention to and not neglecting social withdrawal and social isolation. *Merrill-Palmer Quarterly, 50, 506–534*.

Sanson, A., Hemphill, S. A., & Smart, D. (2004). Connections between temperament and social development: A review. *Social Development, 13, 142–170*.

Schneider, B. H. (1999). A multimethod exploration of the friendships of children considered socially withdrawn by their school peers. *Journal of Abnormal Child Psychology, 27, 115–123*.

Skinner, D., Bryant, D., Coffman, J., & Campbell, F. (1998). Creating risk and promise: Children's and teachers' co-constructions in the cultural world of kindergarten. *Elementary School Journal, 98, 297–310*.

Smart, D., & Sanson, A. (2001). Children's social competence: The role of temperament and behaviour, and their "fit" with parents' expectations. *Family Matters, 59, 10–15*.

Snyder, J., Schrepferman, L., Oeser, J., Patterson, G., Stoolmiller, M., & Snyder, A. (2005). Deviancy training and association with deviant peers in young children: Occurrence and contribution to early-onset conduct problems. *Development and Psychopathology, 17, 397–413*.

Snyder, J., West, L., Stockemer, V., Gibbons, S., & Almquist-Parks, L. (1996). A social learning model of peer choice in the natural environment. *Journal of Applied Developmental Psychology, 17, 215–237*.

Spinrad, T. L., Eisenberg, N., Harris, E., Hanish, L. D., Fabes, R. A., & Kupanoff, K. et al. (2004). The relation of children's everyday nonsocial peer play behavior to their emotionality, regulation, and social functioning. *Developmental Psychology, 40, 67–80*.

Sroufe, A. L. (2000). Early relationships and the development of children. *Infant Mental Health Journal, 21, 67–74*.

Strayer F. F., & Santos A. J. (1996). Affiliative structures in preschool peer groups. *Social Development, 5, 117–130*.

Strayer, F. F., & Strayer, J. (1976). An ethological analysis of social agonism and dominance relations among preschool children. *Child Development, 47, 980–989*.

Strayer, F. F., & Trudel, M. (1984). Developmental changes in the nature and function of social dominance among young children. *Ethology and Sociobiology, 5, 279–295*.

Sullivan, H. S. (1953). *The interpersonal theory of psychiatry*. New York: Norton.

Sutherland, K. S., & Oswald, D. P. (2005). The relationship between teacher and student behavior in classrooms for students with emotional and behavioral disorders: Transactional processes. *Journal of Child and Family Studies, 14, 1–14*.

Thomas, A., & Chess, S. (1977). *Temperament and development*. New York: Brunner/ Mazel.

Tomada, G., Schneider, B. H., de Domini, P., Greenman, P. S., & Fonzi, A. (2005). Friendship as a predictor of adjustment following a transition to formal academic instruction and evaluation. *International Journal of Behavioral Development, 29*, 314–322.

Van Acker, R., & Wheby, J. H. (2000). Exploring the social contexts influencing student success or failure: Introduction. *Preventing School Failure, 44*, 93–96.

Vaughn, B. E., Colvin, T. N., Azria, M. R., Caya, L., & Krzysik, L. (2001). Dyadic analyses of friendship in a sample of preschool-age children attending Head Start: Correspondence between measures and implications for social competence. *Child Development, 72*, 862–878.

Vaughn, B. E., Vollenweider, M., Bost K. K., Azria-Evans, M. R., & Snider, J. (2003). Negative interactions and social competence for preschool children in two samples: Reconsidering the interpretation of aggressive behavior for young children. *Merrill-Palmer Quarterly: Journal of Developmental Psychology, 49*, 245–278.

Wang, Q. (2003). Emotion situation knowledge in American and Chinese preschool children and adults. *Cognition & Emotion, 17*(5), 725–746.

Wentzel, K. R. (2002). Are good teachers like good parents? Teaching styles and student adjustment in early adolescence. *Child Development, 73*, 287–301.

Wiener, J. (2004). Do peer relationships foster behavioral adjustment in children with learning disabilities? *Learning Disability Quarterly, 27*, 21–30.

Wolfberg, P. J., Zercher, C., Lieber, J., Capell, K., Matias, S., Hanson, M., et al. (1999). "Can I play with you?" Peer culture in inclusive preschool programs. *Journal of the Association for Persons with Severe Handicaps, 24*(2), 69–84.

Xie, H., Swift, D. J., Cairns, B. D., & Cairns, R. B. (2002). Aggressive behaviors in social interaction and developmental adaptation: A narrative analysis of interpersonal conflicts during early adolescents. *Social Development, 11*, 205–224.

Youniss, J. (1980). *Parents and peers in social development: A Sullivan-Piaget perspective.* Chicago, IL: University of Chicago Press.

CHAPTER 3

THE DEVELOPMENT OF SOCIAL IDENTITY AND INTERGROUP ATTITUDES IN YOUNG CHILDREN

Kurt Kowalski

Answering the question, "Who am I?" is a life long process that has important implications for personal well being as well as social behavior. Although seemingly obvious at first, the answer to this question is not always so clear since after further consideration it becomes apparent that our sense of self, of who we are, is actually quite complex and made up of multiple components (Markus & Wurf, 1987; Turner, Oakes, Haslam & McGarty, 1994). Our unique constellation of personal characteristics (e.g., personality traits, abilities, reactions to events, etc.) can be thought of as composing our *personal identity,* or the part of our self that makes us different from others. Another aspect of our self, our *social identity,* can be thought of as that part of the self that we have in common with others, and that is derived from our membership in groups. The present chapter examines the development of this social identity in young children and discusses its implication for interpersonal relations and educational practice in early childhood.

Of course not all groups are the same. Some are relatively trivial with respect to self definition, whereas, others have greater social and psychological import. With this in mind, the present chapter focuses largely on

Contemporary Perspectives on Social Learning in Early Childhood Education, pages 49–82
Copyright © 2007 by Information Age Publishing

those group memberships, such as gender and ethnicity, that have the greatest impact on children's social development. It is clear that membership in these groups has far reaching implications for children's socialization from an early age. For example, research indicates that the way parents perceive and interact with infants is heavily influenced by a child's gender and this differential treatment continues throughout childhood (Seavey, Katz & Zalk, 1975; Ruble & Martin, 1998). In addition, teachers' expectations and behavior towards students have been shown to be similarly influenced by children's gender and ethnic group memberships (Dweck, Davidson, Nelson, & Enna, 1978; Minuchin & Shapiro, 1983; Rosenthal & Jacobsen, 1968). These examples illustrate how adult's perceptions of children's group membership clearly influence the environment children interact with, and no doubt the development of their identity. Importantly, however, how children see themselves and others with respect to group membership also has significant implications for development. This later influence, that related to children's own awareness of social group membership, is the primary focus of this chapter. This awareness of group membership will be discussed in the context of previous research in this area and new developments in the application of Social Identity and Self-Categorization Theory (Tajfel & Turner, 1979; Turner, Hogg, Oakes, Reicher, & Wetherell, 1987) to children's social development. Special attention will be given to how awareness of social categories functions in young children's day-to-day social interactions as suggested by the results of a recent naturalistic study in this area conducted by the present author.

CATEGORICAL REPRESENTATION

Putting things into categories is an essential and universal feature of human thinking (Bruner, 1957). This process involves responding to things that are different as if they are the same, based on some shared similarity. This kind of cognitive structuring brings a sense of coherence and stability to the environment and allows for a reduction in the amount of information that must be processed when interacting with new instances of a category. For example, if a friend presents us with a bowl of fruit and we select an apple from it, we are in all likelihood actually picking up a new and distinct object that we have never encountered before. Despite this, we generally do not feel the need to closely examine this new object and learn all of its properties. Rather, we treat it as if it were equivalent to other objects like it that we had encountered in the past and wholeheartedly bite into it. Treating it as a category, rather than a unique thing, allows us to extend past knowledge into the present and make multiple inferences about it that can guide our behavior (e.g., It is eatable. It tastes good. It may keep the doctor away).

This process of categorization, and the cognitive benefits that accrue from it, is not only extended to objects, but also to events and people. Adults divide the social world up into multiple groupings. For example, people are thought of as being young, old, men, women, Black, White, Asian, liberal, conservative, poor, gifted, etc. These categories help simplify a complex social environment and guide behavior. For example, when purchasing a gift for someone we might consider buying quite different things depending on whether that person is young or old, liberal or conservative, a man or a woman. Of course while generalizations based on these categories can be used to predict behavior (e.g., Will they like the gift or not?), they can also lead to negative consequences associated with stereotyping that are not so apparent in our categorization of the physical world. For example, just the act of placing things into categories causes people to exaggerate differences between categories and similarities within them (Tajfel & Wilkes, 1963). For both adults and children, this exaggeration can lead to the distorted perception that members of groups we do not belong to are, "all the same," and more different from us than they really are (Brown, 2000; Katz, 1973; Katz, Sohn, & Zalk, 1975; Messick & Mackie, 1989). Despite these pitfalls, social categorization is pervasive. The world children grow up in is divided by adults into multiple social groupings. Thus, it makes sense to ask, when do children become aware of these categories?

AWARENESS OF SOCIAL CATEGORIES

Studies examining infants' differential looking patterns at photographs of animals or inanimate objects indicate that they clearly possess the capacity to place things into categories (Mandler, 1998; Quinn & Eimas, 1996). When children display this capacity with humans appears to be influenced by a number of factors, including the visibility of the categories and the degree to which adults imbue them with meaning. Both gender and race are social categories that have clear physical correlates (e.g., hair, body type, skin color) and research suggests that children show some sensitivity to these visual cues by the time they reach their first birthday (Katz & Kofkin, 1997; Leinbach & Fagot, 1993). This precocity is revealed by the fact that after being presented with a series of photos of same gender, or same race faces, infants look longer at a new novel face if it is from outside the presented category (i.e., a different gender or different race) than if it is in the same category. This differential looking indicates that, at least under these highly structured conditions of sequential presentation, infants notice the physical cues that mark membership in these groups.

Between two and three years-of-age, children begin to display a clear awareness of gender categories as indicated by their ability to sort photos of people by sex and select the correct photo in response to gender labels (Ruble & Martin, 1998; Yee & Brown, 1994). The ability to do this with racial categories emerges somewhat later with children demonstrating this ability between the ages of three to five (Aboud, 1988; Ocampo, Bernal, & Knight, 1993). This delay in racial awareness, relative to gender, is likely due to differences in the amount of exposure children have to these categories. Virtually all children are exposed to people of both genders from birth. Whereas, depending on their living conditions, many children may have limited exposure to people from different races. In addition, adults emphasize gender categories more than race or ethnicity in their interactions with children. For example, Katz and Kofkin (1997) found that when parents were asked to discuss specially designed picture books with their toddlers that systematically varied the race and gender of the characters, virtually all parents mentioned gender in their discussions (99%), whereas, few mentioned race (6%). Moreover, from infancy on, children are likely to hear themselves being referred to by adults as, "good boys" or "good girls," but rarely as good, "Whites," "Blacks," or "Asians" (Katz, 1983). This kind of labeling likely has a significant impact on children's ability to self identify, an important milestone in the development of social identity.

Most children correctly label their own gender by the time they reach three years-of-age (Ruble et al., 2004; Ruble & Martin, 1998). The ability to identify their racial or ethnic group membership develops somewhat later and varies according to group membership and context. White children correctly identify themselves with respect to racial group membership between the ages of three to five (Aboud, 1988; Ramsey, 1991). This ability appears to vary more among minority children. While some studies report Black children displaying correct self-identification around this same time (three to five), others report considerable development in this ability up until the age of seven (Katz & Kofkin, 1997; McAdoo, 1985; Aboud 1988; Semaj,1980; Spencer, 1984). Studies with Asian children suggest a similarly drawn out pattern of development. Approximately half of the Asian children sampled displayed accurate racial self-identification between the ages of three to five, with this number continuing to grow until seven or eight (Fox & Jordan, 1973; Kowalski & Lo, 2001a; Morland & Hwang, 1981). Importantly, however, this appears to vary across context with Asian children in the United States self-identifying later than those in Taiwan (Kowalski & Lo 2001a; Kowalski & Lo 2001b; Morland & Hwang, 1981). Similar context effects have been found for Black children (McAdoo, 1985; Williams & Morland, 1976).

Perhaps due to the lack of clear physical markers, children's ability to correctly identify their ethnicity is generally reported as emerging somewhat later than race, around seven or eight (Aboud, 1988; Ocampo, Bernal, & Knight, 1993). However, studies have reported Chinese, Indian, and Mexican children correctly identifying their ethnic group membership as early as five or six (Aboud, 1977; Bernal, Knight, Ocampo, Garza, & Cota, 1993; Kowalski, 1998; Kowalski & Kanitkar, 2003) and Maori and Pakeha children as early as four (Vaughan, 1963). Thus, it appears that the ability to accurately identify their racial and ethnic group membership begins to emerge in children between the ages of three to five, but one should expect considerable variability between children, groups, and across contexts.

SOCIAL CATEGORY CONSTANCY

Unlike other more transient social categories such as age, school affiliation, or sports team membership, membership in gender, racial or ethnic categories does not change. This permanence is believed to contribute to the potency that these group memberships have on children's personality development. Ruble et al. (2004) suggests that knowing that these social identities do not change, likely makes them more central to children's overall self conceptions. Kohlberg (1966) argued that this understanding of permanence, combined with children's mastery motivation, leads children to seek out information about these group identities so that they can master them and act in accordance with group norms. Moreover, Kohlberg held that this understanding of permanence develops over an extended period of time and follows a stage-like progression from (a) accurate *identification* of the self and others, to (b) understanding the *stability* of category membership across time, to (c) an appreciation of the *consistency* of the identity across superficial transformations in appearance or context. The attainment of all three stages is called *constancy* and represents what Kohlberg considered to be a mature understanding of category membership linked to developmental changes in children's cognitive abilities akin to those required to master Piaget's classic conservation tasks (Piaget, 1951).

Research examining this suggested progression for gender (e.g., Slaby & Frey, 1975) typically asks children to identify someone as a boy or girl (identification). If they are successful and demonstrate identification, they are then asked about stability. For example, what if the identified person grows up, will they be a man or woman? If stability is displayed, consistency is assessed by asking what would happen if the person started dressing and acting in cross-gendered ways (e.g., a boy growing his hair long, wearing dresses, and playing girl games), would they still be the same gender (e.g., a boy)? Sometimes these questions are accompanied by pictures that demonstrate the actions described (e.g., Gouze & Nadelman, 1980), and children are required to justify their answers (e.g., Emmerich, Goldman, Kirsh, & Sharabany, 1977).

Questions similar in form to those above are used to assess racial and ethnic constancy. For example, Semaj (1980) asked children what would happen if a Black child put on a blond wig and white makeup, would they be Black or White? And, Doyle, Beaudet, and Aboud (1988) showed children photos of a child (initially identified as Italian) as he dressed in a traditional native Indian outfit. After being shown the final photo in the series, in which the child is fully dressed, including wearing a traditional headdress, children were asked if he is now an Italian or an Indian?

A substantial amount of research has been conducted using these types of interviews and this work generally shows a clear developmental progression in the way children respond to these questions, with children moving from identification to constancy as expected. This research indicates that children typically display gender constancy around four to five years-of-age (Bem, 1989; Gouze & Nadelman, 1980; Martin & Little, 1990; Slaby & Frey, 1975). Whereas, racial and ethnic constancy is not typically displayed until children reach eight or nine (Doyle, et al., 1988; Ocampo, et al., 1993; Ocampo, Knight & Bernal 1997; Semaj, 1980). It should be noted, however, that there is quite a bit of variability across studies in the age at which constancy is reported, and how to interpret children's responses to the consistency questions is still open to debate (Ruble et al., 2004; Ruble & Martin, 1998; Hirschfeld, 1995).

Many researchers argue that children's failure to assert the immutability of these social identities, in the face of adult questioning about changing clothes and putting on makeup, reflects young children's tenuous understanding of these categories. This is especially the case for race and ethnicity where it has been argued that children's early identifications represent little more than the application of empty labels (Aboud, 1988; Alejandro-Wright, 1985; Bernal, et al., 1993). This belief that children's early understanding of these categories is severely limited, and lacks an appreciation of permanence, has been reinforced by antidotal accounts of children's racial misconceptions (e.g., stating that skin color can be washed off) and research reporting that, under questioning, children often appeal to fanciful or supernatural explanations for skin color differences until they attain more mature levels of cognitive development (i.e., concrete operations) around age seven (Clark, Hocevar, & Dembo, 1980; Ramsey, 1987).

It now seems, however, that much of the confusion children display in structured interviews concerning the origin and permanence of gender, ethnic or racial categories, stems from limitations associated with young children's language abilities and the methods of inquiry used by researchers. For example, it has been shown that children participating in constancy interviews often do not understand what researchers are really asking them and answer the questions about children changing identity as if the children were playing some sort of game. Thus, children who initially do not display constancy (i.e., who responded that the child in question changed) often change their responses when researches ask them if the child really changed, or is just pretending (Leonard & Archer, 1989; Martin & Halverson, 1983a). Certainly one can see how these interviews, in which strange adults ask children about unusual transformations (e.g., people putting on wigs and elaborate costumes), might be confusing for young children. Moreover, since in normal conversation we generally do not ask questions about the possibility of impossible events, just the fact that an authoritative adult is asking whether a transformed individual might have changed identity, appears to hint that this is indeed possible.

The emphasis on constancy in the identity literature seems to suggest that prior to attaining it, children believe identity changes. However, it is not clear why change rather than stability would be the baseline that children start with, since children's day-to-day experience would appear to support stability (i.e., the people they know do not change). Indeed, research that reflects this daily experience, or that studies children in their natural contexts, indicates that young children know more about the stability and origins of gender and ethnicity/race than previously believed. For example, simple changes, such as using familiar children, or proper names rather than pronouns for the transformed child in gender constancy interviews, reveal that children as young as three understand the stability of gender (Leonard & Archer, 1989; Miller, 1984). Also, by using growth (child to adult) rather than artificial transformations, Hirshfeld (1995) has demonstrated that children as young as three and four expect race to be stable across a person's life span. In addition, recent naturalistic research examining kindergartners' discussions about ethnicity and race in school (Holmes 1995; Kowalski & Kanitkar, 2003) indicates that they clearly expected parents to be the same ethnicity and race as their children because they believe a person's race is transmitted to them by their parents as a result of birth (see also Hirshfeld, 1996 and Van Ausdale & Feagin, 2001). Moreover, even when using a traditional, and arguably confusing measure (e.g., suggesting a change in skin color due to sun exposure), recent research reports that a fairly large percentage of three to five year-olds (41%) expected race to remain stable (Rutland, Cameron, Bennett, & Ferrell, 2005).

The above research, demonstrating considerable knowledge of gender and racial stability in children as young as three to five years-of-age, suggests this knowledge is present soon after identification and that previous results from traditional constancy interviews likely need to be reinterpreted. That is, rather than viewing these procedures as tapping children's already existing beliefs about identity impermanence, it may be more accurate to view them as assessing the degree to which children's expectancy of identity stability can be overridden by adult suggestion that identity can change. This distinction is important for theories of identity development that emphasize the importance of self-identification (e.g., Martin & Halverson, 1981; Tajfel & Turner, 1986). These approaches suggest that mere knowledge of group membership (not unassailable knowledge) is sufficient to put into play a number of potent psychological processes. This notion would seem to be consistent with the fact that most developmental research linking knowledge of identity to changes in other important variables, such as beliefs and behaviors, suggests that identification, or stability, are the important levels of initial understanding, rather than constancy (Doyle et al., 1988; Ocampo et al., 1997; Ruble & Martin, 1998). This is not to imply that continued growth in gender and racial knowledge is unimportant in the development of children's social identity once children have learned to self identify. Rather, it is to suggest that it is growth in knowledge of behaviors, roles, and traits typically associated with group membership (e.g., stereotypes and values) which is most important to children's psychological development after self-identification, not growth in their knowledge about the permanence of identity across artificial transformations suggested in research interviews. The effect of this other important social knowledge will be discussed in a later section.

SOCIAL CATEGORIES IN CHILDREN'S EVERY DAY LIFE

How does awareness of social categories influence young children's developing self perceptions and social interactions? To answer this question we will examine some findings from a recent study that investigated young children's naturally occurring discourse about gender and ethnicity/race in kindergarten (Kowalski & Kanitkar, 2003). This work will serve as a point of departure for reviewing research findings in this area and examining how these findings, often arrived at in the context of highly structured experimental interviews, relate to children's day-to-day social interactions in a natural setting (i.e., school).

The present study was conducted by recruiting two kindergarten teachers to keep audiotape diaries of their students' comments and behaviors relevant to gender and ethnicity/race for a period of three months. Both teachers taught in the same ethnically/racially diverse full-day kindergarten class (one morning and one afternoon) and were trained in how to identify and record target behaviors. The class was composed of 21 five to six year-olds (9 boys and 12 girls) approximately half of whom were children of color (4 Asians, 3 Blacks, 2 Asian Indians, and 1 Latino). A content analysis was performed on the teachers' transcribed audiotape diaries and children's comments were coded according to a theoretically and empirically derived coding system. The results follow.

Category Salience

An examination of the children's comments indicated that they talked about gender almost three times more often than ethnicity and race. Of the 69 social interactions recorded, 51 had to do with gender and 18 with ethnicity or race, suggesting that gender was more salient in the children's naturally occurring social interactions. Previous research examining the relative salience of social categories for young children has generally presented them with photos or drawings of people who vary along multiple dimensions (e.g., race, gender, age). They are then asked to sort the people into groups that are "alike," or "go together," to see which dimensions they find prominent. Young children typically sort people by both gender and race with some studies showing a preference for sorting by gender over race (e.g., Bigler & Liben, 1993) and others showing a preference for race over gender (e.g., Ramsey, 1991).

The above variability across studies likely reflects the fact that the relative salience of specific social identities is highly influenced by the social context children find themselves in. For example, in social contexts where there is considerable racial or ethnic tension among adults, race or ethnicity may be more prominent in children's person perceptions than in places where this conflict is absent (e.g., Trew, 2004). The level of diversity children experience in the classroom, school, or neighborhood, likely also influences the relative salience that gender, race, and ethnicity have in their social interactions. Moreover, this salience can vary from moment to moment and situation to situation. Indeed, Connolly (2001) argues that researchers who ignore the role that context plays in children's use of racial categories, risk reifying these categories by treating them as if they are a stable constant forever present in children's social interactions. To avoid this reification, and appreciate the fluidity of social categorization in children's lives, we now turn to Self-Categorization Theory (Turner et al., 1987). This theory has made significant contributions to our understanding of how social categories function in adults, and has recently been profitably applied to children (Kowalski & Lo, 2005; Sani, Bennett, Mullally, & MacPherson, 2003).

A major tenet of Self-Categorization Theory (SCT) is that our experience of self is dynamic and determined by the specific self-conception that is activated or salient in any given circumstance (Turner et al., 1987). This means that the way we experience ourselves, and others, will vary from situation to situation according to a number of factors. These factors include the comparative context we find ourselves in, our personal goals, and the ease with which different categories are called into consciousness as a result of past experience. For example, if a White boy steps out into a school playground and finds himself among a group of Asian children, he may experience himself as White and the other children as Asian. However, if some of the children are male and some female, and he is looking for someone to engage in ruff-and-tumble play with, he may experience himself and the others in terms of their gender identities (i.e., as boys and girls who may be more or less likely to want to wrestle!). If he wants to ask a question about an upcoming class party, he may experience the group of children as potentially informative classmates, or as members of some other class who would be less likely to answer his question.

The point of the above illustration is that the social category that becomes salient for a child can change according to context. For example, when Kowalski and Lo (2005) asked Chinese-American children to select potential playmates from photos of same sex children identified as either White, Black, or Japanese, they showed a preference for Japanese children and their justifications for their choices suggested that they did so because they perceived themselves and the Japanese children as being in the same group (e.g., "they're Asian like me"). However, when the photo of the Japanese child was presented in the context of two other Asians (i.e., Taiwanese and Chinese) the children seldom chose the Japanese child. Instead they preferred the Chinese child, and they referred to ethnicity in their justifications (e.g., "they're Chinese like me"). Thus, whether they perceived themselves, and children in the photos, in terms of racial or ethnic group membership was determined by the context they were presented with.

This fluidity of social identity in childhood has been described by others (e.g., Ramsey, 1987) and suggests the importance of not viewing these identities as merely fixed, or static across all situations. Moreover, it can explain why children in structured interviews, like the one described above, have been observed to express clear bias for their own ethnic group in the interview, and then leave the interview situation and cheerfully select a child from a different ethnic group to play with. That is, these interviews are generally structured to highlight ethnicity or race (e.g., the children presented in photographic arrays only vary on this dimension and not with respect to age, gender, attractiveness, facial expression, etc.). Thus, the identities that become salient in the interview context may be very different from what emerges in children's typical social interactions where peers and self can be conceptualized along a number of dimensions (e.g., gender, friendliness, interest, sports ability, etc.). Hence, when considering which identities are salient in young children's day-to-day social interactions, it is helpful to observe them interacting in a natural context as was done in the diary study described in the present chapter.

Another study (Holmes, 1995) that examined kindergartners in a natural setting (i.e., school), found much the same as the diary study—that gender was more prominent than race or ethnicity in the children's self-conceptions and social exchanges. This confluence of findings with respect to the important role that gender plays in young children's self-conceptions is probably at least partially a reflection of the way that social contexts consistently highlight gender group membership from an early age, as noted in the previous discussion of self-identification. Gender is used in overtly functional ways much more often than race or ethnicity in our current society. Thus, things like the rest rooms people can use, or the clothes that they can wear, are determined by gender group membership. Indeed, teachers often use gender in functional ways in the classroom. For example, by having children line up according to gender (e.g., "girls on the left, boy on the right"), or by instructing children to use gender as a criteria for selecting classmates to participate in classroom activities (e.g., "a boy just had a turn, choose a girl next time"). Research indicates that this kind of functional use of social categories in the classroom elevates their salience for children and can unknowingly facilitate the formation of stereotypes and group bias (Bigler, 1995; Bigler, Jones, & Lobliner, 1997). Adult use of the categories appears to send a signal to children about their importance that then leads children to start using the categories to organize their social experience. This is consistent with the SCT belief that children form and use these categories, not only to reduce their information processing load in new situations, but also to create meaning and orient themselves in the social landscape.

Children's Use of Social Categories

The comments about gender and ethnicity/race that the teachers observed kindergartners make in the present study were further analyzed to examine their content. Those comments that referred to group role behaviors or characteristics were coded as stereotypic. Most of children's gender comments, 97%, fell into this category, whereas, only 17% of their ethnic/racial comments were of this kind. Two examples, one for gender and the other for ethnicity, are presented below.

A Group of children are putting on a puppet show. Boy ONE has a dinosaur puppet. Boy TWO has a butterfly puppet. They talk back and forth and boy ONE says, "Well, you need to have a boy puppet, and give that girl puppet to a girl." He then proceeds to say which puppets boy ONE could have that are boy puppets.

> Girl ONE comes into class and says she is not going to eat morning snack because she had a "really, really, good breakfast." Girl TWO asks, "What did you have?" Girl ONE, "Rice with bacon, it's my favorite." Girl TWO, "Well it must be Chinese breakfast food, but it's not American breakfast food." Girl ONE is Chinese.

Children's stereotypic comments were further analyzed to determine the degree to which they conformed with common adult stereotypes concerning these groups. The majority of children's gender stereotypic comments, 47 (96%) were consistent with adult gender stereotypes. Whereas, just one (33%), of the only three ethnic stereotypes expressed, was adult consistent (see above example). Taken together, the sheer number of children's gender stereotypic comments, and their consistency with adult forms, suggests that kindergartners possess considerably more information about gender roles and characteristics than ethnicity/race. This difference in information is consistent with previous research indicating that by the time children reach kindergarten they possess a great deal of knowledge about gender roles, behaviors, and traits (Ruble & Martin, 1998). In comparison, studies suggest young children's knowledge of ethnic or racial behaviors, values, and traits is relatively impoverished (Aboud, 1988; Bernal, Knight, Garza, Ocampo, & Cota, 1990). That is, while young children are clearly aware of ethnic/racial group membership, the few studies that have assessed their knowledge of ethnic practices and behaviors (Bernal et al., 1990; Ocampo et al., 1997) suggest children possess little information about these prior to entering middle childhood. As with the differences in age of self-identification and salience discussed in the previous section, this difference in knowledge about gender and ethnicity/race appears to reflect differences in both the amount of exposure children have to category members and the way these categories function in society. For example, a number of social roles and behaviors are overtly linked to gender group membership (e.g., family roles, occupations, types of emotional expression, etc.), while associations between ethnicity and race and these kinds of behaviors are relatively fewer and often more subtle. As a result, children seem to learn roles and behaviors for gender much earlier than they do for ethnicity and race. And, as we will see, they actively use this gender knowledge to regulate their social interactions, whereas, knowledge of racial and ethnic group membership appears to have fewer behavioral implications for young children. It seems likely, however, that as children move towards adolescence and acquire more ethnic and racial knowledge, that knowledge, in addition to being an important component of their identity, will also be used to regulate their behavior (e.g., Fordham & Ogbu 1986; Knight, Cota, & Bernal, 1993; Rotheram & Phinney, 1987).

Cognitive theories of social identity (e.g., Kohlberg, 1966; Martin & Halverson, 1981) suggest that self-identification and stereotype knowledge play an important role in children's social development. These theories contend that once children learn they are members of a group (e.g., gender), they use learned information about group characteristics and behaviors (e.g., stereotypes) to make choices that influence both their present behavior and future development. As a result, boys and girls will tend to select activities and behave in ways that they believe are consistent with their male or female group identities. Furthermore, this seeking out and participation in what they perceive to be "boy" or "girl" activities has implications for the kinds of learning experiences they have and ultimately the skills, abilities, and traits they develop. For example, the skills developed by playing with dolls, a stereotypic girl activity (e.g., nurturance), are different from those developed by playing with trucks, a stereotypic boy activity (e.g., instrumentality). Consequently, children's knowledge of gender stereotypes and their desire to conform to them (i.e., to be a "boy" or a "girl") causes them to seek out learning experiences and act in ways that over time confirm the stereotypes. Thus, children are not merely passive products of adult shaping, but rather active participants in their own socialization seeking out information about their social identities and using that information in ways that have important implications for their future development (Martin, Ruble, & Szkrybalo, 2002).

The children's active, and often spirited, discussions about gender in the present study support the cognitive position described above. These discussions portray a group of five-year-olds actively concerned with specifying what was appropriate and inappropriate behavior for males and females, and seeing to it that those specifications were followed by themselves as well as their peers. Boys refused to dance to what they labeled as "girl music" and girls demonstrated to their peers the proper way for girls to sit verses boys (i.e., legs crossed verses legs open).

When specific children acted in ways that violated gender stereotypes (e.g., the boy playing with the butterfly puppet), their peers tended to respond in one of three ways. In five cases they corrected the child (e.g., "you need to have a boy puppet, and give that girl puppet to a girl"). In two cases they laughed at the violator. And in four cases, they engaged in what we called identity negation, that is, insisting that the violator is no longer who he or she is (e.g., "Jeff is a girl"). These reactions are consistent with previous work indicating that young children tend to negatively evaluate those who violate stereotypic norms (Abrams, Rutland, & Cameron, 2003; Levy, Taylor, & Gelman, 1995; Martin, 1989) and indicate a kind of self-policing of gender boundaries that no doubt has an important impact on children's behavior.

Boundary work of this kind was not observed in the children's ethnic or racial interactions. This absence appears to be at least partially a reflection of the previously noted fact that while children had clear ideas about how one acts like a proper girl or boy, for the most part, they did not claim similar knowledge with respect to how one acts like a proper White, Asian, or Black (for an exception see the comment about breakfast food above). In effect then, it appears that for young children ethnicity and race is something you are, whereas, gender is something you are and something you do.

Children's investment in adhering to group norms at this age appears to reflect an almost moralistic belief in the prescriptive quality of stereotypes that seems to be associated with a lack of experience and limitations in their cognitive abilities. When confronted with counter examples to their stereotypic beliefs (e.g., a female teacher who liked stock car racing), children in the current study almost always (92% of the time) resisted the new counter example (e.g., "You don't like race cars. Only boys like race cars."). This kind of rigidity with respect to stereotypic beliefs is characteristic of young children and appears to peak around five or six years-of-age. It then begins to decline around seven or eight when children begin to show more flexibility with respect to their willingness to accept variability among group members and across different cultures (Ruble & Martin, 1998). This appreciation of within group variability (i.e., that not all members of a group share the same characteristics) appears to reflect accumulated social experience and developmental advances in cognitive abilities (e.g., classification skills, decentration, and perspective taking). These cognitive advances emerge in middle childhood (e.g., Piaget, 1951), and are believed to contribute to older children's more flexible social orientation (Bigler, 1999; Bigler & Liben, 1993; Doyle et al., 1988).

In addition to cognitive limitations, the desire to maintain the integrity of self defining categories and bring coherence and structure to their social experience may also motivate young children to insist that group stereotypes be adhered to. Social Identity Theory (Tajfel & Turner, 1986) notes that social categories are useful for self definition to the degree that they differentiate group members from others. Thus, when members of either your own group (the in-group) or another group that serves as a comparison (the out-group) act in ways that violate group norms (e.g., girls liking cars, or boys liking butterflies), it blurs differences between groups and, as a result, erodes the usefulness of group membership for self definition (Abrams, Rutland, & Cameron, 2003; Prentice, 2005). In effect then, these individuals who act in ways that violate group norms, and blur group boundaries, threaten both our sense of self and the sense of security we gain from inhabiting a predictable social environment. It is no wonder then that young children, trying to cope with the developmental task of achieving self definition and finding order in an often confusing and complex social landscape, should find deviation from what they believe to be accepted ways troublesome, since psychologically these deviations may represent a threat to both self and security. Of course, the same structure and predictability in their social world that brings children comfort and security may also, if too rigid, stifle their development. Thus, when confronting children's stereotypic social beliefs adults may do well to try and balance young children's need for security and order with their additional need for unique self expression and the freedom to pursue multiple life ways. In practice this may mean accepting as normal some level of rigidity in young children's discussions about social categories, while at the same time gently challenging them to move beyond this rigidity and embrace more flexible world views.

Prejudice and Group Bias

Researchers writing on young children's intergroup attitudes often characterize the relations between groups as containing a good deal of animosity. For example, some have referred to relations between boys and girls as, "the gender wars" (e.g., David, Grace, & Ryan, 2004. p. 135) while others suggest that, "it has been long known that young children hold negative attitudes about other ethnic groups" (Doyle et al., 1988, p. 3). Despite these characterizations, the results of the present study did not reveal a great deal of animosity between groups, a finding consistent with Holmes's (1995) earlier naturalistic study of kindergartners' intergroup behavior. This is not to say, however, that children's interactions were free of evaluative comments, but rather that the amount and intensity of the comments were not what one might expect based on previous studies employing structured interviews. This divergence of findings is likely due to the fact that earlier studies using these interviews often misinterpreted children's positive feeling toward their own group as signaling an overt rejection of out-groups, a point we will return to later.

Of the 51 comments concerning gender, only three expressed negative evaluations of an out-group. On two occasions girls negatively evaluated boys (i.e., "Boys can't be friends. Boys fight." and "I don't like boys, only my brother."), and on one occasion a boy noted that he would not want to, "kiss a stupid girl." Although the number of these evaluative comments were few, the pattern of responses with respect to boys and girls is consistent with previous research indicating girls show stronger own group bias than boys (Egan & Perry, 2001; Heyman, 2001; Powlishta et al., 1994; Silvern, 1977; Yee & Brown, 1994). This greater bias in girls may reflect the fact that boys are generally more aggressive (Maccoby & Jacklin, 1974; Ruble & Martin, 1998), resist girls' attempts to influence cross-sex interactions and tend to dominate these interactions, potentially leading to resentment on the part of girls (Charlesworth & LaFreniere, 1983; Glick & Hilt, 2000; Serbin, Sprafkin, Elman, & Doyle, 1984). These differences in interaction style, as well as differences in play style and interests (O'Brien & Huston, 1985; Pellegrini & Perlmutter, 1989), appear to contribute to the clear gender segregation seen in children's playmate choices that begins in preschool and increases as children move towards middle childhood (Leaper, 1994; Maccoby & Jacklin, 1987).

With respect to evaluative comments, the results for ethnicity and race in the present study suggest that the children's social interaction around this topic may have been somewhat more contentious. However, given the small number of comments recorded about ethnicity or race (i.e., only 18), one should be wary of over interpretation. Of the 18 ethnic/racial comments, 4 involved negative evaluations of an out-group. These involved White children's negative statements towards children of color (e.g., "I don't like Brown people"). These results, though few in number, are consistent with previous research indicating that young White (i.e., majority group) children show greater preference for their own group than minority children (Aboud, 1988; Brown, 1995; Cameron, Alvarez, Ruble, & Fuligni, 2001; Katz, 1983). This own group bias in majority group children emerges in the preschool years and increases until children are around five or six years-of-age, and then appears to decrease as they move into middle childhood around seven or eight (Bigler & Liben, 1993; Black-Gutman & Hickson, 1996; Doyle & Aboud, 1995; Doyle et al., 1988).

Like flexibility with respect to stereotypes, the decrease in majority group children's own group bias reported in the above studies has been linked to developmental advances in children's cognitive functioning (e.g., classification skills, ability to consider multiple features at the same time, and perspective taking). These abilities appear to reduce the pull of any one specific group membership by allowing children to appreciate that people belong to multiple groups simultaneously, and that while people may differ with respect to observable features like skin color, they can be the same with respect to other, often not immediately visible features, like interests, beliefs, or feelings (Aboud, 1988; Doyle & Aboud, 1995; Katz & Kofkin, 1997). In general then, the cognitive advances that emerge at the beginning of middle childhood seem to set the stage for more flexible and egalitarian social thinking in children. Importantly, however, while these developmental advances may provide the potential for a reduction in own group bias in middle childhood, they (in and of themselves) do not necessitate such a reduction since in some studies this bias is reported as staying the same, or actually increasing, during this same time period (e.g., Bartel, Bartel, & Grill, 1973; Davey, 1983; Kowalski & Lo, 2001a; Rice, Ruiz, & Padilla, 1974).

In-Group Verses Out-Group Attitudes

When considering children's attitudes about social groups it is important to distinguish between positive feelings towards their own group and
negative feelings towards out-groups. Unfortunately, many of the early
studies that investigated group attitudes in children employed forced-
choice methods that confounded these two dimensions. With respect to
race or ethnicity, these studies typically involved requiring children to
choose between their own group and an out-group when assigning positive
and negative traits (e.g., Williams, Best, Boswell, Mattson, & Graves, 1975),
selecting dolls they liked (e.g., Clark & Clark, 1947), or selecting potential
playmates (e.g., Morland & Hwang, 1981). If children displayed a preference for their own group (e.g., by assigning positive traits to it and not
assigning negative, or by selecting it as liked) this was often interpreted as
indicating a negative attitude towards the out-group.

Recent reexamination of this work indicates, however, that children's
preference for their own group in these studies does not necessarily entail
the rejection of out-groups (see, Cameron et al., 2001). For example, Kowalski (2003) recently demonstrated that when preschoolers were forced by
a traditional attitude measures to assign positive and negative traits to
either their own group or an ethnic out-group, they tended to assign positive traits to their own group and negative traits to the out-group (a pattern
often interpreted as out-group prejudice). Importantly, however, when
they were not forced to choose between groups, these same children
tended to evaluate the out-groups positively. This pattern of findings indicates that their performance on the forced-choice measures (e.g., giving
the negative traits to the out-groups) reflected their desire to evaluate their
own group favorably (i.e., avoid giving it the negative traits), rather than a
desire to derogate the out-groups. This is an important finding because it
indicates that children can develop positive feelings for their own group
without necessarily feeling negatively towards out-groups, a core component of multiculturalism. It also suggests that past research using forced-
choice measures likely exaggerated the degree to which young children
harbor negative attitudes towards out-groups. This exaggeration explains
why naturalistic observations of children, like the current diary study, generally do not reveal the kind of group animosities one might expect from
the earlier research.

According to social identity theory (Tajfel & Turner, 1986), the way we
view the groups we belong to is heavily influenced by our desire to see ourselves favorably. If I am in a group, I want that group to be viewed positively, because what is true of the group must be, by extension, true of me.
Thus, we try to enhance the status of groups we belong to in order to
enhance our own self-esteem. This enhancement of status can be accom-

plished in several ways. For example, by (a) switching to, or joining, high status groups (an option not readily available for race or gender), (b) by competing with, and prevailing over, other groups, (c) by focusing on dimensions for making intergroup comparisons that favor our own group (e.g., physical strength for males, sensitivity for females), or (d) by distorting or exaggerating the positive features of our group. This last strategy involving distortion may be particularly relevant to young children whose group appraisals often appear to be influenced as much by their desires or feelings as their actual experience (Nesdale & Flesser, 2001; Ramsey, 1987; Yee & Brown, 1992).

It is easy to see how young children, who lack an appreciation for within group variability, could be influenced by the self-categorization processes discussed above. These children would embrace the notion that if my group is good, I am good; or perhaps alternatively, if I am good, then my group must be good (Doise & Sinclair, 1973). Consistent with this view, research using a minimal groups paradigm indicates that when children are placed in groups, even on the basis of relatively unimportant criteria (e.g., color of tee shirt, or speed at an egg carrying game), they develop distinct biases in favor of the particular groups they are a part of (Bigler, Jones, & Lobliner, 1997; Nesdale & Flesser, 2001; Yee & Brown, 1992; Vaughan, Tajfel, & Williams, 1981). This tendency to view the groups they belong to favorably appears to play an important role in the formation of ethnic and gender bias in young children as suggested by the fact that this bias often emerges, or becomes stronger, when children learn their own group membership. Thus, awareness of own group membership (e.g., labeling, self-identification, and stability) has been associated with children showing greater liking for their own sex and same sex peers (Fagot, 1985; Martin & Little, 1990; Yee & Brown, 1994) and displaying preference for same race children as potential playmates in structured interviews (Kowalski & Lo, 2001a, 2001b). Moreover, own group bias has been linked to self-esteem, with higher self-esteem children tending to display more own group bias (Bigler, 1995; Bigler et al., 1997; Stephan & Rosenfield, 1979; Yee & Brown, 1992).

In addition to knowledge of own group membership, social information about the differential status of various groups can also influence children's feelings towards their own group (Bennett, Lyons, Sani, & Barrett, 1998; Bigler, Brown, & Markell, 2001; Yee & Brown, 1992; Nesdale & Flesser, 2001). This status effect may explain why young minority group children, as previously noted, often show less own group bias than their majority group counterparts. That is, in accordance with the social identity processes discussed above (Tajfel & Turner, 1986), awareness of negative social judgments about their group may cause minority children seeking positive self regard to feel ambivalent about their group membership, and even foster in them a wish that they could switch to the higher status majority group. Some researchers (e.g., Katz & Kofkin, 1997) suggest that the psychological conflict that accompanies this situation makes accurate self-identification more difficult for young minority children and thus explains why they typically display self-identification at a later age than majority group children. This awareness of status differences has also been used to explain why young minority children have often displayed a preference for the majority group in past studies that required them to choose between groups (e.g., Aboud, 1977; Clark & Clark, 1947; Rice et al., 1974). The impact that social information probably had on these choices is further illustrated by the fact that, likely due to historical changes, more recent studies tend to show a change in this behavior with young minority children often showing either no bias at all, or a preference for their own group (Aboud, 1980; Brown, 1995; Cross, 1985; Kowalski, 2003; Newman, Liss, & Sherman, 1983). However, this change is not universal and recent interpretive work with immigrant preschoolers in Australia suggests that the influence of differential group status continues to exert an important influence on their group identifications (MacNaughton, 2001). One should be cautious, however, in attributing the findings discussed above solely to psychological conflict in minority children concerning their group membership, since neutral or cross race preference in the above studies may actually represent an adaptive response to a social context that requires these children to identify with both groups, majority and minority, in order to be successful (Banks, 1976; Cross, 1985).

The negative racial comments made by some White children in the present study, although few in number, do indicate that the minority children present were aware that others sometimes view their group negatively. Indeed, this was forcefully illustrated by the fact that one boy used his group membership (most likely in error) to explain why a White friend did not want to play with him at that moment (i.e., "You don't want to play with me because I'm Black."). Connolly (2001), reporting on primary school students social interactions, has described similar negative racial comments made by majority group children, despite the fact that they often played with children from the groups they made the negative comments about. These findings indicate that unfortunately young minority group children are not always insulated from the direct expression of negative comments towards their group. This awareness of negative social judgments about their group increases as children get older (McKown & Weinstein, 2003; Quintana & Vera, 1999) and may help explain why minority group children show an increase in own group bias as they move into middle childhood (Davey, 1983; Kowalski & Lo, 2001b; Newman et al., 1983; Rice et al., 1974; Semaj, 1980). That is, growing awareness of prejudice likely increases the salience of ethnic/racial group membership for these children, and may cause them to feel threatened when interacting with others who may judge them negatively merely because of their minority group status (Marx, Brown, & Steele, 1999; Steele & Aronson, 1995). Thus, these children show an increasing preference for their own group. In addition, feeling threatened by an out-group is one of the factors that can move people from merely feeling preference for their own group, to actively disliking the out-group (Brewer, 2001).

In a recent study, Nesdale, Maass, Durkin, & Griffiths (2005) demonstrated that children as young as seven move from positive to negative appraisals of an out-group if they believe that out-group has negative feelings towards their group. Children's appraisals of out-groups were also influenced by whether they thought others in their own group would like or dislike the out-group. That is, when children were told that others in their group would not like the out-group, they tended to express more negative feelings towards that group themselves. This finding suggests that children's identification with their own group can facilitate negative attitudes towards an out-group, if they believe that it is normative for others in their group to not like the out-group in question (e.g., a child expressing distaste for girls because he is a boy and that is what he thinks other boys feel). This research indicates that exposure to social information about what one's own, and other groups, believe with respect to inter group attitudes can influence children's feelings towards out-groups. Consistent with this notion, Kowalski (2003) found that while both majority and minority group preschoolers tended to positively evaluate ethnic out-groups, their out-group appraisals did vary somewhat depending on the specific group being evaluated and appeared to mirror the ethnic dynamics of the local context suggesting that these children were influenced by the type of social information about intergroup relations noted above. Rutland et al., (2005) reported similar findings with preschoolers displaying differing levels of bias depending on the particular ethnic out-group they were presented with. Taken together, this research suggests that it is the prolonged exposure to social information about the differential status of various groups, and existing animosities between them, and not merely knowledge of own group membership, that over time breeds negative out-group attitudes in children.

The negative ethnic comments that young children in current, as well as other studies (e.g., Connolly, 2001) sometimes make, suggests that these children inhabit social contexts where exposure to this kind of information is present, and will with time, likely lead to prejudice in many children. It should be noted, however, that these comments alone, since they are often highly contextual and inconsistently applied, do not appear to indicate the kind of stable well formed negative attitudes towards out-groups that we generally associate with prejudice in older children or adults (Nesdale,

2001; Ramsey, 1987). This difference is illustrated by an observation from Connolly in which a White girl, who often played with two Indian girls, indicated that the reason the three of them did not want to include a fourth girl was, "Cos she's Indian" (p. 224). Ethnicity here seemed to be an after thought, or way to justify the exclusionary behavior, rather than the cause of it, since the girl making the comment was engaged in play with her Indian friends at the time. This sort of sporadic and functional use of ethnicity and race by young children to justify behavior that seems to be driven by something else (e.g., the desire to play alone, exclude a particular child, or get their way, etc.) has been reported by others (Rydland, 2006; Van Ausdale & Feagin 2001) and suggests an emerging awareness in young children that ethnicity and race can have explanatory power in social situations. However, as the above example illustrates, despite these sporadic comments, actual observation of preschoolers and kindergartners' playmate preferences in school do not seem to support the presence of pervasive and strong out-group prejudice. Observational studies often find that race and ethnicity are not related to playmate selection (Porter, 1971; Stevenson & Stevenson, 1960; Swadener, 1991), or that when children do show some preference for their own group (Howes & Wu, 1990; Finkelstein & Haskins, 1983) they still form cross ethnic friendships and readily play with children in other groups.

In summary, the research reviewed above indicates that in the absence of strong negative messages concerning their group, positive own group feelings (i.e., own group bias) emerges quickly in young children with awareness of own group membership. However, attitudes towards outgroups appear to develop at a slower rate as children are exposed to social information, both about the out-groups in question, and what is normative for their own group. As a result, attitudes towards ethnic and racial outgroups do not appear to become well formed and stable until children enter middle childhood or perhaps later (Cameron et al., 2001; Katz, 1976; Nesdale, 2001).

CONCLUSION AND IMPLICATIONS FOR PRACTICE

Despite the fact that it was once popular to view young children as "color blind" (Allport, 1954), children are aware of social categories, including race and ethnicity, from a fairly young age. It should be recognized then that what practitioners do in the classroom interacts with this early awareness and likely has an important role in shaping children's social understandings. Brewer (1979) notes that, "the effect of in-group–out-group categorization is one of differentiating the in-group from the out-group" (p. 322). This statement suggests that when first learning about social categories, children's interest and attention will likely be focused on the articulation and differentiation of their own group from others. Their desire to establish a positive social identity (and the positive self regard that accompanies it) should propel young children to be interested in, and seek out, information that supports the positive distinctiveness of their group (Nesdale, 2004). Thus, those wishing to support young children's developing sense of self should make certain that this kind of group information is readily available in their environment. The school and classroom environment, and the curricular materials children interact with, should provide information about, and positively represent, all social groups present. This positive representation is especially important for minority children, since learning about one's group is an important component of social identity development and this development can be an important source of psychological strength that can help buffer these children from the negative effects of prejudice and discrimination (Caughy, O'Campo, Randolph, & Nickerson, 2002; Spencer & Markstrom-Adams, 1990; Thomas, Townsend, & Belgrave, 2003). This idea that schools represent all groups is certainly not new (e.g., Banks, 1988), however, the research and theory reviewed in this chapter underscores its importance.

This research and theory also suggests that since young children are primarily focused on their own group, and own group bias emerges with knowledge of own group membership, we should be modest in our expectations that these same curricular materials, that can likely powerfully support children's feelings towards their own group, will have an equally powerful effect on their attitudes towards out-groups. A recent review of empirical studies evaluating the effectiveness of interventions using multicultural curricula and materials on children's out-group attitudes supports this notion by concluding that the effect of these programs on out-group attitudes has generally been minimal or even nonexistent (Bigler, 1999). For example, Kowalski (1998) found that after conducting a three month long cultural exchange program between preschoolers in the United States and Japan—during which the U.S. children read books about, and exchanged videos, pictures, letters, and art work with their "sister school friends" in Japan—the U.S. preschoolers were not significantly more positive towards Japanese children than they were prior to the programs beginning. Moreover, ten days after the programs completion, when participants were explicitly questioned about their attitudes towards Japanese children, they did not spontaneously mention the program or their "sister school friends." In fact, when at the end of the interview they were directly asked if they knew any Japanese children, they often said no or confused the category Japanese with Chinese. This seeming imperviousness to an educational experience about an out-group appeared to be a reflection of the children's immature level of cognitive development and the above noted suggestion that young children's primary focus at this age is their own group. This own group focus is illustrated by the fact that one of the few significant effects of the cultural exchange program was that children showed greater liking for their own group at the end of the program than they did at the beginning, likely because participation in the program increased the salience of their own group membership. Importantly, however, this liking for their own group was not related to their rejection of out-groups. Rather, it just appeared that presenting the children with information about others, actually taught them about themselves.

The failure of programs like the one described above to have a substantial impact on children's out-group attitudes suggests that influencing these attitudes probably requires a more sustained effort over time. Longer term and more comprehensive approaches may be more effective at shaping children's out-group attitudes (e.g., Brown, 1998). The sister school intervention, like many others (see Bigler, 1999), was relatively short in duration. Since out-group attitudes appear to develop slowly over time, short term approaches seem likely to be ineffective. In fact, some argue that these kinds of "add-on" programs, which act as supplements to the regular classroom curriculum, represent a kind of "tourist" approach to multiculturalism that can actually misrepresent diverse groups by presenting them in overly simplistic ways that feed the formation of stereotypes (Derman-Sparks, 1989). It is easy to see how this could happen, especially with children under seven who, because of their level of cognitive development, are likely to focus on surface features like appearance that make people different, rather than attending to nonobvious things like traits and feelings that we all share (Aboud, 1988). And who also, because of their difficulty dealing with multiple classifications, may tend to represent others in a unitary or simplistic way (e.g., All Japanese wear kimonos.).

These kinds of cognitive limitations make it difficult for young children to deal with things like abstraction and multiple perspectives and likely have a big impact on how they experience educational materials aimed at introducing them to diversity. For example, complex themes concerning fairness and equity in children's stories about diversity may be lost on young children who do not abstract out the general principals the stories are trying to convey. This was recently brought home to me by a visit to a first grade classroom where, after reading *The Three Little Pigs*, the teacher asked the children, "What are the important lessons in this story?" Rather than noting themes such as, it is important to do a good job when you do something, or if you try to hurt someone you will be hurt in the end, the children said things like, "Don't live in straw houses," or "Don't mess with pigs!" This kind of concrete and literal thinking by young children suggests teachers would do well to explicitly highlight and discuss with them in a direct way the messages they hope children will take away from educational materials dealing with diversity, rather than assuming that children are getting these messages on their own through inference and abstraction. Children's thinking should be closely monitored through questioning and careful observation to determine how they are interpreting these materials and lessons so that their messages are not lost or, worst yet, distorted in ways unintended. This monitoring is especially important since research demonstrates that when children are presented with counter stereotypic stories and images (e.g., a girl sawing wood, or a Black child working hard while a White child rests), they often distort this information so that it fits their preexisting stereotypes and later recall it in a very different form (e.g., a boy sawing wood, or White child working hard while a Black child rests) (Bigler & Liben, 1993; Martin & Halverson, 1983b). Thus, stories intended to counter stereotypes, can actually reinforce them for some children, especially if the children's interpretations are not carefully monitored.

Since our desire to achieve a distinctive social identity appears to focus us on differences between our own group and others (Tajfel & Turner, 1979), teachers might want to try and balance this tendency by emphasizing the similarities between people when teaching children about diversity, especially when these similarities have to do with nonobvious features like traits or desires. In addition, since just the act of categorizing causes us to minimize within group differences, and children seem especially adept at this, we should try to develop ways that children can learn to appreciate the variability within groups so that group boundaries are not drawn too narrowly (e.g., Derman-Sparks & ABC Task Force, 1989; McCracken, 1993). This potential narrowing is important because, as we have seen, children's beliefs about what group members can, or can not do (e.g., boys playing with butterfly puppets, Americans eating rice with bacon) can influence behavior. Moreover, these beliefs about group membership can later extend to academic choices children make concerning the degree to which they invest in their studies, or pursue certain disciplines or activities such as math or joining the student newspaper, all which can have important implications for achievement and later life choices (Eccles, 1989; Fordham & Ogbu 1986). Thus, children should be presented with numerous models of group members engaged in a diversity of tasks so that aspiring to be like their group will serve to broaden children's educational and occupational horizons rather than narrow them.

Although it has been suggested that young children's negative outgroup comments do not seem to represent prejudice in the sense of well-formed stable attitudes towards out-groups, an examination of the situations in which these comments arise does provide insight into how social categories often function in young children's social interactions, and for that matter, in society as a whole. That is, as in the previous example of the girl using ethnicity to justify the exclusion of another girl from their play group, "Cos she's Indian," children in the diary study also used social categories to justify acts of exclusion or to hurt others by name calling (e.g., "This is a girl table, only girls," or "You have to leave because you're brown."). Van Ausdale and Feagin (2001) have also documented similar acts of exclusion among preschoolers. They interpret these acts as attempts to exert power over others, and as such, suggestive of our larger social structure that often uses social categories, like race and gender, to maintain existing power relations that advantage some groups over others.

While, as previously noted, it is important to be cautious in attributing adult meanings and motives to young children's exclusionary behavior, it is also important that these acts should not go unaddressed. Research indicates that what separates prejudiced from nonprejudiced adults is not their knowledge of negative stereotypes. Both groups know these. It is, that nonprejudiced adults also possess countervailing beliefs endorsing the value of equality and the injustice of discrimination that result in them consciously inhibiting discriminatory thoughts that might arise because of their knowledge of stereotype content (Devine, 1989; Devine & Monteith, 1993). Thus, learning to be nonprejudiced in a society where prejudice exists appears to depend on more than just fostering positive attitudes towards out-groups. It also requires fostering negative attitudes towards prejudice and discrimination.

Children should be taught that excluding or hurting others because of their group membership is wrong and cannot be tolerated. Since self-categorization processes predispose children to invest heavily in their own group, it may be unrealistic to think we can socialize them to have this same level of enthusiasm for all out-groups. It does not seem unreasonable, however, to assume that we can teach them to be fair and to embrace universally valued principals like equity, kindness, and tolerance that can insure that their liking for their own group is not used to justify the unfair treatment of others. Indeed, research examining children's beliefs about exclusion based on social group membership indicates that children appreciate its negative impact on others and suggests that they would be more than receptive to adult teaching in this area (Killen, Lee-Kim, McGlothlin, & Stangor, 2002).

In closing, it is important to note that social categories, and our identifications with them, are not only a source of separation and potential divisiveness, but also a source of personal meaning, cooperation, and unity (Oakes & Haslam, 2001; Turner et al., 1987). Among the potent psychological forces related to self-categorization is a sense of belonging and connectedness to fellow category members that can motivate us to self-sacrifice, cooperation, and empathy for others. As we have seen, the salience of specific social categories can vary from situation to situation. Moreover, teachers' behavior can influence this process (e.g., functional use of gender in the classroom). By creating common activities and goals for children (e.g., cooperative learning) teachers can create classroom contexts that highlight group memberships which bring children together. Belonging to a common group has a powerful impact on children's feelings towards fellow group members. Conditions in school can be set up to invoke a sense of common purpose and connectedness among children so that some of the social identities that become habitually salient are those associated with being members of a common community of learners (e.g., classmate, young author, teammate, student of a particular school, etc.). Perhaps then, a sense of unity and cooperation can be created among children, not by trying to ignore or down play group memberships, but rather by encouraging them. Thus, as children develop and their capacity to categorize themselves in multiple ways increases (e.g., girl, Asian, Japanese, American, Californian, student, classmate, team member, skater, music lover, human, etc.), the accumulation of these multiple group memberships will allow children to answer our initial question, "Who am I?" with both a strong sense of self definition and connectedness to others.

REFERENCES

Aboud, F. E. (1977). Interest in ethnic information: A cross-cultural developmental study. *Canadian Journal of Behavioral Science, 9*, 134–146.

Aboud, F. E. (1980). A test of ethnocentrism with young children. *Canadian Journal of Behavioral Science, 12*, 195–209.

Aboud, F. E. (1988). *Children and prejudice.* Oxford, UK: Basil Blackwell.

Abrams, D., Rutland, A., & Cameron, L. (2003). The development of subjective group dynamics: Children's judgments of normative and deviant in-group and out-group individuals. *Child Development, 74*(6), 1840–1856.

Alejandro-Wright, M. N. (1985). The child's conception of racial classification: A socio-cognitive developmental model. In M. B. Spencer, G. K. Brookins, & W. R. Allen (Eds.), *Beginnings: The social and affective development of Black children* (pp. 185–200). Hillsdale, NJ: Erlbaum.

Allport, G. W. (1954). *The nature of prejudice.* Cambridge, MA: Addison-Wesley.

Banks, J. (1988). *Multiethnic education: Theory and practice.* Boston: Allyn & Bacon.

Banks, W. C. (1976). White preference in Blacks: A paradigm in search of a phenomenon. *Psychological Bulletin, 83*, 1179–1186.

Bartel, H. W., Bartel, N. R., & Grill, J. J. (1973). A sociometric view of some integrated open classrooms. *Journal of Social Issues, 29*, 159–173.

Bem, S. L. (1989). Genital knowledge and gender constancy in preschool children. *Child Development, 60*, 649–662.

Bennett, M., Lyons, E., Sani, F., & Barrett, M. (1998). Children's subjective identification with the group and in-group favoritism. *Developmental Psychology, 34*, 902–909.

Bernal, M. E., Knight, G. P., Garza, C. A., Ocampo, K. A., & Cota, M. K. (1990). The development of ethnic identity in Mexican-American children. *Hispanic Journal of Behavioral Sciences, 12,* 3–24.

Bernal, M. E., Knight, G. P., & Ocampo, K., Garza, C. A., & Cota, M. K. (1993). The socialization of cooperative, competitive, and individualistic preferences among Mexican American children: The mediating role of ethnic identity. *Hispanic Journal of Behavioral Sciences, 15*(3), 291–309.

Bigler, R. S. (1995). The role of classification skill in moderating environmental influences on children's gender stereotyping: A study of the functional use of gender in the classroom. *Child Development, 66,* 1072–1087.

Bigler, R. S. (1999). The use of multicultural curricula and materials to counter racism in children. *Journal of Social Issues, 55*(4), 687–705.

Bigler, R. S., Brown, C. S., & Markell, M. (2001). When group are not created equal: Effects of group status on the formation of intergroup attitudes in children. *Child Development, 72,* 1151–1162.

Bigler, R. S., Jones, L. C., & Lobliner, D. B. (1997). Social categorization and the formation of intergroup attitudes in children. *Child Development, 68,* 530–543.

Bigler, R. S., & Liben, L. S. (1993). A cognitive-developmental approach to racial stereotyping and constructive memory in Euro-American children. *Child Development, 64,* 1507–1518.

Black-Gutman, D., & Hickson, F. (1996). The relationship between racial attitudes and social-cognitive development in children: An Australian study. *Developmental Psychology, 32,* 448–456.

Brewer, M. B. (1979). In-group bias in the minimal intergroup situation: A cognitive motivational analysis. *Psychological Bulletin, 86,* 307–324.

Brewer, M. B. (2001). Ingroup identification and intergroup conflict: When does ingroup love become outgroup hate? In R. D. Ashmore, L. Jussim, & D. Wilder (Eds.), *Social identity intergroup conflict, and conflict reduction* (pp.17–41). New York: Oxford University Press.

Brown, B. (1998). *Unlearning discrimination in the early years.* Starfordshire, UK: Trentham Books.

Brown, R. (1995). *Prejudice: Its social psychology.* Cambridge, MA: Blackwell.

Brown, R. (2000). Social identity theory: Past achievements, current problems, and future challenges. *European Journal of Social Psychology, 30,* 745–778.

Bruner, J. S. (1957). On perceptual readiness. *Psychological Review, 64,* 123–152.

Cameron, J. A., Alvarez, J. M., Ruble, D. N., & Fulgini, A. J. (2001). Children's play theories about ingroups and outgroups: Reconceptualizing research on prejudice. *Personality and Social Psychology, 5,* 118–128.

Caughy, M. O., O'Campo, P. J., Randolph, S. M., & Nickerson, K. (2002). The influence of racial socialization practices on the cognitive and behavioral competence of African American preschoolers. *Child Development, 73*(5), 1611–1625.

Charlesworth, W. R., & LaFreniere, P. (1983). Dominance, friendship, and resource utilization in preschool children's groups. *Ethology and sociobiology, 4,* 603–615.

Clark, K. B., & Clark, M. P. (1947). Racial identification and preference in Negro children. In T. M. Newcombe & E. L. Hartley (Eds.), *Readings in social psychology* (pp. 169–178). New York: Holt.

Clark, A., Hocevar, D., & Dembo, M. H. (1980). The role of cognitive development in children's explanations and preferences for skin color. *Developmental Psychology, 16*(4), 332–339.

Connolly, P. (2001). Qualitative methods in the study of children's racial attitudes and identities. *Infant and Child Development, 10*(4), 219–233.

Cross, W. E. (1985). Black identity: Rediscovering the distinction between personal identity and reference group orientation. In M. B. Spencer, G. K. Brookins, & W. R. Allen (Eds.), *Beginnings: The social and affective development of Black children* (pp. 155–171). Hillside, NJ: Erlbaum.

Davey, A. (1983). *Learning to be prejudiced.* London: Edward Arnold.

David, B., Grace, D., & Ryan, M. K. (2004). The gender wars: A self-categorization theory perspective on the development of gender identity. In M. Bennett & F. Sani (Eds.), *The development of social self* (pp. 135–157). Hove and New York: Psychology Press.

Derman-Sparks, L. (1989). How well are we nurturing racial and ethnic diversity? *Connections, 18*(1), 3–5.

Derman-Sparks, L., & ABC Task Force. (1989) *Anti-bias curriculum: Tools for empowering young children.* Washington DC: National Association for the Education of Young Children.

Devine, P. G. (1989). Stereotypes and prejudice: Their automatic and controlled components. *Journal of Personality & Social Psychology, 56*(1), 5–18.

Devine, P. G., & Monteith, M. J. (1993). The role of discrepancy associated affect in prejudice reduction. In D. M. Mackie & D. L. Lewis (Eds.), *Affect, cognition, and stereotyping: Interactive processes in group perception* (pp. 317–344). San Diego, CA: Academic Press.

Doise, W., & Sinclair, A. (1973). The categorization process in intergroup relations. *European Journal of Social Psychology, 3*(2), 145–157.

Doyle, A. B., & Aboud, F. E. (1995). A longitudinal study of White children's racial prejudice as a social-cognitive development. *Merrill-Palmer Quarterly, 41,* 209–228.

Doyle, A., Beaudet, J., & Aboud, F. (1988). Developmental patterns in the flexibility of children's ethnic attitudes. *Journal of Cross-Cultural Psychology, 19*(1), 3–18.

Dweck, C. S., Davidson, W., Nelson, S., & Enna, B. (1978). Sex differences in learned helplessness: II. The contingencies of evaluative feedback in the classroom. III. An experimental analysis. *Developmental Psychology, 14*(3), 268–276.

Eccles, J. S. (1989). Bringing young women to math and science. In M. Crawford & M. Gentry (Eds.), *Gender and thought* (pp. 36–58). New York: Springer-Verlag.

Egan, S. K., & Perry, D. G. (2001). Gender identity: A multidimensional analysis with implications for psychosocial adjustment. *Developmental Psychology, 37,* 451–463.

Emmerich, W., Goldman, K. S., Kirsh, B., & Sharabany, R. (1977). Evidence for a transitional phase in the development of gender constancy. *Child Development, 48,* 930–936.

Fagot, B. I., (1985). Changes in thinking about early sex role development. *Developmental Review, 5,* 83–98.

Finkelstein, N. W., & Haskins, R. (1983). Kindergarten children prefer same-color peers. *Child Development, 54,* 502–508.

Fordham & Ogbu (1986) Black students' school success: Coping with the burden of "acting White." *Urban Review, 18,* 176–206.

Fox, D. J., & Jordan, V. D. (1973). Racial preference and identification of Black, American Chinese, and White children. *Genetic Psychology Monographs, 88,* 229–286.

Glick, P., & Hilt, L. (2000). Combative children to ambivalent adults: The development of gender prejudice. In T. Eckes & H. M. Trautner (Eds.), *The developmental social psychology of gender* (pp. 243–272). Mahwah, NJ: Erlbaum.

Gouze, K. R., & Nadelman, L. (1980). Constancy of gender identity for self and others in children between the ages of three and seven. *Child Development, 51,* 275–278.

Heyman, G. D. (2001). Children's interpretation of ambiguous behavior: Evidence for a "boys are bad" bias. *Social Development, 10,* 230–247.

Hirshfeld, L. A. (1995). Do children have a theory of race? *Cognition, 54,* 209–252.

Hirshfeld, L. A. (1996). *Race in the Making: Cognition, culture, and the child's construction of human kinds.* Cambridge, MA: The MIT press.

Holmes, R. M. (1995). *How young children perceive race.* Thousand Oaks, CA: Sage.

Howes, C., & Wu, F. (1990). Peer interactions and friendships in an ethnically diverse school setting. *Child Development, 61,* 537–541.

Katz, P. A. (1973). Perception of racial cues in preschool children: A new look. *Developmental Psychology, 8*(2), 295–199.

Katz, P. A. (1976). The acquisition of racial attitudes in children. In P. A. Katz (Ed.), *Towards the elimination of racism* (pp. 125–153). New York: Pergamon.

Katz, P. A. (1983). Developmental foundations of gender and racial attitudes. In R. L. Leahy (Ed.), *The child's construction of social inequality* (pp. 41–78). New York: Academic Press.

Katz, P. A., & Kofkin, J. A. (1997). Race, gender, and young children. In S. S. Luthar, J. A. Burack, D. Cicchetti, & J. Weisz (Eds.), *Developmental psychopathology: Perspectives on adjustment, risk, and disorder* (pp. 51–74). New York: Cambridge University Press.

Katz, P. A., Sohn, M., & Zalk, S. R. (1975). Perceptual concomitants of racial attitudes in urban grade-school children. *Developmental Psychology, 11,* 135–144.

Killen, M., Lee-Kim, J., McGlothlin, H., Stanor, C. (2002). How children and adolescents evaluate gender and racial exclusion. *Monographs of the Society for Research in Child Development, 67*(4), 1–119.

Knight, G. P., Cota, M. K., & Bernal, M. E. (1993). The socialization of cooperative, competitive, and individualistic preferences among Mexican American children: The mediating role of ethnic identity. *Hispanic Journal of Behavior Sciences, 15*(3), 291–309.

Kohlberg, L. A. (1966). A cognitive-developmental analysis of children's sex role concepts and attitudes. In E. E. Maccoby (Ed.), *The development of sex differences* (pp. 82–173). Stanford, CA: Stanford University Press.

Kowalski, K. (1998). The impact of vicarious exposure to diversity on preschoolers' emerging ethnic/racial attitudes. *Early Child Development and Care, 146,* 41–51.

Kowalski, K. (2003). The emergence of ethnic/racial attitudes in preschool-age children. *The Journal of Social Psychology, 143*(6), 677–690.

Kowalski, K., & Kanitkar, K. (2003, April). *Ethnicity and gender in the kindergarten classroom: A naturalistic study.* Poster session presented at the Biennial Meeting of the Society for Research in Child Development, Tampa, Florida.

Kowalski, K., & Lo, Y. (2001a). The influence of perceptual features, ethnic labels, and sociocultural information on the development of ethnic/racial bias in young children. *Journal of Cross-Cultural Psychology, 32,* 444–455.

Kowalski, K., & Lo, Y. (2001b, April). *The development of ethnic/racial bias in Chinese American children.* Poster session presented at the Biennial Meeting of the Society for Research in Child Development, Minneapolis, MI.

Kowalski, K., & Lo, Y. (2005, April). *The influence of social context on the expression of ethnic/racial bias in Chinese American children.* Poster session presented at the Biennial Meeting of the Society for Research in Child Development, Atlanta, GA.

Leaper, C. (1994). Exploring the correlates and consequences of gender segregation: Social relationships in childhood, adolescence, and adulthood. In B. Damon (Series Ed.) & C. Leaper (Vol. Ed.), *New directions for child development. The development of gender relationships.* San Francisco: Jossey-Bass.

Leinbach, M. D., & Fagot, B. I. (1993). Categorical habituation to male and female faces: Gender schematic processing in infancy. *Infant Behavior and Development, 16,* 317–332.

Leonard, S. P., & Archer, J. (1989). A naturalistic investigation of gender constancy in three- to four-year-old children. *British Journal of Developmental Psychology, 7,* 341–346.

Levy, G. D., Taylor, M. G., & Gelman, S. A. (1995). Traditional and evaluative aspects of flexibility in gender roles, social, conventions, moral rules, and physical laws. *Child Development, 66,* 515–531.

Maccoby, E. E., & Jacklin, C. N. (1974). *The psychology of sex differences.* Stanford, CA: Stanford University Press.

Maccoby, E. E., & Jacklin, C. N. (1987). Gender segregation in children. In H. Reese (Ed.), *Advances in child development and behavior, Vol. 20* (pp. 239–288). New York: Academic Press.

MacNaughton, G. (2001). Silences and subtexts of immigrant and nonimmigrant children. *Childhood Education, 78*(1), 30–36.

Mandler, J. M. (1998). Representation. In D. Kuhn & R. S. Siegler (Eds.), *Handbook of child psychology (5ᵗʰ ed.): Vol 2: Cognition, perception, and language* (pp. 255–308). New York: Willey.

Markus, H., & Wurf, E. (1987). The dynamic self-concept: A social psychological perspective. *Annual Review of Psychology, 38,* 299–337.

Martin, C. L. (1989). Children's use of gender-related information in making social judgments. *Developmental Psychology, 25,* 80–88.

Martin, C. L., & Halverson, C. E. (1981). A schematic processing model of sextyping and stereotyping in children. *Child Development, 52,* 1119–1134.

Martin, C. L., & Halverson, C. F. (1983a). Gender constancy: A methodological and theoretical analysis. *Sex Roles, 9,* 775–790.

Martin, C. L., & Halverson, C. F. (1983b). The effects of sex-typing schemas on young children's memory. *Child Development, 54,* 563–574.

Martin, C. L., & Little, J. K. (1990). The relation of gender understanding to children's sex-typed preferences and gender stereotypes. *Child Development, 61*, 1427–1439.

Martin, C. L., Ruble, D. L., & Szkrybalo, J. (2002). Cognitive theories of early gender development. *Psychological Bulletin, 128*(6), 903–933.

Marx, D. M., Brown, J. L., & Steele, C. M. (1999). Allport's legacy and the situational press of stereotypes. *Journal of Social Issues, 55*(3), 491–502.

McAdoo, H. P. (1985). Racial attitude and self-concept of young Black children over time. In H. P. McAdoo & J. L. McAdoo (Eds.), *Black children: Social, educational, and parental environments.* Beverly Hills, CA: Sage.

McCracken, J. B. (1993). *Valuing diversity: The primary years.* Washington, DC: National Association for the Education of Young Children.

McKown, C., & Weinstein, R. S. (2003). The development and consequences of stereotype consciousness in middle childhood. *Child Development, 74*(2), 498–515.

Mesick, D. M., & Mackie, D. M. (1989). Intergroup relations. *Annual Review of Psychology, 40*, 45–81.

Miller, A. (1984). A Transitional phase in gender constancy and its relationship to cognitive level and sex identification. *Child Study Journal, 13*, 259–275.

Minuchin, P. P., & Shapiro, E. K. (1983). The school as a context of social development. In P. H. Mussen (Ed.), *Handbook of child psychology (4th ed.), Vol. 4: Socialization, personality, and social development* (pp. 197–274). New York: Wiley.

Morland, J. K., & Hwang, C. (1981). Racial/ethnic identity of preschool children: Comparing Taiwan, Hong Kong, and the United States. *Journal of Cross-Cultural Psychology, 12*, 409–423.

Nesdale, D. (2001). The development of prejudice in children. In M. A. Augoustinos & K. J. Reynolds (Eds.), *Understanding prejudice, racism, and social conflict* (pp. 57–73). London: Sage.

Nesdale, D. (2004). Social identity processes and children's ethnic prejudice. In M. Bennett & F. Sani (Eds.), *The development of social self* (pp. 219–246). London: Psychology Press.

Nesdale, D., & Flesser, D. (2001). Social identity and the development of children's group attitudes. *Child Development, 72*, 506–517.

Nesdale, D., Maass, A., Durkin, K., & Griffiths, J. (2005). Group norms, threat, and children's racial prejudice. *Child Development, 76*(3), 652–663.

Newman, M. A., Liss, M. B., & Sherman, F. (1983). Ethnic awareness in children: Not a unitary concept. *Journal of Genetic Psychology, 83*, 28–34.

Oakes, P. J., & Haslam, S. A. (2001). Distortion v. meaning: Categorization on trial for inciting intergroup hatred. In M. A. Augoustinos & K. J. Reynolds (Eds.), *Understanding prejudice, racism, and social conflict* (pp. 179–194). London: Sage.

O'Brien, M., & Huston, A. C. (1985). Development of sex-typed play behavior in toddlers. *Developmental Psychology, 21*, 866–871.

Ocampo, K. A., Bernal, M. E., & Knight, G. P. (1993). Gender, race, and ethnicity: The sequencing of social constancies. In M. E. Bernal & G. P. Knight (Eds.), *Ethnic identity: Formation and transmission among Hispanics and other minorities* (pp.11–30). New York: State University of New York Press.

Ocampo, K. A., Knight, G. P., & Bernal, M. E., (1997). The development of cognitive abilities and social identities in children: The case of ethnic identity. *International Journal of Behavioral Development, 21*(3), 479–500.

Pellegrini, A. D., & Perlmutter, J. C. (1989). Classroom contextual effects on children's play. *Developmental Psychology. 25*(2), 289–296.

Piaget, J. (1951). *The child's conception of the world.* New York: Humanities.

Porter, J. D. R. (1971). *Black child White child.* Cambridge, MA: Harvard University Press.

Powlishta, K. K., Serbin, L. A., Doyle, A., & White, D. R. (1994). Gender, ethnic, and body type biases: The generality of prejudice in childhood. *Developmental Psychology, 30*, 526–534.

Prentice, D. (2005). *The social enforcement of gender norms.* Paper presented at the American Psychological Society Annual Convention, Los Angeles, CA.

Quinn, P. C., & Eimas, P. D. (1996). Perceptual organization and categorization in young infants. In C. Rovee-Collier & L. P. Lipsitt (Eds.), *Advances in infancy research* (Vol. 10, pp. 1–36). Norwood, NJ: Ablex.

Quintana, S. M., & Vera, E. M. (1999). Mexican American children's ethnic identity, understanding of ethnic prejudice, and parental ethnic socialization. *Hispanic Journal of Behavioral Sciences, 21*, 387–404.

Ramsey, P. G. (1987). Young children's thinking about ethnic differences. In J. S. Phinney & M. J. Rotheram (Eds.), *Children's ethnic socialization: Pluralism and development* (pp. 33–56). Newbury Park, CA: SAGE publications.

Ramsey, P. G. (1991). The salience of race in young children growing up in an all-White community. *Journal of Educational Psychology, 83*, 28–34.

Rice, A. S., Ruiz, R. A., & Padilla, A. M. (1974). Person perception, self-identity, and ethnic group preference in Anglo, Black, and Chicano preschool and third grade children. *Journal of Cross-Cultural Psychology, 5*, 100–108.

Rosenthal, R., & Jacobsen, L. (1968). *Pygmalion in the classroom: Teacher expectation and pupils' intellectual development.* New York: Holt, Rinehart, & Winston.

Rotheram, M. J., & Phinney, J. S. (1987). Ethnic behavior patterns as an aspect of identity. In J. S. Phinney & M. J. Rotheram (Eds.), *Children's ethnic socialization: Pluralism and development* (pp. 201–218). Newbury Park, CA: Sage.

Rutland, A., Cameron, L., Bennett, L., & Ferrell, J. (2005). Interracial contact and racial constancy: A multi-site study of racial intergroup bias in 3–5 year old Anglo-British children. *Applied Developmental Psychology, 26*, 699–713.

Ruble, D. N., Alvarez, J., Bachman, M., Cameron, J., Fuligni, A., Garcia Coll, C., et al. (2004). The development of a sense of "we": The emergence and implications of children's collective identity. In M. Bennett & F. Sani (Eds.), *The development of the social self* (pp. 219–246). London: Psychology Press.

Ruble, D. N., & Martin, C. L. (1998). Gender development. In W. Damon & N. Eisenberg (Eds.), *Handbook of Child Psychology, Vol. 3* (5th ed.). New York: John Wiley & Sons.

Rydland, V. (2006, April). *Teachers' and children's talk about ethnic and linguistic diversity in preschool and first grade classrooms.* Paper presented at the annual meeting of the American Educational Research Association, San Francisco, CA.

Sani, F., Bennett, M., Mullally, S., & MacPherson, J. (2003). On the assumption of fixity in children's stereotypes: A reappraisal. *British Journal of Developmental Psychology, 21,* 113–124.

Seavey, C. A., Katz, P.A., & Zalk, S. R. (1975). Baby X: The effect of gender labels on adult responses to infants. *Sex Roles, 1,* 103–109.

Semaj, L. (1980). The development of racial evaluations and preference: A cognitive approach. *Journal of Black Psychology, 6,* 59–79.

Serbin, L. A., Sprafkin, C., Elman, M., & Doyle, A. B. (1984). The early development of sex differentiation patterns and social influence. *Canadian Journal of Social Science, 14,* 350–368.

Silvern, L. E. (1977). Children's sex-role preferences: Stronger among girls than boys. *Sex Roles, 3,* 159–171.

Slaby, R. G., & Frey, K. S. (1975). Development of gender constancy and selective attention to same-sex models. *Child Development, 46,* 849–856.

Spencer, M. B. (1984). Black children's race awareness, racial attitudes, and self-concept: A reinterpretation. *Journal of Child Psychology and Psychiatry, 24,* 433–441.

Spencer, M. B., & Markstrom-Adams, C. (1990). Identity processes among racial and ethnic minority children in America. *Child Development, 61,* 290–310.

Steele, C. M., & Aronson, J. (1995). Stereotype threat and the intellectual test performance of African-Americans. *Journal of Personality and Social Psychology, 68,* 797–811.

Stephan, W. G., & Rosenfield, D. (1979). Black self-rejection: Another look. *Journal of Educational Psychology, 71,* 708–716.

Stevenson, H. W., & Stevenson, N. G. (1960). Social interaction in an interracial nursery school. *Genetic Psychology Monographs, 61,* 37–75.

Swadener, E. B. (1991). Race, gender, and exceptionality: Peer interactions in two child care centers. In L. Weise, P. G. Altbach, G. P. Kelly, & H. G. Petrie (Eds.), *Critical perspectives on early childhood education* (pp. 101–118). New York: State University of New York Press.

Tajfel, H., & Wilkes, A. L. (1963). Classification and quantitative judgment. *British Journal of Psychology, 54,* 101–114.

Tajfel, H., & Turner, J. (1979). An integrative theory of intergroup conflict. In W. G. Austin & S. Worchel (Eds.), *The social psychology of intergroup relations* (pp. 33–47). Belmont, CA: Wadsworth, Inc.

Tajfel, H., & Turner, J. (1986). The social identity theory of intergroup behavior. In S. Worchel & W. G. Austin (Eds.), *Psychology of intergroup relations* (2nd ed.). Chicago: Nelson-Hall.

Thomas, D. E., Townsend, T. G., & Belgrave, F. Z. (2003). The influence of cultural and racial identification on the psychosocial adjustment of inner-city African American children in school. *American Journal of Community Psychology, 32*(3/4), 217–228.

Trew, K. (2004). Children and socio-cultural divisions in northern Ireland. *Journal of Social Issue, 60*(3), 507–522.

Turner, J. C., Hogg, M. A., Oakes, P. J., Reicher, S. D., & Wetherell, M. S. (1987). *Rediscovering the social group: A self-categorization theory.* Oxford: Blackwell.

Turner, J. C., Oakes, P. J., Haslam, S. A., & McGarty, C. (1994). Self and collective: Cognition and social context. *Personality and Social Psychology Bulletin, 20*(5), 454–463.

van Ausdale, D., & Feagin, J. R. (2001). *The first R: How children learn race and racism.* Lanham, MD: Rowman & Littlefield.

Vaughan, G. M. (1963). Concept formation and the development of ethnic awareness. *Journal of Genetic Psychology, 103*, 93–103.

Vaughan, G. M., Tajfel, H., & Williams, J. (1981). Bias in reward allocation in an intergroup and an interpersonal context. *Social Psychology Quarterly, 44*(1), 37–42.

Williams, J. E., Best, D., Boswell, D., Mattson, L., & Graves, D. (1975). Preschool racial attitude measure II. *Educational and Psychological Measurement, 35*, 3–18.

Williams, J. E., & Morland, J. K. (1976). *Race, color, and the young child.* Chapel Hill, NC: The University of North Carolina Press.

Yee, M. D., & Brown, R. (1994). The development of gender differentiation in young children. *British Journal of Social Psychology, 33*, 183–196.

Yee, M. D., & Brown, R. (1992). Self-evaluations and intergroup attitudes in children aged three to nine. *Child Development, 63*, 619–629.

CHAPTER 4

EXECUTIVE FUNCTION, BEHAVIORAL SELF-REGULATION, AND SOCIAL-EMOTIONAL COMPETENCE

Links to School Readiness

**Megan M. McClelland, Claire E. Cameron,
Shannon B. Wanless, and Amy Murray**

Each year, hundreds of thousands of children in the United States move from preschool to a more structured kindergarten environment, a transition that can be stressful and emotionally challenging for children who have not mastered the skills needed to thrive in formal schooling. Kindergartners who enter school without adequate social and self-regulatory skills are at significantly greater risk for difficulties, including peer rejection and low academic achievement. Moreover, teachers report that children begin school with differing levels of skills critical for success (Lin, Lawrence, & Gorrell, 2003). In one study, 46% of teachers reported at least half of children entering kindergarten lacked basic competencies needed to do well in school, such as following directions, working independently, and having

Contemporary Perspectives on Social Learning in Early Childhood Education, pages 83–107
Copyright © 2007 by Information Age Publishing

adequate academic skills (Rimm-Kaufman, Pianta, & Cox, 2000). There is strong evidence that *learning-related skills* (including executive function, behavioral self-regulation, and social-emotional competence), predict early academic achievement and are found in resilient children (Blair, 2002; McClelland, Morrison, & Holmes, 2000; NICHD, 2003). Thus, it is likely that promoting learning-related skills in preschoolers will prepare them for a more successful transition to kindergarten.

The Committee on Integrating the Science of Early Childhood Development maintains that multiple aspects of children's learning-related skills (including the areas of executive function, behavioral self-regulation, and social-emotional competence), are necessary for early school success (Shonkoff, Phillips, & National Research Council, NRC, 2000). The learning-related skills construct describes skills related to the ability to control, direct, and plan actions in an academic context. It is unclear, however, how these skills are shaped by child, family, and teacher factors, and how each aspect of learning-related skills supports academic achievement. By understanding the factors that influence learning-related skills, and the effects of each learning-related skill area on academic achievement, early childhood educators will be better equipped to prepare children for early school success.

The present chapter has four goals aimed at identifying how learning-related skills are related to early academic achievement in preschool and elementary school. First, we briefly discuss family and child influences in children's social, self-regulatory, and academic development. Second, we unpack the learning-related skills construct including executive function, behavioral self-regulation, and social-emotional competence; discuss their characteristics; and describe how they each relate to early achievement. Third, we examine the complex relations between these areas, which support a broad learning-related skills construct. Fourth, we examine how teaching factors influence children's learning-related skills, and offer practical implications for early childhood educators to improve children's learning-related skills and early school success.

SOURCES OF INFLUENCE IN EARLY DEVELOPMENT

Substantial differences between individual children's early social, self-regulatory, and academic skills emerge even before formal schooling (Morrison, Bachman, & Connor, 2005; NRC, 2000). To ensure that children are prepared for the demands of formal schooling, sources of influence in the child, family, and school that shape early development must be identified well before children enter kindergarten. Our current understanding of how children progress highlights a broad range of influential individual and sociocultural factors (McClelland, Kessenich, & Morrison, 2003;

NICHD, 2003; 2004; Rimm-Kaufman & Pianta, 2000). The bulk of the chapter focuses on early schooling, but we begin our discussion by summarizing potential influences within children, as well as within families.

Child Influences

Research reveals that children's characteristics, including brain development and temperament, are critical for their social, self-regulatory, and academic competence (Calkins, 2004).

Brain Development

One of the most important influences in early childhood is neurological maturation in the parts of the brain that help children control, direct, and plan their actions. Evidence from brain research shows these skills are associated with particular patterns of frontal lobe activity, specifically located in the prefrontal cortex (Blair, 2002). Rapid development in the prefrontal cortex in the years from 3 to 6 mean the preschool period is a crucial time for acquiring skills important for successful functioning in school settings (NRC, 2000). The capacity for individual children to function successfully in early childhood environments varies widely, in part because of differences in prefrontal cortex development, which helps explain why not all children enter kindergarten ready to learn (Calkins, 2004).

Temperament

Child temperament also has biological bases and plays a significant role in the development of young children. The effortful control temperament dimension is seen as "a major form of self-regulation" (Rothbart & Rueda, 2005, p. 169). Kochanska, Murray, and Harlan (2000) have defined effortful control as "a class of self-regulatory mechanisms" that "underpins a broad range of domains of functioning, including, cognitive, social, emotional, motor, and behavioral performance" (p. 220). Moreover, effortful control and self-regulation may be especially critical for children's early learning and school achievement (McClelland et al., 2003). However, although these characteristics are important, they also interact with family processes to influence children's social, self-regulatory, and academic development.

Family Influences

Parenting

A large body of research has examined the vital role that parents play in the development of their children (e.g., Collins, Maccoby, Steinberg, Hetherington, & Bornstein, 2000; Jewkes & Morrison, this volume; NICHD, 2004). Although many aspects of parenting are important for children's development, we briefly discuss two: attachment and the home learning environment.

1. *Attachment.* The quality of the parent–child attachment relationship is an important predictor of the skills children need to succeed in school. A number of researchers have found that having a secure attachment with a parent allows children to express emotion and develop strong self-regulatory skills (e.g., Calkins, 2004). Moreover, studies of attachment highlight the importance of the child's own behavior, including reactivity and responsiveness, in helping to shape the attachment relationship (Maccoby, 1992).

2. *Home Learning Environment.* The quality of the home learning environment is also important for children's early development. One study found that children in homes providing high levels of learning stimulation had higher reading and math skills (Bradley, Corwyn, Burchinal, McAdoo, & García Coll, 2001). A recent study also found that the quality of the home environment predicted first graders' performance on cognitive tasks (NICHD, 2004). Finally, research has found that more stimulating home learning environments, as rated by parents, predicted stronger behavioral self-regulation in children, and that a stimulating home learning environment and good self-regulation were associated with higher levels of emergent literacy and math skills at four years (McClelland & Wanless, 2006).

Although space limits a full discussion, it is clear that multiple factors shape children's social, self-regulatory, and academic functioning in preschool and once children enter kindergarten (see Figure 5.1). In this chapter, we focus on children's learning-related skills which include aspects of executive function, behavioral self-regulation, and social-emotional competence. Together, these skills help children thrive in educational environments and are influenced by child, parent, and teacher factors. For example, as shown in Figure 5.1, it is likely that children's characteristics such as brain development and temperament influence their learning-related skills and achievement. Parenting and teaching influences are also important for children's learning-related skills and school success. However, although these factors are significant predictors of children's school readiness, it is necessary to define the learning-related skills that help children benefit from learning opportunities in school, and describe the implications for teachers. Thus, the remainder of the chapter will focus on defining learning-related skills and how educators can influence these skills.

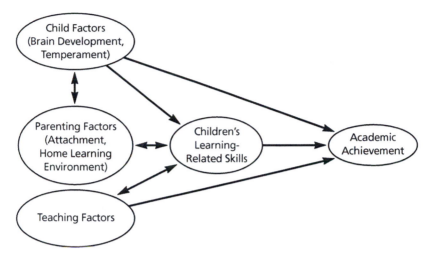

Figure 4.1.   Child, parent, and teching influences on learning-related skills and achievement. *Note:* This is not an exhaustive list of all possible influences on academic achievement.

LEARNING-RELATED SKILLS AREAS

The learning-related skills construct describes a set of skills related to the ability to control, direct, and plan actions in an academic context. These skills are necessary for children to achieve academically, but there remains substantial inconsistency in their definition and terminology (Pintrich, 2000). Thus, the second goal of this chapter is to define and differentiate the areas making up learning-related skills, which we call *executive function, behavioral self-regulation,* and *social emotional competence.* We describe and agree with the existing research base demonstrating that these areas, although separate, are interrelated. We argue that the broad learning-related skills construct is a useful way of conceptualizing these three areas. Clarifying the areas of learning-related skills and eliminating overlap is an important first step toward making more effective recommendations for educational practice.

One way to distinguish the learning-related skill areas is to see how they are used in classroom environments. Executive function (including working memory, attention, and inhibitory control), is just beginning to be studied in classrooms, although children clearly need memory, focused attention, and self-control skills to succeed in school. Executive function is usually studied in laboratories, often using split-second reaction times during a relatively brief session (e.g., Miyake, Friedman, Emerson, Witzki, & Howerter, 2000), and has historically been the least situated in classroom contexts of the three learning-related skill areas. In contrast, behavioral self-regulation includes *applying* executive function to behavioral actions; a child who is successful in this area is able to integrate executive function skills to complete tasks, clean up after herself, and plan future actions. Behavioral self-regulation is studied with tasks requiring judgments from raters on children's motor or oral responses in game-like assessments, as well as with observer reports of behavior at home or in the classroom (Cooper & Farran, 1988; Cameron et al., in press). Social-emotional competence (including cooperation, independence, and responsibility) is also important for classroom functioning, since it has to do with children's success when interacting with or working among other people (Ladd, Birch, & Buhs, 1999).

The broader construct, learning-related skills, encompasses all three areas (executive function, behavioral self-regulation, and social-emotional competence). We argue that each area is important for children's success in school and must be considered a distinct set of skills. In addition, it seems likely that these areas build on each other and that to enhance children's learning-related skills, educators must understand the overall construct, while simultaneously recognizing differences among the areas. Based on recent research and a need to precisely specify distinctions among these areas, we hypothesize a hierarchical structure among the three areas comprising learning-related skills (see Figure 5.2). We predict that children's executive function leads to behavioral self-regulation, which enables broader social-emotional competence (all of which are subject to environmental influence), to shape academic achievement (Rueda, Rothbart, McCandliss, Saccomanno, & Posner, 2005). We focus on research supporting these pathways to early school success and present a conceptual model (see Figure 5.2) describing specific relations among teaching factors, individual learning-related skill areas, and early achievement. In the next section, we briefly discuss components of each area and present evidence for their unique contributions to children's academic functioning in early educational settings.

Executive Function

The first area of learning-related skills is executive function. Drawing from Blair's (2002) definition, we consider executive function "a [cognitive] construct that unites working memory, attention, and inhibitory control for the purposes of planning and executing goal-directed activity" (p. 113). These skills (attention, working memory, and inhibitory control) predict social-emotional and academic success in children's early school environments (Barkley, 1994; Gathercole & Pickering, 2000; Howse, Lange,

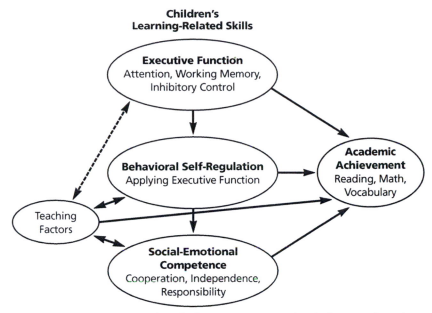

Figure 4.2.   Conceptual model of relations among teacher influences, learning-related skills, and early achievement. Dotted line represents a possible, but untested link.

Farran, & Boyles, 2003). They are also highly interrelated and work together as managerial or "executive" cognitive skills that drive behavior. In executive function research (particularly in neuroscience), individual skills are defined and measured independently from one another, to the extent this is possible, since we use multiple skills in any executive function task (Miyake et al., 2000). We argue that integrating and applying executive function manifests itself in behavioral self-regulation. Before elaborating on the definition of behavioral self-regulation, we first describe three individual executive function components relevant for young children and connect them directly to school success.

Attention

Children are driven to make sense of the world around them, and actively explore their environments to find new and meaningful information (NRC, 2001). Attention involves focusing on important aspects of a situation while ignoring distractions and filtering irrelevant information (Barkley, 1994). Switching focus from one thing to another is also a significant part of attention. In a busy classroom, attention plays a central role in determining what children notice and learn. Children who have trouble identifying important information or ignoring distractions have trouble succeeding in complex classroom settings. For example, in one study, children were required to ignore an entertaining game while focusing their attention on a tedious computer task. Socio-economically disadvantaged kindergartners showed poorer attention compared with students not at-risk, and lower attention predicted lower achievement skills in the at-risk group (Howse, Lange et al., 2003).

Working Memory

In the classroom, children need to remember what they are doing as they work. In other words, they need working memory, which means they must choose and pay attention to important information as they participate in activities or work at a center. At the same time, they must remember their progress in an activity (Miyake et al., 2000). This cognitive skill is crucial for children to understand, process, and act upon the many pieces of information they encounter in a classroom setting. Gathercole and Pickering (2000) found that 6- and 7-year-old low achieving students had more difficulty on a working memory task that required them to keep track of visual information, compared to higher achieving students. In another study, good working memory was uniquely associated with high mathematical ability in children aged 6 to 8 years (Bull & Scerif, 2001). Finally, Adams, Bourke, and Willis (1999) demonstrated that working memory predicted language comprehension skills in 4- to 5-year-olds. Thus, working memory is important for many areas central to early childhood environments, including processing visual information, learning math skills, comprehending oral language, and early literacy development.

Inhibitory Control

Before acting on information in working memory, children need to remember and plan appropriate responses. We define inhibitory control as stopping a natural but unnecessary response and instead demonstrating less automatic, but more adaptive, behavior. In the classroom, inhibitory control helps children remember to clean up materials before moving on to another project, raise their hand before talking, and wait their turn before participating in a group setting. Inhibitory control predicts positive adaptation to preschool environments, including teacher-reported social competence, early in children's lives (Blair, 2002) and is also associated with more regulated emotion control (Kochanska et al., 2000).

Behavioral Self-Regulation

Executive function supports the second area of learning-related skills—behavioral self-regulation. Successful behavioral self-regulation in early childhood involves applying executive function in situations where the important or measured outcome is behavioral, such as cleaning up materials while remembering the teacher's instructions about what to do next. We focus on children's application of executive function, and integration of executive function components (i.e., attention, working memory, and inhibitory control), as a key determinant of behavioral self-regulation. Like behavioral self-regulation, executive function includes multiple skills, but mostly operates and has been primarily studied in the cognitive domain of functioning. In contrast, behavioral self-regulation operates and has been studied in the behavioral domain. The two are related because executive function regulates thought processing and is essential to children's ability to control their behavior.

Behavioral self-regulation in classroom contexts involves the child independently creating and acting on plans for her own behavior. Successfully designing and carrying out behavioral plans is an important goal for children in early school settings (Bronson, 2000). Some academic activities, such as independent assignments managed by individual children, place relatively high demands on behavioral self-regulation (Rimm-Kaufman & Chiu, in press), in part because the options for possible behaviors in such a setting vary widely (e.g., the child could choose to work, interact with friends, or wander aimlessly around the classroom).

Behavioral self-regulation is important for children's early school success. In one study, kindergarten behavioral self-regulation, rated by teachers, predicted early achievement (Howse, Calkins, Anastopoulos, Keane, & Shelton, 2003). In addition, results from our own work demonstrated that a recently developed observational assessment of behavioral self-regulation, the *Head-to-Toes Task*, showed developmental differences in performance with two sites of young children ($N = 353$) from distinct geographical regions (Cameron et al., in press). We also found that children who improved on the Head-to-Toes Task over prekindergarten also grew in early literacy, language, and math skills (McClelland et al., in press). We argue that behavioral self-regulation forms the basis for children's social-emotional competence, which is discussed next.

Social-Emotional Competence

The third area of skills comprising the learning-related skill construct is social-emotional competence, which includes cooperation, independence, and responsibility. As shown in Figure 5.2, social-emotional competence resides at the most contextualized level; its components are the outward manifestations of both executive function and behavioral self-regulation, with a particular focus on social interactions. Social-emotional competence is especially important at school entry, when interacting effectively with others is critical for later success (Raver, 2002). Studies reveal specific aspects of children's social-emotional competence are important for early school performance and the transition to school (McClelland et al., 2000). In particular, getting along well with other children can serve as a protective factor for preschoolers at risk for school difficulties. For example, the NICHD (2004) found that children with strong social competence scored higher in reading and math in first grade compared with preschoolers with poor social skills, even if they came from families with less responsive parenting. Thus, social-emotional competence facilitates early school success through multiple pathways.

Preschool children without basic social-emotional competence have difficulty navigating kindergarten entry (Blair, 2002; Ladd et al., 1999), and are at increased risk for academic difficulties (Alexander, Entwisle, & Dauber, 1993). Deficiencies in this area can negatively affect a child's relationships with teachers and peers. For example, children with patterns of aggressive behavior form fewer peer friendships, and are more likely to be rejected by peers (Raver, 2002). In addition, kindergarten teachers provide less positive feedback to disruptive children than to cooperative children (Arnold, McWilliams, & Arnold, 1998). Furthermore, research reveals a significant portion of children enter kindergarten without these important skills (Blair, 2002). We propose that the specific social-emotional competencies of cooperation, independence, and responsibility are particularly relevant for learning-related skills.

Cooperation

Many studies addressing children's social-emotional competence use the terms *prosocial behavior* or *social competency* to describe measured outcomes (e.g., Eisenberg, Fabes, Guthrie, & Reiser, 2000; Diener & Kim, 2003). We identify the specific social behaviors assessed in these studies as cooperation. Cooperation refers to working and playing well with other children, following directions, and sharing toys and materials (Gresham & Elliott, 1990). In one recent study, less cooperation measured by more solitary play was related to significantly lower literacy skills in preschool (Doctoroff, Greer, & Arnold, 2006).

Independence

In addition to being able to interact appropriately with others, children also need to be able to work on their own, and to direct their own activities, even in the midst of a busy classroom environment. Independence, a manifestation of behavioral self-regulation in a social context, refers to a child's ability to problem-solve alone before asking for help, and to spontaneously begin a task according to instructions (Bronson, 2000). Ladd and colleagues (1999) found that children who functioned more independently in the classroom had significantly higher rates of peer acceptance, and also had higher ratings on teacher–child relationship quality. Moreover, independence (which was part of a classroom participation composite) predicted early academic achievement.

Responsibility

The third component of the social–emotional competence area of learning-related skills is responsibility, which is closely linked to independence. Responsibility refers to being able to select an appropriate workspace, choose and organize materials, and complete tasks successfully when working among other children (Bronson, 2000). McWayne, Fantuzzo, and McDermott (2004) found that children with low levels of independence and responsibility, and high levels of classroom behavior problems, scored lower on measures of academic achievement than children who had similar levels of behavior problems, but higher levels of independence and responsibility. Taken together, these components of social-emotional competence demonstrate how children's behavioral self-regulation is expressed in broader social contexts such as the classroom environment. Although distinct from one another, the components of social-emotional competence (cooperation, independence, and responsibility) relate and often overlap. The next step is to specify how executive function, behavioral self-regulation, and social-emotional competence connect to each other and early school success.

RELATIONS AMONG EXECUTIVE FUNCTION, BEHAVIORAL SELF-REGULATION, AND SOCIAL-EMOTIONAL COMPETENCE

Converging research from multiple disciplines has supported the assertion that executive function, behavioral self-regulation, and social-emotional competence are each important for early school success, but how the three areas are connected remains unclear. Specifying relations among these skills likely has important implications for enhancing children's chances for academic success (see Figure 5.2).

We conceptualize executive function as a building block of behavioral self-regulation, both of foundational importance in early childhood. In concert with conceptual advancements (NRC, 2001) and language development (Bronson, 2000), it seems likely that executive function leads to behavioral self-regulation, enabling children to plan and carry out their future actions (Blair, 2002). In preschool classrooms, these actions often need to reflect a consideration of other people. In other words, children must integrate and apply executive function to behavioral actions (behavioral self-regulation) and subsequently exhibit cooperation, independence, and responsibility when they work with or near others (social-emotional competence). For example, completing tasks requires remembering teacher directions, choosing an appropriate workspace, and filtering attention distractions. Sometimes activities are completed alongside or in cooperation with others and require responsibility and the ability to work independently without distracting other children. In addition, deciding how to react appropriately in a difficult situation means deliberately thinking through possible consequences and controlling strong emotional impulses. Although separate, research indicates that executive function, behavioral self-regulation, and social-emotional competence are interrelated areas that build on each other and are reflected in children's learning-related skills.

Results from our recent research, which represent a preliminary effort at validating the conceptual models in Figures 5.1 and 5.2, indicate that aspects of executive function are significantly related to social-emotional competence in preschool children (McClelland, 2007). In one study, 72 mostly Caucasian, middle-class children, were followed for one year when children were 3 and 4 years. At both time points, children with high parent-rated inhibitory control were also rated by teachers as being more cooperative in the classroom. In addition, at 4 years, children who were able to focus their attention were also more likely to be described as cooperative, independent, and responsible in the classroom. Having strong attention and inhibitory control may help children self-regulate and thus cooperate with others. Attention skills likely help children be more independent and responsible in the classroom by helping them process and encode relevant instructions. Taken together, we found that executive function and social-emotional competence are separate, yet functionally related domains.

Moreover, we replicated this pattern of results in the fall and spring of the prekindergarten year in a second sample of 93 children from families demonstrating educational and ethnic diversity. In this sample, the mean parent education level was approximately equivalent to an associate's degree ($M = 14.63$ years) and 52% of the sample consisted of children from ethnic minorities, including a Spanish-speaking group (McClelland, 2007). We measured executive function with a parent-rated temperament scale assessing attention and inhibitory control, behavioral self-regulation with an observational task, and social-emotional competence with teacher ratings of cooperation, independence, and responsibility. Results from this study indicated that in addition to links between executive function and social-emotional competence, children's behavioral self-regulation significantly predicted a number of social-emotional competencies, including higher levels of children's responsibility in the fall of the prekindergarten year and greater cooperation and independence in both fall and spring. Together, these results suggest that aspects of executive function and behavioral self-regulation are linked to social-emotional competence and may indicate specific paths to academic achievement. In addition, this evidence suggests that these areas form a broad learning-related skills construct.

We propose that the three learning-related skill areas (executive function, behavioral self-regulation, and social-emotional competence) are distinct and should be conceptualized as such in order to individualize educational strategies and meet the needs of children in early school contexts. The idea of unity and diversity within a particular area has been used to describe executive function (Blair, Zelazo, & Greenberg, 2005; Miyake et al., 2000). In this chapter we apply the same idea to learning-related skills. The learning-related skills construct has conceptual appeal as a way to summarize skills needed to benefit from learning opportunities, but the areas comprising learning-related skills are also separable, in the ways they are conceptualized, measured, and most importantly for this chapter, addressed by educators.

LEARNING-RELATED SKILLS
AND EARLY ACADEMIC ACHIEVEMENT

Our recent research has suggested that aspects of *learning-related skills* form a broader construct. Although most educational research has not employed laboratory measures of executive function skills, it has supported a learning-related skills construct in elementary (Cooper & Farran, 1988) and preschool children based on teacher ratings of behavioral self-regulation, and the social-emotional competencies of cooperation, independence, and responsibility. In a study of preschoolers, confirmatory factor analyses found evidence for a learning-related skills construct, which showed variability across children and stability within children over a 1-year period (McClelland & Morrison, 2003). This construct is useful as a means of conceptualizing all three domains (executive function, behavioral self-regulation, and social-emotional competence) important for children's early academic success.

We have also found that teacher-rated learning-related skills uniquely predicted academic outcomes at kindergarten and second grade after controlling for the effects of children's IQ, age at school entrance, amount of preschool experience, ethnicity, parents' education, and the family learning environment (McClelland et al., 2000). In addition, results of a recent study supported the long-term predictability of learning-related skills on children's reading and math scores between kindergarten and sixth grade

(McClelland, Acock, & Morrison, 2006). However, these studies are limited because specific aspects of executive function were not measured and only teacher ratings were included. Future studies should incorporate methods that fully reflect theoretically-based relations among learning-related skill areas.

In this chapter, we have focused on describing and differentiating executive function, behavioral self-regulation, and social-emotional competence, as well as specifying how they relate to each other and to early school success. We next present a conceptual model that highlights the importance of the learning-related skills construct and its individual areas for academic achievement, with the ultimate goal of offering concrete suggestions for practitioners.

CONCEPTUAL MODEL OF EXECUTIVE FUNCTION, BEHAVIORAL SELF-REGULATION, SOCIAL-EMOTIONAL COMPETENCE, AND EARLY ACHIEVEMENT

Findings from our own research, as well as recently published research of others (NRC, 2000), underscore the complex interplay of child variables that influence early social and academic progress (see Figure 5.2). As shown in Figure 5.2, academic success stems from relations among the learning-related skills areas and teaching influences. Research supports the argument that children's executive function underlies behavioral self-regulation, which together shape children's social-emotional competence and achievement. In our conceptual model, we predict that children's executive function is linked to achievement directly and that this relation also depends on levels of behavioral self-regulation, which we argue is the behavioral manifestation of executive function. Consistent with this view, executive function links to children's achievement (NICHD, 2003) and behavioral self-regulation predicts achievement in preschool and early elementary school (Howse, Calkins et al., 2003; McClelland et al., in press).

Research also demonstrates that children's behavioral self-regulation promotes social-emotional competence in broader social contexts (see Figure 5.2). Specifically, as noted above, children's behavioral self-regulation as well as social-emotional competence predict achievement (Ladd et al., 1999). In addition, Bellanti and Bierman (2000) found that children who had trouble paying attention had lower levels of social-emotional competence. Having higher levels of social-emotional competence was also related to higher cognitive scores. Having strong behavioral self-regulation supported by executive function components (i.e., attention) may help children develop social-emotional competence, which helps them with cognitive development.

Finally, as shown in Figure 5.2, we propose that aspects of teaching are linked to children's executive function, behavioral self-regulation, social-emotional competence, and achievement. Although we do not know of research that has specifically examined relations between teaching factors and executive function, it seems plausible that these influences can help support specific executive function components. Thus, we use a dotted line to indicate this possible link, which needs to be tested empirically. We also propose that teaching factors affect children's achievement directly and indirectly through children's behavioral self-regulation and social-emotional competence. This view has been supported by research showing that teaching factors such as teacher warmth and responsiveness to children's needs have been positively linked to stronger social-emotional competence in children (Howes, Hamilton, & Matheson, 1994), and to stronger vocabulary and early reading skills in children at the end of preschool (Connor, Morrison, & Slominski, 2006). It is also likely that relations between teaching factors, executive function, children's behavioral self-regulation, and social-emotional competence are bidirectional, where children's behaviors help shape how teachers behave, just as teacher actions influence children (see Figure 5.2).

Overall, the learning-related skills construct is a useful way to conceptualize a set of skills (executive function, behavioral self-regulation, and social-emotional competence) vital for early achievement, which are likely related to teaching factors. We describe these possible pathways below, following each with practical implications based on current knowledge in the area.

CONNECTING TEACHING FACTORS TO LEARNING-RELATED SKILLS

Teaching factors are linked in multiple ways to children's early academic achievement. Although children's characteristics and parenting are vitally important, we focus the rest of our discussion on how teachers can facilitate children's learning-related skills. Research findings indicate that positive teacher–child interactions, instructional climate, and child-centered classrooms, are associated with improved social and academic competence (Pianta, La Paro, Payne, Cox, & Bradley, 2002). In one study, children whose teachers were warm and responsive had stronger vocabulary and early reading skills at the end of first grade (Connor, Son, Hindman, & Morrison, 2005). These findings reveal that in addition to the child and family, teachers are influential players in cultivating academic success. Teachers also play an essential role in supporting the development of learning-related skills, as a means of promoting children's academic achievement in the early years (Cameron, Connor, & Morrison, 2005; Lin et al., 2003). Although the learning-related skills perspective has not yet been systematically applied in research within classrooms, below we review some potential mechanisms by which teachers can support individual learning-related skill areas. We follow each section with practical implications that emerge from the present findings.

Teaching Factors and Executive Function

Executive function in young children has been primarily studied in laboratory and clinical settings rather than school contexts. Nonetheless, evidence shows that young children's executive function is amenable to environmental influences (Blair et al., 2005). For example, an experimental intervention revealed that after three training sessions in a sorting game requiring executive function (i.e., a modified Wisconsin card sort task), children's inhibitory control skills improved significantly (Dowsett & Livesey, 2000). This shows that the opportunity to play games requiring complex rule use produces improvement in an aspect of executive function important for school success. Other work reveals that children with poor inhibitory control can be taught to talk to themselves as a means of directing their behavior, when thought processes are first modeled aloud by an adult (Meichenbaum & Goodman, 1971). Finally, one study demonstrated that 3- to 4-year-old children had better memory for toys they liked, showing that young children's attention differs depending on how much they are interested in an object (Renninger & Wozniak, 1985).

Promoting Executive Function

Although much of the research on executive function is experimental, findings point to certain recommendations for teachers. First, providing opportunities for children to play games with complex rules is one way that teachers can promote inhibitory control skills, one aspect of executive function. For example, teachers may offer children structured games such as Duck Duck Goose or London Bridge to give them practice mastering a set of rules. Second, it seems important that children be given opportunities to solve problems and be encouraged to talk themselves through completing tasks, sometimes known as private speech (Berk & Spuhl, 1995). Vygotskians propose that private speech serves as a useful tool for children until they can work out their thoughts without the mediator of language (Bodrova & Leong, 2006). To encourage the use of private speech, teachers can model this skill aloud or ask children to talk through the steps as they work on a problem. Third and finally, studies of attention and interest show that teachers who take the time to assess what children like may find that incorporating individualized elements into classroom activities helps children attend to instructions and activities, learn, and retain what they learn. Therefore, early childhood educators who get to know children individually and select materials and activities based on this knowledge will likely promote children's attention to classroom activities.

Teaching Factors and Behavioral Self-Regulation

Compared with executive function, behavioral self-regulation appears more frequently in research in educational settings. In one study, high-quality child care settings, which included enriching activities and experiences, were positively related to children's behavioral self-regulation. In contrast, children in low-quality child care settings had more behavioral self-regulation problems (Arnold et al., 1998; Burchinal, Peisner-Feinberg, Bryant, & Clifford, 2000). Another study examined classroom quality, defined by the emotional and instructional support teachers offered kindergartners, in settings that demanded varying levels of behavioral self-regulation. High-quality instructional and emotional support from teachers, which included providing feedback and conversation about academic activities, decreased students' off-task behavior, even in settings that demanded high levels of behavioral self-regulation skills (Rimm-Kaufman, La Paro, Downer, & Pianta, 2005).

Finally, two interventions using a Vygotskian approach, *Tools of the Mind* and *Scaffolding Early Literacy*, aim to improve young children's behavioral self-regulation by emphasizing the importance of sociodramatic or make-believe play (Bodrova & Leong, 2006). One study indicated that preschoolers who persistently and frequently engaged in complex sociodramatic play demonstrated increased behavioral self-regulation later in the school year (Elias & Berk, 2002). It is possible that pretending to be someone else, who is self-regulated, such as an adult, helps chilren learn perspective-taking (Bodrova & Leong, 2006). Based on these findings, we make recommendations for promoting behavioral self-regulation in early childhood classrooms.

Promoting Behavioral Self-Regulation

Teachers can positively influence the development of behavioral self-regulation in young children by striving to provide high-quality learning environments. There are two important aspects of high-quality early childhood environments. First, stimulating experiences where children can practice behavioral self-regulation in child-centered activities are important. Second, high-quality environments provide emotional and instructional support such as talking with the children about the activities they are engaged in, and giving them relevant feedback. For example, when a child becomes frustrated with an activity, such as completing a puzzle, teachers may promote behavioral self-regulation by asking her what the next step could be. If the next step is finding a piece with a certain shape, the teacher can help the child describe and find the missing piece. Third, teachers may promote behavioral self-regulation by creating frequent opportunities in which children can practice behaving in self-regulated ways, such as in complex sociodramatic play. Pretending to play "school," for example, allows children the opportunity to practice sitting patiently while the "teacher" reads a story. Also, pretending to wait in line at a grocery store offers an opportunity to extend behavioral self-regulation skills. In both of these scenarios, children take on roles that require greater self-regulation skills than they may typically express. Creating appropriate and beneficial sociodramatic play practices, however, requires professional training. Thus we also encourage proper teacher preparation and ongoing support for early childhood educators (NRC, 2001).

Teaching Factors and Social-Emotional Competence

Research demonstrates connections across the early school years between teacher–child relationships and social-emotional competence (Hamre & Pianta, 2001; Howes et al., 1994). In a study with very young children, warm teacher–toddler relationships were associated with more cooperative toddlers and less hostile aggressive behavior (Howes et al., 1994). In other work, kindergarten teachers who had positive relationships with their students (including reporting being sensitive to children's needs and feeling attached to the children), noted that those students exhibited greater social-emotional competence (Pianta et al., 2002). Finally, organizing kindergartners in small groups in a classroom with a warm and sensitive teacher promoted cooperation and social conversation (Rimm-Kaufman et al., 2005). Other work revealed that teacher-reported negativity in kindergarten was related to behavior problems including difficulty listening, cooperating, and participating through eighth grade (Hamre & Pianta, 2001). Thus, across early childhood, teachers may facilitate or hinder the development of social-emotional competence through the relationships that they cultivate with and among the children in their care.

Promoting Social-Emotional Competence

To strengthen social-emotional competence, teachers can work to promote positive teacher–child relationships, which are characterized by warmth and responsiveness to children's needs, and a sense of attachment to individual children. First, teachers can help strengthen these relationships by getting to know each child and his or her family. Through observation, speaking to families and caregivers, and direct interaction with children, teachers will better understand their preferences, interests, backgrounds, and cultures. As a result, teachers will be able to interact with children in a manner that is relevant and respectful (Joseph & Strain, 2003). Second, teachers can build strong teacher–child relationships by offering affirming statements alongside constructive feedback. Children who are the most difficult to build relationships with have often heard few affirming statements from adults in the past. These children frequently are most in need of strong teacher–child relationships. From the research reviewed, it is not clear whether positive teacher–child relationships promote learning-related skills, or whether children with stronger learning-related skills are more likely to develop positive teacher–child relationships. Nonetheless, since teachers play the relatively more powerful role in shaping the tone of early childhood classrooms, we emphasize the importance of intentionally cultivating positive relationships with all of the children in order to promote social-emotional competence

GENERAL RECOMMENDATIONS

Accumulating research reveals the importance of learning-related skills for early academic achievement. Evidence also demonstrates independent contributions of executive function, behavioral self-regulation, and social-emotional competence to early school achievement and reveals a new perspective for structuring research questions and shaping classroom practices with young children in early care and education settings. We propose that certain techniques, such as choosing topics of interest to children to promote attention, and creating interactive classrooms where children can practice behavioral self-regulation, relate with specific components or areas of learning-related skills. A few common themes run throughout these skill areas, however, and to emphasize their importance we end the chapter with three general recommendations.

Our first recommendation is to embed techniques to promote aspects of learning-related skills throughout daily routines and learning activities. This is exemplified in some current interventions (French, 2004; Bodrova & Leong, 2006). To accomplish this, teachers must intentionally create opportunities for children to use executive function or private speech, for example, and take advantage of naturally-occurring opportunities. This means children should practice learning-related skills in different contexts such as circle time, the playground, and small group activities. For example, when the class listens to a set of instructions about an upcoming activity, they must use working memory to remember the order of the activity's steps as they tackle individual portions of the task. Making sure that all children can hear instructions, with minimal outside distractions, ensures they can take advantage of the opportunity to practice their working memory skills.

Second, research shows that educational efforts individualized to particular constellations of attributes are more effective than are programs that do not take differences between children into account (Connor & Morrison, 2005). Thus, we ask teachers to consider learning-related skills as another area of individual difference. We encourage observation and formative assessment in learning-related skill areas as a way to identify and promote each individual's success. For example, if a child is struggling to learn, a number of sources could be considered for intervention. Lack of knowledge or familiarity with educational settings could explain the child's trouble, but deficits in a learning-related skill area may be at work to prevent learning as well. If a child is frustrated with a task, teachers should consider whether it is because she has trouble remembering the directions (executive function), difficulty attending and remembering what to do when there is an attractive water table nearby where she would rather play (behavioral self-regulation), or difficulty sharing her materials with peers (social-emotional competence). Three different strategies would be appropriate depending on the source of trouble. In the first case, the teacher need only review the directions. In the second, the child may need to be moved from the water table or assured she can use it when she finishes her other learning task, and in the third, the child may benefit from practicing skills for cooperating with others, which may include a perspective-taking exercise.

We urge teachers to consider one final suggestion from learning-related skills research, which demonstrates it is typical for children to struggle with the three skill areas in early childhood, because this is when skills are developing. Based on informal observations of children, teachers can adjust activities and their own expectations for behavior, so that children are appropriately challenged and can practice their skills in constructive ways.

CONCLUSIONS

This chapter examined how learning-related skills relate to children's early academic achievement. We defined three areas including executive function, behavioral self-regulation, and social-emotional competence, and described how each relates to early school success. We also examined complex relations among these skills and argued that these areas support a broad learning-related skills construct, reviewing research describing the role that teachers play in children's learning-related skills and academic achievement. Based on our systematic exploration of an important but broad construct, we presented a conceptual model describing relations among specific learning-related skill areas, teaching factors, and early achievement. We ended with practical implications for improving children's learning-related skills and school success. Continued research that clarifies definitions, explores specific skill areas, and offers solutions gleaned from working with practitioners reveals an important avenue for promoting children's learning-related skills as they begin their academic careers.

REFERENCES

Adams, A. M., Bourke, L., & Willis, C. (1999). Working memory and spoken language comprehension in young children. *International Journal of Psychology, 34,* 364–373.

Alexander, K. L., Entwisle, D. R., & Dauber, S. L. (1993). First-grade classroom behavior: Its short- and long-term consequences for school performance. *Child Development, 64,* 801–814.

Arnold, D. H., McWilliams, L., & Arnold, E. H. (1998) Teacher discipline and child misbehavior in day care: Untangling causality with correlational data. *Developmental Psychology, 34.* 276–87.

Barkley, R. A. (1994). The assessment of attention in children. In G. R. Lyon (Ed.), *Frames of reference for the assessment of learning disabilities: New views on measurement issues* (pp. 69–102). Baltimore, MD: Paul H. Brookes.

Bellanti, C. J., & Bierman, K. L. (2000). Disentangling the impact of low cognitive ability and inattention on social behavior and peer relationships. *Journal of Clinical Child Psychology, 29,* 66–75.

Berk, L. E., & Spuhl, S. T. (1995). Maternal interaction, private speech, and task performance in preschool children. *Early Childhood Research Quarterly, 10,* 145–169.

Blair, C. (2002). School readiness: Integrating cognition and emotion in a neurobiological conceptualization of children's functioning at school entry. *American Psychologist, 57,* 111–127.

Blair, C., Zelazo, P. D., & Greenberg, M. T. (2005). The measurement of executive function in early childhood. *Developmental Neuropsychology, 28,* 561–571.

Bodrova, E., & Leong, D. J. (2006). Self-regulation as a key to school readiness: How early childhood teachers can promote this critical competency. In M. Zaslow & I. Martinez-Beck (Eds.), *Critical issues in early childhood professional development* (pp. 203–224). Baltimore, MD: Paul H. Brookes.

Bradley, R. H., Corwyn, R. F., Burchinal, M., McAdoo, H. P., & García Coll, C. (2001). The home environments of children in the United States part II: Relations with behavioral development through age thirteen. *Child Development, 72,* 1868–1886.

Bronson, M. B. (2000). *Self-regulation in early childhood: Nature and nurture.* New York: Guilford Press.

Bull, R., & Scerif, G. (2001). Executive functioning as a predictor of children's mathematics ability: Inhibition, switching, and working memory. *Developmental Neuropsychology, 19*, 273–293.

Burchinal, M. R., Peisner-Feinberg, E., Bryant, D. M., & Clifford, R. (2000). Children's social and cognitive development and child-care quality: Testing for differential associations related to poverty, gender, or ethnicity. *Applied Developmental Science, 4*, 149–165.

Calkins, S. D. (2004). Early attachment processes and the development of emotional self-regulation. In R. F. Baumeister & K. D. Vohs (Eds.), *Handbook of self-regulation: Research, theory, and applications* (pp. 324–339). New York: Guilford Press.

Cameron, C., Connor, C. M., & Morrison, F. J. (2005). Effects of variation in teacher organization on classroom functioning. *Journal of School Psychology, 43*, 61–85.

Cameron, C. E., McClelland, M. M., Jewkes, A. M., Connor, C. M., Farris, C. L., & Morrison, F. J. (in press). Touch your toes! Developing a behavioral measure of preschool self-regulation. *Early Childhood Research Quarterly.*

Collins, W. A., Maccoby, E. E., Steinberg, L., Hetherington, E. M., & Bornstein, M. H. (2000). Contemporary research on parenting: The case for nature and nurture. *American Psychologist, 55*, 218–232.

Connor, C. M., & Morrison, F. J. (2005). Grant: Examining causal implications of child X instruction interactions in early reading: U.S. Department of Education IES Grant # R205H04013.

Connor, C. M., Morrison, F. J., & Slominski, L. (2006). Preschool instruction and children's emergent literacy growth. *Journal of Educational Psychology, 98*(4), 665–689.

Connor, C. M., Son, S.-H., Hindman, A. H., & Morrison, F. J. (2005). Teacher qualifications, classroom practices, family characteristics, and preschool experience: Complex effects on first graders' vocabulary and early reading outcomes. *Journal of School Psychology, 43*(4), 343–375.

Cooper, D. H., & Farran, D. C. (1988). Behavioral risk factors in kindergarten. *Early Childhood Research Quarterly, 3*, 1–19.

Diener, M. L., & Kim, D. (2003). Maternal and child predictors of preschool children's social competence. *Applied Developmental Psychology, 25.* 3–24.

Doctoroff, G. L., Greer, J. A., & Arnold, D. A., (2006). The relationship between social behavior and emergent literacy among preschool boys and girls. *Applied Developmental Psychology, 27*, 1–13.

Dowsett, S. M., & Livesey, D. J. (2000). The development of inhibitory control in preschool children: Effects of "executive skills" training. *Developmental Psychobiology, 36*, 161–174.

Eisenberg, N., Fabes, R. A., Guthrie, I. K., & Reiser, M. (2000). Dispositional emotionality and regulation: Their role in predicting quality of social functioning. *Journal of Personality and Social Psychology, 78.* 136–157.

Elias, C. L., & Berk, L. E. (2002). Self-regulation in young children: Is there a role for sociodramatic play? *Early Childhood Research Quarterly, 17*, 216–238.

French, L. (2004). Science as the center of a coherent, integrated early childhood curriculum. *Early Childhood Research Quarterly, 19*, 138–149.

Gathercole, S. E., & Pickering, S. J. (2000). Working memory deficits in children with low achievements in the national curriculum at 7 years of age. *British Journal of Educational Psychology, 70,* 177–194.

Gresham, F. M., & Elliott, S. N. (1990). *Social Skills Rating System.* Circle Pines, MN: American Guidance Service.

Hamre, B. K., & Pianta, R. C. (2001). Early teacher–child relationships and the trajectory of children's school outcomes through eighth grade. *Child Development, 72,* 625–638.

Howes, C., Hamilton, C. E., & Matheson, C. C. (1994). Children's relationships with peers: Differential associations with aspects of the teacher–child relationship. *Child Development, 65,* 253–263.

Howse, R. B., Calkins, S. D., Anastopoulos, A. D., Keane, S. P., & Shelton, T. L. (2003). Regulatory contributors to children's kindergarten achievement. *Early Education and Development, 14,* 101–119.

Howse, R. B., Lange, G., Farran, D. C., & Boyles, C. D. (2003). Motivation and self-regulation as predictors of achievement in economically disadvantaged young children. *Journal of Experimental Education, 71,* 151–174.

Jewkes, A. M., & Morrison, F. J. (in press). Parenting and schooling influences on early self-regulation development. In O. N. Saracho & B. Spodek (Eds.), *Contemporary perspectives in early childhood education: Vol. 7. Social learning in early childhood education.*

Kochanska, G., Murray, K. T., & Harlan, E. T. (2000). Effortful control in early childhood: Continuity and change, antecedents, and implications for social development. *Developmental Psychology, 36,* 220–232.

Ladd, G. W., Birch, S. H., & Buhs, E. S. (1999). Children's social and scholastic lives in kindergarten: Related spheres of influence? *Child Development, 70,* 1373–1400.

Lin, H. L., Lawrence, F. R., & Gorrell, J. (2003). Kindergarten teachers' view of children's readiness for school. *Early Childhood Research Quarterly, 18,* 225–237.

Maccoby, E. E. (1992). The role of parents in the socialization of children: An historical overview. *Developmental Psychology, 28,* 1006–1017.

McClelland, M. M. (2007). *Specific relations among executive function, behavioral self-regulation and social-emotional competence.* Unpublished manuscript.

McClelland, M. M., Acock, A. C., & Morrison, F. J. (2006). The impact of kindergarten learning-related skills on academic trajectories at the end of elementary school. *Early Childhood Research Quarterly, 21,* 471–490.

McClelland, M. M., Cameron, C. E., Connor, C. M., Farris, C. L., Jewkes, A. M., & Morrison, F. J. (in press). Links between early self-regulation and preschoolers' literacy, vocabulary and math skills. *Developmental Psychology.*

McClelland, M. M., Kessenich, M., & Morrison, F. J. (2003). Pathways to early literacy: The complex interplay of child, family, and sociocultural factors. In R. V. Kail & H. W. Reese (Eds.), *Advances in child development and behavior* (pp. 411–447).

McClelland, M. M., & Morrison, F. J. (2003). The emergence of learning-related social skills in preschool children. *Early Childhood Research Quarterly, 18,* 206–224.

McClelland, M. M., Morrison, F. J., & Holmes, D. H. (2000). Children at-risk for early academic problems: The role of learning-related social skills. *Early Childhood Research Quarterly, 15*, 307–329.

McClelland, M. M., & Wanless, S. B. (2006, July). Child and parenting influences on early reading and mathematics skills. In C. Huntsinger (Chair), *Parental contributions to young children's language, reading, and mathematics development.* Symposium presented at the 19th Biennial Meeting of the International Society for the Study of Behavioural Development, Melbourne, Australia.

McWayne, C. M., Fantuzzo, J. W., & McDermott, P. A. (2004). Preschool competency in context: An investigation of the unique contribution of child competencies to early academic success. *Developmental Psychology, 40*, 633–645.

Meichenbaum, D. H., & Goodman, J. (1971). Training impulsive children to talk to themselves: A means of developing self-control. *Journal of Abnormal Psychology, 77*, 115–126.

Miyake, A. U., Friedman, N. P., Emerson, M. J., Witzki, A. H., & Howerter, A. (2000). The unity and diversity of executive functions and their contributions to complex 'frontal lobe' tasks: A latent variable analysis. *Cognitive Psychology, 41*, 49–100.

Morrison, F. J., Bachman, H. J., & Connor, C. M. (2005). *Improving literacy in America: Guidelines from research.* New Haven, CT: Yale University Press.

National Research Council (U.S.). Committee on Early Childhood Pedagogy., Bowman, B. T. (2001). *Eager to learn: Educating our preschoolers.* Washington, DC: National Academy Press.

NICHD Early Child Care Research Network. (2003). Do children's attention processes mediate the link between family predictors and school readiness? *Developmental Psychology, 39*, 581–593.

NICHD Early Childhood Research Network. (2004). Multiple pathways to early academic achievement. *Harvard Educational Review, 74*, 1–29.

Pianta, R. C., La Paro, K. M., Payne, C., Cox, M. J., & Bradley, R. (2002). The relation of kindergarten classroom environment to teacher, family, and school characteristics and child outcomes. *Elementary School Journal, 102*, 225–239.

Pintrich, P. R. (2000). Issues in self-regulation theory and research. *Journal of Mind & Behavior, 21*, 213–219.

Raver, C. C. (2002). Emotions matter: Making the case for the role of young children's emotional development for early school readiness. *Social Policy Report, 16*, 3–18.

Renninger, K. A., & Wozniak, R. H. (1985). Effect of interest on attentional shift, recognition, and recall in young children. *Developmental Psychology, 21*, 624–632.

Rimm-Kaufman, S. E., & Chiu, Y. J. I. (in press). Promoting social and academic competence in the classroom: An intervention study testing the effectiveness of the Responsive Classroom approach. *Psychology in the Schools.*

Rimm-Kaufman, S. E., La Paro, K. M., Downer, J. T., & Pianta, R. C. (2005). The contribution of classroom setting and quality of instruction to children's behavior in kindergarten classrooms. *The Elementary School Journal, 105*, 377–394.

Rimm-Kaufman, S. E., & Pianta, R. C. (2000). An ecological perspective on the transition to kindergarten: A theoretical framework to guide empirical research. *Journal of Applied Developmental Psychology, 21,* 491–511.

Rimm-Kaufman, S. E., Pianta, R. C., & Cox, M. J. (2000). Teachers' judgments of problems in the transition to kindergarten. *Early Childhood Research Quarterly, 15,* 147–166.

Rothbart, M. K., & Rueda, M. R. (2005). The development of effortful control. In U. Mayr, E. Awh, & S. Keele, (Eds.), *Developing individuality in the human brain: A tribute to Michael I. Posner* (pp. 167–188). Washington, DC: American Psychological Association.

Rueda, M. R., Rothbart, M. K., McCandliss, B. D., Saccomanno, L., & Posner, M. I. (2005). Training, maturation, and genetic influences on the development of executive attention. *PNAS, 102,* 14931–14936.

Shonkoff, J. P., Phillips, D., & National Research Council (U.S.). Committee on Integrating the Science of Early Childhood Development. (2000). *From neurons to neighborhoods: The science of early child development.* Washington, DC: National Academy Press.

CHAPTER 5

CAPITAL AT HOME AND AT SCHOOL AS DETERMINANTS OF CHILD SOCIAL ADJUSTMENT[1]

Toby L. Parcel

INTRODUCTION

This chapter has several interrelated purposes. First, I will argue that child social adjustment is important both for its own sake and for its implications across the life course, particularly in terms of school success. Second, I will argue that the capital to which the child has access, both at home and at school, will be a major determinant of his/her social adjustment. This approach explicitly acknowledges that both the family and the school are influential contexts in shaping social behavior. Following Bronfenbrenner and Morris (1998), I believe that a child's experience is shaped by multiple contexts throughout the course of development. Of course, the family is the first context the child experiences, but within a few years, the school becomes a second context that also will be important. I will review several perspectives that help to illuminate how various forms of capital located at home and at school can be so influential. In doing so, I will distinguish

Contemporary Perspectives on Social Learning in Early Childhood Education, pages 109–131
Copyright © 2007 by Information Age Publishing
109

between perspectives focusing on social capital from those focusing on social class; I will also explore their intersection.

I will also review literature to bring evidence to bear on the importance of these contexts. In doing so, first I will review findings about capital and class at home and their effects on child social adjustment. Second, I will summarize findings regarding the effects of capital at school, and then make some statements regarding the relative strength of each context, the family and the school, in promoting child social adjustment. In summarizing the literature, as much as possible I will confine myself to studies that both inform major theoretical perspectives bearing on the study of capital's effects on children, and that also study children in the age range zero to eight. In a number of cases, however, relevant studies also include older children in their samples. Unless there is evidence to suggest that the studies' findings are confined to children older than age eight, I include some of these studies in this review. Finally, I will explore the practical implications of these findings for families and for schools and chart directions for future research.

In all of these analyses, my focus generally will be on the social adjustment of normal children. The analysis of social adjustment of abused children, those from families characterized by extreme poverty or violence, or those with psychopathologies is important. However, comprehensive coverage of these studies is beyond the scope of this chapter. In a few cases, studies of behavior problems of children in extreme circumstances will be instructive, and thus will be included. In general, this review highlights the critical role of social adjustment in promoting well-being and educational attainment for children not at high risk as a function of prior trauma or deprivation. As such, the review underscores the importance of social adjustment for all children as a critical foundation for social life.

In adopting this framework, I regretfully neglect several other vital perspectives, many of which may be covered elsewhere in this volume. First, this review is explicitly sociological, and thus does not cover a number of factors that psychologists have identified as important to understanding social adjustment. For example, Thomas and Chess and colleagues are leaders in providing evidence that child temperament is important in influencing behavior, and that overreliance on maternal, parental, or institutional influences as determinants of behaviors is inappropriate (Chess & Thomas, 1959; Thomas & Chess, 1977; Thomas, Chess, & Birch, 1968). Werner and Smith (1982) provide important insights into how among a group of vulnerable children, a notable subset prove to be resilient, with social support from significant adults being a key mechanism in helping them to develop this resiliency. Willard Hartup's work (e.g., Hartup, 2005) identifies another major factor: the role of peer interaction in promoting social adjustment, while Asher and Coie (1990) and Guerra, Asher, & De Rosier (2004) find that rejection by peers can be both cause and effect of aggressive behavior. Hastings, Zahn-Waxler, Robinson, Usher, & Bridges (2000) trace the effects of empathy on changes in behavior problems, while the NICHD Early Child Care Research Network (2003a; 2003b) identifies several factors that influence social adjustment in first grade, including child gender, maternal education and depressive symptoms, sensitivity of mothering, and time spent in nonmaternal care. Taken together, these researchers highlight some of the psychological causes of social adjustment, while my review focuses on sociological factors. Clearly, any behavioral outcome is complex. This review helps to illuminate one piece of the puzzle.

WHY IS SOCIAL ADJUSTMENT IMPORTANT?

Social adjustment is important at any age past infancy because poor adjustment can impair well-being into adolescence and adulthood. Children who are aggressive, or undercontrolled, during early childhood often persist in this pattern (Caspi, Elder, & Bem, 1987; 1988; Fischer, Rolf, Hasazi, & Cummings, 1984; Kohlberg, Lacrosse, & Ricks, 1972; Patterson, DeBaryshe, & Ramsey, 1989), with long-term implications including negative labels from teachers, difficulties with achievement, and rejection by peers. These consequences disrupt opportunities to develop better social skills, thus encouraging the persistence of aggression (Patterson & Bank, 1989; Patterson et al., 1989). At the other end of the behavioral continuum, the anxiety, fearfulness, and social withdrawal that characterize overcontrolled behavior also tend to persist because such behaviors impede normal assertiveness in social situations (Caspi et al., 1987). These behavioral styles also have negative implications for school adjustment and academic achievement, given the importance of social adjustment for facilitating achievement, particularly as schooling continues.

Several recent studies elaborate on these points. In a study of 2,580 infants enrolled in the Coventry Cohort Study in 1996, Spencer and Coe (2003) demonstrate strong continuity in behavior problems detected at eight months (e.g., tantrums, sleep or feeding problems) to those that show up at eighteen months and at three years of age. These findings are in the presence of background controls. In addition, McLeod and Kaiser (2004) clearly show how behavior problems among six- to eight-year-old children have negative implications for high school graduation and college attendance up to 14 years later. Specifically, both internalizing and externalizing behavior problems strongly diminish the probability of high school graduation, owing largely to academic failures in middle and high school. Assuming high school graduation, externalizing behaviors reduce the probability of college enrollment, with the key mechanisms appearing to be persisting effects of early behavioral and academic predispositions. Hawkins, Guo, Hill, Battin-Pearson, and Abbott (2001) also document continuity in behavior problems from elementary school through age 18, and Entwistle, Alexander, and Steffel Olson (2005) show that noncognitive resources of first-graders play an important role in promoting academic achievement by age 22. These findings suggest that it is important to analyze the determinants of social adjustment, with a particular eye towards its implications for academic achievement. Social adjustment is important for its own sake, but becomes all the more important once we take into account the role of social adjustment in facilitating success at school.

To preview my central arguments, I suggest that children grow in the context of financial, human, and social capital, both at home and at school. Each form of capital can be viewed as parallel across the contexts of home and school; all forms of capital, regardless of context, can be potentially influential in promoting child social adjustment. Social capital and social class are not identical; rather, they are intersecting concepts. Social class most directly intersects with financial and human capital. Intersection between social class and social capital is closest if we consider the linking concept of occupation. Norms, a form of social capital, vary by parental occupation and influence how directly parents control their children, with attendant effects on child social adjustment. I begin with further elaboration regarding the role of capital at home.

CAPITAL AND CLASS AS DETERMINANTS OF CHILD SOCIAL ADJUSTMENT

Capital at Home

At the most general level, capital refers to resources that generate returns that improve the well-being of investors. The home is the context in which children initially live, and there is capital at home relevant to child well-being. As Coleman (1988; 1990) notes, family background consists of a) financial capital, i.e., financial resources used for the household and the child; b) human capital, i.e., parents' cognitive skills and educational attainment; and c) social capital, defined as relations among actors that "inhere in family relations and in community organization and that are useful for the cognitive or social development of a child or young person" (Coleman, 1990, p. 300). The first two elements of this trichotomy have long histories of theory and research in sociology and economics; Coleman's uniquely sociological contribution is in championing the role of social capital as a resource in the socialization process; his claims regarding the role of social capital in this process provide important theoretical guidance for this review. I first, however, more briefly discuss the roles of financial and human capital in promoting child social adjustment.

Sufficient material support is important for family well-being, and studies regarding the effects of poverty on child outcomes clearly establish that material deprivation is inimical to favorable child development (Duncan & Brooks-Gunn, 1997). Material deprivation causes parental distress that threatens constructive parent–child interaction, with implications for child social behavior (Elder, Van Nguyen, & Caspi, 1985; Kessler, Turner, & House, 1988; McLoyd, 1989; 1990; Mirowsky and Ross, 1986; Siegal, 1984; Whitbeck et al., 1991). Within more typical ranges of material support, variations in socioeconomic standing likely lead to variations in parental affect and mood, with predictable consequences for child social adjustment. Corwyn and Bradley (2005) provide corroborating evidence using structural equation modeling and growth curve analyses.

In addition, higher levels of parental human capital provide assets upon which children can draw to facilitate social adjustment throughout childhood and adolescence. Some of this effect may be due to more educated parents having expectations for certain kinds of social behavior, where such expectations likely included getting along well with others and not acting out or exhibiting withdrawn or clingy behaviors (Lareau, 2001). In addition, parents with higher levels of schooling may do a better job at managing children's behavior (Gecas, 1989), and stronger maternal self concept has a protective effect against behavior problems of young children (Parcel & Menaghan, 1994b). Taken together, these arguments clearly suggest that financial and human capital at home is important in determining child social adjustment.

But what is the scope of social capital? Most generally, social capital inheres in the structure of relations between and among actors, and can occur at any level of social aggregation. Within the family, it clearly includes the time and effort that parents spend on children. *Stronger bonds* between parents and children are a form of social captial that demands both the physical presence of parents and their attention and involvement. Thus, whereas human capital refers to characteristics of individuals, social capital refers to characteristics of relationships. It denotes both the quantity and quality of interaction and the bonds that develop among family members. Coleman, however, also states that *norms* are a critical form of social capital. My focus is primarily upon the *bonds* between parents and children as well as the *norms* parents use in child rearing. Below I develop the argument that human capital and background characteristics may be associated with norms, a form of social capital, that facilitate child socialization.[2]

Social Class and Social Behavior

How do these arguments regarding family capital interface with those regarding the importance of social class and child social behavior? Two areas of intersection appear obvious. First, social scientists typically view parents with higher levels of financial and human capital as having higher social class standing, because measures of education, a central dimension of human capital, and measures of economic well-being, or financial capital, are used to reflect socioeconomic status. Thus, two key forms of capital form the basis for discerning higher versus lower social class.

It is through parental occupation, however, that we see a second critical area of intersection. Specifically, occupations vary in their levels of substantive complexity, which forms a critical link between forms of social control that parents experience on the job and parenting styles that transmit norms of social control to children. Those parents in high complexity occupations may promote stronger social behavior among children than those in lower complexity occupations. Kohn and his colleagues argue that the substantive complexity and the opportunities for self-direction and autonomy that occupations offer affect parents' child-rearing values and the kinds of behavior they encourage in their children because parents encourage the styles of behavior most conducive to success in their own type of work (Kohn, 1977; Kohn & Schooler, 1982; 1983; Kohn, Slomczynski, & Schoenback, 1986; Miller, Schooler, Kohn, & Miller, 1979; Schooler, 1987). Parents in high complexity occupations place less emphasis on direct parental control; instead they promote children's internalization of parental norms, thus reducing the frequency of "acting out" behavior problems by creating stricter internal controls within the children themselves. Two mechanisms appear to be at work. First, these parents appear to be less restrictive towards their children, display greater warmth and involvement, and report reduced use of physical punishments compared to parents in low complexity occupations (Luster, Rhoades, & Haas, 1989). Second, their child-rearing style stresses general principles of behavior that the child can use to guide behavior in specific instances, including during parents' absences. Thus, I argue that the complexity of parental occupation is associated with variation in styles of interaction and norms relevant to children's socialization. This reference to norms helps to link the concepts of social class and social capital.

However, Coleman argues that social capital at home is not related perfectly to parents' socioeconomic status; for example, indicators of socioeconomic standing are related only weakly to direct measures of the quality children's home environments (Bradley & Caldwell, 1984), one form of social capital (Parcel & Menaghan, 1994a; 1994b). Coleman argues that unless parents use their economic resources and human capital as resources in their parental roles, children's socialization may suffer. Parents with less abundant economic and human capital resources still may use them efficiently in the child-rearing process, with attendant positive effects on social behavior. Thus, the relationship between social class and social capital is imperfect.

Formation and Diffusion of Capital at Home

A number of theorists and researchers have been concerned about the implications of capital formation and diffusion for child social adjustment. For example, Coleman (1990) worries that early maternal work will limit the time that mothers can spend networking with neighbors and creating bonds with children, thus weakening the social capital, both at home and in the community, on which children can draw. He also notes that children benefit from capital characterized by "time closure," which he defines as occurring when both parents have enduring attachments to one another. Thus, single parent households have lower levels of social capital with which to facilitate child social adjustment. Of course, maternal work in dual earner households increases the financial capital for the household, thus benefiting child well-being. In addition, in single-earner households, maternal work may be the sole source of financial capital. These facts speak to the importance of recognizing all forms of capital as relevant to child outcomes. In addition, several strands of literature point to the importance of resource diffusion as a negative factor in promoting child well-being. Increased numbers of children in the family will cause all forms of capital—financial, human, and social—to be diffused more finely across children (Coleman, 1990; Downey, 1995). Thus, capital becomes too diluted to be effective for individual children. Such diffusion raises the question of whether there is a critical minimum quantity of capital below which child social adjustment is clearly threatened. Indeed, the literature on poverty and child well-being suggests that while deep poverty is inimical to child development, once the child's basic material needs are met, increases in material well-being may not produce linear improvements in child outcomes (Mayer, 1997). However, Yeung, Linver, and Brooks-Gunn (2002) find that family income is associated with behavior problems scores of 3- to 5-year-old children through pathways including maternal emotional distress and parenting practices. Thus, social capital at home is critical, a topic to which I now turn.

Recent Literature

A number of studies bring evidence to bear on the importance of social capital at home in facilitating the social adjustment of young children. These studies capture aspects of parenting at home, speaking to the types of bonds parents form with children at home, as well as studying the possibly different roles of mothers and fathers in promoting child social adjustment. They derive intellectual inspiration from literatures on parenting styles (for example, see Baumrind, 1966; 2005; Hoffman, 1989; and Hoffman & Kloska, 1995) while focusing more squarely on social capital in the home. In an early analysis of family social capital and children's behavior problems, Parcel and Menaghan (1993) study 524 six- to eight-year-old children in married couple families in 1988 derived from the National Longitudinal Survey of Youth's (NLSY) study of mothers and children. They also study change in behavior problems between 1986 and 1988 for this same group. They find that higher levels of maternal mastery and stronger home environments protect children from behavior problems. Over time, children from homes where fathers had higher levels of occupational complexity in 1986 do better, while those children who experienced the birth of additional siblings or had mothers at very low work hours placed children at risk.

Davies, Harold, Goeke-Morey, and Cummings (2002) also provide support for the notion that weakened family social capital can have deleterious effects on child social adjustment. They investigate the effects of interparental conflict on child emotional security among sixth through eighth graders in a middle and working class suburb of Rochester, NY. When family social capital is strong, interparental conflict has minimal negative effects on child social adjustment. When such capital is weak, conflict has more negative implications. Finally, McLoyd and Smith (2002) studied 1,990 children of the NLSY who were 4- to 5-years-old in 1988, and followed them until they were 10 to 11 in 1994. They find that maternal spanking of young children predicted an increase in behavior problems over time within the context of low maternal emotional support, but not in the context of high emotional support; these findings hold for African American, European American, and Hispanic children. Taken together, these studies suggest that the bonds that parents form at home with their children influence child social adjustment.

Several studies allow us to investigate whether paternal vs. maternal social capital may be operating differently for children. Aldous and Mulligan (2002) study the effects of fathers' child care on children's behavior problems. Using the National Survey of Families and Households, they begin with children younger than five years in 1988 and follow them through 1999. When children were described as difficult to raise, fathers' care made a positive difference in reducing behavior problems when children were older, particularly for sons. Contrary to worries by Coleman that high levels of parental work hours would handicap children, they found that fathers' hours on the job was not significant, nor was parental SES. Maternal care also made a positive difference. Parcel and Menaghan (1994b) find that a combination of maternal and paternal overtime hours, or paternal overtime hours in combination with a new baby in the family, can be detrimental to target children's social adjustment.

A related but distinct topic concerns the effects of family social capital when the child is not part of a two-parent household. King (1994) finds that nonresident father involvement does not generally produce positive effects on child social adjustment, suggesting that once social capital, or time closure, is broken owing to the father's departure, continued paternal involvement is not necessarily helpful to promoting child social adjustment. A review of 64 studies by Amato and Gilbreth (1999) where the offspring vary in age from 0 to 30 years suggests, however, that while frequency of paternal contact was generally not related to child outcomes, feelings of closeness and authoritative parenting were negatively associated with both internalizing and externalizing behavior problems.

Brannigan, Gemmell, Pevalin, and Wade (2002) also study social capital at home. Their sample includes 13,067 children aged 4–11 from households selected on a probability basis as part of the National Longitudinal Survey of Children and Youth undertaken by Statistics Canada in 1986. Looking at both misconduct and aggression as dependent variables, they find that having one as opposed to two parents in the home as well as hostile parenting contribute to poor social adjustment throughout childhood. Their findings point to the importance of several aspects of social capital—norms that guide interaction at home as well as the formation and structure of social capital—that are influential.

We recall Coleman's concerns that maternal labor force participation would disrupt formation of social capital at home with deleterious effects on child well-being. Greenstein's (1993) classic study of maternal employment and child behavior problems highlights a number of issues concerning the formation of social capital at home and its effects on child social adjustment. Studying 1,657 four- and five-year-old children from either the 1986 or 1988 NLSY, he finds no support for the notion that early maternal work has an effect on child behavior problems. Specifically, continuous maternal employment actually reduces behavior problems compared to children of mothers who are not employed. He does find that children from higher income households who received substitute care during infancy have higher levels of behavior problems than comparable children from lower income households, possibly because such care substitution becomes increasingly imperfect as household income rises. Similarly, children with a highly supportive mother benefit more from her continual attention than if his/her mother works. Overall, however, maternal employment is not associated with negative behavioral effects for young children.

In another study of early parental work and child behavior, Parcel and Menaghan (1994a), using a sample of 526 four- to six-year-old children of

NLSY employed mothers, find only weak evidence to suggest that early maternal work handicaps children. Mothers with stronger internal locus of control, Black mothers, and those providing stronger home environments have children with fewer behavior problems. Also, children with married mothers have better social adjustment, while an unstable maternal marital history is detrimental. Low paternal work hours are detrimental. Mothers with both overtime work hours as well as low complexity jobs have children who are especially at risk. Low work hours were more helpful to unmarried than to married mothers. Han, Waldfogel, and Brooks-Gunn (2001) find maternal employment in the child's first year of life has some negative effects on behavior problems as assessed at ages 7 or 8, but only among White children. However, in general, early maternal work did not appear to inhibit child social adjustment.

One additional study highlights the role that family capital plays in promoting child social adjustment. Parcel, Campbell, and Zhong (2005) provide a cross-cultural comparison of family capital effects on behavior problems for children in the United States and Great Britain. Using comparable samples of children from the NLSY in the United States and the National Child Development Study (NCDS) in Great Britain, they investigate the role of parental work, children's home environments, family structure and family human capital on behavior problems among 5- to 13-year-old children in the two societies. The findings suggest that maternal and child human capital matters more in the United States than in Great Britain. For example, children with health limitations are at greater risk for behavior problems in the United States than in Great Britain, while in the United States, having a mother whose family of origin is intact has a protective effect, one that is absent for British children. However, family social capital may matter more in Great Britain than in the United States. While children's home environments are equally protective in both societies, and having a divorced mother is detrimental in both, increased family size is a risk factor for British children but not those in the United States. Similarly, in Britain, having a mother who is single is a risk factor that is absent in the United States. This type of analysis is useful because it helps us to consider how macro level differences across societies may be conditioning how capital operates within families. In this analysis, it does not appear that the more developed welfare state in Great Britain is compensating for capital deficits at home in promoting child social adjustment. Had this been the case, then we would not have seen British children at greater risk for behavior problems in families headed by single mothers or in families with higher numbers of children.

Capital at School

I now turn to the notions of capital and class at school, and in doing so make direct analogies with our arguments regarding capital at home. We can characterize schools as varying in human, financial, and social capital. For example, schools with a higher proportion of teachers who have masters degrees have stronger bases of human capital upon which children can draw. A more substantial literature, however, calls attention to the role of financial capital at school and its role in facilitating child outcomes. Schools with more financial capital may provide more books and higher teacher salaries to promote child social well-being. Finally, social capital associated with schools most directly refers to bonds between parents and schools that can facilitate educational outcomes. Of primary importance are the relationships that parents and children form with schoolteachers. These bonds can also reflect community ties, a concept that also intertwines with the role of school social capital in promoting child well-being. Arguments regarding the superiority of Catholic schools are based on the notion that the community ties associated with a common religion for many attendees and their families promote group norms useful in supporting appropriate social behavior (Coleman, 1988; 1990).

Formation and Diffusion of Capital at School

We can make the same arguments regarding formation and diffusion of capital at school as we did for capital at home. Higher student–teacher ratios speak to diffusion of resources, including teachers' time and attention and teachers' stores of human capital used in the classroom. Such diffusion is often a function of limited school financial capital. In addition, schools in which there is considerable teacher and student turnover can be said to lack time closure that is associated with both teacher and residential stability in other districts, sometimes across generations of students. Following arguments above, attending a Catholic school also may enhance social capital; parents of students may be more likely to have relationships outside of school, in this case through church attendance with parents of other students. Thus, both capital at home and at school can each be conceptualized in terms of formation and diffusion; better formed and less diffused capital, both at home and at school, promotes better child social adjustment.

Recent Literature

The empirical literature regarding school capital effects has two critical features. First, it is overwhelmingly concerned with student achievement and not with student social well-being. Although this is understandable given that the central mission of schools is to promote achievement, it nonetheless represents a significant gap, because schools function as important social environments as well as locations for learning. Second, the origins of this literature are heavily oriented to the question of whether financial status of schools matters in promoting children's achievement. This emphasis on financial capital has only been partially redressed by more recent research. My review reflects both of these features.

Initial studies of school capital focused largely on resource arguments, with key indicators including teacher salaries and student–teacher ratios, the latter referring to resource diffusion (Coleman et al., 1966; Hallinan, 1988). These variables are closely related to financial capital, although studies failed to support the notion that school characteristics themselves are important predictors of educational achievement. They also failed to study student *social* outcomes. Additional work also suggested that lowering the level of conceptualization and measurement even further to the track within a school or to the classroom did show schooling to have effects on educational outcomes even when schools did not (Bidwell & Kasarda, 1980). Recent research debates whether school financial resources promote achievement (Elliott, 1998; Greenwald, Hedges, & Laine, 1996; Hanushek, 1989; 1994). Although there has been less attention devoted to school capital effects on child social adjustment, the findings concerning capital effects on child achievement may suggest possible effects on social behavior as well.

Empirical studies have also focused on the effects of Catholic school attendance on measures of student achievement. These analyses are important because they reason that the common norms, or common social capital, held by teachers, parents, and students, promote child well-being. Some studies of this type show positive effects (Coleman, Hoffer, & Kilgore, 1982; Jensen, 1986), while others show effects are modest in the presence of background controls (Raudenbush & Bryk, 1986; Wilms, 1985). Again, these analyses neglect to study the effects on social adjustment. However, thinking about social capital at home and at school, Buysse (1997) finds that lack of social capital in these contexts places students at high risk for antisocial behavior.

Additional studies that focus on the concept of "mismatch" between students and teachers suggest that reduced social capital as reflected in mismatched norms between White teachers and Black students have implications for child social adjustment. Downey and Pribesh (2004) study classroom behavior in both kindergarten and the eighth grade, and focus both on externalizing behavior problems as well as on approaches to learning. Black children are perceived as behaving more poorly, a function of student–teacher racial mismatching. Those Black students who are evaluated by White teachers earn particularly low evaluations, and this finding occurs at both grade levels, thus bolstering the notion that White teachers' bias is a constant in the child's academic life. Similarly, Alexander, Entwistle, and Thompson (1987) find that Black students are vulnerable to low evaluations of maturity when mismatched to high SES or White teachers. Entwistle and Alexander (1993) also highlight the role of such mismatch in hindering child outcomes in their longitudinal study of Baltimore first graders.

THE RELATIVE IMPORTANCE OF CAPITAL AT HOME AND CAPITAL AT SCHOOL

An important challenge for the study of capital effects on child social adjustment is to understand the relative roles of capital at home and capital at school in predicting such adjustment. Parcel and Dufur (2001) provide evidence on this question in their study of children in the NLSY Child–Mother data set who attended the first through eighth grades in both 1992 and 1994. The findings suggest that although school capital effects are present, family social capital and maternal and child human capital effects are more important in promoting child social adjustment. In particular, when parents know their child's whereabouts and know their child's friends by name, behavior problems are reduced, while they increase as family size increases. Regarding human capital, low birth weight and longer term child health problems promote behavior problems, while teacher skill also reduced behavior problems. At the same time, there are interactive effects between home and school factors that render problematic a strictly competitive test of whether it is capital at home or at school that is more influential. For example, higher levels of maternal mental ability combine with the child attending a private school to boost social adjustment, while higher levels of maternal mental ability and better student–teacher ratios reach a threshold in the positive effects that they contribute to promoting social adjustment. Nonetheless, this study provides some evidence to suggest that capital at home is more important than capital at school in promoting social adjustment of young children.

From work by Lareau (2001) we also catch a glimpse of the relative importance of the school and the home in promoting child well-being. Her work documents what happens when parents and teachers are not "on the same page" regarding expectations for appropriate child behavior. Middle class parents find themselves in tune with the underlying assumptions of teachers for child behavior, while working class parents find themselves at odds with these assumptions. Although the work is couched within the rhetoric of "cultural capital," the clear juxtaposition of working versus middle class norms speaks to our concerns with how social class undergirds parental child rearing practices. From the child's point of view, being in two environments with consonant norms is likely to allow each to reinforce the other in promoting social adjustment, while being in discordant environments is likely to retard it. These findings also speak to the concept of mismatch where there is a discrepancy in norms.

PRACTICAL IMPLICATIONS

It is also important to suggest what practical difference these studies may make for parents, educators, and clinicians as they try to promote strong social adjustment in young children. Several studies highlight the importance of interventions early in childhood, while behavior patterns of both parents and children may be more responsive to corrective action. McLeod and Kaiser's (2004) study noted above suggests that the early elementary years are a critical time for identifying behavior problems and that if so identified, interventions must begin early, given the importance of academic achievement in middle school and high school for facilitating high school graduation. Barlow and Stewart-Brown (2000) highlight the importance of parent education as a vehicle for promoting child social adjustment. In a review of 16 articles looking at the effects of parental education programs on reducing child behavior problems, they conclude that structured parental education programs can improve both parental perceptions of behavior problems as well as reduce objective measures of such problems. These changes are maintained over time. While the programs they reviewed were aimed at treatment of behavior problems, they conclude that parental programs should be aimed at prevention.

Along those lines, Hawkins et al. (2001) focus on an important but relatively neglected aspect of intervention—the importance of school bonding. Bonding was defined as attachment and commitment to school. They investigate the long term effects of school bonding in a study beginning with students in grades 1–4 in eight elementary schools in Seattle. They followed these children until they were 18, and found that changes in school bonding in the adolescent years predicted health and behavior outcomes at age 18, independent of race, poverty, gender, and baseline academic achievement. They conclude that preventive interventions should begin in elementary school. In this study, school bonding was treated more as an individual characteristic rather than a reflection of relationships at school, as we have defined school social capital. However, attachment implies that there are social ties to others in the school setting characterized by temporal continuity, which implies the presence of social capital. Finally, Gottfredson and Gottfredson (2001) study how schools act to prevent behavior problems and promote school security. They document a number of steps that elementary schools can take to promote social adjustment; they also stress the importance of prevention of behavior problems.

LIMITATIONS TO THIS REVIEW

In addition to the restrictions noted at the front of this chapter, I take note of two additional literatures that I was not able to cover. First, space limitations preclude covering studies of community effects on child social adjustment. Researchers have been concerned with the effects of low-income communities on child well-being, and have analyzed the strategies some parents employ in order to compensate for such limitations. These include building strong networks with family and neighbors to increase monitoring of children, and obtaining resources from community sources that help children build human capital useful both in promoting academic achievement as well as social adjustment (Jarrett, 1999). Many of these studies focus on older children and adolescents, probably because the researchers recognize that community influences are likely to be more salient for older as compared with younger children. Still, it is worth noting that in addition to family and school influences, young children's social adjustment may still be influenced by the larger communities in which they live; Kohen, Brooks-Gunn, Leventhal, and Hertzman (2002) and Leventhal and Brooks-Gunn (2000) provide supportive evidence on this point. Second, I have not covered the growing literature on the effects of child care on child social adjustment. This literature is also potentially within the scope of this review because for many young children, child care substitutes for parental care when parents work, and may vary in quality in ways that mirror the quality of parental care, including social capital. Interested readers should consult NICHD Early Child Care Research Network (2003a; 2003b) and associated articles in *Child Development* (2003, Vol. 74, No. 4) for important treatments of how the capital associated with various child care arrangements can influence child social adjustment. I now turn to deficits in the literature that are within the scope of this review.

DIRECTIONS FOR FUTURE RESEARCH

This review has pointed to several deficiencies in relevant literature. Perhaps most glaring is a relative dearth of studies suggesting how social capital at school can promote child social adjustment. Instead, attention has been disproportionately focused on school financial capital, and especially its effects of child achievement. Important though these links are, major longitudinal studies (see especially McLeod & Keiser, 2004 and Entwistle et al., 2005) have clearly documented that social adjustment is an important determinant of achievement, thus highlighting the importance of studying capital effects on social adjustment as well as on academic outcomes. Additional indirect evidence on these points also comes from works on delinquency and related work on social outcomes in young adulthood. For example, McLanahan and Sandefur's (1994) classic work on the effects of single parent households on both academic and social outcomes shows that girls who grow up in a single parent household are more likely to engage in early childbearing. Given what we know about continuity of behavior problems over the life course, these findings imply that as children, these youths may also have had adjustment problems. What roles did their schools play in determining these outcomes? In sum, I recommend that researchers focus more closely on how school social capital, including bonds among young children in school, affects child social well-being.

Compared to these deficits, studies of the effects of family capital on child social adjustment are more abundant and more evenly distributed across the effects of financial, human, and social capital. Parental human capital effects on children, including their social adjustment, are frequently included as controls in a variety of studies; thus, if such effects are not at center stage, neither are they neglected. The literature on child poverty has been both ongoing and voluminous enough for us to know that poverty has deleterious effects on child social well-being, while increments in financial resources after basic material needs are met have nonlinear and decreasingly positive effects on improving child social adjustment. Finally, a growing literature on family social capital is addressing how the formation, diffusion, and nature of family social ties can affect child social well-being.

Two additional gaps in our knowledge are notable. First, we have a relatively poor understanding of the relative importance of capital at home and capital at school in affecting child social adjustment. For young children, it is logical to think that capital at home is more influential, given that schooling has just started and even during the school year, children remain importantly influenced by the capital characteristics of their families. Indeed, Parcel and Dufur (2001) provide supportive evidence on this point, although their statistical modeling does not allow them to definitively conclude that capital at home is more important. The presence of interactive effects does not negate our responsibility to consider which institution may be the most important, even though such findings suggest caution in drawing conclusions. Additional work in progress (Dufur, Parcel, & Troutman, 2005) provides a cleaner test, although that study focuses on achievement. One possibility is for researchers who are interested in capital effects for young children to make an explicit decision to study both their achievement and their social adjustment. Such work would allow us to know more conclusively how capital affects young children.

A second gap is highlighted by the work of Parcel et al. (2005) who study how family capital may operate differently depending on the country in which the family resides. In finding that family social capital may be more consequential for social adjustment in Great Britain than in the United States, while human capital may be more consequential in the United States and Great Britain, the authors provide a glimpse into what type of capital matters where (see also McCulloch, Wiggins, Joshi, & Sachdev, 2000). These findings should be replicated with studies of several types of capital affecting a variety of child outcomes, including social adjustment, across additional societies so that we may more fully understand how the macro-level context may be conditioning the operation of capital within families. While the demands of such studies are considerable given the need for longitudinal data on families and comparable measures of key constructs for both parents and children across cultures, the rewards of such analyses would be considerable in illuminating theory as well as providing important guidance for policymakers as well as families.

CONCLUSIONS

My purpose has been to review the effects of capital at home and at school on the social adjustment of young children. The findings suggest strong continuities in social adjustment across the years of childhood, through adolescence and into young adulthood. In addition, social adjustment affects academic achievement, thus highlighting the importance of social well-being even beyond the realm of social relationships themselves. Social class and social capital are not identical, but rather related concepts. Findings regarding the effects of family financial, human, and social capital are abundant, while comparable findings regarding capital effects at school are more uneven. My central focus has been on the effects of social capital. Higher quality parent–child interaction at home does promote child social adjustment, while resource diffusion across higher numbers of children weakens it. Variations in financial capital are at least partly mediated by social capital, specifically, the bonds between parents and children as well as the norms parents use in constructing interaction with their children at home. There is only scattered evidence that early maternal labor force participation harms child social adjustment.

Turning to school capital effects, a disproportionate focus on the effects of financial capital at school on child achievement leaves relatively neglected the study of how social ties at school may be influential for children, particularly in affecting child social adjustment. I have recommended that new studies redress this imbalance so that we can more fully understand how schools' social environments affect child well-being. I look forward to these studies as a vehicle both for furthering social theory as well as for illuminating more specifically the role that families and schools play in promoting child social well-being.

NOTES

1.   Helpful comments were provided by Elizabeth G. Menaghan and Mikaela Dufur; Deborah Coe provided research assistance. The remaining errors are my own. Support for this review was provided by the Provost's Office at Purdue University.

2.   Social capital is a very broad concept that has been invoked across a variety of disciplines besides sociology, including economics and political science. For example, Fukuyama (1996) argues that differentials in trust across societies as evidenced by the types and strengths of network associations are associated with differentials in economic development, such that those nations with stronger bonds of trust have an easier time promoting economic development. He also has a useful critique of social capital (Fukuyama, 2001). However, trust is not an aspect of social capital that I am able to treat in this review. In addition, Fukuyama's work speaks more to macrolevel issues such as economic development, and has nothing to say about child social adjustment, while Coleman's work speaks directly to child socialization. For these reasons as well as those of parsimony, I cannot broaden the review of social capital theorists beyond Coleman.

REFERENCES

Aldous, J., & Mulligan, G. M. (2002). Fathers' child care and children's behavior problems: A longitudinal study. *Journal of Family Issues, 23*, 624–647.

Alexander, K. L., Entwisle, D. R., & Thompson, M. S. (1987). School performance, status relationships and the structure of sentiment: Bringing the teacher back in. *American Sociological Review, 52*, 665–682.

Amato, P. R., & Gilbreth, J.G. (1999). Nonresident fathers and children's well-being: A meta-analysis. *Journal of Marriage and the Family, 61*(3), 557–573.

Asher, S. R., & Coie, J. D. (1990). *Peer rejection in childhood.* New York: Cambridge University Press.

Barlow, J., & Stewart-Brown, S. (2000). Behavior problems and group-based parent education programs. *Developmental and Behavioral Pediatrics, 21*, 356–370.

Baumrind, D. (1966). Effects of authoritative parental control on child behavior. *Child Development, 37*(4), 887–907.

Baumrind, D. (2005). Patterns of parental authority and adolescent autonomy. *New Directions for Child and Adolescent Development, 108*, (Summer), 61–69.

Bidwell, C. E., & Kasarda, J. D. (1980). Conceptualizing and measuring the effects of school and schooling. *American Journal of Education, 88*, 401–450.

Bradley, R. H., & Caldwell, B. M. (1984). The HOME inventory and family demographics. *Developmental Psychology, 20*, 315–320.

Brannigan, A., Gemmell, W., Pevalin, D. J., & Wade, T. J. (2002). Self-control and social control in childhood misconduct and aggression: The role of family structure, hyperactivity, and hostile parenting. *Canadian Journal of Criminology,* (April), 119–142.

Bronfenbrenner, U., & Morris, P. A. (1998). The ecology of developmental process. In R. M. Lerner (Ed.), *Handbook of child psychology* (5 ed., Vol. 1, pp. 993–1028). New York: Wiley.

Buysse, W. H. (1997). Behavior problems and relationships with family and peers during adolescence. *Journal of Adolescence, 20*, 645–659.

Caspi, A., Elder, G. H., Jr., & Bem, D. J. (1987). Moving against the world: Life-course patterns of explosive children. *Developmental Psychology, 23*, 308–313.

Caspi, A., Elder, G. H., Jr., & Bem, D. J. (1988). Moving away from the world: Life-course patterns of shy children. *Developmental Psychology, 24*, 824–831.

Chess, S., & Thomas, A. (1959). Characteristics of the individual child's behavioral responses to the environment. *American Journal of Orthopsychiatry, 29*, 791–802.

Coleman, J. (1988). Social capital in the creation of human capital. *American Journal of Sociology, 94*, S95-S120.

Coleman, J. (1990). *Foundations of social theory.* Cambridge, MA: Belknap Press.

Coleman, J. S., Campbell, E. Q., Hobson, C. J., McPartland, J., Mood, A. M., Weinfeld, F. D., & York, R. L. (1966). *Equality of educational opportunity.* Washington, DC: US Congressional Printing Office.

Coleman, J. S., Hoffer, T. S., & Kilgore, S. (1982). *High school achievement: Public, Catholic, and private schools compared.* New York: Basic Books.

Corwyn, R. F., & Bradley, R. H. (2005). Socioeconomic status and childhood externalizing behaviors: A structural equation framework. In V. L. Bengtson, A. C. Acock, K. R. Allen, P. Dilworth-Anderson, & D. M. Klein (Eds.), *Sourcebook of family theory and research* (pp. 469–483). Thousand Oaks, CA: Sage.

Davies, P. T., Harold, G. T., Goeke-Morey, M. C., & Cummings, E. M. (2002). Child emotional security and interparental conflict. *Monographs of the Society for Research in Child Development, 67*(3, Serial No. 270).

Downey, D. B. (1995). When bigger is not better: Family size, parental resources and children's educational performance. *American Sociological Review, 60*, 746–761.

Downey, D. B., & Pribesh, S. (2004). When race matters: Teachers' evaluations of students' classroom behavior. *Sociology of Education, 77*(4), 267–282.

Dufur, M. J., Parcel, T. L. & Troutman, K. P. (2005). Using social capital at home and at school to predict child academic achievement. Unpublished.

Duncan, G. J., & Brooks-Gunn, J. (Eds.). (1997). *Consequences of growing up poor.* New York: Russell Sage Foundation.

Elder, G. H., Jr., Van Nguyen, T., & Caspi, A. (1985). Linking family hardship to children's lives. *Child Development, 56*, 361–375.

Elliott, M. (1998). School finances and opportunities to learn: Does money well spent enhance student achievement? *Sociology of Education, 71*, 223–245.

Entwistle, D. R., & Alexander, K. L. (1993). Entry into school: The beginning school transition and educational stratification in the United States. *Annual Review of Sociology, 19*, 401–423.

Entwistle, D. R., Alexander, K. L., & Steffel Olson, L. (2005). First grade and educational attainment by age 22: A new story. *American Journal of Sociology, 110*, 1458–1502.

Fischer, M., Rolf, J. E., Hasazi, J. E., & Cummings, L. (1984). Follow-up of a preschool epidemiological sample: Cross-age continuities and predictions of later adjustment with internalizing and externalizing dimensions of behavior. *Child Development, 55*, 137–150.

Fukuyama, F. (1996). *Trust: The social virtues and the creation of prosperity.* New York: Free Press.

Fukuyama, F. (2001). Social capital, civil society, and development. *Third World Quarterly, 22*(1), 7–20.

Gecas, V. (1989). The social psychology of self-efficacy. *Annual Review of Sociology, 15*, 291–316.

Gottfredson, G. D., & Gottfredson, D. C. (2001). What schools do to prevent problem behavior and promote safe environments. *Journal of Educational and Psychological Consultation, 12*, 313–344.

Greenstein, T. N. (1993). Maternal employment and child behavioral outcomes: A household economics analysis. *Journal of Family Issues, 14*, 323–354.

Greenwald, R. L., Hedges, V., & Laine, R. D. (1996). The effect of school resources on student achievement. *Review of Educational Research, 66*, 361–396.

Guerra, V. S., Asher, S. R., & DeRosier, M. E. (2004). Effect of children's perceived rejection on physical aggression. *Journal of Abnormal Child Psychology, 32*(5), 551–563.

Hallinan, M. T. (1988). Equality of educational opportunity. In W. R. Scott & J. Blake (Eds.), *Annual Review of Sociology* (Vol. 14, pp. 249–268). Palo Alto, CA: Annual Reviews.

Han, W.-J., Waldfogel, J., & Brooks-Gunn, J. (2001). The effects of early maternal employment on later cognitive and behavioral outcomes. *Journal of Marriage and Family, 63*, 336–354.

Hanushek, E. A. (1989). The impact of differential expenditures on school performance. *Educational Researcher, 18*, 45–51.

Hanushek, E. A. (1994). Money might matter somewhere: A response to Hedges, Lane, and Greenwald. *Educational Researcher, 23*, 5–8.

Hartup, W. W. (2005). Peer interaction: What causes what? *Journal of Abnormal Child Psychology, 33*(3), 387–394.

Hastings, P. D., Zahn-Waxler, C., Robinson, J., Usher, B., & Bridges, D. (2000). The development of concern for others in children with behavior problems. *Developmental Psychology, 36*(5), 531–546.

Hawkins, J. D., Guo, J., Hill, K. G., Battin-Pearson, S., & Abbott, R. D. (2001). Long-term effects of the Seattle social development intervention on school bonding trajectories. *Applied Developmental Science, 5*, 225–236.

Hoffman, L. W. (1989). Effects of maternal employment in the two-parent family. *American Psychologist, 44*(2), 283–292.

Hoffman, L. W., & Kloska, D. D. (1995). Parents' gender-based attitudes toward marital roles and child rearing: Development and validation of new measures. *Sex Roles, 32*(5/6), 273–295.

Jarrett, R. L. (1999). Successful parenting in high-risk neighborhoods. *The Future of Children, 9*, 45–50.

Jensen, G. F. (1986). Explaining differences in academic behavior between public-school and Catholic-school students: A quantitative case study. *Sociology of Education, 59*, 32–41.

Kessler, R., Turner, J. B., & House, J. S. (1988). Effects of unemployment on health in a community survey: Main, modifying, and mediating effects. *Journal of Social Issues, 44*, 69–85.

King, V. (1994). Variation in the consequences of nonresident father involvement for children's well-being. *Journal of Marriage and the Family, 56*, 963–972.

Kohen, D. E., Brooks-Gunn, J., Leventhal, T., & Hertzman, C. (2002). Neighborhood income and physical and social disorder in Canada: Associations with young children's competencies. *Child Development, 73*, 1844–1860.

Kohlberg, L., LaCrosse, J., & Ricks, D. (1972). The predictability of adult mental health from childhood behavior. In B. B. Wolman (Ed.), *Manual of child psychopathology* (pp. 1217–1284). New York: McGraw-Hill.

Kohn, M. L. (1977). *Class and conformity: A study in values* (2nd Ed.). Chicago: University of Chicago Press.

Kohn, M. L., & Schooler, C. (1982). Job conditions and personality: A longitudinal assessment of their reciprocal effects. *American Journal of Sociology, 87*, 1257–1286.

Kohn, M. L., & Schooler, C. (1983). *Work and personality: An inquiry into the impact of social stratification.* Norwood, NJ: Ablex.

Kohn, M. L., Slomczynski, K. M., & Schoenback, C. (1986). Social stratification and the transmission of values in the family: A cross-national assessment. *Sociological Forum, 1*, 73–102.

Lareau, A. (2001). Linking Bourdieu's concept of capital to the broader field: The case of family–school relationships. In B. J. Biddle (Ed.), *Social class, poverty, and education: Policy and practice* (pp. 77–100). New York: Routlege-Falmer.

Leventhal, T., & Brooks-Gunn, J. (2000). The neighborhoods they live in: The effects of neighborhood residence on child and adolescent outcomes. *Psychological Bulletin, 126*, 309–337.

Luster, T., Rhoades, K., & Haas, B. (1989). The relation between parental values and parenting behavior: A test of the Kohn hypothesis. *Journal of Marriage and the Family, 51*, 139–147.

Mayer, S. E. (1997). *What money can't buy.* Cambridge, MA: Harvard University Press.

McCulloch, A., Wiggins, R. D., Joshi, H. E., & Sachdev, D. (2000). Internalising and externalising children's behavior problems in Britain and the U.S.: Relationships to family resources. *Children and Society, 14*, 368–383.

McLanahan, S., & Sandefur, G. D. (1994). *Growing up with a single parent: What hurts, what helps.* Cambridge, MA: Harvard University Press.

McLeod, J. D., & Kaiser, K. (2004). Childhood emotional and behavioral problems and educational attainment. *American Sociological Review, 69*, 636–658.

McLoyd, V. C. (1989). Socialization and development in a changing economy. *American Psychologist, 44*, 293–302.

McLoyd, V. C. (1990). The impact of economic hardship on Black families and children: Psychological distress, parenting, and socioemotional development. *Child Development, 61*, 311–346.

McLoyd, V. C., & Smith, J. (2002). Physical discipline and behavior problems in African American, European American, and Hispanic children: Emotional support as a moderator. *Journal of Marriage and Family, 64*, 40–53.

Miller, J., Schooler, C., Kohn, M. L., & Miller, K. A. (1979). Women and work: The psychological effects of occupational conditions. *American Journal of Sociology, 85*, 66–94.

Mirowsky, J., & Ross, C. E. (1986). Social patterns of distress. *Annual Review of Sociology, 12*, 23–45.

NICHD Early Child Care Research Network. (2003a). Does amount of time spent in child care predict socioemotional adjustment during the transition to kindergarten? *Child Development, 74*, 976–1005.

NICHD Early Child Care Research Network. (2003b). Social functioning in first grade: Associations with earlier home and child care predictors with current classroom experiences. *Child Development, 74*, 1639–1662.

Parcel, T. L., Campbell, L. A., & Zhong, W. (2005). The effects of capital at home on children's behavior problems in the United States and Great Britain. Manuscript submitted for publication.

Parcel, T. L., & Dufur, M. J. (2001). Capital at home and at school: Effects on child social adjustment. *Journal of Marriage and Family, 63*, 32–47.

Parcel, T. L., & Menaghan, E. G. (1993). Family social capital and children's behavior problems. *Social Psychology Quarterly, 56*, 120–135.

Parcel, T. L., & Menaghan, E. G. (1994a). Early parental work, family social capital, and early childhood outcomes. *American Journal of Sociology, 99*, 972–1009.

Parcel, T. L., & Menaghan, E. G. (1994b). *Parents' jobs and children's lives.* New York: Aldine.

Patterson, G. R., & Bank, L. (1989). Some amplifying mechanisms for pathological processes in families. In M. R. Gunnar & E. Thelen (Eds.), *Systems and development* (pp. 167–209). Hillsdale, NJ: Erlbaum.

Patterson, G. R., DeBaryshe, B. D., & Ramsey, E. (1989). A developmental perspective on antisocial behavior. *American Psychologist, 44*, 329–335.

Raudenbush, S. W., & Bryk, A. S. (1986). A hierarchical model for studying school effects. *Sociology of Education, 59*, 1–17.

Schooler, C. (1987). Psychological effects of complex environments during the life span: A review and theory. In C. Schooler & K. W. Schaie (Eds.), *Cognitive functioning and social structure over the life course* (pp. 24–49). Norwood, NJ: Ablex.

Siegal, M. (1984). Economic deprivation and the quality of parent–child relations: A trickle-down framework. *Journal of Applied Developmental Psychology, 5*, 127–144.

Spencer, N., & Coe, C. (2003). Social patterning and prediction of parent-reported behavior problems at 3 years in a cohort study. *Child: Care, Health, and Development, 29*, 329–336.

Thomas, A., & Chess, S. (1977). *Temperament and development.* New York: Brunner/ Mazel.

Thomas, A., Chess, S., & Birch, H. G. (1968). *Temperament and behavior disorders in children.* New York: New York University Press.

Werner, E. E., & Smith, R. S. (1982). *Vulnerable, but invincible: A longitudinal study of resilient children and youth.* New York: McGraw-Hill.

Whitbeck, L. B., Simons, R. L., Conger, R. D., Lorenz, F. O., Huck, S., & Elder, G. H., Jr. (1991). Family economic hardship, parental support, and adolescent self-esteem. *Social Psychology Quarterly, 54,* 353–363.

Wilms, J. D. (1985). Catholic-school effects on academic achievement: New evidence from the High School and Beyond follow-up study. *Sociology of Education, 58,* 98–114.

Yeung, W. J., Linver, M. R., & Brooks-Gunn, J. (2002). How money matters for young children's development: Parental investment and family processes. *Child Development, 73,* 1861–1879.

CHAPTER 6

PARENTING AND SCHOOLING INFLUENCES ON EARLY SELF-REGULATION DEVELOPMENT

Abigail M. Jewkes and Frederick J. Morrison

"Critics Attack Suspension of Thirty-three Philadelphia Kindergartners" (Rimer, *The New York Times*, 2002)

"Study Charges NJ Preschools Kicking Kids Out" (Brody, *The Record*, 2005)

"With Mayhem at Home, They Call a Parent Coach" (Belluck, *The New York Times*, 2005)

"Expulsion Rate Highest for Preschoolers, Study Shows" (Garza, *Fort Worth Star-Telegram*, 2005)

These select headlines highlight how issues related to self-regulation have become a media and public interest issue. The last headline references a study report released in May 2005 that received tremendous media attention due to its alarming finding that school expulsion rates were highest in the prekindergarten year (Gilliam, 2005; Gilliam & Shahar, 2006). According to a national survey of kindergarten teachers, more than half of their students enter school without the necessary social skills (Rimm-Kaufman & Pianta, 2000), and social immaturity is a frequent reason for parents delay-

Contemporary Perspectives on Social Learning in Early Childhood Education, pages 133–148
Copyright © 2007 by Information Age Publishing
All rights of reproduction in any form reserved.

ing their children's (primarily boys) kindergarten entry (Stipek, 2002). Statistics like this beg for an answer to the question of what is causing children to be kicked out of classrooms prior to actually beginning school (if it is indeed the case that this problem has escalated in the last five years). Are children less self-regulated today than twenty years ago? Do parents and/or early childhood educators lack the knowledge and skill to address self-regulatory issues? While answering these questions is beyond the scope of this chapter (see Morrison, Bachman, & Connor, 2005 for a discussion), they point to the need for an examination of the environmental influences on children's self-regulation development. Since the majority of children spend their time prior to kindergarten in a combination of parental and early childhood programs[1], we find it necessary to explore these specific aspects of children's environments in order to better understand the influences of parenting and early schooling on self-regulation development. We review the extant literature in these two domains across the early childhood period (birth to age 8), including findings from large nationally-representative research studies and recent research conducted as part of our longitudinal study of young children's literacy development, and conclude with intriguing cross-cultural research that may help illuminate our understandings of early self-regulation development.

ENVIRONMENTAL SOURCES OF SELF-REGULATION

As with other aspects of early development, self-regulation is influenced by a combination of biological and environmental sources (Bronson, 2000). Thus, two especially relevant contexts during early childhood are the home and school (preschool and elementary) settings. While there are multiple perspectives regarding what constitutes self-regulation, we view self-regulation as a complex construct within the larger domain of social/emotional development. In general terms, self-regulation is the control of one's emotions and behaviors, and difficulties in learning to do so can result in behavior problems (emotion regulation, self-control). More specifically, during the early childhood period, self-regulation can be understood as the controlling, directing, and planning of behavior and emotions, which together are an essential aspect of early childhood development, especially in relation to school preparation (Shonkoff & Phillips, 2000). For example, it is important that children control their behavior (not hit a classmate) and follow teacher instructions (stop playing with the blocks when it is time to clean up) in the classroom in order to be a successful learner. With an increasing emphasis on the teaching of academic skills at younger ages, most notably in preschool, as one way to better prepare children for success upon school entry, self-regulation skills are all the more important in the years prior to formal schooling (Bowman, Donovan, & Burns, 2001). In fact, variability in self-regulation exists as early as age three (McClelland & Morrison, 2003). Given the lack of consensus in defining the components of self-regulation, valid and reliable measures of these skills are limited, especially in early childhood (see Cameron et al., 2005b for a discussion). Thus, previous research has primarily utilized broader measures of social-emotional skills, as we discuss in our reviews below.

PARENTING

As the primary caregivers of children prior to school entry, parents can potentially influence, both directly and indirectly, children's self-regulation development. In attempting to understand if these relationships exist and if so, explicating these pathways, it is important to conceptualize parenting as a multifaceted, rather than a global, construct that has domain-specific impacts. Additionally, the definition of terms informs methodological approaches, and ultimately the relationships with our outcome of interest. Thus, the goals of our review of the parenting literature were twofold. First, we were interested in empirical research that examined how specific dimensions of parenting influence children's self-regulation development. And secondly, we focused on studies that employ a range of parenting measures.

Specificity of Parenting

Darling and Steinberg (1993) identified three aspects of parenting—goals/beliefs, practices, and style—as relevant to child outcomes. Building on this framework, numerous studies have examined particular aspects of parenting and their relationships with self-regulation. Morrison and Cooney (2002) developed a parenting questionnaire that included 50 closed questions describing parenting beliefs and practices on a scale from 1 (not at all like me) to 5 (very much like me). Factor analysis resulted in four distinct aspects of parenting: strength of beliefs, control, warmth/responsivity, and quality of family learning environment. Of these, strength of parental beliefs directly influenced children's social skills. Parental warmth/responsivity and the quality of the family learning environment had indirect influences via kindergarten academic skills.

Recent work in our laboratory reinforces the importance of specific aspects of parenting. The same parenting questionnaire used by Morrison and Cooney (2002) was given to a sample of approximately 300 ethnically diverse parents (African American, Asian American, Arab/Middle Eastern, and Hispanic/Latino) in our longitudinal study of children's literacy development (mean age = 4.4 years). Exploratory factor analysis provided strong support for three independent dimensions of parenting: (a) parental warmth and responsiveness, (b) parental control/discipline, and (c) the quality of the home learning environment. Together, these factors explained 30% of the variance in parent responses and are reflective of parenting beliefs and practices prior to and after kindergarten entry.

Eisenberg and colleagues' (2003) longitudinal study of children's self-regulatory behavior from age 4.5 to 8 pinpoints another important aspect of parenting—emotional expressivity. The study ($N = 208$) employed direct-observation and parent- and teacher-reported data and found that maternal expressivity (positive and negative) influenced children's self-regulation, which in turn, influenced externalizing behavior problems and social competence.

While outside the early childhood period, Grolnick and Ryan's (1989) study of parenting style and self-regulation in grades 3 to 6 lends further support to the specificity of parenting influences. Maternal ($N = 64$) and paternal ($N = 50$) interviews were coded for three parenting dimensions—autonomy support, involvement, and structure—and parental autonomy support positively predicted child-reported self-regulation.

In a nationally representative study of over 1,000 children, there was a unique contribution of parenting to self-regulation at age 54 months, as measured by the Social Skills Questionnaire of the Social Skills Rating System (SSRS; Gresham & Elliott, 1990). The parenting context was a combination of two measures collected at 6, 15, 24, 36, and 54 months of age: the HOME (Caldwell & Bradley, 1984) and coded videotaped mother–child interactions resulting in a maternal sensitivity composite. It is noteworthy that the parenting context was directly and significantly related to social skills, but the child care context had no such relationship (NICHD ECCRN, 2004a).

Follow-up analyses also using the NICHD Study of Early Child Care and Youth Development ($N = 648$) included paternal and maternal data—parent–child interactions and parental beliefs (as measured by the Parental Modernity Scale of Child Rearing and Educational Beliefs; Shaefer & Edgerton, 1985)—and assessment of children's social skills with the Child Behavior Checklist (Achenbach, 1991) and SSRS, both completed by children's teachers in kindergarten, first, and second grade. Results of hierarchical linear models indicated that fathers' interactions with their children, both prior to kindergarten entry and in first and second grade, predicted teachers' ratings of children's behavior problems and social skills (NICHD ECCRN, 2004b). Not surprisingly, the interaction styles of fathers and mothers were related to parenting beliefs, although for fathers they were not predictive of child social outcomes. These findings underscore the important and unique role of fathers, a generally understudied figure in parenting research, in children's early self-regulation development, and lend support to others' call for additional research differentiating between maternal and paternal influences (Grolnick & Farkas, 2002).

Parent responsivity in the infant, toddler, and preschool years and its relationship to social development at age four for preterm and full-term children was examined by Landry, Smith, Swank, Assel, & Vellet (2001). Consistency in maternal responsiveness across the first years of life was important for children's social development (specifically responsiveness to their mothers during home observations), especially preterm children. Furthermore, full-term children with mothers who were initially high in responsiveness but switched to low responsiveness by ages three and four had a decrease in their social development. These findings highlight the need for consistency in a specific aspect of parenting early in life, which may indicate a necessity throughout the early childhood years in order to promote social skills development, including self-regulation.

Methodological Approaches

In their review chapter, Grolnick and Farkas (2002) identify difficulties in studying parenting and self-regulation, including analytic techniques that capture the complex bidirectional relationships between parents and children. A recent investigation of longitudinal parenting and social skills among low-income African American families ($N = 278$) evaluated the use of multiple methodologies to study parenting (Zaslow et al., 2006). Maternal reports, the HOME-SF, and direct observations were collected during preschool and followed up with maternal, teacher, and self-reports of children's social skills five years later. While all three measures of parenting predicted children's social skills (although not across all informants), direct observation was the strongest and most consistent predictor. In addition to demonstrating the impact of parenting on children's social skills across the early childhood years, this study provides important information for future studies of parenting.

While the majority of studies have examined self-regulation under the broader social-emotional skills construct, a few investigations have focused on self-regulation in early childhood. Dennis (2006) studied 113 three- and four-year-olds and their mothers in order to understand the relationships among child reactivity and control (viewed as aspects of temperament), parenting, and emotional self-regulation. These constructs were measured via parent report with the Child Behavior Questionnaire (Rothbart, Ahadi, & Hershey, 1994) and SSRS, coded mother–child interactions, and two challenging tasks designed to elicit child persistence and frustration. Results presented a dynamic relationship between parent and child behavior that was context-specific and predictive of children's self-regulation.

A recent study utilized direct observation in the home and school settings to connect parenting behaviors and self-regulation in kindergarten (Neitzel & Stright, 2003). Mothers' scaffolding during four problem-solving tasks with their children was coded for metacognitive content and manner of instruction (cognitive support), emotional support, and transfer of responsibility, while children's classroom behaviors were coded for metacognitive talk, task persistence, behavior self-control, monitoring progress, and seeking assistance. Maternal cognitive support predicted children's cognitive strategies in school (metacognitive talk, monitoring, and seeking assistance), and maternal emotional support and transfer of responsibility were important for children's behavior control. Slightly different patterns of translation were found in a study with third-graders (Stright, Neitzel, Sears, & Hoke-Sinex, 2001). While parental manner of instruction, but not metacognitive content of instructions, predicted children's attention to instructions and seeking assistance, parental metacognitive content predicted children's monitoring and metacognitive talk in school. Together, these studies specify how parental support in a specific learning context can translate to academic self-regulation skills and how these processes change over the early elementary grades. Furthermore, these findings may be used to inform parenting programs aimed at improving children's self-regulation.

In summary, these studies indicate that certain aspects of parenting indeed contribute to children's early self-regulation directly and indirectly. The findings underscore the domain specificity of parenting across the early childhood period, the need to further examine paternal influences, and the importance of definitions and measurement of parenting and self-regulation.

SCHOOLING

With the creation of universal state-funded pre-kindergarten (pre-K) programs and the increasing numbers of children attending preschool (54% of three- to five-year olds in 2003; Child Trends Databank, 2006), we found it necessary to examine this specific aspect of children's early environments in order to better understand the influences of early schooling on self-regulation development. While self-regulation is understood as part of larger social and biological developmental processes, and there is abundant evidence of the importance of self-regulation skills for academic success (see McClelland et al. [in press] in this volume for a discussion), less is known about the influence of schooling on these skills. A recent report on the first year of the Head Start Impact Study found positive effects on three-year-old (but not four-year-old) Head Start participants' social-emotional outcomes

(Administration for Children & Families, 2005). While the report does not address explanations for this finding, it may be due to a combination of children's entering skills and previous experiences (participation in Early Head Start, for example), the specific kinds of activities children engaged in, something unique about children enrolled in Head Start at age three, or even methodological flaws. Similarly, the evaluation of Early Head Start found positive effects on participating children's social-emotion skills in comparison to control children (Love et al., 2005). We remain hopeful that future analyses of these study data will further illuminate the reasons.

Preschool and kindergarten teachers may focus on skills such as following directions and classroom routines, paying attention, standing in line, and sitting properly (whether on the floor on in a chair) that promote self-regulation, yet it is not clear how these kinds of organizing structures may or may not be effective strategies for individual children. A recent study of first-grade classroom practices offers a way to examine this question (Cameron, Connor, and Morrison, 2005). The more time teachers spent in orient–organize activities (such as explaining the daily classroom schedule or providing instructions about how to complete an activity), the less time children spent transitioning between activities. Similarly, the more time teachers spent orienting and organizing children at the beginning of the school year, and modifying this instructional time over the course of the year, the greater the amount of time children were able to spend in child-managed (independent) activities by the spring. An equally important finding in this study was the variability of teachers in one grade in one school district, which suggests that practices related to self-regulation development are far from uniform.

In the next section of this chapter we describe an alternative methodological approach to disentangle the influences of schooling from those of general development and review studies that have utilized this technique to examine self-regulation.

The School Cutoff Technique

One analytic approach that has been used primarily to examine children's cognitive and academic skills may be informative for investigations of self-regulation. This technique, referred to as the school cutoff, takes advantage of the arbitrary school cutoff dates for kindergarten entry (Morrison, Griffith, & Frazier, 1996). For any group of children of the same chronological age, some will "make" the cutoff while others will "miss" it, resulting in children who have differential amounts of schooling. By selecting a sample of children with birth dates immediately before and after the cutoff date and controlling for any differences in background characteristics between the two groups of children, it is possible to separate age-related from schooling-related influences.

In our review of the literature we found only one published study that utilized the school cutoff technique to examine self-regulation. This study found schooling effects in second and third grade for executive functions (McCrea, Mueller, & Parrila, 1999). Our recent analyses also employed the school cutoff methodology to examine schooling effects on preschoolers' behavioral self-regulation skills. This analytic technique, while used with school-age children (Alexander & Martin, 2004; Crone & Whitehurst, 1999; Morrison, Griffith, & Alberts, 1997; Morrison, Smith, & Dow-Ehrenberger, 1995), has yet to be utilized with children prior to kindergarten. Furthermore, previous investigations of preschool self-regulation have relied on teacher or parent reports. Thus, our two research questions were: (a) How do children's self-regulation skills change from the fall to the spring of the prekindergarten year? and (b) To what extent is self-regulation learning influenced by general developmental processes versus specific preschool or prekindergarten experiences?

Children were part of a longitudinal study of development in multiple contexts from preschool through the early elementary grades in a diverse suburban school district in a midwest state and included 82 four-year-olds ($M = 3.86$ and 4.43 years in the fall and spring, respectively) with birth dates two months before or after the state kindergarten entry date of December 1st. The sample was divided into two subgroups based on children's birthdays resulting in 49 young prekindergartners (birthdays before or on December 1) and 33 old preschoolers (birthdays after December 1). Thus, the children were almost identical in age, but had different educational experiences allowing us to examine developmental and schooling influences separately. Children were predominately Caucasian (83%), female (56%), native English speakers (89%), from middle-to-upper SES backgrounds, and attended part-day prekindergarten (65%). Propensity score matching (Rosenbaum & Rubin, 1983) was used to equate children in the old preschool and young prekindergarten groups on key background characteristics.

Children's self-regulation was assessed with the Head-to-Toes Task, a direct observational measure for use with preschool children (Cameron, Connor, et al., 2005). Scores on this task reflect the total number of correct responses out of ten items, with a maximum score of 10. Mean comparisons of children's scores from the fall to spring revealed significant differences ($p < .001$). Subgroup analyses of young prekindergartners and old preschoolers consistently favored the young prekindergartners in the fall and spring. We used Hierarchical Linear Modeling (HLM version 6.01; Raudenbush, Bryk, & Congdon, 2005) to create a two-level model with children nested in classrooms. The mean Head-to-Toes scores were 3.50 ($SD = 3.94$) and 5.88 ($SD = 4.06$) in the fall and spring. Children's classification as old preschoolers or young prekindergartners did not significantly predict their spring self-regulation scores; however, children's fall scores significantly predicted their spring scores (see Table 7.1).

Table 6.1.   HLM Results for Pre-kindergarten Spring Behavioral Self-Regulation Scores

Fixed effects	Coefficient	Standard error	t-ratio (df)	p value
Head-to-Toes				
Intercept	4.53	1.44	3.14 (40)	.004
Old preschooler	.935	.951	.984 (40)	.332
Propensity score	1.43	2.16	.660 (66)	.511
Random effects	Variance	df	χ^2	
Head-to-Toes				
Intercept	.045	38	41.56	.318
Level-1, R	14.75			

This study demonstrated variability in four-year-olds' self-regulation skills, with most children unable to complete the task in the fall, but successful in the spring. While children's scores increased from fall to spring, indicating growth in behavioral self-regulation skills, this growth is attributable to general developmental rather than specific schooling effects. This finding is consistent with the NICHD ECCRN (2004a) study where the child care context did not influence early social skills, but parenting did. Thus, in the absence of preschool schooling effects, parenting is the primary environmental influence on early self-regulation development. It is important to note the sample this study included children from middle- to upper-SES families and the overall above-average performance of children as a whole across a variety of academic and social skills. It is possible that a different pattern of results may emerge with a more variable sample of young children. Together, these results have direct implications for preschool and prekindergarten curricula, including the increasing emphasis on literacy learning prior to kindergarten entry and the need to address social/emotional development along with academic learning. We are currently investigating the specific instructional practices used by the teachers in these preschool classrooms (via coding of videotaped classroom observations) to better understand the present findings and how they ultimately may enhance children's educational experiences prior to kindergarten.

In a another study using the cutoff design, Burrage, Cameron, Sims, Shah, and Morrison (2006) examined kindergarten and first-grade schooling effects on two different measures of self-regulation that are important for school-based performance (Shallice, Marzocchi, Del Salvo, Meuter, &

Rumiati, 2002): (a) working memory (from the Auditory Working Memory subtest of the Woodcock-Johnson Tests of Achievement; Woodcock & Mather, 2000) and (b) response inhibition (the Complicated Head-to-Toes task). Participants were 45 children (18 "old" prekindergartners, 27 "young" kindergartners) whose dates of birth fell either just before or after the arbitrary cutoff date of December 1st for kindergarten entry in their school district in the Midwest. Researchers assessed children individually on a battery of tasks in a 30-minute session, once in the fall and once in the spring. In addition to the working memory and response inhibition measures, the Letter-Word Identification subtest of the Woodcock-Johnson was also included as a control task because researchers have consistently shown the skill is affected by schooling (Christian, Bachman, & Morrison, 2001). We conducted a 2 (Group) × 2 (Testphase) ANOVA on the three tasks. There was a main effect of Testphase for all tasks (Complicated Head-to-Toes $F = 10.49$, $p < .01$; Auditory Working Memory $F = 19.65$, $p < .001$; Letter–Word $F = 76.59$, $p < .001$). Performance on the tasks improved from fall to spring for both groups. There was a main effect of Group for the Letter–Word ID task, $F = 11.83$, $p = .001$, and the Auditory Working Memory task, $F = 4.16$, $p = .05$, with kindergartners performing better in fall and spring. There was a significant interaction effect for the Complicated Head-to-Toes task, $F = 4.54$, $p = .04$, with kindergartners performing better in the fall, but prekindergartners performing as well as the kindergartners by the spring.

These results demonstrate significant schooling (i.e., Group) effects on specific aspects of self-regulation, as well as word decoding. Kindergartners outperformed prekindergartners of the same age on both the Auditory Working Memory and Letter–Word ID tasks in both the fall and spring. In the fall, kindergartners outperformed prekindergartners on the Complicated Head-to-Toes task, but, by the spring, this was not the case, suggesting that prekindergartners were able to "catch up" with kindergartners during their prekindergarten year. Our findings suggest that word decoding skills and auditory working memory improve as a result of both prekindergarten and kindergarten-related experience. Response inhibition, however, appears to change as a result of prekindergarten experience, but not kindergarten experience. Furthermore, the different patterns of schooling effects for the two self-regulation tasks support the idea that they are distinct and separate, although related, components of early self-regulation.

In summary, very few studies have employed the cutoff technique to examine how schooling influences children's self-regulation. Those studies that have been conducted found support for schooling effects on *some* aspects of self-regulation during the preschool, prekindergarten, and kindergarten years. While the evidence is preliminary, there is an emerging sense of a limited or no focus on self-regulatory skills in early childhood classrooms. Furthermore, one study demonstrated how first-grade classroom practices can assist children in developing self-regulation, thus making us hopeful that early, explicit, and focused approaches to promoting self-regulatory may benefit young children.

BROADENING THE PERSPECTIVE: CROSS-CULTURAL RESEARCH

In international comparisons of children's academic achievement, Asian children repeatedly outperform their American peers. Stevenson and Lee (1990) documented that differences in school practices across Chinese (Taipei, Taiwan), Japanese (Sendai), and American (Minneapolis) cultures were present in first grade and attributed this finding, in part, to parenting (or other experiences at home). Another source of these differences may be significant differences in self-regulation learning at young ages, and in their discussion of the schooling environments, the authors noted the organized and efficient nature of the Asian classrooms, especially in comparison to the American classrooms (Stevenson & Lee, 1990). Furthermore, these teacher practices were positively linked to children's attention, a finding consistent with a recent U.S. study of first grade classrooms (Cameron, Connor, et al., 2005).

Along similar lines, Lan, Cameron, and Miller (2006) investigated the development of behavioral self-regulation in school by comparing students' on-task, self-regulated behavior and its relation with group size and teacher instructions in China and the United States.

Thirteen first-grade classrooms (six suburban U.S. and seven urban Chinese classrooms, with children from middle-SES families) were coded for teacher and student behaviors during 30-second time intervals (1,051 intervals total) from videotapes of mathematics lessons (each class is 35 minutes long). During each interval, classroom-level behavioral self-regulation was coded as either *on-task* (70% of the students were actively or passively on-task for longer than 20 seconds in the 30-second interval, examples of on-task behaviors include answering/asking questions, examples of passive on-task include listening or writing) or *off-task* (other than on-task). Group size (whole class or small group) and teacher's instructions including (a) *preparatory* instructions (given prior to the student behavior) or (b) *correctional* instructions (given after an activity) for oral and gestural instructions were also coded. Average interrater reliability was 0.92. Chinese teachers were more likely to use whole-class structures and give preparatory instructions compared to the U.S. teachers. One striking difference was the greater use (70% of self-regulatory instructions) by Chinese teachers of direct commands (e.g., "pay attention to me," "sit properly," and "stop"), which were very rare in the American classrooms. In contrast, 72% of instructions given by American teachers were correctional. Chinese students showed a larger percent of on-task behaviors than their American counterparts. Results of logistic regression analysis revealed that time significantly predicted on-task behavior (b = –0.02, t(985) = –3.31, $p < 0.01$), with U.S. students' decreasing on-task behavior over time and Chinese students' on-task behavior remaining stable. Chinese students showed significantly more on-task behaviors than their U.S. counterparts (b = 2.74, t(985) = 4.78, $p < 0.01$). In addition, group size had a significant effect on student on-task behavior (b = –0.96, t(985) = –4.70, $p < 0.01$): The larger the group was, the more likely students were on-task. Teacher instructions also had a significant effect on student on-task behavior (b = –0.3, t(985) = 2.209, $p < 0.05$). This study reveals compelling differences in both student and teacher behaviors associated with behavioral self-regulation in the classroom, raising the possibility for classroom interventions focused on varying group size and explicit teacher instructions.

Recent comparative research between North American (Portland, Oregon and Ontario, Canada) and Chinese children provides additional insight into the processes by which young children develop self-regulation skills. Two studies, one examining parental attitudes and toddlers' behavioral inhibition and the other investigating executive function in preschoolers, are discussed.

Chen and colleagues (1998) examined Chinese and Canadian toddlers' behavioral inhibition (measured through coded mother–child interactions) in relation to mother-reported child-rearing attitudes. Not surprisingly, there were significant differences in children's inhibitory behaviors, with Chinese toddlers' more inhibited than Canadian toddlers, and mothers' attitudes across the two cultures. Examination of the interaction between children's behaviors and mothers' attitudes also indicated significant cultural differences. For Canadian children, maternal punishment and overprotectiveness was associated with increased inhibition behavior, while the opposite was true for Chinese children. Mothers' acceptance, encouragement, and lack of punishment were positively related to children's inhibition.

In their study of preschoolers, Sabbagh, Xu, Carlson, Moses, & Lee (2006) examined differences between Chinese and American children's executive functioning. Children aged 3 to 5 were administered seven different executive function tasks. Results demonstrated improvement with age for all children (except on one task), and Chinese children's superiority compared to American children across all measures.

These two studies highlight the larger effect of culture on children's self-regulation and have important implications for understanding the multiple contextual influences. Given the increasing diversity of families in the United States, it will be necessary to conduct studies examining how parenting is related to self-regulation across cultural groups.

CONCLUSION

In this chapter, we reviewed literature examining parenting and schooling influences on children's self-regulation development in early childhood. We conclude that parenting predicts self-regulation through multiple pathways and in specific ways. While there is limited evidence for early schooling effects, attention to self-regulation in early childhood classrooms is often not a specific focus, and therefore, is variable. Furthermore, emerging cross-cultural research is indicative of specificity in development.

NOTES

1.   While participation in child care is at an all-time high, this aspect of children's early environment will not be addressed; rather, we focus on preschool, pre-K, and early elementary school.

REFERENCES

Achenbach, T. M. (1991a). *Manual for the child behavior checklist and revised child behavior profile.* Burlington: University of Vermont, Department of Psychiatry.

Administration for Children and Families. (2005). *Head Start impact study: First year findings.* Washington, DC: U.S. Department of Health and Human Services.

Alexander, J. R. M., & Martin, F. (2004). The end of the reading age: Grade and age effects in early schooling. *Journal of School Psychology, 42,* 403–416.

Belluck, P. (2005, March 13). With mayhem at home, they call a parent coach. *The New York Times,* p. A1.

Bowman, B. T., Donovan, M. S., & Burns, M. S. (Eds.) (2001). *Eager to learn: Educating our preschoolers.* Washington, DC: National Academy Press.

Brody, L. (2005, May 17). Study charges NJ preschools kicking out kids. *The Record (Bergen County, NJ),* p. A01.

Bronson, M. (2000). *Self-regulation in early childhood: Nature and nurture.* New York: Guilford Press.

Burrage, M., Cameron, C. E., Sims, B. C., Shah, P., & Morrison, F. J. (2006). *A natural experiment of schooling effects on executive functions.* Paper presented at the Conference on Human Development, Louisville, KY.

Caldwell, B. M., & Bradley, R. H. (1984). *Home observation for the measurement of the environment.* Little Rock: University of Arkansas.

Cameron, C. E., Connor, C. M., & Morrison, F. J. (2005). Effects of variation in teacher organization on classroom functioning. *Journal of School Psychology, 43,* 61–85.

Cameron, C. E., McClelland, M. M., Jewkes, A. M., Connor, C. M., Farris, C., Morrison, F. J. (in press). Touch your toes! Developing a behavioral measure of preschool regulation. *Early Childhood Research Quarterly.*

Chen, X., Hastings, P. D., Rubin, K. H., Chen H., Cen, G., & Stewart, S. L. (1998). Child-rearing attitudes and behavioral inhibition in Chinese and Canadian toddlers: A cross-cultural study. *Developmental Psychology, 34*(4), 677–539.

Child Trends Databank. (2006). *Preschool and prekindergarten programs.* [Data file]. Available from http://www.childtrendsdatabank.org/indicators/103prekindergarten.cfm

Christian, K., Bachman, H. J., & Morrison, F. J. (2001). Schooling and cognitive development. In R. J. Sternberg & E. L. Grigorenko (Eds), *Environmental effects on cognitive abilities* (pp. 287–335). Mahwah, NJ: Erlbaum.

Crone, D. A., & Whitehurst, G. J. (1999). Age and schooling effects on emergent literacy and early reading skills. *Journal of Educational Psychology, 91*(4), 604–614.

Darling, N., & Steinberg, L. (1993). Parenting style as context: An integrative model. *Psychological Bulletin, 113,* 487–496.

Dennis, T. (2006). Emotional self-regulation in preschoolers: The interplay of child approach reactivity, parenting, and control capacities. *Developmental Psychology, 42*(1), 84–97.

Eisenberg, N., Valiente, C., Morris, A. S., Fabes, R. A., Cumberland, A., Reiser, M., et al. (2003). Longitudinal relations among parental emotional expressivity, children's regulation, and quality of socioemotional functioning. *Developmental Psychology, 39*(1), 3–19.

Garza, C. L. (2005, May 17). Expulsion rate highest for preschoolers, study shows. *Fort Worth Star-Telegram.*

Gilliam, W. S. (2005). Prekindergartners left behind: Expulsion rates in state prekindergarten systems. Report prepared for the Foundation of Child Development. http://www.fcd-us.org/PDFs/NationalPreKExpulsionPaper03.02_new.pdf

Gilliam, W. S., & Shahar, G. (2006). Preschool and child care expulsion and suspension: Rates and predictors in one state. *Infants & Young Children, 19*(3), 228–245.

Gresham, F. S., & Elliot, S. N. (1990). *Social skills rating system.* Circle Pines, MN: American Guidance Service.

Grolnick, W. S., & Farkas, M. (2002). Parenting and the development of children's self-regulation. In M. H. Bornstein (Ed.), *Handbook of parenting (Vol. 5): Practical issues in parenting (pp. 89–110).* Mahwah, NJ: Erlbaum.

Grolnick, W. S., & Ryan, R. M. (1989). Parent styles associate with children's self-regulation and competence in school. *Journal of Educational Psychology, 81*(2), 143–154.

Lan, X., Cameron, C. E., & Miller, K. F. (2006). *A cross-cultural investigation of teachers' instructions about self-regulation in elementary math classrooms.* Paper presented at the Conference on Human Development, Louisville, KY.

Landry, S. H., Smith, K. E., Swank, P. R., Assel, M. A., & Vellet, S. (2001). Does early responsive parenting have a special importance for children's development or is consistency across early childhood necessary? *Developmental Psychology, 37*(3), 387–403.

Love, J. M., Kisker, E. E., Ross, C., Raikes, H., Constantine, J., Boler, K., et al. (2005). The effectiveness of early Head Start for 3-year-old children and their parents: Lessons for policy and programs. *Developmental Psychology, 41*(6), 885–901.

McClelland, M. M., & Morrison, F. J. (2003). The emergence of learning-related social skills in preschool children. *Early Childhood Research Quarterly, 202*, 1–19.

McClelland, M. M., Cameron, C. E., Wanless, S. B., & Murray, A. (in press). Executive function, self-regulation, and social emotional skills: Links to school readiness. In O. N. Saracho & B. Spodek (Eds.), *Contemporary perspectives on research in social learning in early childhood education.*

McCrea, S. M., Mueller, J. H., & Parrila, R. K. (1999). Quantitative analyses of schooling effects on executive function in young children. *Child Neuropsychology, 5*(4), 242–250.

Morrison, F. J., Bachman, H. J., & Connor, C. M. (2005). *Improving literacy in America: Guidelines from research.* New Haven, CT: Yale University Press.

Morrison, F. J., & Cooney, R. R. (2002). Parenting and academic achievement: Multiple paths to early literacy. In J. G. Borkowski (Ed.), *Parenting and the child's world* (pp. 141–160). Mahwah, NJ: Erlbaum.

Morrison, F. J., Griffith, E. M., & Alberts, D. M. (1997). Nature-nurture in the classroom: Entrance age, school readiness, and learning in children. *Developmental Psychology, 33*(2), 254–262.

Morrison, F. J., Griffith, E. M., & Frazier, J. A. (1996). Schooling and the 5 to 7 shift: A natural experiment. In A. J. Sameroff & M. M. Haith (Eds.), *The five to seven year shift: The age of reason and responsibility* (pp.161–186). Chicago: University of Chicago.

Morrison, F. J., Smith, L., & Dow-Ehrenberger, M. (1995). Education and cognitive development: A natural experiment. *Developmental Psychology, 31*(5), 789–799.

Neitzel, C., & Stright, A. D. (2003). Mothers' scaffolding of children's problem solving: Establishing a foundation of academic self-regulatory competence. *Journal of Family Psychology, 17*(1), 147–159.

NICHD ECCRN (2004a). Multiple pathways to early academic achievement. *Harvard Educational Review, 74*(1), 1–29.

NICHD ECCRN (2004b). Fathers' and mothers' parenting behavior and beliefs as predictors of children's social adjustment in the transition to school. *Journal of Family Psychology, 18*(4), 628–638.

Raudenbush, S., Bryk, A. S., & Congdon, R. (2005). *HLM 6: Hierarchial linear and nonlinear modeling.* Lincolnwood, IL: Scientific Software International, Inc.

Rimer, S. (2002, December 16). Critics attack suspension of 33 Philadelphia kindergarteners. *The New York Times*, pp. A16, A18.

Rimm-Kaufman, S. E., and R. C. Pianta. 2000. Teacher's judgments of problems in the transition to kindergarten. *Early Childhood Research Quarterly, 15*(2), 147–166.

Rosenbaum, P. R., & Rubin, D. B. (1983). The central role of the propensity score in observational studies for causal effects. *Biometrika, 70*, 41–55.

Rothbart, M. K., Ahadi, S., & Hershey, K. L. (1994). Temperament and social behavior in children. *Merrill-Palmer Quarterly, 40,* 21–39.

Sabbagh, M. A., Xu, F., Carlson, S. M., Moses, L. J., & Lee, K. (2006). The development of executive functioning and theory of mind: A comparison of Chinese and U.S. preschoolers. *Psychological Science, 17*(1), 74–81.

Shaefer, E. S., & Edgerton, M. (1985). Parent and child correlates of parental modernity. In I. E. Sigel (Ed.), *Parental belief systems* (pp. 287–318). Hillsdale, NJ: Erlbaum.

Shallice, T., Marzocchi, G. M., Del Salvo, M., Meuter, R. F., Rumiati, R. I. (2002). Executive function profile of children with attention deficit hyperactivity disorder. *Developmental Neuropsychology, 21*(1), 43–71.

Shonkoff, J. P., & Phillips, D. A. (Eds.). (2000). *From neurons to neighborhoods: The science of early childhood development.* Washington, DC: National Academy Press.

Stevenson, H. J., & Lee, S. (1990). Contexts of achievement: A study of American, Chinese, and Japanese children. *Monographs of the Society for Research in Child Development, 55,* 1–2.

Stright, A. D., Neitzel, C., Sears, K. G., & Hoke-Sinex, L. (2001). Instruction begins in the home: Relations between parental instruction and children's self-regulation in the classroom. *Journal of Educational Psychology, 93*(3), 456–466.

Stipek, D. 2002. *At what age should children enter kindergarten? A question for policy makers and parents* (Social Policy Report, Volume XVI, Number 2). Ann Arbor, MI: Society for Research in Child Development.

Woodcock, R. W., & Mather, N. (2000). *Woodcock Johnson psycho-educational battery-III.* Itasca, IL: Riverside.

Zaslow, M. J., Weinfield, N. S., Gallagher, M., Hair, E. C., Ogawa, J. R., Egeland, B., et al. (2006). Longitudinal prediction of child outcomes from differing measures of parenting in a low-income sample. *Developmental Psychology, 42*(1), 27–37.

CHAPTER 7

PARENT–PROVIDER RELATIONSHIPS IN EARLY CARE SETTINGS

Angela M. Tomlin

All learning takes place in the context of relationships and is critically affected by the quality of those relationships. (Norman-Murch, 1996, p. 17)

INTRODUCTION

Young children learn directly through acting on and observing their environment, but this learning requires adult mediation of children's experiences (Odom & Wolery, 2003). For most young children, primary caregivers, including parents, are the admired persons who provide scaffolding, prompting, and other bridges to learning. In some families, however, a poor parent–child relationship may blunt the effectiveness of the parent as a model or the parent may lack the critical skills to support their child's development, often as a result of their own difficult early histories. Programs intended to improve infant and child outcomes, therefore, often include a parent support component, achieved by a relationship with a provider. This paper will use constructs from social learning theory in tandem with concepts from the attachment literature to discuss the importance of parent–child relationships to child development and offer a

Contemporary Perspectives on Social Learning in Early Childhood Education, pages 149–172
Copyright © 2007 by Information Age Publishing

perspective on the many ways in which providers from a variety of early childhood programs use relationship-based approaches to improve parent–child relationships.

ORIGINS OF PARENTING BEHAVIORS AND BELIEFS

Most human behavior is learned observationally through modeling; from observing others one forms an idea of how new behaviors are performed. (Bandura, 1977, p. 22)

In order to help parents and children attain a positive and nurturing relationship, providers must understand how parenting behaviors and beliefs originate and are sustained. An important source of our understanding of the basis of many behaviors, attitudes, and emotional reactions, including those related to parenting, is social learning theory. Bandura's formulation of social learning theory (1977) highlights the value of models and observation in learning new behaviors and ways of thinking about the self and others. With regard to the development of complex behaviors such as parenting, social learning clearly plays an important role, as both clinicians and researchers agree that a person's first and perhaps most enduring model of how to parent is one's own parent (Berlin, 2005).

The way that one was parented has broad effects, informing how one thinks about oneself and how one thinks about relationships in general (Bowlby, 1988). Parents' actions provide a model of both parenting behavior (e.g., nurturance, discipline) and beliefs about parent–child relationships that in turn form the child's ideas about relationships, in a cognitive structure that attachment theorists have called an *internal working model* (IWM) (Bowlby, 1988). The IWM not only informs thinking about relationships, but also influences present and future relationship behavior (Berlin, 2005). Efforts to support and enhance relationships between parents and children will be most effective when they address the parent's IWM (Bowlby, 1988; Lieberman & Van Horn, 2005).

Supportive adult to adult relationships are recognized to have an important role in initiating and furthering child–adult relationships, including attachment (Bronfenbrenner & Morris, 1997). Bronfenbrenner and Morris (1997) propose that the parent–child relationship is enhanced when the supportive adults provide direct caregiving assistance as well as actions that increase the status of the parent (e.g., expressions of admiration and affection). Caregivers and other helpers within and outside of the family can provide this support to parents (Marty, Readdick, & Walters, 2005), which must be ongoing (Lieberman & Van Horn, 2005).

Social learning theory principles provide additional information about the kind of relationship that leads most effectively to cognitive and behavioral changes, stating that new behaviors are most efficiently learned when the model or coach is a person that is similar to the observer and/or a person that the observer likes or admires (Bandura, 1977). This notion fits well with the idea that the quality of a parent's relationships with other people plays a role in the parent's ability to develop and sustain an appropriate and satisfying relationship with their child (Bronfenbrenner & Morris, 1997).

The social learning theory construct of *self-efficacy* provides another way to think about a parent's beliefs about their capacities and relationships. Self-efficacy relates to beliefs about one's ability to handle situations by organizing and implementing a necessary course of action (Bandura, 1997). Therefore, both knowledge about how to do a task and confidence in one's ability to complete the task are necessary. Similar to the origins of IWM, self-efficacy beliefs are generated by successful past experiences, witnessing other's success in such instances, positive verbal judgments of others about one's competence, and physiological events (e.g., anxiety, stress, mood) (Bandura, 1997). With regard to parenting, self-efficacy is demonstrated when parents have confidence in their ability to carry out parenting behaviors in addition to knowledge about behaviors related to child rearing. The research literature on parental self-efficacy beliefs is sparse and almost exclusively relates to mothers (DesJardin, Eisenberg, & Hodapp, 2006). However, at least one study indicated that higher maternal self-efficacy was linked to increased responsiveness with infants, a behavior that is seen as critical to a positive attachment relationship (Teti & Gefland, 1991).

Beliefs about self-efficacy can be changed through modeling, supportive verbal statements (verbal persuasions) and encouraging reflection on one's feelings and capacities, actions that are integral to a relationship-based approach based on attachment theory. Thus, it seems likely the provider who uses relationship-based methods may support parental self-efficacy and thereby benefit the parent–child attachment. In the next section we will turn our attention to the factors that make a positive attachment relationship so important.

WHY FOCUS ON THE PARENT–CHILD RELATIONSHIP?

Successful parenting is a principal key to the mental health of the next generation.
(Bowlby, Retrieved February 6, 2006 from www.circleofsecurity.org)

Intervention programs that focus on improving the parent–child relationship often use attachment theory and research as a foundation. Attachment is very well researched because the development of a secure attachment to one or more primary caregivers is considered the most important task of the first year of life. A secure attachment also has long-term value because it provides a template for future relationships and it is associated with many other positive outcomes, including capacity for emotional regulation (Sroufe, 1996).

Attachment may be defined as an enduring emotional bond that develops between a child and a specific adult who is in a caregiver role with that child (Bowlby, 1969/1982). Attachments are unique to a dyad, although a child can have more than one attachment. Regular interactions with a specific adult over time are needed for attachment to develop. Bowlby (1969/1982) proposed that the child is born prepared to develop an attachment relationship. Therefore, some type of an attachment will always develop, although the quality of the attachment can vary (Ainsworth, Blehar, Waters, & Wall, 1978).

In the last 15 to 20 years, animal researchers have made links between brain development and experience (Schore, 2001). The brain of the newborn is understood to be "designed to be molded by the environment it encounters" (Thomas et al., 1997, p. 209). The concept of the brain as "experience expectant" (Bruer & Greenough, 2001) emphasizes the viewpoint that the baby needs to encounter specific environmental and interpersonal experiences in order for the brain to mature. In some cases, an expected capacity may fail to develop if anticipated experiences are not received. This is easily seen in studies from the 1970s that demonstrated that kittens prevented from using one eye had normal activity in both eyes, but fewer cortical cells devoted to binocular vision with subsequent deficits in depth perception compared to control animals (Blake & Hirsch, 1975). Newer research suggests that more complex experiences can also have specific effects on brain function. Importantly, for this discussion, regular social interactions are now considered the most essential kinds of experiences not only for the development of attachment, but also for the development of the brain (Schore, 2001). This means that everyday, routine caregiving interactions are critical in determining how the infant's brain is structured and functions.

As conceptualized in the Ainsworth-Bowlby model and expanded by Main and colleagues (Ainsworth et al., 1978; Main & Solomon, 1990), attachment relationships are termed *secure* or *insecure*. Identification of secure and insecure attachment patterns occurs in a research setting by observing the child and caregiver in a structured series of activities called the *strange situation* (Ainsworth et al., 1978). The episodes in the strange situation paradigm press for attachment behaviors by putting the infant into mildly stressful situations, including brief separations from the parent and the introduction of a stranger. Observation of the baby's response when the parent returns (reunion episode) is considered very important as it indicates the child's ability to recover from the stressor with the caregiver's support. The parent's behaviors during the strange situation may be understood as a reflection of their typical behavior in the home setting. In this way, the strange situation provides a window into the parent–child relationship.

Secure attachment patterns are characterized by the infant's ability to use the caregiver as a secure base and a secure haven (Ainsworth et al., 1978). In practical terms, this means that a baby is best able to explore and learn in the presence of the attachment figure (relative to alone or with the stranger) and that the baby will turn to the attachment figure for comfort and when upset, hurt, or frightened. Although the securely attached baby is expected to protest separation and to be upset when the parent is unavailable, she will quickly calm and regain regulation when the parent returns and provides comfort. In low risk populations, approximately 60% of infants are expected to have a secure attachment pattern (Ainsworth et al., 1978).

A secure attachment is believed to be facilitated by nurturing caregiving actions that are consistent and timely. Through these caregiving actions the baby comes to feel confident that his or her needs will be met. An important long-term function of a secure attachment relationship is the infant's growing capacity for self-regulation (Sroufe, 1996). When the parent repeatedly and consistently fails to provide the needed positive social interactions, nurturing, and scaffolding, an insecure attachment may form. Insecure attachments may lead to serious long-term emotional and behavioral consequences, which escalate in the presence of multiple risk factors. As infants grow into toddlers and preschoolers, problems stemming from the primary relationship and subsequent deficits in social and emotional regulation appear in the form of challenging behaviors, including self injurious behavior, tantrums, aggression toward others, and disrupted sleep. Difficult behavior can occur in any population, although stressful experiences, environments, and relationships increase the risk (Knitzer & Lefkowitz, 2006). Concern with the behavior problems of young children crosses systems and has been identified as a priority for children who participate in Part C early intervention services (i.e., those with delays and those at risk for disabilities) (Gilkerson & Kopel, 2005; Hadadian, Tomlin, & Sherwood-Puzzello, 2005), otherwise typically developing children who are accessing child care (Rusby, 2002), young children entering school programs (Mashburn & Pianta, 2006), and many at risk populations (Knitzer & Lefkowitz, 2006; Tomlin & Hadadian, in press).

Three types of insecure attachments have been identified: resistant (ambivalent), avoidant, and disorganized. Babies who have a resistant attachment represent 12% of American samples (Ainsworth et al., 1978). In research settings, these babies are less able to use their caregiver's safe haven function, shown by less exploration and more difficulty being calmed by their parents. Although the child is upset and appears to need help to calm down, the resistant infant is likely to struggle and try to get away from the parent who is attempting to comfort him. Avoidant patterns occur in about 18% of American samples (Ainsworth et al., 1978). These infants appear to have little to no difficulty separating from attachment figures and may actually ignore them when they return. Interestingly, these babies can have physiological indicators that separation stresses them, even when they do not show it behaviorally. Increases in heart rate and the stress hormone cortisol during separation have been demonstrated for some avoidant infants (Spangler & Grossman, 1993).

A later but important addition to the attachment categories is disorganized attachment (Main & Solomon, 1990). The attachment behavior of these children is described as unusual or odd. Behavior that is a combination of behaviors found in the other groups may occur. Other babies may demonstrate behaviors such as screaming, freezing, or self-stimulation. It is felt that disorganized attachment is more likely to occur when infants have experienced maltreatment or extremely poor caregiving. Between 10 and 14% of dyads show this pattern (Main & Solomon, 1990).

Research on attachment has a rich history that informs many programs and interventions for parents and their young children by emphasizing the centrality of the parent–child relationship to other child outcomes. The theory forms the basis for programs that use improvements in parent–child interactions as a platform for progress in other developmental areas. Observation of secure or well-functioning parent–child dyads also provides information about strategies that may support parents and children whose relationships are challenged. The next section will review the links between support provided to parents, parent–child relationships, and child outcomes.

SUPPORTING CHILDREN MEANS SUPPORTING PARENTS

She needed to talk and I needed to listen. (Weatherston, 1997, p. 6)

When attempting to influence child outcomes through supports to parents, it becomes important to understand how parent characteristics are related to child attachment status. Research on parent contributions to the quality of the parent–child relationship is summarized as the *transmission model* (van IJzendoorn, 1995). As originally conceptualized, the transmission model postulated that the parent's IWM influenced parenting behaviors, which in turn directly impacted the child's attachment behaviors. However, a meta-analysis revealed that the parenting behaviors actually accounted for a small proportion of the association between parental IWM and child attachment (van IJzendoorn, 1995). Although this transmission gap continues to be studied, at this point the majority of researchers agree that parental IWMs by themselves are a strong predictor of child attachment behaviors (Berlin, 2005). In fact, the relationship is so robust that parent IWMs have been found to predict a child's attachment status even when assessed prior to the birth of the child (Benoit & Parker, 1994).

Research that connects parental IWM with child attachment status underlies our understanding how change is possible through relationships. As discussed earlier, one's IWM develops as a result of experiences with relationships and once established, guides the person's expectations about future relationships. Regular exposure to and participation in healthier relationships and interactions, including, for example, modeling of appropriate parenting practices, will result in changes to parental thinking and behavior that are beneficial to parents and their children (Gowen & Nebrig, 2002). From a social learning theory perspective, the interventionist (model or coach) that can develop rapport with the parent will be most effective. Therefore, provider behaviors that enhance relationship are critical.

The new relationship that the parent develops with the provider has been called a *corrective attachment relationship* because it serves to replace maladaptive relationship patterns (Lieberman, Silverman, & Pawl, 2000). Over time, the corrective attachment relationship changes the parent's thinking about relationships. Through a mechanism called *parallel process*, the new relationship also results in changes to other relationships (Parlakian, 2002). Jeree Pawl's simple but effective description of parallel process is frequently quoted: "Do unto others as you would have them do unto others" (Pawl & St. John, 1998, p.7) and it underscores the importance of both the provision of support and the modeling functions of the parent–provider relationship. In the context of family work, parallel process is understood to mean that a worker who provides a supportive relationship to a parent is helping the parent to better support his or her child.

Regardless of a provider's training background, initial tasks for establishing parent and provider partnerships typically include gaining access to the family, establishing an initial working relationship with clear boundaries, developing trust through consistency, emotional availability, and a nonjudgmental stance, and then maintaining the relationship over time (Landy & Menna, 2006). Gaining the parent's trust and establishing a therapeutic relationship can be challenging. Barriers are many, especially for high risk families, those from cultures different from the interventionist, and families headed by very young parents. The provider must work to show the parent she can be trusted, by being sensitive, consistent, reliable, and responsive to the parent's needs and concerns. It is no accident that the provider's behavior mirrors that of a sensitive and caring parent.

Once a relationship is in place, the provider and parent work together to understand how the dysfunctional IWM of self and of others developed (Bowlby, 1988). From this basic understanding, change is possible. Gaining this knowledge requires reflecting on difficult and perhaps painful memories and is thus most likely to happen within the context of a supportive relationship. The most important functions of the intervener continue to be provision of a secure base from which to explore past and present relationships, including those with one's children, and acting as a model of supportive and empathic behaviors (Bowlby, 1988; Berlin, 2005).

As the relationship develops, the parent will be helped to gain more complex skills needed for a better relationship, such as reflective function, empathy for their child, ability to recognize and tolerate feelings, a realistic and balanced view of the child, and appropriate and successful child-rearing skills (Landy & Menna, 2006; Lieberman & Van Horn, 2005). Strategies for achieving these diverse goals are borrowed from infant mental health approaches and may not be appropriate for all workers. Providers must know and adhere to the boundaries of their own discipline when engaged in relationship-based work with families. However, some methods can be used by many disciplines, including addressing basic needs, working from family strengths, and using questions to help parents reflect on their own and child's experiences (Weatherston, 2005). The next section of the paper will review some of these strategies and how they can be adapted for work in nonmental health contexts.

RELATIONSHIP-BASED STRATEGIES: WAYS ANYONE CAN HELP

As infant–family practitioners, we must be holders of hope; ...we must communicate a belief in possibilities. (Weston, 2005, p. 346)

It is important to recognize that families can benefit from supports given by all kinds of early care providers, including teachers, early interventionists, and child care professionals (Gowen & Nebrig, 2002). Any professional or paraprofessional who interacts regularly has the potential to support parent–child relationships and foster social and emotional development through the positive relationship that is developed with the parents (Tomlin & Viehweg, 2003). Having made this assertion, it is acknowledged that front-line workers may worry that working with families around relationship is the purview of mental health professionals, perhaps because they associate mental health or emotional development with mental illness. It is true that relationship-based work has its roots in psychotherapy (Fraiberg, Adelson, & Shapiro, 1975). However, a relationship-based approach can be adapted and implemented by many kinds of workers at many levels from prevention through mental health intervention. As these adaptations have been adopted into the work of many family providers, there is growing evidence that with training and supervision many different workers from nonmental health backgrounds are capable of providing parental support within a relationship-based structure that may prevent problem relationships or result in positive changes to the parent–child relationship (Gowen & Nebrig, 2004; Landy & Menna, 2006).

Researchers and clinicians have advocated for building relationship-based practices borrowed from infant mental health into all child and family services. As a result, the range of programs and intervention methods that utilize relationship-based approaches in one way or another is broad. Programs may be home-based or clinic-based, short-term or intensive, provided by nonprofessionals, paraprofessionals, or highly trained professionals, target all families, those at risk or those with documented parental mental health or addictions challenges, or designed to serve families of children with disabilities or delays. Similarly, programs that support families can offer an array of services. These may include concrete assistance, helping families to connect to other resources, and developmental guidance. With regard to relationship-based approaches, four principles that can span all child–family programs have been identified: strengthening the parent–child relationship, responsive caregiving, continuity of care, and emotional nurturance (Graham, White, Clarke, & Adams, 2001).

Relationship-based and infant mental health techniques that are appropriate for use by a broad range of providers have been identified as building skills, providing support, and promoting positive interactions (Tomlin & Viehweg, 2003). Building parenting skills includes helping the parent learn to notice the baby's cues. Often this is done by "speaking for the baby," or giving voice to the baby's needs by saying something such as "I'm crying because I'm hungry." Providers can also help parents in more direct ways by teaching about expected skills of young children and gently correcting misconceptions. Supportive strategies include active listening, wondering with the parent about the baby's experiences, and highlighting family, parent, and child strengths by helping the parent to notice and enjoy positive experiences with their child. To help promote positive parent–child interactions, a provider may first help parents understand that what they do with their babies matters. Emphasizing the value of simple, everyday routines and interactions and then encouraging parents to do those actions is also beneficial.

RELATIONSHIP-BASED APPROACHES
AND REFLECTIVE PRACTICE

The action is in the interaction. (Shahmoon-Shanok, 2000, p. 368)

Relationship-based approaches to infant–family work are closely allied with reflective practice models. Although reflective practice is most associated with clinical supervision, professionals can also utilize the strategies from reflective practice to build relationships with parents. The three core principles of reflective supervision are reflection, collaboration, and regularity (Parlakian, 2001). Reflection refers to stepping back from a situation in order to look at and think about what is really happening in the situation. It means a constant reappraisal of what one is seeing and doing (Fenichel, 1992). This may happen during clinical supervision with one's supervisor, but it should also occur on the spot when working with a child and family.

The "look, listen, and learn approach" is recommended to help the nonmental health provider build and use reflective skills (Parlakian, 2002). Providers are encouraged to look at all aspects of the situation, listen to what the parent is telling about the situation in overt and unspoken ways, and to learn by making a hypothesis about what is going on that is open to revision as one learns more. The provider gathers information by asking open-ended questions intended to help a parent step back and look at the situation. Giving careful attention to the parent's responses allows the provider to learn more about the family and their situation as she refines her hypothesis.

Collaboration refers to the fact that providers and parents work together, sharing responsibility and control for the outcomes for the family (Parlakian, 2002). This feature of reflective practice is consistent with family-centered position of most infant-family programs. Regularity is the final component of reflective practice. This feature mirrors the importance of consistent responsiveness by the parent in the developing parent-infant relationship. Similarly, a positive parent-provider relationship is built over time by the provider behaving in consistent ways. This includes practical consistency, such as keeping regular appointments and bringing promised information or resources, and consistency in behavior, therapeutic stance, and responsiveness.

In a recent article Heffron, Ivins, and Weston (2005) provided an excellent discussion of relationship-based methods that providers can use both during intervention activities and supervision. The strategies are presented within the context of the concept of *use of self*, meaning the professional's ability to recognize the importance of self-awareness and willingness to explore how one is affected by a particular situation (Bertacchi & Coplon, 1992). One use of self strategy is *perspective taking*, which is especially useful with issues such as child-rearing practices. When using perspective taking, the provider will work with the parent to understand a given practice from the parent's viewpoint, even though the provider does not agree with the practice and plans to work with the parent to introduce changes (Heffron et al., 2005). For example, when discussing discipline methods, a parent might assert that physical discipline (spanking) is their method of choice. Instead of correcting the parent, a provider using perspective taking could ask the parent to talk more about their use of spanking and how they believe it will help their child (Lieberman & Van Horn, 2005).

PROGRAMS THAT USE
A RELATIONSHIP-BASED APPROACH

The quality of the relationship matters as much as the specific information, guidance, and assistance that is offered. (Gowen & Nebrig, 2002, p. 4–5)

Efforts to improve child outcomes through programs that include parents have a long history in the United States. For example, the roots of home visiting programs can be traced back more than 125 years, with the earliest published documentation in the 1880's (see Charity Organization Society, 1883, in Sweet & Appelbaum, 2004). Across the many early childhood specialties, researchers and clinicians have documented connections between healthy parent–child relationships, competence in social and emotional skills and self-regulation, and positive developmental outcomes, resulting in a near universal emphasis on interventions that support relationships. For example, with regard to early intervention and early childhood education and special education services, fundamental tenets include the family and home as the primary nurturing context and strengthening relationships between parents and children as an essential feature of programs designed to increase the child's learning and development (Odom & Wolery, 2003). Therefore, support provided to families through professional interactions is emphasized in these fields. For families struggling with or at risk for domestic violence or child abuse, relationship enhancing strategies have been a significant component of both prevention and intervention or remediation approaches (Daro & Harding, 1999; Dozier, Dozier, & Manni, 2002; Zeanah & Smyke, 2005). In child care, seasoned providers are valued for their teaching, modeling, mentoring, and support to vulnerable parents as much as for the care given to children (Musick & Stott, 2000).

Many relationship-based programs are entirely or partially set in the home. As a recent meta-analysis of home visiting programs pointed out, what occurs during sessions with individual families and individual providers is highly variable and therefore difficult to quantify (Sweet & Appelbaum, 2004). Fidelity to program design is a concern as is the rigor of evaluation methods (Chaffin, 2004). As a result of the variability among programs and variability of implementation within programs, research on effectiveness has been difficult and therefore scarce. There is some global data to indicate that home visiting programs provide at least some benefit to families (Sweet & Appelbaum, 2004). For programs that targeted families at risk for child maltreatment, an impressive median rate of 39% reduction of violence toward children has been reported (Bilukha et al., 2006). In this study, higher levels of provider training and increased length of family participation in the program were both related to successful attainment of outcomes. With these successes and challenges in mind, the next part of the chapter will provide a sampling of current programs and services for very young children and families that use relationship-based methods.

RELATIONSHIP-BASED SYSTEMS, SERVICES, AND PROGRAMS

If a community values its children it must cherish their parents. (Bowlby, 1951, p. 84)

Early Intervention/Part C

Part C of the revision to the Individuals with Disabilities Education Improvement Act (IDEA) (2004) is intended to help states identify and serve young children with disabilities or at risk for disabilities in order to maximize their developmental outcomes. Services for families accessing Part C are mandated to be comprehensive, coordinated, and family centered. According to the federal legislation, services are to be provided in the child's natural environment, which means that services often occur in the home. In many instances, the provider's role is to teach parents how to enhance their child's development during everyday, routine activities (Gowen & Nebrig, 2002).

For many providers, working in early intervention (EI) brings experiences their training did not prepare them for, such as teaching parents to implement an intervention instead of working directly with the child themselves. In addition, being in a home setting provides access to information and family needs the provider may feel unprepared to tackle (Tomlin & Hadadian, 2007). Although early intervention professionals who do not have mental health backgrounds should not provide mental health services, they can learn to use relationship-based approaches within their scope of practice (Jones & Lythcott, 2005). Including relationship-based strategies can be especially important in early intervention as parents report that emotional support is one of their biggest unmet needs (Gilkerson & Kopel, 2005). Furthermore, recent research has made relationship-based practices a priority in early intervention by showing that relationships serve to organize development and form the basis of all intervention efforts (Weston, Ivins, Heffron, & Sweet, 1997).

The benefits of relationship-based strategies within EI has been addressed in many states including Florida, Indiana, and Michigan (Tomlin

& Viehweg, 2003). In Illinois, supporting the social and emotional (SE) development of children participating in Part C in order to more effectively identify and serve those children with SE concerns has been a recent priority (Gilkerson & Kopel, 2005). An important goal of the Illinois program is fostering positive parent–child relationships. To achieve these ends, relationship-based training and reflective consultation and supervision opportunities have been provided to case managers and service coordinators. In addition, networking and training is available to direct service providers. Starting as a pilot, the program has shown cost effectiveness, positive changes in staff knowledge, practice, and role satisfaction for providers. There has also been an increase in identification of children with SE concerns and provision of needed services (Gilkerson & Kopel, 2005). As a result of this success, the program has been funded for rollout statewide.

Child Care

Recent estimates suggest that more than half of U.S. children under 5 years participate in a regular child care situation (U.S. Census Bureau, 2005). As participation rates increased, research efforts followed, often with the disparate results that flow from differences in research design and theory. A good example is the research focused on the effects of child care attendance on mother–child attachment, with some researchers finding that repeated separation between mother and child for child care may lead to problems with attachment (Belsky, 1988), while others reporting no differences in quality of attachment for low risk mother–baby dyads who utilize or do not utilize good quality child care (Caruso, 1996). Adding to our difficulty in obtaining good answers to important questions about child care participation are design limitations, such as small sample sizes, short follow up periods, and lack of needed controls (NICHD, 2005). To address the need for more useful and integrated information, the National Institute of Child Health and Human Development (NICHD) planned and implemented a collaborative study of the effects of child care on infants and toddlers (later expanded to preschool and beyond). Beginning in 1987, this longitudinal study was designed to address the limitations of previous work in the field, using a sophisticated research design and newer, more powerful statistical techniques. The studies address a broad range of issues related to child care participation, including quality of care, effects on families, relationships and child health, and behavioral and developmental outcomes—a thorough review of which would be impossible in this chapter. Abridged versions of studies completed to date and an overview of the project were published in a readily available volume (NICHD, 2005). For this paper, we will focus aspects of child care participation that consider adult-to-adult relationships: parent–provider partnerships and child care consultation.

Although it seems likely that children benefit when child care providers and parents partner, there is surprisingly little research to directly support this assertion. Many recommendations come from theory or clinical experience. For example, specific adult directed behaviors such as modeling, role-sharing, and direct parent support are believed to yield benefits to the child in the form of better parent–child relationships (Marty et al., 2005; Musick & Stott, 2000). Daily routines and activities are recommended as opportunities for caregivers to enhance parent–infant relationships for both high and low risk populations. Marty et al. (2005) grouped relationship-enhancing strategies into three categories: increasing daily parent–child face-to-face time, reinforcing the baby's attachment to parents, and reinforcing the parents' close relationship with the baby. The authors advise that making center policy congruent with attachment theory will increase opportunities to implement these strategies. For example, childcare providers could encourage visiting practices and breast feeding to increase parent–child time together. Other recommendations relate to center environment and practice around communication with parents, arrival and departure, and caregiver modeling of behaviors that support attachment, specifically "warmth and affection, sensitivity, responsiveness, consistency, and autonomy-promotion" (Marty et al., 2005, p. 281).

Available empirical studies about parent–caregiver partnerships most often address the general attitudes that parents and providers have about each other, rather than specific parent–provider relationships (Elicker, Noppe, Noppe, & Fortner-Wood, 1997). One measure that addresses this limitation is the Parent–Caregiver Relationship Scale (PCRS), which assesses parent and caregiver perceptions of their relationship with regard to care of an infant (Elicker et al., 1997). In the initial field study, parents and providers identified issues including confidence in the other and collaboration as important components of their relationships. Parents and providers had similar, but not identical reports, resulting in less than perfect congruence in their ratings of components of their relationships. However, it is interesting that factors related to competence in caring for an infant (knowledge, skills) and interpersonal factors such as respect, caring, trust, and communication were identified by both parents and providers. These results acknowledge that parent–caregiver partnerships include skills related to taking care of the child and skills related to initiating and maintaining the adult to adult relationship.

The relationship between parent–provider partnerships and parent/caregiver–child interactions has also been empirically supported (Owen, Ware, & Barfoot, 2000). This study of mother–caregiver communication combined direct observation of the quality of the caregiver child interaction, the quality of mother–child interaction, and parent and provider reports of their child rearing beliefs and partnership behaviors (specifically sharing and seeking information). The results indicated that increases in mother–caregiver communication about the child was associated with higher quality caregiving (e.g., more sensitive, supportive, and stimulating interactions) by the provider and by the mother. The authors indicate that this is apparently the first study to empirically link parent–provider partnership behavior with positive mother–child interaction quality.

In addition to supports that result in better child outcomes, caregiver actions may also result in direct personal benefit to parents. Indeed in one study parents, but not providers, indicated that their relationships with their child care providers had important "friendship" aspects (Elicker et al., 1997, p. 96). Perhaps most poignantly for young and single mothers, this kind of nurturing relationship may be "doubly meaningful" as the trusted care provider takes the place of mother, teacher, or mentor (Musick & Stott, 2000, p. 445).

Another way for parents and providers to work together to support a child in care is to utilize mental health consultation. Although child-care consultation activities are frequently initiated by child behavior or adjustment concerns, the adult relationships that surround the child are seen as the port of entry for this work. In other words, the child is viewed as the "hub" of interconnected relationships among many caregiving adults. There is considerable focus on adult to adult relationships, because, as explained by Johnston and Brinamen (2006), "The health of adult relationships thoroughly affects their children's well-being" (p. 147).

The consultant's role is to make sure that all voices are heard, including the child, parent, providers, and supervisors (Pawl, 2000). To be able to address all of these constituents, the mental health consultant should understand child development, child care, adult relationships, and parent needs (Johnston & Brinamen, 2006). Mental health consultants use many of the strategies described earlier to build a sense of cooperative partnership between the child care provider and the parent for the benefit of the child (Johnston & Brinamen, 2006). From this sense of cooperation and partnership, a plan to support both providers and the child emerges.

One example of successful mental health consultation is the Day Care Consultants program, which is part of the Infant–Parent Program at the University of California, San Francisco. Johnston and Brinamen (2006) have recently published a practical guide to mental health consultation in child care based on 20 years of work at Day Care Consultants. The text explains how to implement the principles and practices of relationship-based mental health consultation in child care, and includes a useful chapter on adult relationships.

Programs for At Risk Families

A large number of programs have been developed that target low income families whose children have already experienced, or who are at risk for, negative outcomes, including delayed development, behavior problems, and abuse and neglect. Programs typically include outcome measures related to parent–child interactions or relationship quality, in addition to changes in parenting behavior, parental mental health, and home environment, among others (Brooks-Gunn, Berlin, & Fuligni, 2000). A thorough review of home-visiting programs for high risk families is beyond the scope of this paper; for our purposes it is useful to state that positive effects on parent–child interactions have been demonstrated and that one pathway to improved child outcomes is more positive parent–child relationships. Instead we will briefly review two current national projects that have explicit goals for enhancing parent–child relationships: Healthy Families America and Early Head Start (for fuller reviews, see Brooks-Gunn et al., 2000; Landy & Menna, 2006).

Healthy Families America

Healthy Families America (HFA) is an intensive home visiting program intended to reduce the rates of child maltreatment and other negative outcomes for young children and their families (Daro & Harding, 1999). Although various state programs may have unique features, the overall program designs are similar. The common program design layers various support services onto a "universal" relationship-based foundation provided to the mother–child dyad. The program is home-based, begins during pregnancy or early in the child's life, and lasts for 3 to 5 years depending on family needs. Additional family resources are added as appropriate and include: parent support groups, early childhood education, parent education, and family counseling.

Making positive change in parent–child relationships is an explicit goal of HFA. HFA recommends that programs select providers for their ability to establish positive relationships with parents, then provides both didactic training and reflective supervision to support them in this work. In outcome studies, participating parents have reported that the workers provided them with needed social supports (Daro & Harding, 1999). Through these positive parent–professional relationships, parents learn how to interact with their children, how to understand a child's developmental skills, and positive discipline methods. Parents also learn the importance of parent–child relationships, and to be more sensitive, responsive, and nurturing toward their children (Prevent Child Abuse America, 2002).

Outcomes of HFA programs in individual states with summaries can be found on the HFA website (www.healthyfamiliesamerica.org). Users may download various research reports, by topic, including positive parenting. The positive parenting research summary indicates that participation yields improvement including increases in parent's empathic awareness of their child's needs, decreases in experienced parental stress, and better parent–child interaction, bonding, and communication (Prevent Child Abuse America, 2002). Daro and Harding (1999) provided a complete summary of the available outcomes including child abuse and neglect, child health, child development, and maternal life course, in addition to parent–child interactions. Although findings vary by program, overall, improvements to parent–child interaction were viewed as "robust" (Daro & Harding, 1999, p. 170). For example, improvements are reported in parent sensitivity to child cues and parents report less distress in the relationship.

Early Head Start

Early Head Start (EHS), like its sister program Head Start, is a federally funded intervention program that targets children whose families have income at or below the federal poverty level. At least 10% of available spaces must serve children with disabilities (Administration for Children, Youth, and Families). EHS programs are often designed to have strong parent support components, because of the expected indirect benefits to the child's developmental outcomes (Love et al., 2005). EHS programs may begin serving families during the mother's pregnancy and continue until the identified child is 3-years-old.

In response to a national forum on infant mental health, EHS partnered with Zero to Three to develop a National Resource Center to provide training, research, technical assistance, and information dissemination in infant mental health areas. Materials are available on a dedicated website (http://www.ehsrc.org) and provide a discussion of how to infuse infant mental health practices in EHS, including the value of supports to parents (Zero to Three, n.d.).

A recent analysis of the effectiveness of EHS was conducted using data from the first wave of program grantees (Love et al., 2005). Measures included child outcomes at age three years (cognitive, language, and social emotional) and parenting behavior. Overall, participating families demonstrated significant favorable outcomes compared to control families. Best outcomes were found for programs that involved a combination of in-home and center-based approaches and those that began earlier in the child's life. EHS programs can document benefits to children's social and emotional competence both by parent report and direct observation of parent–child interactions. Gains in self-regulation capacity included less aggression, better attention to objects, and more engagement with parents during play.

BEYOND EARLY CHILDHOOD: PARENT-PROFESSIONAL
RELATIONSHIPS IN EDUCATION SETTINGS

The importance of support to families does not stop at age 5 years; relationships between children, their family members, and school staff have been a focus of research and intervention efforts in early education for many years (Rimm-Kaufman & Pianta, 2005). In a recent integration, Mashburn and Pianta (2006) use a developmental systems model to discuss how the direct effects of parents and indirect effects of parent–school professional relationships impact young children's school readiness and other competencies. The model reviews multiple layers of relationships and sources of effects, including features of the individual child, direct caregivers, family characteristics, parent–teacher and parent–administrator relationships, and teacher–child relationships. As can be seen from even this brief discussion, a thorough review of this rich and complex literature is beyond the scope of this paper. However, the model's explanation of the indirect effects of the parent–school relationship on the child's school experience provides support to our discussion of how parent–professional relationships affect children and families.

In 1998, the National Education Goals Panel (NEGP) published a set of recommendations that acknowledged the importance of strengthening connections between schools and families as a way to help children make better transitions and adaptations in school (NEGP, 1998). These recommendations highlight the value of parent–teacher relationships and family–school communication in enhancing child outcomes. Following the publication of the recommendations, the National Center for Early Development Learning (NCEDL) designed an intervention to enhance family and school relationships in early school years (Pianta & Kraft-Sayre, 2004). The intervention is flexible such that individual programs address their goals by selecting and adapting practices derived from a set of basic principles. The family friendly principles include "fostering relationships and resources, promoting continuity from preschool to kindergarten, focusing on family strengths, tailoring practices to individual needs, and forming collaborative relationships" (Rimm-Kaufman & Pianta, 2005, p. 289). Comparison of the NCEDL principles with best practices in infant mental health, relationship-based practices, and best practices in other early care fields reflects good agreement.

Children benefit when families receive support from schools and perceive the school as supportive, because parents become more involved and better understand their role in their child's education (Rimm-Kaufman & Pinata, 2005). In particular, parent report of increased trust in teachers was associated with greater likelihood of active parent involvement in school (Adams & Christenson, 1998). In turn, when parents are more involved at school, children had more positive behavioral outcomes including better self-regulation, fewer classroom behavior problems, and higher social competence (Rimm-Kaufman & Pianta, 2005).

Communication is an important method of building the parent–school relationship. Teachers and families report a decline in communication from preschool to kindergarten and into early grade school, suggesting that early communication is most critical (Rimm-Kaufman & Pianta, 2005). Although most commonly used passive contacts (brochures, flyers, open houses) have value (Early, Pianta, Taylor, & Cox, 2001), parents prefer personal contacts that give specific information about how to help their children be ready for school (Pianta & Kraft-Sayre, 2004). Unfortunately, but not surprisingly, teachers are similar to other professionals in reporting a lack of training in how to foster relationships with families (Mashburn & Pianta, 2005). Nevertheless, this literature supports the connection between positive parent–professional relationships and successful child outcomes in school settings.

SUMMARY

In addition to being intuitively appealing, the notion that good relationships lead to more good relationships rests on a solid framework of theory and research in attachment and social learning theory stretching back for over 60 years. More recent research regarding the effects of early experiences on brain development and function lends additional support. Ongoing clinical investigations with vulnerable populations have the potential to provide more evidence, including the related idea that exposure and experience with positive relationships can help mend the damage incurred through negative early relationships. Strong interdisciplinary interest in relationship-based practice brings the promise of continuing research on the effects of provider supports to parents on parent–child interactions. Future clinical research would be strengthened by use of larger sample sizes, longer follow-up periods, direct observations of parent–child interactions, and attention to cost effectiveness of the programs. Finally, the effects of doing this intense work on providers would be worth study, given practical concerns with provider retention and burnout.

Research available to date does seem to support the concept that efforts to improve child outcomes must always consider supports to parents. Practices by providers who work to influence child outcomes through parental support may be seen as consistent with basic social learning theory principles, including learning through observation and modeling, the importance of connection between the model and the observer, and the effect of individual concepts of self-efficacy. These practices are also congruent with attachment theory, especially with regard to the effects of a positive, healthy, early attachment and the benefits of a corrective attachment experience. This chapter has provided an overview of research and practice issues related to supports to parent–child relationships in education, early intervention systems, child care, and programs for high risk families. Other systems, such as medical fields (Johnson, Kent, & Leather, 2005; Turner, 2005) and child welfare (Haight, Kagle, & Black, 2003; Mennen & O'Keefe, 2004) are incorporating understanding of attachment and the importance of supports to parent–child relationships into their practices. Across systems, families will benefit as providers increasingly understand how support to parents results in support to children.

REFERENCES

Adams, K. S., & Christenson, S. L. (1998). Differences in parent and teacher trust levels: Implications for creating collaborative family–school relationships. *Special Services in the Schools, 14(1),* 1–22.

Ainsworth, M., Blehar, M., Waters, E., & Wall, S. (1978). *Patterns of attachment: A psychological study of the strange situations.* Mahwah, NJ: Erlbaum.

Bandura, A. (1977). *Social learning theory.* New York: General Learning Press.

Belsky, J. (1988). Infant day care and social emotional development: The United States. *Journal of Child Psychology and Psychiatry, 29(4),* 397–406.

Benoit, D. & Parker, K. C. H. (1994). Stability and transmission of attachment across three generations. *Child Development, 65,* 1444–1457.

Berlin, L. (2005). Interventions to enhance early attachments: The state of the field today. In L. Berlin, Y. Ziv, L. Amaya-Jackson, & M. Greenberg, (Eds.), *Enhancing early attachments: Theory, research, intervention, and policy* (pp. 3–33). New York: Guilford.

Bertacchi, J., & Coplon, J. (1992). The professional use of self in prevention. In E. Fenichel (Ed.), *Learning through supervision and mentorship to support the development of infants, toddlers, and their families: A sourcebook* (pp. 84–90). Washington, DC: Zero to Three.

Bilukha, O., Hahn, R. A., Crosby, A., Fullilove, M. T., Liberman, A., Moscicki, E., et al. (2006). The effectiveness of early childhood home visitation in preventing violence. *American Journal of Preventive Medicine, 28(281),* 11–39.

Blake, R. & Hirsch, H. V. (1975). Deficits in binocular depth perception in cats after alternating monocular depth perception. *Science, 190(4219),* 1114–6.

Bowlby, J. (1951). *Maternal care and mental health* (World Health Organization Monographs Serial No.2). *Bulletin of the World Health Organization, 3,* 355–534.

Bowlby, J. (1969/1982). *Attachment and loss: Volume 1: Attachment.* New York: Basic Books.

Bowlby, J. (1988). *A secure base: Parent–child attachment and healthy human development.* New York: Basic Books.

Bronfenbrenner, U., & Morris, P. A. (1997). The ecology of developmental processes. In W. Damon & R.M. Lerner (Eds.), *Handbook of child psychology* (5th ed., Vol. 1, pp. 993–1028). New York: Wiley.

Brooks-Gunn, J., Berlin, L., & Fuligni, A. (2000). Early childhood intervention programs: What about the family? In J. Shonkoff & S. Meisels (Eds.), *Handbook of early childhood intervention, 2nd ed.* (pp. 549–588). Cambridge: Cambridge University Press.

Bruer, J. T. & Greenough, W. T. (2001). The subtle science of how experience affects the brain. In D. B. Bilay, J. T. Bruer, F. J. Symons, & J. W. Lichtman (Eds.), *Critical thinking about critical periods* (pp. 209–221). Baltimore: Brookes.

Caruso, D. A. (1996). Maternal employment status, mother–infant interaction, and infant development in day care and non-day car groups. *Child & Youth Car Forum, 25(2),* 125–133.

Chaffin, M. (2004). Is it time to rethink Healthy Start/Health Families? *Child Abuse and Neglect, 28(6),* 589–595.

Daro, D. A., & Harding, K. A. (1999). Healthy Families America: Using research to enhance practice, Home visiting: Recent program evaluations. *The Future of Children, 9(1),* 152–176.

DesJardin, J. L., Eisenberg, L. S., & Hodapp R. M. (2006). Supporting families of young deaf children with cochlear implants. *Infants and Young Children, 19(3),* 179–189.

Dozier, M., Dozier, D., & Manni, M. (2002). Attachment and biobehavioral catch-up: The ABCs of helping foster infants cope with early adversity. *Zero to Three, 22,* 7–13.

Early, D. M., Pianta, R. C., Taylor, L. C., & Cox, M. J. (2001). Transition practices: Findings from a national survey of kindergarten teachers. *Early Childhood Education Journal, 28,* 199–206.

Elicker, J., Noppe, I. C., Noppe, L. D., & Fortner-Wood, C. (1997). The Parent-caregiver relationship scale: Rounding out the relationship system in infant child care. *Early Education and Development, 8(1),* 83–100.

Fenichel, E. (1992). *Learning through supervision and mentorship to support the development of infants, toddlers, and their families.* Washington: DC Zero to Three.

Fraiberg, S., Adelson, E., & Shapiro, V. (1975). Ghosts in the nursery: A psychoanalytic approach to the problems of impaired infant–mother relationships. *Journal of the American Academy of Child Psychiatry, 14,* 397–421.

Gilkerson, L., & Kopel, C. C. (2005). Relationship-based systems change: Illinois' model for promoting social-emotional development in Part C Early Intervention. *Infants and Young Children, 18(4),* 349–365.

Gowen, J. W., & Nebrig, J. B. (2002). *Enhancing early emotional development: Guiding parents of young children.* Baltimore, MD: Brookes.

Graham, M. A., White, B. A., Clarke, C. C., & Adams, S. (2001). Infusing infant mental health practices into front-line caregiving. *Infants & Young Children, 14,* 14–23.

Hadadian, A., Tomlin, A. M., & Sherwood-Puzzello, C.M. (2005). Early intervention service providers: What do they say about their infant mental health training needs? *Early Child Development & Early Care, 175(5),* 431–444.

Haight, W. L., Kagle, J. D., & Black, J. E. (2003). Understanding and supporting parent–child relationships during foster care visits: Attachment theory and research. *Social Work, 48(2)*, 195–207.

Heffron, M. C., Ivins, B. & Weston, D. (2005). Finding an authentic voice. Use of Self; Essential learning processes for relationship-based work. *Infants and Young Children, 18(4)*, 323–336.

Individuals with Disabilities Education Improvement Act (IDEA) Amendments of 2004, Pub. L. No. 108–446 (2004).

Johnson, G., Kent, G., & Leather, J. (2005). Strengthening the parent–child relationship: A review of family interventions and their use in medical settings. *Child: Care, Health, & Development, 31(1)*, 25–32.

Johnston, K., & Brinamen, C. (2006). *Mental health consultation in child care: Transforming relationships among directors, staff, and families.* Washington, DC: Zero to Three Press.

Jones, B. H., & Lythcott, M. (2005). Kitchen therapy and beyond: Mental health services for young children in alternative settings. In K. M. Finello (Ed.), *The handbook of training and practice in infant and preschool mental health* (pp. 256–286). San Francisco, CA: Jossey-Bass.

Knitzer, J., & Lefkowitz, J. (2006). *Pathways to early school success: Helping the most vulnerable infants, toddlers, and their families.* New York: The National Center for Children in Poverty.

Landy, S. & Menna, R. (2006). *Early intervention with multi-risk families: An integrative approach.* Baltimore: Brookes.

Lieberman, A., Silverman, R., & Pawl, J. H. (2000). Infant–parent psychotherapy: Core concepts and current approaches. In C. H. Zeanah (Ed.), *Handbook of infant mental health, 2nd ed.* (pp. 472–484). New York: Guilford.

Lieberman, A. F., & Van Horn, P. (2005). *Don't hit my mommy: A manual for child–parent psychotherapy with young witnesses of family violence.* Washington, DC: Zero to Three.

Love, J. M., Kisker, E. E, Ross, C., Raikes, H, Constantine, J., Boller, K. et al. (2005). The effectiveness of Early Head Start for 3-year-old children and their parents: Lessons for policy and programs. *Developmental Psychology, 41(6)*, 885–901.

Main, M., & Solomon, J. (1990). Procedures for identifying infant as disorganized/disoriented during the Ainsworth Strange Situation. In M. T. Greenberg, D. Cicchetti, & E.M. Cummings (Eds.), *Attachment in the preschool years* (pp. 121–160). Chicago: University of Chicago Press.

Marty, A. H., Readdick, C. A., & Walters, C. M. (2005). Supporting secure parent–child attachments: The role of the non-parental caregiver. *Early Child Development and Care, 175(3)*, 271–283.

Mashburn, A., & Pianta, R. (2006). Social relationships and school readiness, *Early Education and Development, 17(1)*, 151–176.

Mennen, F. E., & O'Keefe, M. (2004). Informed decisions in child welfare: The use of attachment theory. *Children and Youth Services Review, 27*, 577–593.

Musick, J., & Stott, F. (2000). Paraprofessionals revisited and reconsidered. In J. P. Shonkoff & S. J. Meisels (Eds.), *Handbook of early childhood intervention, 2nd Ed.* (pp. 439–455). New York: Cambridge University Press.

National Education Goals Panel (NEGP). (1998). *National education goals report executive summary: Improving education through family-school-community partnerships.* Washington, DC: U.S. Government Printing Office.

National Institute of Child Health and Development (NICHD) Early Child Care Research Network. (2005). *Child care and child development.* New York: Guilford.

Norman-Murch, T. (1996). Reflective supervision as a vehicle for individual and organizational development. *Zero to Three,* 17(2), 16–20.

Odom, S. L., & Wolery, M. (2003). A unified theory of practice in early intervention/early childhood special education: Evidence-based practices. *The Journal of Special Education, 37(3),* 164–173.

Owen, M. T., Ware, A. M., & Barfoot, B. (2000). Caregiver–Mother partnership behavior and the quality of caregiver–child and mother–child interactions. *Early Childhood Research Quarterly, 15,* 413–428.

Parlakian, R. (2001). *The power of questions: Building quality relationships with families.* Washington, DC: Zero to Three.

Parlakian, R. (2002). *Reflective supervision in practice: Stories from the field.* Washington, DC: Zero to Three.

Pawl, J. (2000). The interpersonal center of the work that we do. *Zero to Three, 20,* 5–7.

Pawl, J. H., & St. John, M. (1998). *How you are is as important as what you do....In making a positive difference for infants, toddlers, and their families.* Washington, DC: Zero to Three.

Pianta, R. C., & Kraft-Sayre, M. K. (2004). *Successful kindergarten transition: Your guide to connecting children, families, and schools.* Baltimore: Brookes.

Prevent Child Abuse America (2002). *Research Folder.* Retrieved February 5, 2006, from www.preventchildabuse.org.

Rimm-Kaufman, S. E., & Pianta, R. C. (2005). Family–school communication in preschool and kindergarten in the context of a relationship-enhancing intervention. *Early Education & Development, 16(3),* 287–316.

Schore, A. (2001). Effects of a secure attachment relationship on right brain development, affect regulation, and infant mental health. *Infant Mental Health Journal, 22,* 7–66.

Shahmoon-Shanok, R. (2000). The action is in the interaction: Clinical practice guidelines with parents of children with developmental disorders. In Interdisciplinary Council on Developmental and Learning Disorders (Eds.), *Clinical practice guidelines* (pp. 333–370). Bethesda, MD: Interdisciplinary Council on Developmental and Learning Disorders.

Spangler, G., & Grossman, K. E. (1993). Biobehavioral organization in securely and insecurely attached infants. *Child Development, 64(5),* 1439–1450.

Sroufe, L. A. (1996). *Emotional development: The organization of emotional life in the early years.* New York: Cambridge University Press.

Sweet, M. A., & Appelbaum, M. I. (2004). Is home visiting an effective strategy? A meta-analytic review of home visiting programs for families with young children. *Child Development, 75(5),* 1435–1456.

Teti, D. M., & Gelfand, D. M. (1991). Behavioral competence among mothers of infants in the first year: The mediational role of maternal self-efficacy. *Child Development, 62,* 918–929.

Thomas, D. G., Whitaker, E., Crow, C. D., Little, V., Love, L., Lykins, M. S., et al. (1997). Event-related potential variability as a measure of information storage in infant development. *Developmental Neuropsychology, 13*, 205–232.

Tomlin, A. M., & Hadadian, A. (2007). Early intervention and early care provider experiences with high risk families. *Early Child Development and Care, 177*(2), 187–194.

Tomlin, A., & Viehweg, S. (2003). Infant mental health: Making a difference. *Professional Psychology, 34(6)*, 617–625.

Turner, J. C. (2005). A place for attachment theory in child life programming: The potential to assess the quality of parent–child relationships. *Child & Youth Care Forum, 34(3)*, 195–207.

U.S. Census Bureau. (2005). *Who's minding the kids? Child care arrangements, Winter, 2000.* Retrieved July 28, 2006, from http://www.census.gov/prod/2005pubs/p70-101.pdf.

van IJzendoorn, M. H. (1995). Adult attachment representations, parental responsiveness, and infant attachment: A meta-analysis on the predictive validity of the Adult Attachment Interview, *Psychological Bulletin, 117*, 387–403.

Weatherston, D. (1997). She needed to talk and I needed to listen. *Zero to Three, 18(3)*, 6–12.

Weatherston, D. J. (2005). Returning the treasure to babies: An introduction to infant mental health service and training. In K. M. Finello (Ed.), *The handbook of training and practice in infant and preschool mental health* (p. 3–30). San Francisco: Jossey-Bass.

Weston, D. R., Ivins, B., Heffron, M., & Sweet, N. (1997). Formulating the centrality of relationship in early intervention: An organized perspective. *Infants & Young Children, 9*, 1–12.

Weston, D. (2005). Training in infant mental health: Educating the reflective practitioner. *Infants and Young Children, 18(4)*, 337–348.

Zeanah, C. H., & Smyke, A. T. (2005). Building attachment relationships following maltreatment and severe deprivation. In L. Berlin, Y. Ziv, L. Amaya-Jackson, & M. Greenberg, (Eds.), *Enhancing early attachments: Theory, research, intervention, and policy* (pp. 195–216). New York: Guilford.

Zero to Three. (n.d.). *Pathways to prevention: A comprehensive guide to supporting infant mental health.* Retrieved February 2, 2006, from http://www.ehsnrc.org/highlights/mentalhealth.htm.

CHAPTER 8

PROMOTING SCHOOL READINESS IN FOSTER CHILDREN

**Katherine C. Pears, Philip A. Fisher,
Cynthia V. Heywood, and Kimberly D. Bronz**

School entry is an important developmental milestone for children. Those who lack the social and academic skills to succeed in kindergarten are likely to exhibit trajectories of increasing academic failure and behavior problems across their school years (Entwisle & Alexander, 1999; Williamson, Appelbaum, & Epanchin, 1991). In contrast, success in kindergarten and in first grade is a protective factor associated with positive outcomes in elementary school and beyond (Ensminger & Slusarcick, 1992; Gutman, Sameroff, & Cole, 2003). Foster children are at particularly high risk for difficulties in school, faring worse than their peers on many indicators of school performance, including academic achievement, social competence, high school completion, and need for special education services (Blome, 1997; Wodarski, Kurtz, Gaudin, & Howing, 1990; Zima et al., 2000). Therefore, helping to prepare foster children for school entry by focusing on the skills necessary to succeed in kindergarten could be a key window for early intervention.

This chapter reviews the need for interventions to address school readiness deficits in foster children. Evidence for the effectiveness of several programs designed to enhance school readiness in children at risk for

Contemporary Perspectives on Social Learning in Early Childhood Education, pages 173–198
Copyright © 2007 by Information Age Publishing

abuse and neglect (and thus for entry into foster care) is then summarized. The programs featured here all include a focus on the use of social learning-based parenting techniques (e.g., consistent, clear limits and reinforcement) and on the development of school readiness skills. It is posited that, although many of these programs have been shown to be effective with high-risk children in general, they have not been tailored to the needs of foster children, and no evidence currently exists of their effectiveness with this population. Thus, a preventive intervention that has been specifically designed to enhance foster children's psychosocial and academic school readiness is outlined. Finally, the need for further development of school readiness programs specifically designed for foster children is discussed.

SCHOOL OUTCOMES FOR FOSTER CHILDREN

The foster care population in the United States has grown substantially over the past two decades. This growth likely results from a combination of changes in child abuse and neglect reporting requirements, higher foster care entrance (vs. exit) rates, and the impact of poverty, family violence, mental illness, and substance abuse in the face of decreasing budgets for social services (Barbell, 1997). The U.S. Department of Health and Human Services (U.S. DHHS, 2004) reported that there were more than 500,000 children in foster care in the United States and that children enter the foster care system at a rate of more than 230,000 a year.

Foster children display problems requiring mental health and other services at much higher rates than the general population (Pilowsky, 1995). For instance, Trupin, Tarico, Low, Jennelka, and McClellan (1993) found that 72% of child welfare children in their sample were statistically indistinguishable from children in intensive mental health treatment programs. Studies have also documented high rates of developmental delays among young foster children (Horwitz, Simms, & Farrington, 1994; Pears & Fisher, 2005). Landsverk, Davis, Ganger, Newton, and Johnson (1996) found that 60% of children under age 6.5 years in kinship care scored in the questionable or abnormal range on the Denver Developmental Screening Test II (Frankenburg, Dodds, Archer, Shapiro, & Bresnick, 1992) and that 72% residing in nonrelative foster care showed similar deficits.

Given the pervasiveness of psychosocial and developmental problems among foster children, it is not surprising that they fare poorly on indicators of school performance. Indeed, evidence suggests that foster children may have particular difficulty in school settings. Zima et al. (2000) found that 69% of foster children screened positive for a behavior problem, academic skill delay, or school failure. Others have found that foster children frequently lag behind their peers in academic skills (Fanshel, 1978; Wodarski et al., 1990). Receipt of special education services is also disproportionately high in foster care: An estimated 30–37% of foster children receive special education services, 3–4 times the rate for the general population (Goerge, Van Voorhis, Grant, Casey, & Robinson, 1992; Sawyer & Dubowitz, 1994). Moreover, foster children are disproportionately diagnosed with emotional disturbance as a condition for special education eligibility (Goerge et al., 1992; Parrish et al., 2001). School dropout rates are also very high among foster children. For example, Berry and Barth (1990) reported that 35–66% of foster children fail to complete high school, compared to 22% in the general population. In sum, given the high rates of academic difficulties and the increasing size of the foster population, improving these children's performance in school is an issue of public health importance.

SCHOOL READINESS AS A FOCUS OF PREVENTIVE INTERVENTIONS FOR FOSTER CHILDREN

From a prevention perspective, the preschool period is an ideal time to initiate programs to improve foster children's school outcomes. School readiness during the preschool years predicts kindergarten performance and is associated with academic achievement and behavior through adolescence and into adulthood (Entwisle & Alexander, 1999; Shonkoff & Phillips, 2000; Williamson et al., 1991). For instance, Kurdek and Sinclair (2000) found that school readiness measured at kindergarten entry significantly predicted academic outcomes between first and fifth grades. In a sample of high-risk children, Ensminger and Slusarcick (1992) found that academic performance in first grade was strongly associated with high school graduation, even when background factors were controlled. Further, Ensminger, Juon, and Fothergill (2002) found that boys with lower levels of school readiness were more likely to use cocaine as adults.

At present, little is known about the school readiness skills of foster children specifically. One study found that, in the fall of the kindergarten year, children in foster care had lower scores on social competence and self-regulatory skills and higher scores on self-reported loneliness than did their age- and SES-matched nonmaltreated peers who had never experienced foster care (Pears, Heywood, Takahasi, & Fisher, 2007). Thus, in terms of socioemotional skills, foster children were less prepared for school. Studies have shown that maltreated children in general have difficulties with academic skills and behavior in kindergarten (Keiley, Howe, Dodge, Bates, & Pettit, 2001; Rowe & Eckenrode, 1999). For example, Keiley et al. found that children who had histories of maltreatment prior to age 5 years were rated as having more externalizing and internalizing behaviors than their peers in kindergarten. Similarly, studies of children at risk for maltreatment and involvement in the child welfare system have found that these children are less prepared for school entry than their peers (Alexander & Entwistle, 1998). Thus, given the links between school readiness and later school success and the research suggesting that maltreated children and foster children might be particularly ill-prepared for school entry, interventions targeting school readiness in this population could help to prevent a number of later academic and psychosocial problems.

KEY COMPONENTS OF SCHOOL READINESS

Before discussing interventions aimed at improving school readiness in foster children, the skills and contextual factors that contribute to school readiness for children more generally should be specified. There has been debate on which specific skills are needed for school readiness (Meisels, 1999). School readiness interventions for the general population, however, typically focus on socioemotional readiness, emergent literacy, or both. These areas may be further subdivided into multiple components. There is also a large body of literature supporting the notion that caregiver involvement in schooling is crucial to early and lasting school success (Christenson, Rounds, & Gorney, 1992). For a more comprehensive review of various conceptualizations of school readiness, see Meisels (1999).

Socioemotional Readiness

Key areas of socioemotional readiness in childhood include the following: reciprocal social interaction (Bierman & Montminy, 1993; Coie et al., 1993; French, 1988; Howes, 1988; Ladd & Price, 1993; Odom, McConnell, & McEvoy, 1992), social problem-solving strategies (Bierman & Welsh, 1997; Odom et al., 1992; Welsh, Bierman, & Pope, 2000), and emotion recognition skills (Denham, McKinley, Couchoud, & Holt, 1990; Dunn & Hughes, 1998; Garner, 1996). Social competence is a powerful predictor of later academic achievement. For example, socially rejected children show poorer academic achievement and higher rates of grade retention, truancy, and dropout (Jimerson, Egeland, Sroufe, & Carlson, 2000; Kupersmidt & Coie, 1990; Murray & Greenberg, 2000; Wentzel, 1999). Moreover, children who are rejected by their peers in first grade continue to be rejected through middle school (Brendgen, Vitaro, Bukowski, & Doyle, 2001). Conversely, social competence is associated with a readiness to learn. For example, Coolahan, Fantuzzo, Mendez, and McDermott (2000) found that preschool children who engaged in positive peer play interactions exhibited more competence, motivation, attention, persistence, and positive attitudes toward learning than children with less positive interactions.

Emergent Literacy

Emergent literacy refers to the skills and knowledge that are considered to be precursors to reading and writing (Sulzby & Teale, 1991; Teale & Sulzby, 1986). The development of these skills is essential for successful reading outcomes (Lonigan, Burgess, & Anthony, 2000; Whitehurst & Lonigan, 1998). Such skills include the following: language, understanding of narrative, knowledge of the conventions of print, knowledge of letters, phonological awareness, and understanding of phoneme–grapheme correspondence (also known as alphabetic understanding).

Language-based competencies are strongly associated with academic and social success (Hart & Risley, 1995). Teachers overwhelmingly cite a "deficiency in language" as the greatest barrier to school readiness (Boyer, 1991). Because language delays appear to be pervasive among foster children (Stock & Fisher, 2006), this is a prime intervention target.

The ability to understand text and story narratives is central to reading instruction in elementary school settings (Bowman, Donovan, & Burns, 2000). Comprehension of story narratives requires an understanding of elements of narrative style, characters, dialogue, and sequencing of events (Bowman et al., 2000). Exposure to narrative, through access to books and reading time with adults, has been shown to improve children's emergent literacy skills (Neuman, 1999).

In addition to understanding narratives, book and print awareness are a child's first steps toward reading (Bowman et al., 2000). Literacy development is aided by an understanding of conventions of print (Whitehurst & Lonigan, 1998). Children with greater understanding of such conventions upon entry into first grade have better second-grade reading scores, even when vocabulary is controlled (Tumner, Herriman, & Nesdale, 1988).

Decoding printed words involves the ability to translate units of print into units of sound (Whitehurst & Lonigan, 1998). Children typically begin to recognize some printed alphabet letters and words in preschool (Bowman et al., 2000). Knowledge of letters upon school entry is one of the strongest predictors of short- and long-term reading outcomes (Schatschneider, Fletcher, Francis, Carlson, & Foorman, 2004; Stevenson & Newman, 1986).

Along with knowledge of letters, phonological awareness is an important predictor of later reading ability. Phonological awareness is the ability to hear and manipulate various sound structures of language at the word, syllable, and phoneme level (Whitehurst & Lonigan, 1998). Phonological awareness is strongly associated with reading outcomes (Adams, 1990) and is one of the best predictors of first- and second-grade reading outcomes (Schatschneider et al., 2004).

Phoneme–grapheme correspondence is the ability to understand the links between a letter's sound and its name (Honig, 1996; Whitehurst & Lonigan, 1998). This advanced emergent reading skill is a basic skill needed for conventional reading (Whitehurst & Lonigan, 1998). Better phoneme–grapheme knowledge in kindergarten predicts later reading outcomes (Schatschneider et al., 2004).

Caregiver Effects on School Readiness

A well-established research base supports the notion that caregiver involvement in preschool emergent literacy activities and in school activities is important for child outcomes (Christenson et al., 1992; Entwisle & Alexander, 1999; Pianta, Kraft-Sayre, Rimm-Kaufman, Gercke, & Higgins, 2001; Zill & Nord, 1994). Caregiver involvement has also been associated with higher grades, better attitudes toward schoolwork, increased prosocial behavior, greater participation in classroom learning activities, higher attendance rates, fewer special education placements, and fewer suspensions (Clark, 1993; Collins, Moles, & Cross, 1982; Comer & Haynes, 1991; Fehrmann, Keith, & Reimers, 1987; Lazar & Darlington, 1978). Furthermore, higher caregiver involvement is correlated with higher student achievement (Christenson, 1999). Grolnick and Slowiaczek (1994) conceptualized caregiver involvement as having three main components: behavioral (e.g., attending school open houses), cognitive-intellectual (e.g., exposing the child to books and museums), and personal (e.g., the child's belief that their caregiver cares about school). They found that behavioral involvement and cognitive-intellectual involvement related to children's school performance.

Another well-established evidence base demonstrates the importance of effective parenting skills on outcomes. Longitudinal research examining parenting and family interaction has provided strong evidence that the use of harsh and inconsistent discipline techniques, poor monitoring and supervision of the child, and low rates of encouragement for positive behavior are related to problematic outcomes, including difficulties in school in childhood and adolescence (Patterson & Fisher, 2002; Patterson, Reid, & Dishion, 1992; Patterson, Reid, & Eddy, 2002). Research on the stability of behavior problems suggests that such problems commonly begin at an early age in the context of parent–child relationships (Olweus, 1979, 1980; Patterson, 2002; Robins, 1978). Early failures in discipline, continued child noncompliance, and low levels of prosocial skills set the stage for negative reactions from care-givers and others that cause the child to be rejected and isolated. This further compounds compliance and discipline problems, causing a gradual escala-tion of coercive behaviors used by family members to control family interac-tions. Over time, the effects of family interaction patterns appear to generalize to school and other community settings. Thus, once these interac-tional patterns have been transmitted to the child, they predict subsequent problems from childhood into adulthood (Caspi, Elder, & Bem, 1987; Kaz-din, 1987; Robins, 1966; Walker, Shinn, O'Neill, & Ramsey, 1987).

Integrated Approaches

A growing evidence base supports the use of socioemotional (Olds et al., 1998; Peth-Pierce, 2000; Webster-Stratton, 1992) and emergent literacy (Whitehurst et al., 1988) interventions for the general population. There have also been a number of recent policy statements urging more holistic approaches to school readiness that combine these approaches (Bowman et al., 2000; Shonkoff & Phillips, 2000). Finally, a number of successful school readiness interventions, including Head Start, the Carolina Abece-darian Project, and the Chicago Parent–Child Centers (discussed below; Campbell, Ramey, Pungello, Sparling, & Miller-Johnson, 2002; Reynolds, Temple, & Ou, 2003; Zigler & Styfco, 1995), have also focused on promot-ing parent involvement or teaching effective parenting skills.

SCHOOL READINESS AND THE NEEDS
OF FOSTER CARE CHILDREN

The above section outlined the components of school readiness that might be key for any child entering school and might thus be important foci for interventions targeting school readiness. However, foster children might have particular areas of vulnerability due to the combined effects of early maltreat-ment and out-of-home placements that would necessitate more intensive intervention in specific areas. Two important components of school readiness in which foster children appear to show greater vulnerability than their peers are self-regulation and caregiver involvement in schooling.

Self-Regulation and School Readiness in Foster Children

The ability to control negative emotions and behaviors is vital to school success (McClelland, Morrison, & Holmes, 2000). Numerous aspects of emotional and behavioral regulation, including the abilities to pay attention, follow directions, and work independently, are strongly associated with kindergarten achievement (Cooper & Farran, 1988; Ladd, Birch, & Buhs, 1999; McClelland et al., 2000). Children who cannot control their behavior and who are disruptive are less likely to show independence in learning and are less likely to be perceived by kindergarten teachers and peers as good students. Further, these children tend to have negative relationships with teachers (Ladd et al., 1999). In longitudinal studies, negative child–teacher relationships in kindergarten predicted poor outcomes in child academic achievement and school behavior through middle school (Birch & Ladd, 1998; Hamre & Pianta, 2001; Ladd et al., 1999).

Foster children might have particular difficulties with self-regulation because of the effects of their maltreatment and placement histories on the brain systems underlying their self-regulatory skills. Research on animals and humans has documented the impact of early adversity on these neural systems (De Bellis et al., 1999; Glaser, 2000; Levine, Johnson, & Gonzalez, 1985; Sánchez, Ladd, & Plotsky, 2001; Schneider & Moore, 2000; Suomi, Mineka, & DeLizio, 1983). In particular, foster children might show alterations in the functioning of the hypothalamic pituitary axis, a system that is sensitive to stress (Bruce, Pears, Levine, & Fisher, 2007), and the prefrontal cortex, a system that controls their ability to inhibit impulses (Pears & Fisher, 2005). Such deficits might underlie problems with self-regulation that are seen in these children.

Caregiver Involvement and School Readiness in Foster Children

As is noted above, caregiver involvement in early literacy and in school is an important component of children's school success. Foster children are likely to be at a particular disadvantage in terms of caregiver involvement in school readiness and schooling. These children are likely to have experienced multiple transitions prior to reaching school age. Pears and Fisher (2005) showed that preschool children in foster care experienced an average of 3.47 transitions in their lifetime, each of which can interfere with caregiver involvement in emergent literacy prior to school or with caregiver involvement in school. A survey of foster children who were seniors in high school found that 65% reported that their caregivers had never attended a teacher conference, that more than 73% reported that their caregiver had never visited their class, and that more than 70% reported no caregiver history of volunteering at school (Blome, 1997).

Contextual Variables Specific to Foster Care Affecting School Readiness

Foster children's school readiness might also vary depending on the magnitude and timing of early maltreatment and placement histories. Maltreated children generally display poorer behavioral and academic functioning (Rogosch, Cicchetti, & Aber, 1995). Additionally, the type of maltreatment that a child has experienced might differentially affect school functioning (Trickett & McBride-Chang, 1995). For example, physically abused children have the most significant behavioral difficulties in school, whereas neglected children demonstrate the most significant academic delays (Eckenrode, Laird, & Doris, 1993; Kurtz, Gaudin, Wodarski, & Howing, 1993). Thus, perhaps interventions to promote school readiness in foster children would have differential effects depending on the type and severity of maltreatment.

Foster children's school readiness might also be adversely affected by their experiences with placement transitions. Because transitions between foster placements represent further separations and losses for children whose primary attachment relationship has been disrupted (Dozier, Albus, Fisher, & Sepulveda, 2002), they might impinge on normal social and cognitive development. Multiple transitions might also interfere with the development of emergent literacy skills, as children and caregivers might not have enough time to establish important routines. Characteristics of foster care placement history (e.g., length of time in placement and number of placements) have been related to behavior problems and severe delays in academic skills (Benbenishty & Oyserman, 1995; Cooper, Peterson, & Meier, 1987; Newton, Litrownik, & Landsverk, 2000; Zima et al., 2000).

Taken together, the research suggests that foster children might have specific vulnerabilities that place them at risk for difficulties in the transition to school. Thus, interventions that target the unique needs of foster children at this very early stage of academic life seem warranted. As is noted in the next section, however, very few interventions directly address these needs.

SCHOOL READINESS INTERVENTIONS FOR AT-RISK CHILDREN

Although school readiness in foster children appears to be a promising window for preventive intervention, no existing empirically validated programs are specifically focused on and tailored to the needs of foster children. The following programs were designed to address the needs of at-risk populations of children but have not been targeted to foster children directly. They are reviewed here because they have been shown to be effica-cious in promoting school readiness in children at risk for outcomes such as maltreatment and involvement in the child welfare system and thus could potentially benefit foster children. However, these programs may not consistently address the spectrum of emotional, behavioral, and skill-related needs demonstrated by this population.

In general, early childhood interventions with a focus on preparing chil-dren for school are part of an increasingly large number of preventive interventions being developed for youth across the United States. Studies of the outcomes of a number of these programs have shown short- and long-term academic benefits, including lower incidences of grade reten-tion, placement in special education, and disruptive classroom behavior and greater rates of high school graduation (Barnett, 1995; Lazar, Darling-ton, Murray, Royce, & Snapps, 1982; Schweinhart & Weikart, 1986). Longi-tudinal follow-up studies of the participants in a number of these programs have demonstrated benefits beyond school outcomes, including lower rates of teen pregnancy, delinquent behavior, and substance use, and higher rates of employment (Lazar et al., 1982; Schweinhart & Weikart, 1986). There are also long-term benefits to society in terms of economic savings. Good quality early childhood programs can save over $7.00 for every $1.00 spent as a result of increased literacy, college attendance, and employment, and decreased school dropout rates, welfare usage, and arrests (Schweinhart, Barnes, Weikart, Barnett, & Epstein, 1993).

Raver (2002) noted that, despite the promise of school readiness inter-ventions, few have been evaluated for effectiveness within the highest risk populations. However, there is a growing demand for evidence from experi-mental trials to support the efficacy of prevention interventions, particularly those targeted towards young children (Shonkoff & Phillips, 2000). In vali-dation research, the gold standard is the randomized efficacy trial, involving the comparison of two groups, a treatment group and a control group, to which participants have been randomly assigned. Such trials provide strong evidence because they rule out uncontrolled variables that might affect out-comes. However, randomized efficacy trials are costly and difficult to con-duct, and it is sometimes not feasible to assign participants to groups randomly. Thus, quasiexperimental designs are often used in efficacy research. Such designs involve the comparison of two groups who have not been randomly assigned to receive or not receive the intervention.

We present here a number of school readiness interventions that have been specifically targeted toward children at risk for poor school outcomes by virtue of low-income, poorly educated, and young families who might be involved in substance use or criminal activities. These are also risk factors for involvement with the child welfare system. Thus, the programs target the population from which foster children are most likely to come, although, as is noted above, they have not been specifically designed for foster children. The programs presented here all have been empirically validated through the use of randomized or quasiexperimental trials. They also feature integrated approaches to school readiness, meaning that they have combined foci on emergent literacy skills, socioemotional readiness, and caregiver involvement.

Head Start

Perhaps the most widely recognized early childhood education program is Head Start. The program is designed to foster healthy development in preschool-aged, low-income children through the provision of a range of services, including comprehensive health, educational, nutritional, socialization, and other developmental services promoting school readiness. Staff members coordinate services with community agencies to promote family wellness and economic stability through job training, mental health and social services, and literacy development for parents. Head Start legislation reflects the school readiness goals of the program. All children participating in a Head Start program are expected to achieve the following: develop phonemic, print, and number awareness; understand and use language to communicate for various purposes; understand and use increasingly complex and varied vocabulary; develop and demonstrate an appreciation of books; and, in the case of English language learners, progress toward acquiring the English language (National Head Start Association, 2005). Another distinguishing feature of the program is the coordination of health services to children and their families. Health services, including nutritional education, medical and dental screenings, immunizations, and necessary follow-up services increase children's ability to perform in school and decrease health problems that contribute to poor attendance in subsequent years (Smith, 2003).

Since its inception in 1965, Head Start has provided services to over 22 million low-income children and their families. Head Start children exhibit many of the key skills indicative of a successful transition to kindergarten and a readiness to learn (U.S. DHHS, 1998, 2001, 2005). For example, Head Start children exhibited significant gains in their vocabulary, early writing, and socioemotional skills while in the program; once in kindergarten, they exhibited significant growth in word knowledge, letter recognition, math skills, and writing skills relative to national averages, suggesting that they entered school ready to learn (U.S. DHHS, 2001). The benefits of the program appear to continue beyond the transition to school. For example, in first grade, Head Start children had significantly higher scores on achievement tests and were significantly less likely to have been retained a grade than a comparison group of non-Head Start attendees (Abelson, Zigler, & Deblasi, 1974; Currie & Thomas, 1995). Studies indicate that there is wide variation in the quality of individual Head Start programs and that these variations affect child outcomes (U.S. DHHS, 2001).

Chicago Parent–Child Center Program

Like Head Start, the Chicago Parent–Child Center (CPC) Program is a large-scale, federally funded program. Started in 1967, the program operates out of 24 centers. Participants have been followed since 1985, and outcomes have been reported through age 21 years. The program includes mandatory parental involvement and an educational intervention implemented from preschool through third grade, including self-contained centers at public elementary schools with specialist teachers, smaller classes, and direct instruction in many classrooms (Reynolds, 2000). Because this program is a large-scale public program, participants were not randomly assigned to intervention or nonintervention groups.

Results from quasiexperimental studies show that participants in the CPC programs showed greater success in school than their low-income peers who did not receive treatment. Children who participated in the CPC programs were less likely to be retained in a grade or placed in special education and showed higher school achievement (Reynolds, 2000). Children in this program also showed increased social skills with longer participation resulting in the most lasting effects (Fuerst & Fuerst, 1993; Reynolds, 2000). Rates of high school graduation were higher for children who received the CPC intervention, although only for females. Children in neighborhoods with the highest poverty levels experienced more significant outcomes than those in neighborhoods with less poverty (Reynolds, 2000).

Foster children participating in large-scale programs such as Head Start and the CPC, while not studied directly, would likely benefit from the emphasis on emergent literacy skills and increased caregiver involvement. Addressing their medical and mental health needs along with improving contextual family variables likely to impact healthy family functioning (e.g., employment, parent literacy, and substance use) is an important protective factor in increasing school readiness. As was previously discussed, however, foster children demonstrate deficits in self-regulation abilities that can negatively impact school success, and these programs do not target the development of these skills directly. As a result, there may be persistent needs among foster children that are left unaddressed even after successful participation in Head Start or CPC.

Carolina Abecedarian Project

In addition to large-scale, federally funded programs to promote school readiness, there have been a number of successful smaller-scale interventions for at-risk children. One of the earliest of these was the Carolina Abecedarian Project, which provided comprehensive and individualized education, health care, and family support through a developmental child day care setting (Ramey et al., 2000). The program created stimulus-rich and responsive early child care and home environments to promote school readiness and to prepare children for a successful transition into elementary school (Campbell et al., 2002; Ramey et al., 2000)

Treatment phases included a 5-year preschool phase (infancy to kindergarten) and a 3-year primary school phase. Children were randomly assigned to one of four groups: three treatment groups (one receiving both phases of the intervention, one receiving only the preschool phase, and one receiving only the primary school phase) and a no-treatment group. The preschool phase featured a full-day educational intervention in a child care setting in which cognition, language, and adaptive skills were emphasized. The primary school phase was designed to enhance parent involvement in school through the support of a homeschool resource teacher, home-based activities to enhance learning, and appropriate individualization of instruction to support unique needs.

One hundred and eleven children from low-income families participated in the project, 98% of whom were African-American. Significant and persistent cognitive and academic benefits were seen from early childhood through middle adolescence. Students who received the preschool phase were less likely to be placed in special education programs or to experience grade retention. Preschool treatment demonstrated a larger effect size on reading and mathematics scores than primary school treatment (Ramey et al., 2000). Follow-up assessments at age 21 years indicated that the children who participated in the preschool phase continued to have higher scores on tests of general cognitive ability, math, and reading, attained more years of education, were more likely to attend 4-year colleges, and were less likely to become teen parents than children who received no intervention (Campbell et al., 2002).

High/Scope Perry Preschool Project

The High/Scope Perry Preschool Project, designed for low-income, developmentally delayed 3-year-olds (Schweinhart & Weikart, 1997), was aimed to improve the children's cognitive and social development via daily attendance in an enriched preschool program and weekly home visits by the preschool teachers for 2 years. Participants showed increased early academic achievement in comparison to their peers and, in the long term, showed higher grade completion (Berruta-Clement, Schweinhart, Barnett, Epstein, & Weikart, 1984; Schweinhart & Weikart, 1980). Additionally, the program showed long-term psychosocial consequences. By age 27 years, children who had completed the program had significantly higher monthly earnings, significantly higher percentages of home and second-car ownership, lower rates of dependence on social services, and fewer incidents of arrest, including arrests for drug production and dealing (Schweinhart et al., 1993). This is one of the few programs for which cost effectiveness research to calculate the governmental savings per child (e.g., savings on resources such as public assistance, special education services, and other mental health services) is available: an estimated $25,437 per child would be saved by age 27 years (Karoly et al., 1998).

Several elements of these two long-term intervention programs could be highly beneficial to foster children and for children at risk for entry into foster care: (a) Long-term involvement beginning in infancy or toddlerhood could prevent the escalation of child- and parent-related problems that could result in removal of the child from the biological family; (b) individualization of education and coordination of services would allow service providers to consistently address the unique needs of the participating children; (c) promoting caregiver involvement would serve as a protective factor for foster children who, as is previously discussed, typically experience low caregiver involvement in school-related activities; and (d) consistent program involvement across developmental periods would bring continuity and advocacy for participating foster children over multiple transitions. These potential benefits, however, were not empirically validated with foster children in the efficacy trials. This remains to be done in future school readiness interventions. Additionally, participation in such long-term programs as the Carolina Abecedarian Project and the High/ Scope Perry Preschool Project might be difficult, as foster children experience multiple caregivers who might demonstrate varying willingness to participate in services.

Home Instruction Program for Preschool Youngsters

The programs discussed previously all provided out-of-home care experiences to the participants. The Home Instruction Program for Preschool Youngsters (HIPPY) program provides evidence that the provision of in-home, parent-directed services can also significantly improve children's school readiness. When compared to children from higher income families, children from low-income families have less access to high-quality educational materials and experiences, and their parents tend to be less involved in their schooling experiences (Evans, 2004). The HIPPY focuses on increasing the likelihood of low-income parents' participation in their child's schooling by helping parents to provide daily in-home educational enrichment for their 4- and 5-year-old children. Activities focus on language development, sensory and perceptual discrimination, and problem-solving skills (Baker & Piotrkowski, 1996). Bimonthly home visits by para-professionals and bimonthly group meetings led by a professional program coordinator make up the core elements of parent training (Baker & Piotrkowski, 1996).

Quasiexperimental studies have examined the HIPPY's impact on children's cognitive skills, the home educational environment, and school performance. Participants in the HIPPY were less likely to be retained a grade and showed higher classroom adaptation skills and scores on reading measures (Baker & Piotrkowski, 1996). The intervention also appears to have long-term benefits. Children who received the intervention had fewer school suspensions and better grades, classroom behavior, and achievement test scores in third and sixth grades than their peers who had not received the intervention (Bradley & Gilkey, 2002). Though beneficial for increasing caregiver involvement and improving emergent literacy skills, the HIPPY does not address socioemotional development, which is a key deficit among foster children that is likely to contribute to difficulties in transitioning to school. Thus, like some of the programs discussed above, this program does not target all the areas of vulnerability that are likely to negatively impinge upon school readiness in foster children.

TARGETING SCHOOL READINESS IN FOSTER CHILDREN

The success of the school readiness programs reviewed above suggests that such intervention efforts can not only improve children's school outcomes but also offer long-term benefits to the individuals and to society. Whereas these programs were targeted toward children who might have been at risk for child welfare involvement, none were specifically designed for foster children. As is noted above, foster children evidence specific vulnerabilities that might interfere with school readiness and that should be targeted by interventions with this population.

These vulnerabilities include impairments in self-regulatory abilities that might place children at risk for academic failure, problems in social relations, and disruptive behaviors in school. However, Blair (2002) noted that many school readiness interventions (including those detailed above) lack a specific focus on increasing self-regulatory skills. Given foster children's particular deficits in self-regulation, interventions to address school readiness in this population should contain particular emphasis on promoting these skills.

Also noted above, foster children might be more likely to experience poor caregiver involvement in school due to multiple transitions between different caregivers. Given the importance of caregiver involvement to school success, any program to enhance school readiness in foster children should target caregiver involvement in preparing children for school entry and in kindergarten once the child is enrolled. Additionally, such a program would need to provide contingencies for any transitions that the child might make while in the program, such as providing materials and support to the new caregivers.

An additional potential risk factor for poor caregiver involvement in school is the likelihood of foster children showing mental health problems, many of which involve disruptive behavior (Trupin et al., 1993). Such behavior can increase the likelihood of a placement disruption and another transition for the child. Programs that teach foster caregivers behavior management skills and that offer support and consultation around behavioral problems have been shown to decrease behavior problems in foster children (Chamberlain & Reid, 1998; Fisher, Gunnar, Chamberlain, & Reid, 2000) and to reduce placement disruptions (Fisher, Burraston, & Pears, 2005). Thus, another important component of an intervention designed to improve school readiness in foster children would be to support caregivers in using empirically validated behavior management techniques.

Although many of the programs outlined above feature one or more of the components important to a school readiness intervention targeted towards foster children, none feature all of the components. No research currently exists on the efficacy of these programs specifically for children in foster care. Programs that specifically address all the school readiness needs of foster children might have a better chance for success with this population.

The Kids in Transition to School Program

The recently developed Kids in Transition to School (KITS) Program (Pears, Fisher, & Bronz, 2007) is an intervention specifically designed to enhance foster children's psychosocial and academic school readiness. This program focuses not only on the development of emergent literacy and socioemotional skills but also on the promotion of self-regulation skills and caregiver involvement. The KITS Program consists of four components: (a) a 28-session therapeutic play group that begins in the summer before kindergarten and is designed to facilitate the development of self-regulatory behaviors, social skills, and emergent literacy skills via highly structured environments and activities; (b) a 12-session, bimonthly caregiver information and support group to provide information and skills training for increasing caregiver involvement in the child's school readiness and subsequent schooling and to provide instruction in techniques for effective parenting; (c) developmental assessment and referral to identify children with developmental delays who might need more intensive intervention services in addition to the KITS intervention; and (d) home- and school-based behavioral consultation as needed.

The play group curriculum addresses socioemotional skills (emotional and behavioral regulation and social competence) and emergent literacy skills. Additionally, there is a strong focus on activities that teach children to develop and strengthen self-regulatory skills. Opportunities to practice inhibitory control and maintaining attentional focus (two important aspects of self-regulation) are embedded across activities, and the repeated exposure to a classroom situation and to a group of peers in a school-like setting help to desensitize the child to this source of social stress at school. The KITS caregiver curriculum focuses on teaching caregivers skills to prepare their foster children for school and to support their children's success in school. Additionally, the group facilitators provide behavioral consultation to help caregivers address problems using the behavioral techniques employed in the play groups.

As is noted above, when working with foster children, it is necessary to address the issue of placement transitions. In the KITS Program, if a child transitions to a new caregiver during the intervention or during kindergarten, a clinical staff member visits the home to provide the information and support group curriculum. Additionally, because such transitions frequently involve school changes, the staff facilitates parent–teacher meetings (as needed) to introduce the child and caregivers to the teacher and to address any behavioral and academic difficulties.

Preliminary results from a pilot study of the KITS program, a small-scale randomized efficacy trial conducted with 24 participants, supported the feasibility of offering the KITS program to foster children and their caregivers. Of the children participating, 83% completed all phases of the assessment. The majority of the children in the intervention group attended 80% or more of the play groups. Behaviorally, according to caregiver and observer reports, the intervention children were less emotionally labile after they had completed the play groups, suggesting that they had improved their emotion regulation skills (Pears, Fisher, & Bronz, 2007). That caregivers and observers both noted these changes is particularly encouraging. Additionally, the children who received the intervention showed gains in their social competence as evaluated by their caregivers (Pears, Fisher, & Bronz., 2007). The promising results from the pilot study have led to the inception of a large-scale efficacy trial involving the recruitment of 200 children over a 4-year period at the Oregon Social Learning Center (currently underway).

CONCLUSIONS

Foster children fare much worse than their peers on many indicators of school performance (e.g., academic achievement, social competence, high school completion rates, and need for special education services). From a prevention perspective, efforts must be put forth to improve foster children's school readiness, thereby decreasing the likelihood of later academic and social difficulties. The success of a number of early intervention programs in improving the school readiness and long-term outcomes of at-risk children provides further evidence that systematic programming to enhance foster children's readiness for kindergarten entry is warranted. However, foster children might have particular vulnerabilities due to their histories of maltreatment and out-of-home placement that should be specifically targeted by such interventions: deficits in self-regulatory skills and difficulties in caregiver involvement due to multiple caregiver transitions. Efforts to create programs to improve foster children's school readiness skills should include elements that address the unique needs of these children. Preliminary evidence from the KITS program has shown promising results. Future efforts should focus on testing the efficacy of programs designed specifically for these children. If programs to enhance school readiness in foster children prove to be effective, they have the potential to deflect these children from trajectories of school failure and poor social relations and could positively impact their long-term mental health and psychosocial functioning.

REFERENCES

Abelson, W. D., Zigler, E., & Deblasi, C. L. (1974). Effects of a four-year follow-through program on economically disadvantaged children. *Journal of Educational Psychology, 66*, 756–771.

Adams, M. J. (1990). *Beginning to read: Thinking and learning about print.* Cambridge, MA: MIT Press.

Alexander, K. L., & Entwisle, D. R. (1998). Achievement in the first 2 years of school: Patterns and processes. *Monographs of the Society for Research in Child Development, 53*(2, Serial No. 218).

Baker, A. J., & Piotrkowski, C. S. (1996) *Parent and children through the school years: The effects of the Home Instruction Program for Preschool Youngsters* (Report No. UD031430). Los Altos, CA: David and Lucile Packard Foundation.

Barbell, L. (1997). *Foster care today: A briefing paper.* Washington, DC: Child Welfare League of America.

Barnett, W. S. (1995). Long-term effects of early childhood programs on cognitive and school outcomes, *The Future of Children, 5,* 25–50.

Benbenishty, R., & Oyserman, D. (1995). Children in foster care: Their present situation and plans for their future. *International Social Work, 38,* 117–131.

Berruta-Clement, J. R., Schweinhart, L. J., Barnett, W. S., Epstein, A. S., & Weikart, D. P. (1984). Changed lives: The effects of the Perry Preschool Program on youths through age 19. *Monographs of the High/Scope Educational Research Foundation, 8.*

Berry, M., & Barth, R. P. (1990). A study of disrupted adoptive placements of adolescents. *Child Welfare, 69,* 209–225.

Bierman, K. L., & Montminy, H. P. (1993). Developmental issues in social-skills assessment and intervention with children and adolescents. *Behavior Modification, 17,* 229–254.

Bierman, K. L., & Welsh, J. A. (1997). Social relationship deficits. In E. J. Mash & L. G. Terdal (Eds.), *Assessment of childhood disorders* (3rd ed., pp. 328–365). New York: Guilford Press.

Birch, S. H., & Ladd, G. W. (1998). Children's interpersonal behaviors and the teacher–child relationship. *Developmental Psychology, 34,* 934–946.

Blair, C. (2002). School readiness: Integrating cognition and emotion in a neurobiological conceptualization of children's functioning at school entry. *American Psychologist, 57,* 111–127.

Blome, W. W. (1997). What happens to foster kids: Educational experiences of a random sample of foster care youth and a matched group of non-foster care youth. *Child and Adolescent Social Work Journal, 14,* 41–53.

Bowman, B. T., Donovan, M. S., & Burns, M. S. (Eds.). (2000). *Eager to learn: Educating our preschoolers.* Washington DC: National Academy Press.

Boyer, A. W. (1991). Improving the expository paragraph writing of learning-disabled elementary school students using small group strategies instruction and word processing (Doctoral dissertation, University of Kentucky). *Dissertation Abstracts International, 52,* 129–130.

Bradley, R. H., & Gilkey, B. (2002). The impact of the Home Instructional Program for Preschool Youngsters (HIPPY) on school performance in 3rd and 6th grades. *Early Education and Development, 13,* 301–311.

Brendgen, M., Vitaro, F., Bukowski, W. M., & Doyle, A. B. (2001). Developmental profiles of peer social preference over the course of elementary school: Associations with trajectories of externalizing and internalizing behavior. *Developmental Psychology, 37,* 308–320.

Bruce, J., Pears, K. C., Levine, S, & Fisher, P. A. (2007). *Morning cortisol levels in preschool-aged foster children: Differential effects of maltreatment type.* Manuscript submitted for publication.

Campbell, F. A., Ramey, C. T., Pungello, E., Sparling, J., & Miller-Johnson, S. (2002). Early childhood education: Young adult outcomes from the Abecedarian Project. *Applied Developmental Science, 6,* 42–57.

Caspi, A., Elder, G. H., & Bem, D. J. (1987). Moving against the world: Life-course patterns of explosive children. *Developmental Psychology, 23,* 308–313.

Chamberlain, P., & Reid, J. (1998). Comparison of two community alternatives to incarceration for chronic juvenile offenders. *Journal of Consulting and Clinical Psychology, 6,* 624–633.

Christenson, S. L. (1999) Families and schools. In R. C. Pianta & M. J. Cox (Eds.), *The transition to kindergarten* (pp. 143–177). Baltimore, MD: Paul H. Brookes.

Christenson, S. L., Rounds, T., & Gorney, D. (1992). Family factors and student achievement: An avenue to increase students' success. *School Psychology Quarterly, 7,* 178–206.

Clark, R. M. (1993). Homework-focused parenting practices that positively affect student achievement. In N. F. Chavkin (Ed.), *Families and schools in a pluralistic society* (pp. 85–105). Albany, NY: State University of New York Press.

Coie, J. D., Watt, N. F., West, S. G., Hawkins, J. D., Asarnow, J. R., Markman, H. J., et al. (1993). The science of prevention: A conceptual framework and some directions for a national research program. *American Psychologist, 48,* 1013–1022.

Collins, C. H., Moles, O., & Cross, M. (1982). *The home-school connection: Selected partnership programs in large cities.* Boston: Institute for Responsive Education.

Comer, J. P., & Haynes, N. M. (1991). Parent involvement in schools: An ecological approach. *The Elementary School Journal, 91,* 271–337.

Coolahan, K., Fantuzzo, J., Mendez, J., & McDermott, P. (2000). Preschool peer interactions and readiness to learn: Relationships between classroom peer play and learning behaviors and conduct. *Journal of Educational Psychology, 92,* 458–465.

Cooper, C. S., Peterson, N. L., & Meier, J. H. (1987). Variables associated with disrupted placement in a select sample of abused and neglected children. *Child Abuse and Neglect, 11,* 75–86.

Cooper, D. H., & Farran, D. C. (1988). Behavioral risk factors in kindergarten. *Early Childhood Research Quarterly, 3,* 1–19.

Currie, J., & Thomas, D. (1995). Does Head Start make a difference? *American Economic Review, 85,* 341–346.

De Bellis, M. D., Baum, A. S., Birmaher, B., Keshavan, M. S., Eccard, C. H., Boring, A. M., et al. (1999). A. E. Bennett Research Award: Developmental traumatology: Part I: Biological stress systems. *Biological Psychiatry, 45,* 1259–1270.

Denham, S. A., McKinley, M., Couchoud, E. A., & Holt, R. (1990). Emotional and behavioral predictors of preschool peer ratings. *Child Development, 61,* 1145–1152.

Dozier, M., Albus, K., Fisher, P. A., & Sepulveda, S. (2002). Interventions for foster parents: Implications for developmental theory. *Development and Psychopathology, 14,* 843–860.

Dunn, J., & Hughes, C. (1998). Young children's understanding of emotions within close relationships. *Cognition and Emotion, 12,* 171–190.

Eckenrode, J., Laird, M., & Doris, J. (1993). School performance and disciplinary problems among abused and neglected children. *Developmental Psychology, 29,* 53–62.

Ensminger, M. E., Juon, H. S., & Fothergill, K. E. (2002). Childhood and adolescent antecedents of substance use in adulthood. *Addiction, 97,* 833–844.

Ensminger, M. E., & Slusarcick, A. L. (1992). Paths to high school graduation or drop out: A longitudinal study of a first-grade cohort. *Sociology of Education, 65,* 95–113.

Entwisle, D. R., & Alexander, K. L. (1999). Early schooling and social stratification. In R. C. Pianta & M. J. Cox (Eds.), *The transition to kindergarten* (pp. 13–38). Baltimore, MD: Paul H. Brookes.

Evans, G. W. (2004). The environment of childhood poverty, *American Psychologist, 59,* 77–92.

Fanshel, D. (1978). Historic themes and landmarks in social-welfare research. *Child Welfare, 57,* 455–456.

Fehrmann, P. G., Keith, T. Z., & Reimers, T. M. (1987). Home influences on school learning: Direct and indirect effects of parent involvement on high school grades. *Journal of Educational Research, 80,* 330–337.

Fisher, P. A., Burraston, B., & Pears, K. (2005). The Early Intervention Foster Care Program: Permanent placement outcomes from a randomized trial. *Child Maltreatment, 10,* 61–71.

Fisher, P. A., Gunnar, M. R., Chamberlain, P., & Reid, J. B. (2000). Preventive intervention for maltreated preschool children: Impact on children's behavior, neuroendocrine activity, and foster parent functioning. *Journal of the American Academy of Child and Adolescent Psychiatry, 39,* 1356–1364.

Frankenburg, W. K., Dodds, J., Archer, P., Shapiro, H., & Bresnick, B. (1992). *The DENVER II training manual.* Denver, CO: Denver Developmental Materials.

French, D. C. (1988). Heterogeneity of peer rejected boys: Aggressive and nonaggressive subtypes. *Child Development, 59,* 976–985.

Fuerst, J. S., & Fuerst D. (1993). Chicago experience with an early childhood program: The special case of the Child Parent Center Program. *Educational Research, 35,* 237–253.

Garner, P. (1996). The relations of emotional role-taking, affective/moral attributions, and emotional display rule knowledge to low-income school-age children's social competence. *Journal of Applied Developmental Psychology, 17,* 19–36.

Glaser, D. (2000). Child abuse and neglect and the brain—A review. *Journal of Child Psychology and Psychiatry and Allied Disciplines, 41,* 97–116.

Goerge, R. M., Van Voorhis, J., Grant, S., Casey, K., & Robinson, M. (1992). Special-education experiences of foster children: An empirical study. *Child Welfare, 71,* 419–437.

Grolnick, W. S., & Slowiaczek, M. L. (1994). Parents' involvement in children's schooling: A multidimensional conceptualization and motivational model. *Child Development, 65,* 237–252.

Gutman, L. M., Sameroff, A. J., & Cole, R. (2003). Academic growth curve trajectories from 1st grade to 12th grade: Effects of multiple social risk factors and preschool child factors. *Developmental Psychology, 39,* 777–790.

Hamre, B. K., & Pianta, R. C. (2001). Early teacher–child relationships and the trajectory of children's outcomes through eighth grade. *Child Development, 72,* 625–638.

Hart, B., & Risley, T. R. (1995). *Meaningful differences in the everyday experience of young American children.* Baltimore, MD: Paul H. Brookes.

Honig, B. (1996). *Teaching our children to read: The role of skills in a comprehensible reading program.* Thousand Oaks, CA: Corwin Press.

Horwitz, S. M., Simms, M. D., & Farrington, R. (1994). Impact of developmental problems on young children's exits from foster care. *Journal of Developmental and Behavioral Pediatrics, 15,* 105–110.

Howes, C. (1988). Abused and neglected children with their peers. In G. T. Hotaling & D. Finkelhor (Eds.), *Family abuse and its consequences: New directions in research* (pp. 99–108). Newbury Park, CA: Sage.

Jimerson, S. R., Egeland, B., Sroufe, A., & Carlson, B. (2000). A prospective longitudinal study of high school dropouts examining multiple predictors across development. *Journal of School Psychology, 38,* 525–549.

Karoly, L. A., Greenwood, P. W., Everingham, S. S., Hoube, J., Kilburn, M. R., Rydell, C. P., et al. (1998). *Investing in our children: What we know and don't know about the costs and benefits of early childhood interventions.* Pittsburgh, PA: RAND.

Kazdin, A. E. (1987). Treatment of antisocial behavior in children: Current status and future directions. *Psychological Bulletin, 102,* 187–203.

Keiley, M. K., Howe, T. R., Dodge, K. A., Bates, J. E., & Pettit, G. S. (2001). The timing of child physical maltreatment: A cross-domain growth analysis of impact on adolescent externalizing and internalizing problems. *Development and Psychopathology, 13,* 891–912.

Kupersmidt, J. B., & Coie, J. D. (1990). Preadolescent peer status, aggression, and school adjustment as predictors of externalizing problems in adolescence. *Child Development, 61,* 1350–1362.

Kurdek, L. A., & Sinclair, R. J. (2000). Psychological, family, and peer predictors of academic outcomes in first- through fifth-grade children. *Journal of Educational Psychology, 92,* 449–457.

Kurtz, P. D., Gaudin, J. M., Wodarski, J. S., & Howing, P. T. (1993). Maltreatment and the school-aged child: School performance consequences. *Child Abuse and Neglect, 17,* 581–589.

Ladd, G. W., Birch, S. H., & Buhs, E. S. (1999). Children's social and scholastic lives in kindergarten: Related spheres of influence? *Child Development, 70,* 1373–1400.

Ladd, G. W., & Price, J. M. (1993). Playstyles of peer-accepted and peer-rejected children on the playground. In C. H. Hart (Ed.), *Children on playgrounds: Research perspectives and applications* (pp. 130–161). Albany, NY: State University of New York Press.

Landsverk, J. A., Davis, I., Ganger, W., Newton, R., & Johnson, I. (1996). Impact of child psychosocial functioning on reunification from out-of-home care. *Children and Youth Services Review, 18,* 447–462.

Lazar, I., & Darlington, R. B. (1978). *Summary: Lasting effects after preschool.* Ithaca, NY: Cornell University Consortium for Longitudinal Studies.

Lazar, I., Darlington, R. B., Murray, H., Royce, J., & Snapps, A. (1982). Lasting effects of early education: A report from the consortium for longitudinal studies. *Monographs of the Society for Research in Child Development, 47*(2–3, Serial No. 195).

Levine, S., Johnson, D. F., & Gonzalez, C. A. (1985). Behavioral and hormonal responses to separation in infant rhesus monkeys and mothers. *Behavioral Neuroscience, 99*, 399–410.

Lonigan, C. J., Burgess, S. R., & Anthony, J. L. (2000). Development of emergent literacy and early reading skills in preschool children: Evidence from a latent variable longitudinal study. *Developmental Psychology, 36*, 596–613.

McClelland, M. M., Morrison, F. J., & Holmes, D. L. (2000). Children at risk for early academic problems: The role of learning-related social skills. *Early Childhood Research Quarterly, 15*, 307–329.

Meisels, S. J. (1999). Assessing readiness. In R. C. Pianta & M. J. Cox (Eds.), *The transition to kindergarten* (pp. 39–66). Baltimore, MD: Paul H. Brookes.

Murray, C., & Greenberg, M. T. (2000). Children's relationship with teachers and bonds with school: An investigation of patterns and correlates in middle childhood. *Journal of School Psychology, 38*, 423–445.

National Head Start Association. (2005). *Head Start quality, performance, and outcome: The real story.* Retrieved August 3, 2006, from http://www.nhsa.org/research/research_position_realstory.htm

Neuman, S. B. (1999). Books make a difference: A study of access to literacy. *Reading Research Quarterly, 34*, 286–311.

Newton, R. R., Litrownik, A. J., & Landsverk, J. A. (2000). Children and youth in foster care: Disentangling the relationship between problem behaviors and number of placements. *Child Abuse and Neglect, 24*, 1363–1374.

Odom, S. L., McConnell, S. R., & McEvoy, M. A. (1992). Peer-related social competence and its significance for young children with disabilities. In S. L. Odom, S. R. McConnell, & M. A. McEvoy (Eds.), *Social competence of young children with disabilities* (pp. 3–35). Baltimore, MD: Paul H. Brookes.

Olds, D., Henderson, C. R., Jr., Cole, R., Eckenrode, J., Kitzman, H., Luckey, D., et al. (1998). Long-term effects of nurse home visitation on children's criminal and antisocial behavior: 15-year follow up of a randomized controlled trial. *Journal of the American Medical Association, 280*, 1238–1244.

Olweus, D. (1979). Stability of aggressive reaction patterns in males: A review. *Psychological Bulletin, 86*, 852–875.

Olweus, D. (1980). The consistency issue in personality psychology revisited—with special reference to aggression. *British Journal of Social and Clinical Psychology, 19*, 377–390.

Parrish, T., Delano, C., Dixon, D., Webster, D., Berrick, J. D., & Bolus, S. (2001). *Education of foster group home children, whose responsibility is it?: Study of the educational placement of children residing in group homes.* Palo Alto, CA: American Institutes of Research.

Patterson, G. R. (2002). The early developmental of coercive family process. In J. B. Reid, G. R. Patterson, & J. Snyder (Eds.), *Antisocial behavior in children and adolescents: A developmental analysis and model for intervention* (pp. 25–44). Washington, DC: American Psychological Association.

Patterson, G. R., & Fisher, P. A. (2002). Recent developments in our understanding of parenting: Bi-directional effects, causal models, and the search for parsimony. In M. Bornstein (Ed.), *Handbook of parenting: Vol. 5 Practical and applied parenting* (2nd ed., pp. 59–88). Mahwah, NJ: Erlbaum.

Patterson, G. R., Reid, J. B., & Dishion, T. J. (1992). *A social learning approach. IV. Antisocial boys.* Eugene, OR: Castalia.

Patterson, G. R., Reid, J. B., & Eddy, J. M. (2002). A brief history of the Oregon Model. In J. B. Reid, G. R. Patterson, & J. Snyder (Eds.), *Antisocial behavior in children and adolescents: A developmental analysis and model for intervention* (pp. 3–21). Washington, DC: American Psychological Association.

Pears, K., & Fisher, P. A. (2005). Developmental, cognitive, and neuropsychological functioning in preschool-aged foster children: Associations with prior maltreatment and placement history. *Journal of Developmental and Behavioral Pediatrics, 26,* 112–122.

Pears, K. C., Fisher, P. A., & Bronz, K. D. (2007). *Improving school readiness in foster children: A pilot randomized efficacy trial of a preventive intervention.* Manuscript submitted for publication.

Pears, K. C., Heywood, C. V., Takahashi, A., & Fisher, P. (2007). *School readiness in maltreated foster children.* Manuscript submitted for publication.

Peth-Pierce, R. (2000). *A good beginning: Sending America's children to school with the social and emotional competence they need to succeed.* Bethesda, MD: The Child and Mental Health Foundations and Agencies Network.

Pianta, R. C., Kraft-Sayre, M., Rimm-Kaufman, S., Gercke, N., & Higgins, T. (2001). Collaboration in building partnerships between families and schools: The National Center for Early Development and Learning's Kindergarten Transition Intervention. *Early Childhood Research Quarterly, 16,* 117–132.

Pilowsky, D. (1995). Psychopathology among children placed in family foster care. *Psychiatric Services, 46,* 906–910.

Ramey, C. T., Campbell, F. A., Burchinal, M., Skinner, M. L., Gardner, D. M., & Ramey, S. L. (2000). Persistent effects of early childhood education on high-risk children and their mothers. *Applied Developmental Science, 4,* 2–14.

Raver, C. C. (2002). Emotions matter: Making the case for the role of young children's emotional development for early school readiness. *Social Policy Report: Giving Child and Youth Development Knowledge Away, 16*(3), 3–18.

Reynolds, A. J. (2000). *Success in early intervention: The Chicago Child–Parent Centers.* Lincoln, NE: University of Nebraska Press.

Reynolds, A. J., Temple, J. A., & Ou, S. (2003). School-based early intervention and child well-being in the Chicago Longitudinal Study. *Child Welfare, 82,* 633–656.

Robins, L. N. (1966). *Deviant children grown up: A sociological and psychiatric study of sociopathic personality.* Baltimore: Williams & Wilkins.

Robins, L. N. (1978). Sturdy childhood predictors of adult antisocial behavior: Replications from longitudinal studies. *Psychological Medicine, 8,* 611–622.

Rogosch, F. A., Cicchetti, D., & Aber, J. L. (1995). The role of child maltreatment in early deviations in cognitive and affective processing abilities and later peer relationship problems. *Development and Psychopathology, 7,* 591–609.

Rowe, E., & Eckenrode, J. (1999). The timing of academic difficulties among maltreated and nonmaltreated children. *Child Abuse and Neglect, 23,* 813–832.

Sánchez, M. M., Ladd, C. O., & Plotsky, P. M. (2001). Early adverse experience as a developmental risk factor for later psychopathology: Evidence from rodent and primate models. *Development and Psychopathology, 13,* 419–449.

Sawyer, R. J., & Dubowitz, H. (1994). School performance of children in kinship care. *Child Abuse and Neglect, 18,* 587–597.

Schatschneider, C., Fletcher, J. M., Francis, D. J., Carlson, C. D., & Foorman, B. R. (2004). Kindergarten prediction of reading skills: A longitudinal comparative analysis. *Journal of Educational Psychology, 96,* 265–282.

Schneider, M. L., & Moore, C. F. (2000). Effect of prenatal stress on development: A nonhuman primate model. In C. A. Nelson (Ed.), *The Minnesota Symposia on Child Psychology: The effects of early adversity on neurobehavioral development* (Vol. 31, pp. 201–244). Mahwah, NJ: Erlbaum.

Schweinhart, L. J., Barnes, H. V., Weikart, D. P., Barnett, W. S., & Epstein, A. S. (1993). Significant benefits: The High/Scope Perry Preschool Study through age 27. *Monographs of the High/Scope Educational Research Foundation, 7.*

Schweinhart, L. J., & Weikart, D. P. (1980). Young children grow up: The effects of the Perry Preschool Study through age 15. *Monographs of the High/Scope Educational Research Foundation, 7.*

Schweinhart, L. J., & Weikart, D. P. (1986). Early childhood development programs: A public investment opportunity. *Educational Leadership, 44,* 4–12.

Schweinhart, L. J., & Weikart, D. P. (1997). The High/Scope Preschool Curriculum Comparison Study through age 23. *Early Child Research Quarterly, 12,* 117–143.

Shonkoff, J. P., & Phillips, D. A. (Eds.). (2000). *From neurons to neighborhoods: The science of early childhood development.* Washington, DC: National Academy Press.

Smith, A. (2003). *Position paper: A look at Head Start's health services and their value to our nation's poorest children.* Alexandria, VA: National Head Start Association.

Stevenson, H. W., & Newman, R. S. (1986). Long-term prediction of achievement and attitudes in mathematics and reading. *Child Development, 57,* 646–659.

Stock, C. D., & Fisher, P. A. (2006). Language delays among foster children: Implications for policy and practice. *Child Welfare, 85,* 445–461.

Sulzby, E., & Teale, W. (1991). Emergent literacy. In R. Barr, M. Kamil, P. Mosenthal, & P. D. Person. (Eds.), *Handbook of reading research* (Vol. 2, pp. 727–758). New York: Longman.

Suomi, S. J., Mineka, S., & DeLizio, R. D. (1983). Short- and long-term effects of repetitive mother–infant separations on social development in rhesus monkeys. *Developmental Psychology, 19,* 770–786.

Teale, W. H., & Sulzby, E. (Eds.). (1986). *Emergent literacy: Writing and reading.* Norwood, NJ: Ablex.

Trickett, P. K., & McBride-Chang, C. (1995). The developmental impact of different forms of child abuse and neglect. *Developmental Review, 15,* 311–337.

Trupin, E. W., Tarico, V. S., Low, B., Jennelka, R., & McClellan, J. (1993). Children on child protective service caseloads: Prevalence and nature of serious emotional disturbance. *Child Abuse and Neglect, 17,* 345–355.

Tumner, W. E., Herriman, M. L., & Nesdale, A. R. (1988). Metalinguistic abilities and beginning reading. *Reading Research Quarterly, 23,* 134–158.

U.S. Department of Health and Human Services (U.S. DHHS). (1998). *Head Start program performance measures: Second progress report.* Washington, DC: Author.

U.S. Department of Health and Human Services (U.S. DHHS). (2001). *Head Start FACES: Longitudinal findings on program performance: Third progress report.* Washington, DC: Author.

U.S. Department of Health and Human Services (U.S. DHHS). (2004). *The AFCARS Report: Preliminary FY 2002 Estimates as of August 2004.* Retrieved August 3, 2006, from http://www.acf.hhs.gov/programs/cb/stats_research/afcars/tar/report9.htm

U.S. Department of Health and Human Services (U.S. DHHS). (2005). *Head Start impact study: First year findings.* Washington, DC: Author

Walker, H. M., Shinn, M. R., O'Neill, R. E., & Ramsey, E. (1987). A longitudinal assessment of the development of antisocial behavior in boys: Rationale, methodology, and first-year results. *RASE: Remedial and Special Education, 8,* 7–16.

Webster-Stratton, C. (1992). *The incredible years: A trouble-shooting guide for parents of children aged 3–8.* Toronto, Ontario: Umbrella Press.

Welsh, J. A., Bierman, K., & Pope, A. W. (2000). Play assessment of peer interaction in children. In K. Gitlin-Weiner & A. Sandgrund (Eds.), *Play diagnosis and assessment* (2nd ed., pp. 517–543). New York: Wiley.

Wentzel, K. R. (1999). Social-motivational processes and interpersonal relationships: Implications for understanding motivation at school. *Journal of Educational Psychology, 91,* 76–97.

Whitehurst, G. J., Falco, F. L., Lonigan, C. J., Fischel, J. E., DeBaryshe, B. D., Valdez-Menchaca, M. C., et al. (1988). Accelerating language development through picture book reading. *Developmental Psychology, 24,* 552–559.

Whitehurst, G. J., & Lonigan, C. J. (1998). Child development and emergent literacy. *Child Development, 69,* 848–872.

Williamson, R., Appelbaum, M., & Epanchin, A. (1991). Longitudinal analyses of academic achievement. *Journal of Educational Measurement, 28,* 61–76.

Wodarski, J. S., Kurtz, P. D., Gaudin, J. M., & Howing, P. T. (1990). Maltreatment and the school-age child: Major academic, socioemotional, and adaptive outcomes. *Social Work, 35,* 506–513.

Zigler, E. F., & Styfco, S. (1995). *Head Start and beyond: A national plan for extended childhood intervention.* New Haven, CT: Yale University Press.

Zill, N., & Nord, C. W. (1994). *Running in place.* Washington, DC: Child Trends.

Zima, B. T., Bussing, R., Freeman, S., Yang, X., Belin, T. R., & Forness, S. R. (2000). Behavior problems, academic skill delays and school failure among school-aged children in foster care: Their relationship to placement characteristics. *Journal of Child and Family Studies, 9,* 87–103.

CHAPTER 9

TEACHING HISTORY AND SOCIAL STUDIES TO YOUNG CHILDREN

Gary Fertig

Are children in the primary grades capable of learning history and understanding the past in ways that will make their lives more meaningful in the present? A small but important body of research conducted for purposes of answering this question has focused on the nature and significance of relationships between children's developing sense of time and their ability to engage in historical reasoning. Underlying this research is the belief that: "Without a strong sense of chronology—of when events occurred and in what temporal order—it is impossible for students to examine relations among them or to explain historical causality" (NCHS, 1994, p. 18). The members of any culture, however, have different ways of making temporal distinctions and using time. For example, the Nuer, a pastoral people residing in the Southern Sudan, recognized and lived by two different but related systems of time. One system reflected important ecological cycles that signaled when it was time to move from villages to camps whereas the other was used for purposes of reckoning kinship relations within Nuer social structure: "Both refer to successions of events which are of sufficient interest to the community for them to be noted and related to each other conceptually" (Evans-Pritchard, 1940, p. 94). In many industrialized societies time is viewed as a limited resource and valuable commodity used to

Contemporary Perspectives on Social Learning in Early Childhood Education, pages 199–215
Copyright © 2007 by Information Age Publishing

achieve specific purposes and therefore "we understand and experience time as a kind of thing that can be spent, wasted, budgeted, invested wisely or poorly, saved, or squandered" (Lakoff & Johnson, 1980, p. 8).

In their review of research on the relationship between children's developing understanding of time and emergence of historical understanding, Thornton and Vukelich (1988) focused attention on the temporal concepts of clock time, calendar time, and historical time:

> Clock time involves using numeral notations to estimate or accurately judge units of time on a clock, watch, or digital device. Calendar time requires one to use time language involving days, weeks, months, seasons, holidays, and years, as well as numerical digits, to judge units of time on standard calendars. Historical time requires one to depict a person, place, artifact, or event in the past using some form of time language. (p. 70)

Thornton and Vukelich (1988) concluded that efforts to understand clock time, calendar time, and historical time are related to one another and depend on the child's overall cognitive development. They advised teaching the terms *past* and *present* anytime after four years of age and asserted that five and six year olds understood the cyclical nature of time when schedules and patterns of activities were presented to them from the perspective of daily routines. Between the ages of 8 and 9, children begin to associate certain calendar dates with historically significant people and events, place themselves in correct chronological sequence in relation to other family members by age, arrange a given set of dates in proper numerical order, and estimate how long ago an event took place using general terms such as *long ago* and *way back when*. By ages 10 and 11, children are able to label periods of time and begin using the historical vocabulary of specific eras, such as *during colonial times* and at the time of the *Civil War*. Thornton and Vukelich cautioned teachers to distinguish between *use* and *understanding* during instruction: "Young children may recite abstract time terms in history lessons, but the evidence suggests that dates and some time terms have little meaning for some youngsters" (1988, p. 79).

In a later article Vukelich and Thornton (1990) proposed a set of guidelines for teachers and publishers of history textbooks to follow when presenting temporal concepts to young children based on *pinnacles of time*. These were defined as "singularly important temporal understandings associated with particular age spans" (p. 23). Pinnacles of time for children between the ages of 3 and 5 included the ability to sequence daily events and family members by age; for 6–8 year olds, using numbers to talk about the past and associating favorite holidays, people, and events with certain dates; and during the age span of 9–11, students should begin matching clusters of events and people with conventional historical time descriptors such as colonial times, revolutionary and civil war eras: "It is during the age span of 9–11 years that those time understandings usually associated with understanding history most markedly develop" (Vukelich & Thornton, 1990, p. 23).

Taking into account the four studies used by Thornton and Vukelich (1988) in their review of research on the developing relationship between children's understanding of time and ability to learn history (Bradley, 1947; Friedman, 1944b; Jahoda, 1963; Oakden & Sturt, 1922), Keith Barton and Linda Levstik (1996) were able to locate only seven more empirical research studies that addressed the same relationship (Downey, 1994; Friedman, 1944a; Levstik & Pappas, 1987; McAulay, 1961; Poster, 1973; Saxe, 1992; West, 1978, 1981, 1982). They noted however that, with the exception of Downey (1994) and Levstik and Pappas (1987), none of these studies included "the kind of systematic discussion of methods, materials, or results that would enable the reader to judge the soundness of their conclusions. Without more complete description, such investigations remain suggestive at best" (Barton & Levstik, 1996, p. 421). Lacking solid empirical evidence indicating that understanding any one form of determining time, for example clock or calendar time, was a necessary precondition for understanding historical time, they advised against drawing any firm conclusions about the nature and significance of relationships between children's temporal understanding and their ability to learn history.

Barton and Levstik (1996) also questioned the usefulness of employing *stages* to represent and explain the development of historical time. They referred to studies in the field of cognitive psychology where research over the past 30 years had shown that the form and structure of human thought is much more dependent on and embedded within particular subject matter than previously believed (Sternberg, 1989; Wellman & Gelman, 1992; Holyoak & Spellman, 1993). Considering the importance of content for regulating thought processes in conjunction with the existence of culturally defined constructions of time, Barton and Levstik reasoned that when children are learning how to depict people and events in time, telling the time of day using a clock, and calculating the number of days in a week, they are "simultaneously developing their facility with parallel cultural constructions" (1996, p. 422). Thus, the ability to think in terms of historical time did not appear to represent a single cognitive trait developing in linear fashion through a series of uniform stages where certain fundamental abilities function as necessary prerequisites to more advanced abilities.

Finally, Barton and Levstik (1996) criticized prior research for employing a narrow conception of historical time. Research tasks in which subjects were required to arrange a set of dates in correct chronological order should not be considered valid measures of understanding historical time because children can complete them successfully without knowing the meaning of significant events in history associated with those dates. Conversely, tasks that required subjects to arrange in correct chronological order the names of famous people, inventions or items of technology deemed to be of historical significance by an adult researcher served only as very indirect measures of understanding historical time because children have limited content knowledge of traditional school history. Barton and Levstik's research constituted a radical break with previous studies that sought to evaluate children's ability to learn about the past based on measures of the traditional school history curriculum and extent to which their thinking was consistent with that of professional historians. They focused instead on the kinds of temporal distinctions children did make and their reasons for making them in response to historical photographs, drawings, cartoons, and other visual images. Using in-depth, open-ended interviews, Barton and Levstik elicited a wide range of responses from children that could be considered *historical*. According to this line of research, children's intuitive ways of knowing the past are worthy of serious study, even when they do not comport with the temporal distinctions and professional adult vocabularies of historians.

Barton and Levstik (1996) presented 58 students in grades K–6 with a series of nine historical pictures representing well-known periods of American history: the Colonial Era, Antebellum South, Westward Expansion, the 1950s, 1960s, and 20th century. Each picture contained a rich variety of visual cues related to the social history of fashion, communication, transportation, architecture, and people interacting with one another in mundane activities. Children were asked initially to place two pictures next to each other using the time distinction "longest time ago" and "closest to now" followed by the introduction of additional pictures, "one at a time," and a request to place each picture "in between two of them or at about the same time as one of them" (Barton & Levstik, 1996, pp. 451–452). Children were encouraged "to think out loud" as a way of explaining why they were placing the pictures in a particular order along with identifying what "things in the picture help you to decide which picture happened longest ago, or most recently?" (Barton & Levstik, 1996, p. 451). These researchers were interested in discovering the basis upon which children made time distinctions rather than focusing exclusively on their ability to arrange pictures in a proper historical sequence.

Results from interviews with 34 primary age students—eight kindergartners and 26 first, second, and third graders—indicated that all of the children were able to make the basic temporal distinction between *close to now* and *long ago* (Barton & Levstik, 1996). Kindergartners, first, and second graders used features in the pictures that were familiar in the present to explain why some pictures were *close to now*, because the pictures also included them, and features that were not associated with the present, or maximally different from similar features in the present, to explain why some of the pictures were from *long ago*. In addition to recognizing a dichotomous division of time, several kindergarten and first graders, and all of the second graders created several categories of pictures, explaining them not only in comparison to the present but also in relation to each other. Finding the categories *close to now* and *long ago* to be overly restrictive, these children recognized that some of the pictures were *newer* than other *close to now* pictures and that some of the pictures were *older* than other *long ago* pictures. They also believed that some of the pictures needed to be placed between certain old and new pictures. By grade three all children were dividing the pictures into at least five categories, *older, old, middle, close to now,* and *now* (Barton & Levstik, 1996, p. 432).

Barton and Levstik (1996) concluded that the ability to assign dates to pictures and make accurate use of specific background knowledge increased with age and grade level but consistently lagged far behind children's ability to differentiate periods of time using visual cues. Although third graders were differentiating up to five different time periods, most were unable to associate any of the pictures with specific dates except for two of the most recent pictures.

Kindergartners, first, and second graders who were just beginning to learn the meaning of numbers, used dates reluctantly and only on rare occasion—and when they did assign dates to pictures, they appeared to be guessing or using dates at random. Even when the mathematical meaning of dates was understood, children experienced difficulty when they attempted to relate dates to specific historical events. Third graders were more willing to assign dates to pictures when asked and did so in ways that were consistent with their verbal descriptions, took into account previous estimates, and demonstrated an understanding of the numerical basis for dates. Barton and Levstik remarked that, "children at this level most often estimated dates by naming decades or centuries ("the 1950s" or "back in the 1800s") rather than the more specific but seemingly random guesses ("1522") of younger children" (1996, p. 435). Kindergarten through second graders made use of very general qualitative descriptors for time periods such as *the old days, a long time ago,* and *back then* while third and fourth graders added descriptors such as *old-fashioned, the old West,* and *before the Civil War.*

While the ability to make temporal distinctions became more numerous, detailed, and supported with historical background information across grade levels, Barton and Levstik (1996) found that even the youngest children in their study had some background knowledge about the past, made temporal distinctions to organize their knowledge and, therefore, could benefit from learning history in school prior to fourth grade. They advised teachers to find out what students already know and think they know about the past, how they reason about the past using that knowledge, and to build on children's prior understanding in the following ways:

1. Begin with social history, that is, history related to changes over time in people's material conditions and social relations pertaining to everyday life because this was the most accessible kind of history for young learners.

2. Make use of a variety of visual materials to provide students with images of what people looked like, the kinds of activities they engaged in, and how technology worked in the past.

3. Encourage students to create their own visual images of the past as a means for interpreting history and using the arts to express their insight into what it means to be human.

4. Recognize that the use of dates with students below fifth grade does not evoke the same kinds of historical images and understandings one would expect from adults; when teaching dates and conventionally named periods, therefore, a variety of visual images of the past should be presented within the context of historical situations children find meaningful.

In research carried out with school children in Northern Ireland, Barton (2002) continued his investigation into the kinds of temporal distinctions made by young learners, the reasoning behind their actions, and how understanding historical time changed with age. During interviews with 86 students ranging in age from 6–9 years old, children were asked to arrange a set of pictures in chronological order and explain their reasoning. However, unlike previous studies in which children were asked to interpret visual materials (e.g., Barton & Levstik, 1996; Foster, Hoge, & Rosch, 1999; Harnett, 1993; Hoge & Foster, 2002), Barton analyzed students' responses from the theoretical perspective of mediated action (Wertsch, 1998; Wells, 1999) to determine whether understanding historical time should be considered a prerequisite for history instruction or an outcome of history instruction. Resolving this problem required identifying the cultural tools that children used to make different kinds of temporal distinctions. Cultural tools are the mental and material means by which people engage in purposeful thought and action (Wertsch, 1998). Certain tools of historical time were expected to facilitate children's efforts to make temporal distinctions, others to constrain their efforts by placing limits on chronological reasoning, and some might simply be irrelevant to the task of making distinctions in time. In this regard, Barton viewed the purpose of his research as one of documenting "how students draw from a set of multiple and overlapping tools related to time, and how each of these may expand or limit their ideas about the past" (2002, p. 165).

Barton (2002) asked children to arrange nine pictures representing different times in history in chronological order based on how old the pictures were. Students as young as 6 were able to sequence the pictures using the terms "older," "newer," "closer to now," and "longer ago" with great accuracy (Barton, 2002, p. 167). In addition to sequencing the pictures, which required separating them based on the times they represented, students grouped the pictures into different categories. The older the student the more categories he or she created and used. Six-year-olds divided the nine pictures they were given into anywhere between three and six groups, 7 and 8 year olds placed the same pictures into four to seven groups, and 9 and 10 year olds created eight or nine categories for grouping purposes. The action of grouping pictures was similar to the ways adults group historical phenomena into broad categories or periods of time that seem to go together. Finally, students measured the pictures' distance in time, either from one another or from the present by means of physically separating the pictures farther from or closer to other pictures.

Students in Barton's study used four cultural tools to sequence, group, and measure historical time (2002). The first tool used was *factual knowledge of objects, people, and events*. In sequencing pictures students looked for the presence or absence of objects that were not in use at the same time or differentiated pictures by noting changes in the form or use of the same object, for example, differences in styles of clothing, models of cars, and building materials of homes. The second tool used to sequence and group pictures was *direct experience* or the experiences of people they knew well such as family members. Although using direct experience was not a common strategy and limited due to their age, students were quite confident in the placements when they were able to use direct experiences to make temporal distinctions among the pictures. The third tool used to sequence and group pictures in time, *examples of progress and decline*, was used when there were perceived to be significant changes in people's material conditions, such as advances in architecture or transportation. Barton noted that the use of this tool imposed a constraint on children's efforts to differentiate time periods because advances in architecture and other aspects of material culture are not consistent over time or uniform for people living in all societies. Students used the fourth tool, *anchoring and adjustment*, when asked to date the most recent picture and then arrange the remaining eight pictures back in time using it as an anchor point. Their estimates of the dates of pictures and number of years separating them were inaccurate however, even though they understood the arithmetical basis of numbers making up the dates.

Based on children's use of these four cultural tools to make temporal distinctions, Barton concluded that understanding historical time was not a precondition for learning history, "Quite the contrary: students used the information they had learned about history to make sense of time" (2002, p. 176). Two of the tools, using examples of progress and decline and the anchoring and adjustment strategy, were not used effectively and led to inaccurate placements. Children were most successful making distinctions when they were able to draw upon factual knowledge of the past and direct experience to sequence, group, and measure temporal distances among the pictures.

Three observations made by Barton (2002) have important implications for instruction. First, when making temporal distinctions, children relied on visual cues in the pictures related to changes in people's material conditions over time and social relations associated with everyday life. This finding was consistent with studies conducted in the United States in which American students who had received little or no formal history instruction in school before the fourth grade were also able to differentiate among different time periods represented by pictures (Barton & Levstik, 1996; Hoge & Foster, 2002). This can be explained in light of the fact that the social contexts that influenced children's understanding of historical time most profoundly, family experiences and popular culture, were present in both countries.

A second observation was that the information used by Irish students to differentiate pictures in historical time was not learned from a history curriculum presented to them in any particular chronological sequence (Barton, 2002). Moreover, children in Ireland learn about a greater number of historical phenomena ranging farther back in time and in a greater variety of places compared to American students. The Irish students were more adept at making temporal distinctions than were students of similar ages in the United States, presumably because they were able to draw upon knowledge of a greater number and variety of time periods. American students may have been limited in their ability to make temporal distinctions by a history curriculum organized around a single chronological sequence of events. Barton asserted, therefore, that American students "do not need more chronology so much as they need more information that they will find useful in their own chronological sense-making activities" (Barton, 2002, p. 176).

Finally, even though students in Northern Ireland received formal history instruction earlier in their school careers than American students and learned about a greater variety of people, places, and events ranging much farther back in time, this did not always help them differentiate periods of historical time. What children need to learn about the past to understand historical time in a more relational manner, according to Barton (2002), are factual details and information about multiple time periods and events in association with one another and their dates. Taught and learned in isolation, dates and facts did not help students in either country make greater sense of historical time.

Research that has analyzed children's responses to historical photographs, drawings, artifacts, and historical fiction over the past 25 years has done much to clarify what young learners know about history and how they make sense of the past (Barton & Levstik, 1996; Foster, Hoge, & Rosch, 1999; Harnett, 1993; Levstik & Barton, 1996; Levstik & Pappas, 1987; West, 1981, 1986). Findings from these studies indicate that children as young as 5 years of age possess substantial knowledge of social history and employ a variety of conceptual strategies to organize and understand the past in meaningful ways. Rather than viewing children's unschooled ways-of-knowing the past as impediments to learning history, young learners' prior knowledge and experience may be used as a foundation for scaffolding history curriculum and instruction in increasingly effective ways. The role played by history within the context of an integrated social studies approach is discussed next, followed by a consideration of cultural universals as the most appropriate social studies content for young children. Suggestions for investigating cultural universals using classroom time lines and historical biography are presented as means for connecting with and building on children's prior knowledge of chronology and social history.

HISTORY AND THE SOCIAL STUDIES

Just as the tools of historical time represent only one set of skills used by historians to interpret the meaning of events in the past, history represents only one of the academic disciplines that comprise the social studies. According to the National Council for the Social Studies (NCSS):

> Social studies is the integrated study of the social sciences and humanities to promote civic competence. Within the school program, social studies provides coordinated, systematic study drawing upon such disciplines as anthropology, archaeology, economics, geography, history, law, philosophy, political science, psychology, religion, and sociology, as well as appropriate content from the humanities, mathematics, and natural sciences. The primary purpose of social studies is to help young people develop the ability to make informed and reasoned decisions for the public good as citizens of a culturally diverse, democratic society in an interdependent world. (1994, p. vii)

The guiding mission of all social studies is to prepare children for active and informed citizenship in a democratic society. It is through the social studies that children learn how to become effective citizens by making practical use of key concepts and methods of inquiry from the academic disciplines to deliberate with others over controversial social issues. Ideally, citizens living together in democratic societies collaborate with one another in decision-making processes that contribute to a common good through the exercise of informed participation and reasoned judgment based on a common body of evidence.

Many primary grades teachers teach citizenship in meaningful and authentic ways by relating such abstract ideas as informed participation, reasoned judgment, and a common good to children's personal lives and social interactions within the classroom, school, and community. Opportunities for teaching good character and effective citizenship arise naturally within the context of teaching students how to make and keep friends, interact positively with family members, and engage in cooperative investigations of perplexing problems and interesting events. Teachers who are adept at preparing students for effective citizenship typically transform their classrooms into communities of learners who are motivated to help each other achieve academic success and develop positive self-esteem.

In addition to its mission of civic education, the National Council for the Social Studies (1994) definition emphasizes the importance of an integrated approach to disciplined inquiry. How, then, does a teacher decide which of the disciplines to integrate? It is the particular person, social issue or historical event under investigation that defines the most appropriate combination of individual disciplines to integrate for effective teaching and learning. For example, if the topic a teacher plans to investigate with students involves learning about the characteristics of culture and how various aspects of culture change over time, then anthropology, geography, history, and sociology would all be appropriate disciplines to draw upon for purposes of providing students with the skills and concepts they need to understand the concept of culture change. Given the research indicating what children know and are able to do in regard to wielding the tools of historical time, what is the most appropriate social studies content for students in the primary grades and how might teachers provide meaningful opportunities for students to enrich their understanding of humanity by teaching that content in historical perspective? According to many social studies educators the answer to this question lies in investigations of what are known as cultural universals.

USING THE SOCIAL STUDIES TO INVESTIGATE
CULTURAL UNIVERSALS IN HISTORICAL PERSPECTIVE

One of the most powerful introductions to social studies content occurs when children participate in investigations of cultural universals: "In our view, most of the topics traditionally addressed in the primary grades—families, communities, transportation, and government, among others—provide a sound basis for developing fundamental understandings about the human condition" (Brophy & Alleman, 2002, p. 106). Introducing children to the social studies through inquiries of cultural universals is nothing new for teachers in the primary grades; Brophy and Alleman, however, criticized major textbook treatments of cultural universals for being "limited in scope, trivial in import, and lacking connection to major social education goals" (2002, p. 100). Despite this shortfall of textbooks, they considered cultural universals to be sound social studies content for students in the primary grades because they are found in all societies past and present, constitute a significant part of people's material culture, and can be used to explain human social structure and its organization. Leading students in investigations of cultural universals such as transportation, communication, money, food, clothing, and shelters was considered to be developmentally appropriate because:

> children begin accumulating direct personal experiences with most of these cultural universals right from birth, so that by the time they begin school, they have developed considerable funds of knowledge and experience that they can draw on in constructing understandings of social education concepts and principles. (Brophy & Alleman, 2002, p. 106)

Learning about cultural universals can be made more meaningful for children when they are presented within social contexts that show them being used by interesting people. To acquire an interrelated understanding of cultural universals as integrated systems—learning how innovations in transportation, for example, can change how people work, socialize and communicate with one another—their invention and development must be traced through time. Integrating key concepts and processes of inquiry from different disciplines, capitalizing on children's inclination to make human sense of the past by including people (Donaldson, 1978; Dunn, 1988), and presenting cultural universals in systematic relationships with other cultural universals enhances the meaning of social studies for young learners.

DEVELOPING CLASSROOM TIME LINES

Developing classroom time lines provides opportunities for students to use the tools of historical time to establish temporal relationships among a variety of cultural universals, events, and people in the past. Time lines may also be assembled using historical materials that appeal to the multiple senses of young learners by incorporating documents, artwork, historical artifacts, photographs, paintings, and even music. Built to scale they can represent intervals of time ranging from the hours in a day to the decades in a century. Patterns of continuity and change in the form and functioning of cultural universals over time can be displayed and discussed by students in a more coherent manner using the temporal frameworks made possible by time lines. Issues of the day, relevant cultural and historical conditions, and other types of antecedents leading up to events in the past, together with their consequences—anticipated and unanticipated, positive and negative—can be displayed visually on time lines to aid students in recognizing multiple causes and effects. When time lines are used to document personal and family histories, students can compare and contrast significant events in each other's lives to learn that they all have a past which needs to be interpreted because they do not all share the same personal and family histories, and that each individual in the class is a part of history because it is people that make history. Used in this manner, time lines highlight those elements of diversity among individual students that characterize the class as a unique group.

Juxtaposing two or more time lines provides opportunities for comparing social studies phenomena, for example, the biography of an individual and the events taking place in a city, state, or country during the same time span. Parallel time lines may also be used to establish temporal relationships between cultural universals that have influenced people's values, their social relations, and ways of seeing the world, as with the invention and widespread use of radio, television, and computers in American society. Children should be encouraged to contribute their own ideas and materials to classroom time lines; for example, a student might present an old photograph or toy to the class, recount its history and explain where their artifact should be placed on the time line. Bringing materials from home to place on a classroom time line allows children to become participants in history as well as active members of their classroom community as they collaborate with each other to make sense of the past. The stories students tell about artifacts from home along with personal exploits and narrations of family activities become a catalyst for discussing the past in relation to the present. Class discussions help build a common experience base that becomes background knowledge for supporting the creation of original historical narrative.

USING HISTORICAL BIOGRAPHY
TO LEARN ABOUT CULTURAL UNIVERSALS

Reading and listening to historical biography provides multiple points of imaginative entry for scaffolding instruction that builds on students' prior knowledge and supports integrated applications of the social studies when learning about cultural universals. Consider for example the biography of

John Batterson Stetson, *Boss of the Plains: The Hat That Won the West* (Carlson & Meade, 1998). This delightful biography written for children is about the life and times of the man who established his place in history by inventing the cowboy hat. Students learn about the many different kinds of hats that travelers and settlers brought to the American West; none, however, were as well adapted to this new environment as the Stetson hat, called the Boss of the Plains. In addition to discovering what hats were made of and how they were manufactured in the 1840s, students learn that the clothes people wore in the past were not merely a matter of fashion or the result of arbitrary decisions but rather they were designed to serve very practical purposes.

Despite its relatively high price at the time—an entire month's wages for the typical cowboy—Mr. Stetson's hat was highly valued and considered well worth the cost. It could be used to shield your eyes from the sun, prevent rain and snow from dripping down the back, fan the flames of a campfire, and waved at cattle to drive them into corrals. Here was a hat that doubled as a container for collecting food, carrying oats to a hungry horse, or scooping water from a nearby stream. Used as a pillow to rest one's head or propped on a stick and used as a decoy to evade intruders, the Boss of the Plains was ideally suited to a host of needs resulting from environmental conditions that characterized a particular place and time in history. The story of Mr. Stetson and his hat serves as a very accessible example of innovation in clothing and cultural adaptation for young learners.

As a twelve-year-old boy, John Stetson did not attend school; instead, he worked alongside his eleven brothers and sisters making hats in their family-owned business located in Orange, New Jersey (Carlson & Meade, 1998). Later in life, however, John contracted tuberculosis, and like many others afflicted with this disease at the time he headed to the high and dry plains of the Colorado Territory in hopes of finding relief from his symptoms. Along the way he meets gold prospectors, trappers, cowboys, businessmen, and ordinary families who also were traveling west to take advantage of the many opportunities afforded by the American frontier. Children can learn about the contingent nature of history by asking *what if* questions about the past (Zarnowski, 2003): "What if John Stetson had not become ill with tuberculosis?" "Perhaps then he would no longer feel any need to travel west." "Would we still have the Stetson cowboy hat today?" "Might someone else have invented a similar kind of hat?"

Carlson and Meade (1998) provide readers with colorful illustrations that show people walking through towns and over the prairie, riding horses, traveling by stagecoach and carriage, leading mule teams and transporting their possessions by way of pack dogs, wagons, and oxcarts. In addition to learning about the cultural universal of clothing, opportunities abound for integrating instruction related to the many different types of transportation used by Americans during the mid-nineteenth century. Vehicles at the time were powered by people and animals, steam engines, and by the wind for ships of sail, and each could be adapted to serve a specific purpose. Some modes of transportation were designed to carry raw materials and manufactured goods while others were designed to carry people in quarters ranging from the quite ordinary to the most luxurious for those who possessed great wealth.

Characters in the book are depicted working together in groups and interacting socially at different kinds of jobs and businesses that will interest children. Readers are introduced to bullwhackers, mule-skinners, and drovers along with the town blacksmith, a watchmaker, and a gang of Pikes Peak miners shoveling gold-bearing gravel into long wooden sluice troughs. There is the economic point to be made that, like John Stetson, most people who moved west in 1840s America did not become rich picking up gold by the handful from rivers and steams; rather, most settlers made a living for themselves and families providing others with the goods and services they needed and wanted at a time when wealth was in large measure determined by the amount of land one owned, and that land was particularly valuable when it could be used for farming and ranching. The cultural universals contained in this one book related to clothing, transportation, and careers in the nineteenth-century can all be represented on time lines and compared with similar material conditions and social relations at other times in history or in comparison to how people dress, travel, and work today.

CONCLUSION

Using time lines and historical biography in an integrated approach to teaching and learning social studies challenges children to impose temporal order on their thinking about cultural universals in relation to significant issues, people, and events in the past. When investigations of cultural universals are embedded in compelling stories about interesting people that evoke affective responses as well as intellectual associations, students are more likely to regard their learning as meaningful and memorable. Creating their own visual representations, drawings, models, and paintings of cultural universals in use at different times in the past and collaborating with others in the development of projects they really care about provides the impetus for students to exercise reasoned judgment and the motivation to sustain reflective inquiry. Used as graphic organizers for scaffolding history curriculum and instruction on prior knowledge, time lines enable teachers to take advantage of the chronological reasoning abilities and social history that children have learned outside of school. Their ability to sequence, group, and measure temporal relationships among cultural universals using cues derived from observed changes in people's material conditions and social relations can be used to help students match particular events with specific dates and historical periods.

Understanding how cultural universals work and the role they play in human affairs cuts across disciplinary boundaries and invites teachers and students to employ an integrated approach to learning social studies, one that makes use of the analytical tools and key concepts from different academic disciplines. Studying a culture's geography, for example, can help children understand how cultural universals and human behaviors initially regarded as weird or stupid were really purposeful and intelligent adaptations to particular environmental and social conditions. Conducting inquiry into how people lived during different periods of development in agricultural practices or industrial production can also be used to challenge the commonly held misconception that all people around the world pass through identical stages of development that do not overlap or coexist. Learning for example that Americans in the 1840s lived in cities at the same time settlers were moving west in covered wagons, wearing cowboy hats and building homes made of sod can be a real revelation for young learners.

Effective social studies instruction appeals to children's imaginations, makes connections to their lives outside of school, and builds on prior knowledge (NCHS, 1994; Alleman & Brophy 2001; Seefeldt, 2005). Historical narrative accounts that succeed in cultivating children's empathy encourage reflection on their own and others' emotional responses, and caring about others is an important aspect of citizenship for those who truly value the common good. Perhaps, then, learning how to feel about people, issues, and events that took place in the past leads to just as much social understanding as reflective inquiry designed to develop logical operations and intellectual reasoning.

REFERENCES

Alleman, J., & Brophy, J. (2001). *Social studies excursions, K-3: Powerful units on food, clothing, and shelter.* Portsmouth, NH: Heinemann.

Barton, K. C. (2002). "Oh, that's a tricky piece!": Children, mediated action, and the tools of historical time. *Elementary School Journal, 103,* 161–185.

Barton, K. C., & Levstik, L. S. (1996). "Back when God was around and everything": Elementary children's understanding of historical time. *American Educational Research Journal, 33,* 419–454.

Bradley, N. C. (1947). The growth of knowledge of time in children of school-age. *British Journal of Psychology, 38,* 67–68.

Brophy, J., & Alleman, J. (2002). Learning and teaching about cultural universals in primary-grade social studies. *Elementary School Journal, 103,* 99–114.

Carlson, L., & Meade, H. (1998). *Boss of the plains: The hat that won the west.* New York: DK Publishing.

Donaldson, M. (1978). *Children's minds.* New York: Norton.

Downey, M. T. (1994, April). *After the dinosaurs: Children's chronological thinking.* Paper presented at the Annual Meeting of the American Educational Research Association, New Orleans.

Dunn, J. (1988). *The beginnings of social understanding.* Cambridge: Harvard University Press.

Evans-Pritchard, E. E. (1940). *The Nuer: A description of the modes of livelihood and political institutions of a Nilotic people.* Oxford: Oxford University Press.

Foster, S. J., Hoge, J. D., & Rosch, R. H. (1999). Thinking aloud about history: Children's and adolescents' responses to historical photographs. *Theory and Research in Social Education, 27,* 179–214.

Friedman, K. C. (1944a). The growth of time concepts. *Social Education, 8,* 29–31.

Friedman, K. C. (1944b). Time concepts of elementary school children. *Elementary School Journal, 44,* 337–342.

Harnett, P. (1993). Identifying progression in children's understanding: The use of visual materials to assess primary school children's learning in history. *Cambridge Journal of Education, 23,* 137–154.

Hoge, J. D., & Foster, S. J. (2002, April). *It's about time: Students' understanding of chronology, change, and development in a century of historical photographs.* Paper presented at the annual meeting of the American Educational Research Association, New Orleans.

Holyoak, K. J., & Spellman, B. A. (1993). Thinking. *Annual Review of Psychology, 44,* 265–315.

Jahoda, G. (1963). Children's concepts of time and history. *Educational Review, 15,* 87–107.

Lakoff, G., & Johnson, M. C. (1980). *Metaphors we live by.* Chicago: University of Chicago Press.

Levstik, L. S., & Barton, K. C. (1996). "They still use some of their past": Historical salience in elementary children's chronological thinking. *Journal of Curriculum Studies, 28,* 531–576.

Levstik, L. S., & Pappas, C. C. (1987). Exploring the development of historical understanding. *Journal of Research and Development in Education, 21,* 1–15.

McAulay, J. D. (1961). What understandings do second grade children have of time relationships? *Journal of Educational Research, 54,* 312–314.

National Center for History in the Schools (NCHS). (1994). *National standards: History for grades K-4.* Los Angeles: Author.

National Council for the Social Studies (NCSS). (1994). *Curriculum standards for social studies: Expectations of excellence.* (Bulletin No. 89). Washington, DC: Author.

Oakden, E. C., & Sturt, M. (1922). The development of the knowledge of time in children. *British Journal of Psychology, 12,* 309–336.

Poster, J. B. (1973). The birth of the past: Children's perception of historical time. *History Teacher, 6,* 587–598.

Saxe, D. W. (1992). Resolving students' confusion about indefinite time expressions. *The Social Studies, 83,* 188–192.

Seefeldt, C. (2005). *Social studies for the preschool/primary child.* Columbus: Pearson Prentice Hall.

Sternberg, R. J. (1989). Domain-generality versus domain-specificity: The life and impending death of a false dichotomy. *Merrill-Palmer Quarterly, 35*(1), 115–130.

Thornton, S. J., & Vukelich, R. (1988). Effects of children's understanding of time concepts on historical understanding. *Theory and Research in Social Education, 16,* 69–82.

Vukelich, R., & Thornton, S. J. (1990). Children's understanding of historical time: Implications for instruction. *Childhood Education, 67,* 22–25.

Wellman, H. M., & Gelman, S. A. (1992). Cognitive development: Foundational theories of core domains. *Annual Review of Psychology, 43,* 337–375.

Wells, C. (1999). *Dialogic inquiry: Towards a sociocultural practice and theory of education.* New York: Cambridge University Press.

Wertsch, J. V. (1998). *Mind as action.* New York: Oxford University Press.

West, J. (1978). Young children's awareness of the past. *Trends in Education, 1,* 9–14.

West, J. (1981). Authenticity and time in historical narrative pictures. *Teaching History, 29,* 8–10.

West, J. (1982). Time charts. *Education 3–13, 10*(1), 48–50.

West, J. (1986). The development of primary school children's sense of the past. In R. Fairbrother (Ed.), *History and the primary school. Greater Manchester primary contact* (Special Issue No. 6.). Manchester: Didsbury School of Education.

Zarnowski, M. (2003). *History makers: A questioning approach to reading and writing biographies.* Portsmouth, NH: Heinemann.

CHAPTER 10

PLAY AS GROUP IMPROVISATION

A Social Semiotic, Multimodal Perspective on Play and Literacy

Stacy DeZutter

INTRODUCTION

In recent decades, there has been a "social turn" in the study of literacy (Gee, 2000). Literacy researchers have begun to consider literacy as a social activity, and to attend to the ways literacy develops as children interact with others. Moving beyond traditional approaches that have focused on the acquisition of reading and writing as discrete and separable skills possessed by individuals, this sociocultural approach to literacy studies focuses on the ways in which literacy is a social practice, a process that occurs *between* individuals. Reading and writing, in this view, are deeply bound up with an individual's wider ability to understand and produce texts that are meaningful to others (Gee, 1989; Kress & Street, 2006). Literacy development is understood as a matter of learning to participate in the meaning-making practices of one's social group. From this perspective, it becomes important to attend to the social contexts in which children par-

Contemporary Perspectives on Social Learning in Early Childhood Education, pages 217–241
Copyright © 2007 by Information Age Publishing
All rights of reproduction in any form reserved.

ticipate, in order to understand how they learn the literacy practices of their communities.

One context for literacy learning that has received a great deal of research attention is children's pretend play. Traditionally, play has been explored as an important setting for the development of emergent literacy, in which children develop prerequisite skills for reading and writing, because play shares many common features with written texts, such as the presence of the basic elements of a story. However, the social turn in literacy studies requires a shift in emphasis regarding the benefit of play for literacy development. When literacy is understood as a social practice, play becomes important as a context for literacy development because play is a form of social meaning-making. More specifically, play provides a uniquely beneficial setting for the development of literacy because it is a shared improvisational activity. As I argue in this chapter, because the course of a play episode is undetermined at its start, children must engage in ongoing explicit and implicit negotiations in order to play meaningfully together. This engagement is a critical part of play's benefit for literacy development.

Consider the following play episode. Muhammed, Corinna, and Artie are playing with toy jungle animals in the block area of their preschool classroom.

(1)	Corinna:	Guess what? At the museum, someone is uh robbing us! And they wanta take us to jail!
(2)	Muhammed:	That very bad. How do you know a hippo, is robbing you?
(3)	Artie:	Uh, you saw them?
(4)	Corinna:	Yes, I saw him last night, he was robbing my owner. And I can't get him *[inaudible]* my favorite food, mashed, mashed bugs.
(5)	Artie:	*[inaudible]* to get out of here. The *[inaudible]* took it out. And I can get out, BOOM. I blasted open the door.
(6)	Corinna:	Artie, you killed, you, uh got killed, alright?
(7)	Artie:	And, we found him, OK? He wasn't dead, he just in jail.
(8)	Corinna:	OK.
(9)	Artie:	*[inaudible]* where were you?
(10)	Corinna:	I'm in jail.

(11)   Artie: OK! Boom. And here's the bad guys coming in [*inaudible*]

(12)   Corinna: I wanna thank you

(13)   Artie: Let's pretend when you turned around, the bad guys were [*inaudible*] in back of you, OK?

(14)   Corinna: I love you for saving me!

(adapted from Sawyer, 1997, pp. 160–161)

At Turn 2, Muhammed has several options. He could, for example, have extended Corinna's jail idea by adding more information about going to jail, or he could have introduced a new idea related to the museum. Note, however, that if he wants to keep the play episode going, there are also many things he cannot do—he cannot suddenly begin talking about birthday parties or monster trucks, because these things have no obvious connection to the current play topic. Muhammed's contribution has to be consistent with the evolving play world he and his friends are developing (Curran, 1999; Griffin, 1984). Note also that once Muhammed makes his contribution, his friends also have several options—they could accept his idea of a hippo as the robber (which is what they do), or they could alter it somehow, ignore it, or explicitly reject it (Sawyer, 1997; Verba, 1993b). His friends' response will determine the role of his contribution in the evolving play world, just as his choice of responses to Corinna determines how her contribution in Turn 1 will affect successive play. Of course, Muhammed's friends are no freer than he is to introduce nonsequiturs, if they wish to maintain the flow of play—their responses to his hippo idea are also constrained by what has come before.

Through this process of proposal and response, Muhammed and his friends negotiate the construction of their play world. Negotiation is a key part of the children's play activity, because their play is improvisational—there is no preset storyline for them to act out. Even if they were following a familiar story like the plot of a favorite television show, they would be free to deviate and embellish as they wish (Corsaro, 1992; Sawyer, 1997). In addition to negotiating what they will play, the children also have to negotiate how they will play, for example, which of the materials available in the block corner will stand in for the door and the jail.

As children improvise their play world together, they are participating in a shared meaning-making activity. They are collaborating to enact a story that is meaningful to them, and, in turn, they are using their play as a means to help them make sense of the real world (Corsaro, 1985; Kendrick, 2005; Kliewer et al., 2003; Löhfdahl, 2005; Paley, 1988, 1990, 2004; Rowe, 1998). In so doing, they are learning what it is like to participate in a literate community—a social group who together make meaning of their experiences through the use of shared forms of representation.

In this chapter, I argue that through the processes involved in group improvisation, children's social pretend play provides an important context for the development of their early literacy. As we have seen in the example above, children's play is open-ended and collaborative, and therefore requires ongoing negotiations about what will be played and how to play it. As children play together, they create a shared social product, an emergent play narrative. In this way, pretend play provides a setting for children to engage in the kind of socially shared meaning-making activity that is the basis for the many kinds of literacy in which they will participate throughout their lives. Further, pretend play involves *semiosis*, the process of using symbols and signs to communicate meaning. Semiosis is an important component of literacy from a sociocultural perspective, because in order to successfully engage in the literate practices of one's community, one must become a facile user of the sign systems used by that community. Because play requires children to negotiate their sign use, it allows children to develop an awareness of the semiotic process.

I begin the chapter by reviewing early approaches to researching the connections between play and literacy, in order to set the stage for a discussion of how new ways of thinking about literacy require researchers to focus on the improvisational aspects of play. I then consider how applying concepts used to study improvisation can help us understand the social processes that yield play's contribution to literacy development. Finally, I consider the implications of this discussion for educators.

PLAY AND EMERGENT LITERACY

Researchers have been interested in the connections between play and literacy since the 1980s, beginning with such early studies as Pellegrini and Galda's work on thematic fantasy play and story comprehension (Galda, 1984; Pellegrini, 1984; Pellegrini & Galda, 1982). This line of research flourished in the 1990s (Yaden, Rowe, & MacGillivray, 2000) and continues to be a significant area of inquiry for early childhood researchers (Roskos & Christie, in press). Of course, the idea that play has benefits for cognitive development is not new. The influence of play on children's developing cognitive capacities, including the skills that underlie literacy, is discussed by both Piaget (1962) and Vygotsky (1978). (For reviews of these foundational theorists' work with regard to play and literacy, see Pellegrini & Galda, 1993; Roskos & Christie, 2001b; Smolucha & Smolucha 1998.)

The research on the connections between play and literacy that emerged in the 1980s was influenced by the reconceptualization of literacy development as "emergent literacy." Emergent literacy research departed from earlier views of literacy development, which focused on conventional literacy and "reading readiness" by identifying prerequisite skills for basic decoding and letter-writing, skills that could then be explicitly taught (Lancy, 1994; Mason & Allen, 1986; Teale & Sulzby, 1986; Yaden et al., 2000). From an emergent literacy perspective, children begin the process of becoming literate shortly after birth and continue throughout childhood. Emergent literacy research examines the forms of literate behavior in which children engage before they are able to read and write conventionally, and emphasizes children's active construction of increasingly sophisticated literacy strategies. From this perspective, important literate behaviors are acquired not through explicit training but through engagement in the social world.

Within the emergent literacy scholarship, accounts of play's benefits for literacy development have centered on three aspects of play: symbolic transformation, metaplay, and narrative elements. Work on symbolic transformation considers how the symbolization processes involved in pretend play, for example using a toy banana to stand in for a telephone, function to help children develop "representational competence," the ability to construct and use symbols to communicate meaning. Work on "metaplay" (Fein, 1981) refers to children's talk about the play they are doing ("let's pretend that..."). Metaplay has been conceptually linked to metalinguistic awareness—children's knowledge about the structures and functions of language—and to their ability to use language in decontextualized ways. Researchers have found that children's use of symbolic transformation in play predicts scores on measures of early writing (Pellegrini & Galda, 1991; Pellegrini, Galda, Dresden, & Cox, 1991; Silvern, Williamson, & Waters, 1982), while metaplay is related to story comprehension and predicts reading scores (Dickinson & Beals, 1994; Pellegrini & Galda, 1991, 1993; Silvern et al., 1982).

The connection between narrative and play has been recognized as particularly important to play's contribution to literacy development. Because play contains many of the same features as the narrative texts involved in school-based literacy (such as storybooks and classroom readers), play is thought to help children learn how to think about and respond to such texts (Fein, Ardila-Rey, & Groth, 2000; Pellegrini & Galda, 2000). Researchers have identified several aspects of pretend play that are also present in narrative texts (Branscombe & Taylor, 2000; Eckler & Weiniger, 1989; Galda, 1984; Kavanaugh & Engle, 1998; Pellegrini, 1985; Sachs, Goldman, & Chaille, 1984; Sawyer & DeZutter, in press; Silvern, Taylor, Williamson, Surbeck, & Kelley, 1986; Walker 1999).

Both involve "framing." As they play, children must move between multiple interpretive frames, so that at times their talk refers to the real world and at other times they are talking within the frame of the play world (Bateson, 1971; Garvey & Berndt, 1979; Kane & Furth, 1993). Reading and writing also require facility in moving between multiple frames of reference.

Both involve the production and comprehension of decontextualized language. Decontextualized language is language that can stand alone and be understood without the immediate presence of the things and events that are being referred to. Because pretend play involves communicating about an imagined (non-present) world, it is thought to help prepare children to interact with similar imagined worlds found in school-based texts (Pellegrini, 1985).

Both involve characters and plot elements. In pretend play, children take on roles as characters who have specific points of view and motivations. Play unfolds as the characters engage in a series of actions, resulting in plot events, which may have more or less cohesion and complexity, and may be more or less linked to character identity and motivation, but which nonetheless resemble at a basic level the events that comprise the plot of a story. Some researchers have argued that engaging in pretend play allows children to develop a "story schema," a mental representation of how stories are structured, that would later aid them in comprehension and production of school-based narrative texts (Eckler & Weiniger, 1989; Pellegrini, 1985; Sachs et al., 1984; Silvern et al., 1986).

Research on the relationship between pretend play and narrative competence has primarily focused on documenting the presence of these common features and tracing their development in children's play as they age. In general, it has been found that the presence, coherence, and complexity of all the elements identified above increase between the ages of two and five (Eckler & Weiniger, 1989; Farver, 1992; Galda, 1984; Garvey & Berndt, 1979; Pellegrini, 1985; Sachs et al., 1984; Walker 1999).

Other research on the connections between play and narrative competence has explored the effects of adult-directed book-themed play (sometimes called "thematic fantasy play" or "play training") on story comprehension and production, generally finding that play enactment is somewhat more effective than other interventions at helping children comprehend, recall, and produce coherent stories (Christie, 1991; Galda, 1984; Pellegrini, 1985; Silvern et al., 1986; Williamson & Silvern, 1991). In a related line of inquiry, several researchers have built on the work of Vivian Paley (1988, 1990), who developed a classroom procedure in which children dictate their spontaneously composed stories to a teacher, and then have these stories enacted by peers, a process which is thought to contribute to narrative competence (Fein et al., 2000; Groth & Darling, 2001; Nicolopoulou, 1997, 2002).[1] Other work has looked at various ways in which adults might successfully scaffold children's play in order to increase the coherence or complexity of their play narratives (Galda, 1984; Glaubman, Kashi, & Koresh, 2001; Silvern et al., 1986).

The research described in this section is important work because it recognizes play as a specialized setting in which children can develop and exercise emerging literacy behaviors. Indeed, numerous authors have noted the importance of pretend play among children as a unique communicative context, one in which children have the opportunity to use language to construct and talk about imagined worlds, and one in which children are able to explore a variety of linguistic styles with relatively more freedom than in other conversational settings that tend to be driven by adults (Dickinson & Beals, 1994; Ervin-Tripp, 1991; Farver, 1992; Garvey & Kramer, 1989; Lillard, 1998; Verba, 1993b).

However, the early work on connections between play and literacy is limited in some important ways. First, for the most part, this work focused narrowly on conventional forms of literacy, for example by correlating play behaviors with reading test scores. Second, much of this work was concerned primarily with static features of pretend play, such as the number of plot events or metalinguistic verbs contained in a play episode, without attention to the way the play episode unfolds through time. Third, this work tended to consider the cognition of individual children in isolation, either by treating each child's play behaviors as analytically separable from the play of his or her partners, or by assuming that observations made of children playing alone were generalizable to pretend play with peers. These issues will be addressed in the discussion below, as I consider how new approaches to studying the "play-literacy interface" (Roskos & Christie, 2001a) respond to these concerns. I argue that a key shift in such work is the understanding that play is improvisational, and I offer some concepts developed by Sawyer (1997, 2002) to help researchers think about the ways the improvisationality of social pretend play makes it an ideal environment for literacy development.

NEW DEFINITIONS OF LITERACY

As Yaden et al. (2000) note, discussions of emergent literacy in recent years have become less unified, with many authors recognizing the need to consider broader definitions of what it means to be literate. For example, Bearne (2003) points out the need to respond both to the changing modes of communication that have come with a global, digital age, and to our growing understanding, in the face of an increasingly diverse society, that literacy practices are deeply embedded within the social context in which they occur. For scholars like Bearne (2003), Kress (1997, 2003), Dyson (2003), and Gee (2004), literacy is multimodal, it involves competence in communicating through multiple sign systems. Literacy, in this understanding, means not just the ability to interact with printed texts but to generate and communicate meaning using a range of symbolic tools. Modes of literacy such as still and moving images, music, sound effects, and gesture each have their own expressive affordances, allowing users to communicate different kinds of ideas and relationships (Kress, 1997, 2003; Rowe, 1998). From this perspective, literacy development becomes a matter of developing semiotic competence, the ability to choose forms of symbolic representation that will best afford expression of the meaning one wishes to communicate and that are, at the same time, as transparent as possible to those with whom one is communicating (Kress, 1997; Labbo, 1996).

Researchers who embrace this multimodal, semiotic approach to literacy are situated within the "social turn" in literacy studies, which emphasizes that literacy is a social practice that is deeply embedded within the community in which it occurs (Gee, 2000, 2004; Kress & Street, 2006). These researchers attend to the fact that people, including children, belong to many different literate communities, each with different ways of making meaning out of their experiences and communicating that meaning to one another. An academic department at a university, an ensemble of jazz musicians, and a recreational sports team are examples of communities in which an adult may participate, each involving a different form of literacy. Successful participation in a literacy community involves mastery of that community's literate practices (including their semiotic conventions), as well as awareness of the community's values for what kinds of experiences should be represented (Gee, 1989).

Scholars who assume a social semiotic, multimodal theory of literacy (Kress & Street, 2006) assert that literacy involves creative appropriation, a notion developed by sociocultural psychologists working in the tradition of Vygotsky (e.g., Rogoff, 1990). Creative appropriation means that children don't simply internalize the representational resources of their social group and use them mechanically. Rather, children make adaptive use of culturally available material—both in terms of content and in terms of means of representation—reshaping and redefining that material for their own communicative purposes (Corsaro, 1992, 2003; Dyson, 2003; Kendrick, 2005; Nicolopoulou, 1991, 2002; Rowe, 1998; Sawyer, 1997; Verba, 1993b).

Thus, in a social semiotic, multimodal view, literacy development is a matter of becoming facile with the range of symbolic resources used by the communities in which a child participates. Leland and Harste (1994) explain, "In order to be literate, learners need to be able to orchestrate a variety of sign systems to create texts appropriate to the contexts in which they find themselves." Play is an important setting for developing flexibility in using multiple sign systems, because it is multimodal, involving both verbal and nonverbal communication including modes such as physical enactment and costume design (Kendrick; 2005; Rowe, 1998), and also because it is situated within the child's peer community (Nicolopoulou, 2002).

A number of researchers have begun to explore the relationship between play and social semiotic, multimodal literacy. Kendrick (2005) has argued that play is important for the development of literacy because as children play, they create a "play text" in which they use available cultural resources to make meaning of their own experiences. Play offers children a "space of authorship" in which they "reflect on, and consciously choose, symbols and modes of representation that help them organize and articulate their inner thoughts" (p. 9). Kendrick's case study of five-year-old Leticia explores Leticia's developing literacy by examining the girl's emerging competence as a purposeful user of signs and author of texts during play.

Also adopting a social semiotic, multimodal perspective, Rowe (1998) has looked at the way children integrate content from books in their spontaneous pretend play. Rowe emphasizes the process of transmediation, whereby children move from one sign system to another, for example by using a toy animal to enact movements and postures described in words in a storybook. As children express meaning through alternative sign systems, Rowe argues, they encounter anomalies which "motivate a shift of stance from understanding to reflecting on and reorganizing knowledge through the lens of the new sign system" (p. 30). Because play involves shifting between multiple modes of representation, it presses children to reflect on the representation process itself. Such a metacognitive stance about representation is fundamental to the development of semiotic literacy (Leland & Harste, 1994). Rowe also emphasizes that play with peers is important because it provides a setting for symbolic activity within a community. She points out that while the open-endedness of play offers a centrifugal force, by which children can explore outward into ever more divergent and unconventional uses of signs and deeply idiosyncratic meaning, the peer group serves as a balancing centripetal force. Because they are required to "bring their inventions and transformations into the range of understanding and experience" (p. 33) of their fellow players, the peer group serves to pull children back toward conventionality and the maintenance of shared meaning.

Nicolopoulou (1997, 2002) has explored the role of play in children's development of narrative competence. But unlike other work on narrative competence, Nicolopoulou understands the development of this aspect of literacy not in terms of the static acquisition of a "story schema," but rather in terms of the child's ability to participate in the narrative practices of his community. Echoing Rowe's centripetal/centrifugal analogy, Nicolopoulou asserts that pretend play is an important setting in which children can learn to participate successfully in narrative activity, because they are free to creatively appropriate representational forms from the larger culture, while at the same time they are bound by the requirement of using those forms in ways that their peers understand.

Nicolopoulou's (2002) explanation of the process by which play contributes to narrative development is worth quoting at length, because it summarizes the ways in which play can be understood to contribute to literacy from a social semiotic, multimodal perspective.

> As children come to realize the possible purposes and satisfactions that can be pursued in narrative activity—which are symbolic, expressive, emotional, and social-relational as well as instrumental—they are driven to learn and appropriate the narrative forms culturally available to them and to turn these to their own ends; and they gradually discover that, in order to do so, they must attend to and grasp the (mostly implicit) rule-governed structures inherent in these narrative forms. Children are both impelled and enabled to do this through their participation in practices of shared symbolic activity that serve as collectively constituted fields within which to use and master narrative forms, to explore and extend their inherent possibilities through performances and experimentation, and to push on to greater narrative range and proficiency. (p. 122)

Authors like Kendrick, Rowe, and Nicolopoulou, working from a social semiotic, multimodal perspective, assert that because play allows children to engage in semiotic activity in the context of a community, it prepares them for literate engagement in other contexts, including but not limited to school.[2] From this perspective, the structural features of the play episode are less important to literacy development than the fact that play is both open-ended and social, allowing for the possibility of experimentation with sign use and for the opportunity to negotiate shared meaning with peers. Thus from a social semiotic, multimodal point of view, it becomes important to understand that children's pretend play with peers is a form of group improvisation.

PLAY AS IMPROVISATION

Sawyer (1997, 2002) has compared children's pretend play to forms of adult improvisational performance such as jazz music or improvisational comedy (See also Göncü & Perrone, 2005). He observes that children's play shares all of the defining characteristics of improvisation, including:

- Unpredictability of outcome: There is not a scripted, known endpoint
- Moment-to-moment contingency: The next dialogue turn depends on the one just before
- Openness to collaboration
- Oral performance, without a written product
- Embeddedness in the social context of the performance.
  (adapted from Sawyer, 2002)

Using improvisation as a lens to understand what happens during children's play helps focus our attention on play as a moment-to-moment creation of the play group (Sawyer & DeZutter, in press). Concepts developed by Sawyer for use in understanding group improvisation (2003), then, will be helpful in understanding what happens when children engage together in pretend play.

One such concept is Sawyer's idea of "collaborative emergence." Collaborative emergence describes the process by which a collective social product emerges from the successive, incremental contributions of the participants. Collaborative emergence is found in all group improvisation, including jazz, theater, work groups, and classroom conversations (Sawyer, 2003). In children's pretend play, improvisation results in the collaborative emergence of a play narrative which cannot be attributed simply to the additive contributions of each participant. As Sawyer and DeZutter have explained,

> Improvised narratives are created by the collaborative efforts of the entire group. No single speaker creates the narrative, it emerges from the give and take of conversation. The narrative is constructed turn by turn; one child proposes a new development for the play, and other children respond by modifying or embellishing that proposal. Each new proposal for a development in the narrative is the creative inspiration of one child, but that proposal does not become part of the play until it is evaluated by the other children. In the subsequent flow of dialogue, the group collaborates to determine whether to accept the proposal, how to weave that proposal into the drama that has already been established, and then how to further elaborate on it. (in press)

For example, in the play episode that opened this chapter, Corinna contributed the idea of going to jail, but that in and of itself did not fully determine the future storyline, because her partners were free to respond differently to her contribution, for example by proposing that they got lost on the way or that the jail had burned down. In fact, Artie responded by moving the action forward to a point where his partners' characters had already arrived in jail, so that Corinna's contribution of "they want to take us to jail" served to set the stage for the succeeding jail break.

Sawyer calls the process by which a player's contribution takes on meaning as a result of the way other players build on it "retroactive interpretation" (1997). Because play turns are interpreted retroactively, a player does not know the full meaning of her turn until the other players have responded. In the hippo/jail episode, Corinna did not know that her statement, "someone is robbing us" would refer to the hippo until Muhammed elaborated on her idea with his question, "How do you know a hippo is robbing you?" and Artie implicitly accepted this proposal by asking, "You saw them?" Because of retroactive interpretation, it does not make sense to attribute any particular element in the play narrative to an individual child. The narrative that emerges is the result of the complex process of all the players responding to each other.

Accordingly, an important consequence of understanding the play narrative as collaboratively emergent is that it takes on analytical independence from the actions, intentions, and mental states of each child. The play narrative is a group-level phenomenon, since it results from the complex interactional processes of the group, and it cannot be adequately explained by identifying the actions or mental representations of each individual participant. Further, due to the process of retroactive interpretation, it would not make sense to analyze a play text by inferring a child's goals or intentions at a particular turn, since the ultimate meaning of a child's contribution is not determined until the other players respond. Understanding that the play narrative is collaboratively emergent, and therefore not the conscious creation of any one child, complicates the notion found in earlier research that play is beneficial to literacy development because it allows children to develop or exercise a "story schema," and supports the move to the more robust notion that play is beneficial because it offers a setting for participation in semiotic activity within a community.

Another concept used to understand group improvisation is "downward causation" (Sawyer, 1999). This term describes the process by which the emergent social product that arises from the interactions of a group in turn begins to influence the behavior of the participants. In the case of children's play, as the play narrative emerges, it constrains, at least to some degree, the options of each child for contributing to the play. For example in Turn 4 of the jail break episode, there were many things Corinna could have said to Artie's proposal that she'd seen the hippo do the robbing. However, there were also many things she could not have said, at least if she wanted to maintain the flow of the play (the imperative to do so is in fact understood as an implicit rule of play—Curran, 1999; Garvey, 1993; Griffin, 1984). If she had begun to speak about something that was clearly not connected to the play situation at hand, her partners would likely have either ignored it, responded to the statement as if it were somehow continuous with what they were doing, or stopped playing all together in order to address the breakdown. Thus, if Corinna wants to continue participating successfully in the play, she is not entirely free; she is constrained by the requirement that she operate within the play narrative that has emerged to that point.

DIRECTIONS

As the preceding discussion suggests, when play is understood as group improvisation, it becomes necessary to consider multiple, interdependent levels of analysis. In his work on children's play, Sawyer (1997, 2001) has identified three levels of analysis—the individual, the oral culture, and the peer group. Developmental psychologists interested in play have generally attended solely to the individual level of analysis. But as has been shown above, once play is seen as group improvisation, it becomes difficult to understand literacy development through play in terms of isolated individual cognition.

One way to avoid the problem associated with analyzing play in terms of individual children's cognition is to study the interactional patterns that occur between players. This is particularly helpful from a social semiotic view of literacy, because literacy knowledge is not conceived as static structures in individual heads, but rather as the ability to participate appropriately in the meaning-making practices of one's community. Analyzing the patterns of interaction that occur when children play together can help us understand how children come to participate with increasing facility in joint meaning-making with their peers.

In fact, attention to interactional processes and collaborative meaning making has long been a part of play research. For example, building on Bateson's (2004, 1971) idea of a "play frame" which participants must distinguish from reality, Garvey (Garvey, 1974; Garvey & Berndt, 1979; Garvey & Kramer, 1989) considers the ways that children negotiate and manage the play frame using metacommunication. Griffin (1984) further detailed the metacommunicative behaviors that allow for the coordination of meaning during play. Corsaro (1985) also attended to collaborative meaning making in his study of peer friendship. Verba (1993b) detailed several "cooperative formats," or structures for participation in the joint construction of the play narrative. In a more recent study, Howe, Petrakos, Rinaldi, and LeFebvre (2005) documented the interactional strategies used by kindergartners to construct shared meaning during play. In addition to the work that attempts to identify the interactional structures through which children collaborate, a related line of work explores how children develop the capacity to participate in the collaborative construction of a play text. For example, Farver (1992) examined the communicative strategies used by children ages two through five to create and structure shared meaning during play, detailing the ways that children's strategies for participating in joint meaning construction change as they age. Howes, Unger, and Matheson (1992) trace the development of children's ability to participate in the representation and communication of meaning during play, showing that initially infants are dependent on a more expert partner to endow their actions with meaning, but by the age three children have gained representational independence and are therefore ready to fully participate in joint meaning making with peers.

While the work on peer interaction discussed here does not make explicit connections to literacy learning, it parallels the "social turn," by moving away from a focus on individual cognitive development and toward a concern with the processes by which children collaboratively create meaning during play. In the future, research on play's contribution to literacy development will need to attend to this work, because it offers a foundation for understanding the ways that play serves as a setting for children to engage in the social meaning-making practices that constitute literacy. In addition, work exploring the peer interaction processes involved in collaborative construction of meaning in play might be integrated with investigations into creative appropriation and transmediation, such as the work of Dyson (2003) and Rowe (1998), so that we can better understand how peer interaction during play supports development of facility in socially situated sign use. Similar work has been done with regard to peer collaborative activity during other activities, including Labbo's work on computer-based symbol making (1996), Daiute's work on peer collaboration in story writing (Daiute, 1990; Daiute & Dalton, 1992), and Corsaro and Nelson's (2003) analysis of peer collaboration in various literacy activities in preschool classrooms.

In addition to considering the role of peer interaction in literacy development, researchers will need to consider the ways in which individual development interacts with development at other levels. For example, many authors have observed that among children who play together frequently, an oral culture will emerge, in the form of relatively stable texts or thematic motifs that are revisited, recycled, and embellished in successive play episodes (Corsaro, 1985, 1992; Musatti, 1993; Nicolopoulou, 2002; Opie, 1993; Sawyer, 1997, 2001). An example of oral culture can be observed on a grander scale in the form of playground rhymes and games that are passed down through generations of children, without much participation from adults (Opie & Opie, 1959; Sawyer, 2001; Sutton-Smith, 1989). On a smaller scale, each play group has its own emergent texts that exert some amount of downward causation on the players who use them. Researchers interested in how play contributes to literacy development might explore how this process of downward causation influences the way children participate in the narrative practices of their peer community.

The fruitfulness of such an investigation is suggested by a study by Corsaro and Nelson (2003). They look at the role of peer culture in literacy development in two U.S. and two Italian preschool classrooms, finding that children engage in shared literacy activities when they interact informally with their peers, and that these activities are shaped by the interests, concerns, and values of the classroom peer culture. While Corsaro and Nelson (2003) do not include social pretend play in their discussion, it is clear from Corsaro's other work (1985, 1992) that peer culture exerts a similarly downward causal influence on children's play, and can therefore be understood as an important mediator of literacy learning during play. Paley (1988, 1990) also speaks to the role of emergent peer culture in mediating play. Paley's emphasis on listening carefully to the content of children's play and to how themes emerge, recur, and evolve within a classroom is worthy of attention by literacy researchers. Her work offers a vibrant picture of how play texts result from group improvisation and how these same texts serve as meaning-making tools for children. Another direction relating to the interaction between individuals and emergent peer culture is suggested by Musatti (1993). She observes how modes of representation as well as representational content become both more explicit and more conventionalized as children in a peer group play together. Musatti notes that this process of local emergence within the peer group reproduces at a microphenomenal level the process of cultural formation in larger society. Future research might explore further the way participation in the formation of local peer culture prepares children for participation in cultural formation on a larger scale.

The development of the individual child through play is situated not only within the oral culture of her peers but also within the group-level learning of her peer group. As Sawyer (2001) points out, at the same times as individual children are learning from playing together, the group as a whole is learning, too. For example, in a preschool classroom, the class is learning how to function better as a group. To clarify, consider by analogy an improvisational theatre group. Improv groups rehearse quite a bit before they perform—not to develop material or to improve the skills of the individual actors, but to develop their ability to function as an ensemble (author's field notes, October 11, 2003; Sawyer, 2001). In the same way, the peer group is developing its ability to function as a group. Over time, children in a peer group, such as a preschool classroom, develop collectively-held strategies for communicating, solving problems, and working together, so that the negotiation strategies that children use during group improvisational play might look very different later in the group's history than they do early on. Literacy researchers might explore the ways in which the collectively-held semiotic practices of a peer group develop over time, and how this interacts with the development of individual members.

IMPLICATIONS FOR EDUCATORS

In the decades of research into the connections between play and literacy, many recommendations have been made to educators with regard to how they might facilitate children's play in ways that enhance the benefits for literacy development. Underlying all these suggestions has been the assertion that teachers of preschool-aged children should recognize that literacy, for this age group, involves developing representational competence and the ability to participate in meaning-making activities with peers (Pellegrini & Galda, 1994; Roskos & Christie, 2001b). In this section, I build on the work of other scholars who have made specific recommendations for using play in early educational settings to enhance literacy development, in order to explore three broad implications of understanding play as a form of group improvisation in which children engage in multimodal, semiotic activity.

Provide Ample Time for Peer Play

It has often been suggested that adults might scaffold children's play in strategic ways, in order to introduce and model literacy concepts (Morrow & Rand, 1991; Roskos & Christie, 2001b; Saracho, 2004; Schrader, 1991; Vukelich, 1991). From a social semiotic point of view, adult scaffolding could serve to allow children to engage in more sophisticated semiotic or narrative practices than they could without the assistance of a more expert partner (for example, see Bondioli, 2001; Glaubman et al., 2001). However, from the same perspective, it is equally, if not more, important that children have ample opportunity to play with their peers in ways that are not adult directed. Children learn in different ways from adults than they do from their peers (Daiute & Dalton, 1992; Paley, 1990; Verba, 1993b). On the one hand, adults are more expert at literacy practices, and can scaffold children in using more complex strategies. On the other hand, when children interact with adults, they are more likely to defer to the authority of the adult, and less likely to improvise (Baker-Sennett, Matusov, & Rogoff, 1992; Pellegrini & Galda, 1994).

Because peers have relatively equal status, their representational strategies are more open to negotiation, revision, and collaboration than might be the strategies of an adult partner (Verba, 1993b). Of course, even though peers have relatively equal status, they have differential expertise—each child arrives at the play episode with a slightly different collection of semiotic resources, assembled from her own prior experiences of engagement in the symbolic world. Playing together involves negotiating across these differential states of knowledge. As Verba (1993b) explains, learning processes in peer play are very much like those observed in other forms of peer collaborative learning in which peers reciprocally scaffold each other (Forman, 1992; Tudge & Rogoff, 1989). Further, Verba notes that the direction of asymmetry may shift over the course of interaction, so that at one moment one child may be more competent in relation to the activity at hand, while in the next moment, the roles may be reversed. Christie and Stone (1999) observed that even in a multiage classroom, scaffolding during play was seldom unidirectional, with the younger children providing assistance almost as much as the older children.

In addition to the benefits of collaborative learning, play with peers offers children the opportunity to participate in a community of narrative practice of their own making, in which they can participate fully, as compared to the more peripheral position they hold when participating in meaning-making activity with adults (cf. Musatti, 1993). Because nondirected play with peers offers children benefits that are different from those found in their interactions with adults, and because classrooms are important places where children come together as a community, educators will do well to offer children plenty of opportunity for unconstrained play with their peers.

Create a Classroom Environment That Supports Narrative Activity in Play

While it is important for children to have the opportunity to play together without the intrusion of adults, there are other ways in which educators might intervene in order to support the development of social semiotic, multimodal literacy through play. For example, it might be argued that one reason class groups using the Paley model (see above) achieve such notable gains is that the model creates a formal procedure for making story-based play happen and for inviting children to reflect on their play stories, and also because it supports the development of a classroom narrative culture (Groth & Darling 2001; Nicolopoulou, 1997, 2002; note that the Paley model does not involve explicit instruction about writing or enacting stories). Educators should continue to explore this model, and might also develop other formats for supporting spontaneous peer play and for helping children reflect on the narrative activity of their group. For example, teachers could develop procedures in their classroom that create opportunities for children to talk about their play.

Provide a Play Environment That is "Enriched" With Abstract Objects

Another approach that has been recommended for adult intervention in children's play is the use of literacy enriched play environments (LEPEs). Play centers equipped with objects associated with print-based literacy such as stamps, envelopes, pencils, appointment books, and newspapers, have been shown to be effective in increasing the amount of print-based literacy-related behaviors in which children engage during play, especially when the play environments are staffed with adults skilled at strategic mediation of children's use of the materials (Einarsdottir, 2001; Neuman & Roskos, 1991, 1992, 1997; Saracho, 2001; Vukelich, 1991). From a social semiotic, multimodal perspective, literacy enriched play environments are valuable because they help children learn to engage in the text-based practices of their community.

At the same time, this perspective suggests that children may benefit as well from play environments that have been equipped in a very different way. In contrast to LEPEs, play centers that contain only very abstract objects, such as blocks and scarves, may be valuable to literacy learning because they challenge players' symbolization processes and stretch their abilities to coordinate their sign usage when referents are less obvious (cf. Verba, 1993a). This approach might be especially beneficial once children have become facile in playing with more defined props (Pellegrini & Galda, 1994).

CONCLUSION

In this chapter, I have argued that new approaches to literacy development based on a social semiotic, multimodal perspective require us to attend to pretend play as a form of group improvisation. Play, like all forms of group improvisation, involves the collaborative creation of a shared social product—a play narrative. Because it is both open-ended and collaborative, play requires children to coordinate their semiotic activity; they must arrive at a shared understanding about what they are playing and how they will play it. Play, then, provides an important setting in which children can develop facility in using a range of symbolic resources in the context of a meaning-making community. In this way, engaging in group improvisation with peers during pretend play prepares children for participating in the various literacy communities in which they will engage throughout their lives.

ACKNOWLEDGEMENTS

Melissa Mosley and Heather Hayes, as well as two anonymous reviewers, provided invaluable insights toward the revision of this chapter. I would also like to thank the Mr. and Mrs. Spencer T. Olin Fellowship program at Washington University in St. Louis for their support during the writing of this chapter.

NOTES

1. Paley's own writings (e.g., 1988, 1990) provide a rich ethnographic account of the narrative practices of children in a preschool classroom. While Paley rarely discusses issues of narrative competence and literacy explicitly, her descriptions of children's play are more aligned with the social semiotic multimodal view explored later in this chapter than with the structural approach described here. Her work is included in the Directions section of this chapter.

2. It has been noted that, from a social semiotic, multimodal perspective, play is an especially important context for the literacy development of groups of children who have traditionally been marginalized in schools, because it allows them the opportunity to create a meaning-making system based on their own experiences and abilities. For example, Kliewer et al. (2003) consider the various ways in which children with moderate to severe disabilities engage in meaning-making activities within inclusive classrooms. In this study, pretend play was one of several settings in which students could use a variety of semiotic systems to construct and communicate meaning with peers, each child according to her own ability. Play can also be a particularly useful setting for developing literacy among children whose home literacy practices differ from those traditionally found at school. For example, Dyson (2003) explores how, in play and other informal peer interactions, African American children interweave content, narrative structures, and representational practices from the many spheres in which they participate.

REFERENCES

Baker-Sennett, J., Matusov, E., & Rogoff, B. (1992). Sociocultural processes of creative planning in children's playcrafting. In P. Light & G. Butterworth (Eds.), *Context and cognition: Ways of learning and knowing* (pp. 93–114). Hillsdale, NJ: Erlbaum.

Bateson, G. (1971). The message "This is play." In R. E. Herron & B. Sutton-Smith (Eds.), *Child's play* (pp. 261–266). Malabar, FL: Robert E. Krieger Publishing Company. (Original work published 1956)

Bateson, G. (2004). A theory of play and fantasy. In H. Bial. (Ed.), *The performance studies reader* (pp 121–131). New York: Routledge. (Original work published 1955)

Bearne, E. (2003). Rethinking literacy: Communication, representation, and text. *Reading: Literacy & Language, 37*(3), 98–103.

Bondioli, A. (2001). The adult as a tutor in fostering children's symbolic play. In A. Göncü & E. L. Klein (Eds.), *Children in play, story, and school* (pp. 107–131). New York: The Guilford Press.

Branscombe, N. A., & Taylor, J. B. (2000). "It would be as good as Snow White." Play and prosody. In K. Roskos & J. Christie (Eds.), *Play and literacy in early childhood: Research from multiple perspectives* (pp. 169–188). Mahwah, NJ: Erlbaum.

Christie, J. (1991). Psychological research on play: Connections with early literacy development. In J. Christie (Ed.), *Play and early literacy development* (pp. 27–43). Albany, NY: SUNY Press.

Christie, J. F., & Stone, S. J. (1999). Collaborative literacy activity in print-enriched play centers: Exploring the "zone" in same-age and multi-age groupings. *Journal of Literacy Research, 31*(2), 109–131.

Corsaro, W. A. (1985). *Friendship and peer culture in the early years.* Norwood, NJ: Ablex.

Corsaro, W. A. (1992). Interpretive reproduction in children's peer cultures. *Social Psychological Quarterly, 55,* 160–177.

Corsaro, W. A., & Nelson, E. (2003). Children's collective activities and peer culture in early literacy in American and Italian preschools. *Sociology of Education, 76*(3), 209–227.

Curran, J. M. (1999). Constraints of pretend play: Explicit and implicit rules. *Journal of Research in Childhood Education, 14*(1), 47–55.

Daiute, C. (1990). The role of play in writing development. *Research in the Teaching of English, 24*(1), 4–47.

Daiute, C., & Dalton, B. (1992). *Collaboration between children learning to write: Can novices be masters?* (Report No. CSW-TR-60). Berkeley, CA: National Center for the Study of Writing and Literacy. (ERIC Document Reproduction Service No. ED354522)

Dickinson, D. K., & Beals, D. E. (1994). Not by print alone: Oral language supports for early literacy development. In D. F. Lancy (Ed.), *Children's emergent literacy: From research to practice.* Westport, CT: Praeger.

Dyson, A. H. (2003). *The brothers and sisters learn to write: Popular literacies in childhood and school cultures.* New York: Teachers College Press.

Eckler, J. A., & Weininger, O. (1989). Structural parallels between pretend play and narratives. *Developmental Psychology, 25*(5), 736–743.

Einarsdottir, J. I. (2001). Incorporating literacy resources into the play curriculum of two Icelandic preschools. In K. Roskos & J. Christie (Eds.), *Play and literacy in early childhood: Research from multiple perspectives* (pp. 77–90). Mahwah, NJ: Erlbaum.

Ervin-Tripp, S. (1991). Play in language development. In B. Scales, M. Almy, A. Nicolopoulou, & S. Ervin-Tripp (Eds.), *Play and the social context of development in early care and education* (pp. 84–97). New York: Teachers College Press.

Farver, J. (1992). Communicating shared meaning in social pretend play. *Early Childhood Research Quarterly, 7*(4), 501–516.

Fein, G. G. (1981). Pretend play in childhood: An integrative review. *Child Development, 52*(4), 1095–1118.

Fein, G. G., Ardila-Rey, A. E., & Groth, L. A. (2000). The narrative connection: Stories and literacy. In K. Roskos & J. Christie (Eds.), *Play and literacy in early childhood: Research from multiple perspectives.* Mahwah, NJ: Erlbaum.

Forman, E. A. (1992). Discourse, intersubjectivity, and the development of peer collaboration: A Vygotskian approach. In L. T. Winegar & J. Valsiner (Eds.), *Children's development within social context* (pp. 143–159). Hillsdale, NJ: Lawrence Erlbaum Associates, Inc.

Galda, L. (1984). Narrative competence: Play, storytelling, and story comprehension. In A. D. Pellegrini & T. Yawkey (Eds.), *The development of oral and written language in social contexts* (pp. 105–118). Norwood, NJ: Ablex Publishing.

Garvey, C. (1974). Some properties of social play. *Merrill-Palmer Quarterly, 20* 163–180.

Garvey, C. (1993). Diversity in the controversial repertoire: The case of conflicts and social pretending. *Cognition and Instruction Discourse and shared reasoning, 11*(3–4), 251–264.

Garvey, C., & Berndt, R. (1979). *The organization of pretend play.* Corte Madera, CA: Select Press.

Garvey, C., & Kramer, T. L. (1989). The language of social pretend play. *Developmental Review, 9*(4), 364–382.

Gee, J. P. (1989). Literacies and traditions. *Journal of Education, 171*(1), 26–38.

Gee, J. P. (2000). The New Literacy Studies: from 'socially situated' to the work of the social. In Barton, D., Hamilton, M., & Ivanic, R. (Eds.), *Situated literacies: Reading and writing in context* (pp. 180–196). New York: Routledge.

Gee, J. P. (2004). *Situated language and learning: A critique of traditional schooling.* New York: Routledge.

Glaubman, R. B.-I., Kashi, G., & Koresh, R. (2001). Facilitating the narrative quality of sociodramatic play. In A. Göncü & E. L. Klein (Eds.), *Children in play, story, and school* (pp. 132–157). New York: Guilford Press.

Göncü, A., & Perrone, A. (2005). Pretend play as a lifespan activity. *Topoi, 24*(2), 137–147.

Griffin, H. (1984). The coordination of meaning in the creation of a shared make-believe reality. In I. Bretherton (Ed.), *Symbolic play* (pp. 73–100). Orlando, FL: Academic Press.

Groth, L. A., & Darling, L. D. (2001). Playing "inside" stories. In A. Göncü & E. L. Klein (Eds.), *Children in play, story, and school* (pp. 220–237). New York: Guilford Press.

Howe, N., Petrakos, H., Rinaldi, C. M., & LeFebvre, R. (2005). "This is a bad dog, you know:" Constructing shared meanings during sibling pretend play. *Child Development, 76*(4), 783–794.

Howes, C., Unger, O. A., & Matheson, C. C. (1992). *The collaborative construction of pretend: Social pretend play functions.* Albany, NY: State University of New York Press.

Kane, S. R., & Furth, H. G. (1993). Children constructing social reality: A frame analysis of social pretend play. *Human Development Special Topic: New Directions in Studying Pretend Play, 36*(4), 199–214.

Kavanaugh, R. D., & Engel, S. (1998). The development of pretense and narrative in early childhood. In O. N. Saracho & B. Spodek (Eds.), *Multiple perspectives on play in early childhood education* (pp. 80–99). Albany, NY: SUNY Press.

Kendrick, M. (2005). Playing house: A sideways glance at literacy and identity in early childhood. *Journal of Early Childhood Literacy, 5*(1), 5–28.

Kliewer, C., Fitzgerald, L., Meyer-Mork, J., Hartman, P., English-Sand, P., & Raschke, D. (2003). Citizenship for all in the literate community: An ethnography of young children with significant disabilities in inclusive early childhood settings. *Harvard Educational Review, 74*(4), 373–403.

Kress, G. (1997). *Before writing: Rethinking the paths to literacy.* New York: Routledge.

Kress, G. (2003). *Literacies in the new media age.* New York: Routledge.

Kress, G., & Street, B. (2006). Foreword. In K. Pahl & J. Rowsell (Eds.), *Travel notes from the New Literacy Studies: Instances of practice* (pp. vii–x). Clevedon, UK: Multilingual Matters.

Labbo, L. D. (1996). A semiotic analysis of young children's symbol making in a classroom computer center. *Reading Research Quarterly, 31*(4), 356–385.

Lancy, D. F. (1994). The conditions that support emergent literacy. In D. F. Lancy (Ed.), *Children's emergent literacy: From research to practice* (pp. 1–20). Westport, CT: Praeger.

Leland, C. H., & Harste, J. C. (1994). Multiple ways of knowing: Curriculum in a new key. *Language Arts, 71*(5), 337–345.

Lillard, A. S. (1998). Playing with a theory of mind. In O. N. Saracho & B. Spodek (Eds.), *Multiple perspectives on play in early childhood education* (pp. 11–33). Albany, NY: SUNY Press.

Löhfdahl, A. (2005). 'The funeral': A study of children's shared meaning-making and its developmental significance. *Early years, 25*(1), 5–16.

Mason, J. M., & Allen, J. (1986). A review of emergent literacy with implications for research and practice in reading. *Review of Research in Education, 13*, 3–47.

Morrow, L. M., & Rand, M. (1991). Preparing the classroom environment to promote literacy during play. In J. Christie (Ed.), *Play and early literacy development* (pp. 141–166). Albany, NY: SUNY Press.

Musatti, T. (1993). Meaning between peers: The meaning of the peer. *Cognition and Instruction Discourse and shared reasoning, 11*(3–4), 241–250.

Neuman, S. B., & Roskos, K. (1991). The influence of literacy enriched play centers on preschoolers' conceptions of the functions of print. In J. Christie (Ed.), *Play and early literacy development* (pp. 167–188). Albany, NY: SUNY Press.

Neuman, S. B., & Roskos, K. (1992). Literacy objects as cultural tools: Effects on children's literacy behaviors in play. *Reading Research Quarterly, 27*(3), 202–225.

Neuman, S. B., & Roskos, K. (1997). Literacy knowledge in practice: Contexts of participation for young writers and readers. *Reading Research Quarterly, 32*(1), 10–32.

Nicolopoulou, A. (1991). Play, cognitive development, and the social world: The research perspective. In B. Scales, M. Almy, A. Nicolopoulou & S. Ervin-Tripp (Eds.), *Play and the social context of development in early care and education* (pp. 129–142). New York: Teachers College Press.

Nicolopoulou, A. (1997). Children and narratives: Toward an interpretive and sociocultural approach. In M. Bamberg (Ed.), *Narrative development: Six approaches* (pp. 179–215). Mahwah, NJ: Erlbaum.

Nicolopoulou, A. (2002). Peer-group culture and narrative development. In S. Blum-Kulka & C. E. Snow (Eds.), *Talking to adults: The contribution of multiparty discourse to language acquisition* (pp. 117–152). Mahwah, NJ: Erlbaum.

Opie, I. (1993). *The people in the playground.* New York: Oxford University Press.

Opie, I. & Opie, P. (1959). *The lore and language of schoolchildren.* New York: Oxford University Press.

Paley, V. G. (1988). *Bad guys don't have birthdays.* Chicago: University of Chicago Press.

Paley, V. G. (1990). *The boy who would be a helicopter: The uses of storytelling in the classroom.* Cambridge, MA: Harvard University Press.

Paley, V. G. (2004). *A child's work: The importance of play and fantasy.* Chicago: University of Chicago Press.

Pellegrini, A. D. (1984). Identifying causal elements in the thematic-fantasy play paradigm. *American Educational Research Journal, 21*(3), 691–701.

Pellegrini, A. D. (1985). The relations between symbolic play and literate behavior: A review and critique of the empirical literature. *Review of Educational Research, 55*(1), 107–121.

Pellegrini, A. D., & Galda, L. (1982). The effects of thematic-fantasy play training on the development of children's story comprehension. *American Educational Research Journal, 19*(3), 443–452.

Pellegrini, A. D., & Galda, L. (1991). Longitudinal relations among preschoolers' symbolic play, metalinguistic verbs, and emergent literacy. In J. Christie (Ed.), *Play and early literacy development* (pp. 47–68). Albany, NY: SUNY Press.

Pellegrini, A. D., & Galda, L. (1993). Ten years after: A reexamination of symbolic play and literacy research. *Reading Research Quarterly, 28*(2), 163–175.

Pellegrini, A. D., & Galda, L. (1994). Early literacy from a developmental perspective. In D. F. Lancy (Ed.), *Children's emergent literacy: From research to practice* (pp. 21–28). Westport, CT: Praeger.

Pellegrini, A. D., & Galda, L. (2000). Commentary—Cognitive development, play, and literacy: Issues of definition and development function. In K. A. Roskos & J. F. Christie (Eds.), *Play and literacy in early childhood: Research from multiple perspectives* (pp. 62–74). Mahwah, NJ: Erlbaum.

Pellegrini, A. D., Galda, L., Dresden, J., & Cox, S. (1991). A longitudinal study of the predictive relations among symbolic play, linguistic verbs, and early literacy. *Research in the Teaching of English, 25*(2), 219–235.

Piaget, J. (1962). *Play, dreams, and imitation in childhood* (C. Gattegno & F. M. Hodgson, Trans.). New York: Norton.

Rogoff, B. (1990). *Apprenticeship in thinking: Cognitive development in social context.* New York: Oxford University Press.

Roskos, K., & Christie, J. (2001a). Examining the play-literacy interface: A critical review and future directions. *Journal of Early Childhood Literacy, 1*(1), 59–89.

Roskos, K., & Christie, J. (2001b). Under the lens: The play-literacy relationship in theory and practice. In S. Reifel & M. H. Brown (Eds.), *Early education and care and reconceptualizing play* (pp. 321–338). New York: JAI Press.

Roskos, K., & Christie, J. (Eds.). (in press). *Play and literacy in early childhood: Research from multiple perspectives* (2nd ed.). Mahwah, NJ: Erlbaum.

Rowe, D. W. (1998). The literate potentials of book-related dramatic play. *Reading Research Quarterly, 33*(1), 10–35.

Sachs, J., Goldman, J., & Chaille, C. (1984). Planning in pretend play: Using language to coordinate narrative development. In A. D. Pellegrini & T. Yawkey (Eds.), *The development of oral and written language in social contexts* (pp. 119–128). Norwood, NJ: Ablex.

Saracho, O. N. (2001). Exploring young children's literacy development through play. *Early Child Development and Care, 167*, 103–114.

Saracho, O. N. (2004). Supporting literacy-related play: Roles for teachers of young children. *Early Childhood Education Journal, 31*(3), 201–206.

Sawyer, R. K. (1997). *Pretend play as improvisation: Conversation in the preschool classroom.* Hillsdale, NJ: Erlbaum.

Sawyer, R. K. (1999). The emergence of creativity. *Philosophical Psychology, 12*(4), 447–470.

Sawyer, R. K. (2001). Play as improvisational rehearsal: Multiple levels of analysis in children's play. In A. Göncü (Ed.), *Children in play, story, and school* (pp. 19–38). New York: The Guilford Press.

Sawyer, R. K. (2002). Improvisation and narrative. *Narrative Inquiry, 12*(2), 319–349.

Sawyer, R. K. (2003). *Group creativity: Music, theater, collaboration.* Mahwah, NJ: Erlbaum.

Sawyer, R. K., & DeZutter, S. L. (in press). Improvisation: A lens for play and literacy research. In K. Roskos & J. Christie (Eds.), *Play and literacy in early childhood: Research from multiple perspectives* (2nd ed.). Mahwah, NJ: Erlbaum.

Schrader, C. T. (1991). Symbolic play: A source of meaningful engagements with writing and reading. In J. Christie (Ed.), *Play and early literacy development* (pp. 189–214). Albany, NY: SUNY Press.

Silvern, S. B., Taylor, J. B., Williamson, P. A., Surbeck, E., & Kelley, M. F. (1986). Young children's story recall as a product of play, story familiarity, and adult intervention. *Merrill-Palmer Quarterly, 32*(1), 73–86.

Silvern, S. B., Williamson, P. A., & Waters, B. (1982). Play as a mediator of comprehension: An alternative to play training. *Educational Research Quarterly, 7*(3), 16–21.

Smolucha, L., & Smolucha, F. (1998). The social origins of mind: Post-piagetian perspectives on pretend play. In O. N. Saracho & B. Spodek (Eds.), *Multiple perspectives on play in early childhood education* (pp. 34–58). Albany, NY: SUNY Press.

Sutton-Smith, B. (1989). Children's folk games as customs. *Western Folklore, 48*(1), 33–42.

Teale, W. H., & Sulzby, E. (Eds.). (1986). *Emergent literacy: Writing and reading. Writing research: Multidisciplinary inquiries into the nature of writing series.* Norwood, NJ: Ablex.

Tudge, J., & Rogoff, B. (1989). Peer influences on cognitive development: Piagetian and Vygotskian perspectives. In M. N. Bornstein & J. S. Bruner (Eds.), *Interaction in human development* (pp. 17–40). Mahwah, NJ: Erlbaum.

Verba, M. (1993a). Construction and sharing of meanings in pretend play among young children. In M. Stambak & H. Sinclair (Eds.), *Pretend play among three year olds* (pp. 1–29). Hillsdale, NJ: Erlbaum.

Verba, M. (1993b). Cooperative formats in pretend play among young children. *Cognition and Instruction Discourse and shared reasoning, 11*(3–4), 265–280.

Vukelich, C. (1991). Materials and modeling: Promoting literacy during play. In J. Christie (Ed.), *Play and early literacy development* (pp. 215–232). Albany, NY: SUNY Press.

Vygotsky, L. S. (1978). *Mind in society* (A. Kozulin, Trans.). Cambridge, MA: Harvard University Press.

Walker, C. A. (1999). Playing a story: Narrative and writing-like features in scenes of dramatic play. *Reading Research & Instruction, 38*(4), 401–413.

Williamson, P. A., & Silvern, S. B. (1991). Thematic-fantasy play and story comprehension. In J. Christie (Ed.), *Play and early literacy development* (pp. 69–90). Albany, NY: SUNY Press.

Yaden, D. B. J., Rowe, D. W., & MacGillivray, L. (2000). Emergent literacy: A matter (polyphony) of perspectives. In R. Barr, M. L. Kamil, P. D. Pearson, & P. B. Mosenthal (Eds.), *Handbook of reading research* (Vol. 3, pp. 425–454). Mahwah, NJ: Erlbaum.

CHAPTER 11

SOCIAL ASPECTS IN LANGUAGE AND LITERACY LEARNING

Progress, Problems, and Interventions

**Adriana G. Bus, Maria T. de Jong,
and Marinus H. van IJzendoorn**

The language development of children at the age of three is a good predictor of reading comprehension at the age of nine (Hart & Risley, 2003). Preschoolers, who as infants and toddlers are brought up in a linguistically deprived environment and who not only hear little spoken language but are also given little feedback to spontaneous attempts at speech, are behind in written language skills at the age of 9–10 years. Evidently once ground has been lost it is not easy to regain. Hart and Risley (2003) speak of "an early catastrophe." This chapter is aimed at further specification of which sorts of social experience stimulates written language development. In particular we examine the question which early experiences are necessary to buffer children against reading problems at school. Is the risk for reading problems arising at primary school reduced by reading to children in the infant, toddler, and preschooler phase? We take the position that when adult caregivers read books to children, they enter into a cognitive apprenticeship that scaffolds or supports youngsters' literacy learning. Or

Contemporary Perspectives on Social Learning in Early Childhood Education, pages 243–257
Copyright © 2007 by Information Age Publishing
243

to put it differently, social interaction serves as a major force in the growth of children's literacy competence (Bus, 2001).

In the first part, we try to specify which knowledge developing in the preschool stage prevents reading problems later in school age. We notice for instance that toddlers and preschoolers get better at using the language in books. Although they are not really "reading" text it seems from their approach that children become more and more familiar with the structure and the rhythm that is typical of books (Sulzby, 1985). In the second part, we stress the importance of adult–child interaction in stimulating story comprehension as an incentive to children's literacy development. Related to the social-construction hypothesis (Teale and Sulzby, 1986), we discuss the hypothesis that a negative history of parent–child interactive experiences might inhibit children's reading experiences resulting in a considerably higher risk of developing a problem with reading later at school. In the last part the role of play groups for toddlers and preschoolers in stimulating language and literacy is described and it is discussed which alternative strategies play-group caregivers may use to facilitate effective interaction with young children.

THE INFLUENCE OF ORAL LANGUAGE DEVELOPMENT ON EARLY READING DEVELOPMENT

According to the PSA model (*Phonological Sensitivity Approach*) oral language development stimulates phoneme awareness and via phoneme awareness reading proficiency. The so-called CLA perspective (*Comprehensive Language Approach*) emphasizes that language comprehension is also an important factor in learning to read. This is certainly true for Group 4 and above. Whitehurst's studies show that vocabulary is a good predictor of reading comprehension in the higher school years (Storch and Whitehurst, 2002). Hart and Risley's (2003) findings support the hypothesis that early difference in vocabulary continue to affect reading development later in school. These researchers spent two and half years registering the experiences of young children with spoken language by recording monthly for one hour what happened in families where 1 or 2 young children were learning to speak. The highly diverse vocabularies at the age of 3 years appeared to be a good predictor for the reading proficiency in Group 5 when the children are 9 to 10 years old ($r = .56$).

Dickinson and colleagues (Dickinson, McCabe, Anastasopoulos, Peisner-Feinberg, & Poe, 2003) concluded that even in the very young children there is more support for the CLA perspective than for the notion that especially phoneme awareness is important (the PSA perspective). In their study, knowledge about written language is measured against orthographic knowledge (e.g., NNNNX is not a word, but PLUD is), success in the reading of many frequently occurring words (e.g., McDonalds, Coca Cola, milk, exit, etc.), and name writing. Their subjects were 3 to 4 years old. If the relation between oral and written language development arises via phoneme awareness as the PSA model proposes, then only phoneme awareness could explain the differences. This appeared not to be the case: In addition to phoneme awareness, differences in emergent word recognition were also explained by vocabulary. Thus, even in this group of very young children, phoneme awareness is not a sufficient explanation for the relation between written and oral language. It seems as if understanding written language in the environment and books is already a significant factor. The more the children are successfully representing the content of notices or text, the better they are at guessing letters, as long as the basic skills for recoding are still rudimentary.

A number of researchers (including Sénéchal and LeFevre, 2002; Storch and Whitehurst, 2002) regard reading aloud as a way of stimulating oral language that is relevant to comprehension of written text. Other oral communications situations, which just like reading aloud are characterized by a complex vocabulary and grammar, are probably just as effective. Consider for instance the *"dining table discussions"* about children's experiences in situations where the parents and other table companions are not present. The language is complex because it has to be suitable to providing information about a context with which the listener has only limited or even no experience. In contrast is the belief that children, through being read to, come into contact—to a far greater extent than in other language situations—with a particular sort of language that is typical of written language and that rarely occurs in other language situations. Consider subordinate clauses, quotations that are literally spoken between two characters, passive constructions, unknown expressions, and idioms. This type of language not only characterizes books for adults but also storybooks for the very youngest children. When we recently tested the comprehension of sentences from picture storybooks in a pilot study we realized how difficult the language use is in books for four- and five-year-olds. Sentences like *"that heals every disease and can do no harm"* appeared to be a stumbling block for a very advanced five-year-old preschooler.

SOCIAL EXPERIENCES AROUND STORYBOOKS ARE A STIMULUS TO LEARNING TO READ

Children, who as toddlers and preschoolers are regularly read to, have a considerably lower risk of developing a problem with reading later at school (Bus, van IJzendoorn, and Pellegrini, 1995; Scarborough and

Dobrich, 1994). From a synthesis of all studies between 1950 and 1994 into the relation between being read to in the preschool phase and reading performance it seemed that being read to not only correlated with the early reading development but also with reading performance later in primary school when children read conventionally. Some researchers have correctly questioned the conclusion that being read to stimulates reading development. The finding that being read to is linked to a higher score on reading tests does not mean that these higher scores are the result of being read to. The frequency with which a child is read to, can be the result of greater interest in language-related activities: Children with a stronger predisposition for language and greater cognitive capacities will want to be read to more often. According to this interpretation, interest in books is anchored in biologically determined traits that strengthen the need for language-related activities. In other words, reading to a child may not be the cause but rather the consequence of the language-related developments.

In the perspective of a series of studies into social-emotional aspects of reading aloud (Bus, 2003), the latter hypothesis is less likely. We discovered that very young children with resistance to being read to could be distinguished in particular by the quality of the social relationship with the parent from children who did enjoy being read to. Danny, aged three, illustrates this point. His mother told us that she never read aloud to him because he didn't like it. When we asked her to try in a laboratory setting, her attempt indeed was unsuccessful. Danny refused to sit quietly and listen despite well-intentioned attempts by his mother to get him interested in the book. Short moments of attention alternated with highly rejective reactions. We tested the quality of the emotional bond between parents like this and their children and discovered that a relatively large portion of the children who are read to rarely and who do not much enjoy being read to, have an insecure emotional attachment with the parent. It is typical of such parents that they are fairly insensitive to the interests and needs of their child; when reading to them they are unable to bring to the fore elements from the book that would interest the child and give explanations that would strengthen the interest in how events unfold. A consequence of this is that friction often arises and reading-aloud sessions take a disagreeable direction. Because these parents and children experience less pleasure in reading aloud, it also does not become routine. In other words, pleasure in reading aloud arises when parents are successful at getting children to enjoy books. Whether reading aloud takes place is not only a question of a child's aptitude and interest but mainly of how the parents approach this social interactive challenge.

Such differences are present from the very beginning of parental attempts to read to children. By way of illustration, we will discuss results of a study with 1-year-old infants' interest in books as a function of attachment security. Similarly to other studies of book reading to babies (van Kleeck et al., 1996), we found that most maternal energy was devoted to getting and keeping the baby's attention and encouraging participation in the routine (Bus and van IJzendoorn, 1997). However, the insecurely attached children were less attentive than the secure ones: They were more likely to look at other objects in the environment or to make attempts to escape from the mother's lap. Insecurely attached children responded less to the book content by referencing: They were less inclined to make animal sounds, touch the pictures (for example, caressing an animal picture), or make movements to represent a pictured object (like horse-riding in response to a picture of a horse). Their mothers seemed occupied with controlling their child's negative behaviors by putting an arm around the child, thus restricting the infant's movements, or by keeping the book out of reach. We expect to find similar but probably smaller differences between securely and insecurely pairs when this study would have been carried out in the home instead of the laboratory. At home parents may relax more and allow their child more freedom than in the laboratory.

ENGAGING CHILDREN IN THE WORLD OF THE BOOK

According to the book reading paradigm (Teale and Sulzby, 1986), social interaction serves as a major force in engaging young children in the world of the book. In attempting to read to a very young child one knows that it is insufficient to just read the text. Whilst reading aloud, other than in the majority of oral language situations, immediate support can be offered if preschoolers are not yet successful at grasping the complex events, in making links between events and understanding the language. During reading aloud, a subtle question and answer game with adults arises through which toddlers and preschoolers get better and better at grasping the structure of texts. Adults stress the relation between the text and what can be seen in the pictures, they ask questions and explain things to children to set them on the trail of the links between the various events.

Only as preschoolers get closer to school age, their parents read more and talk less about the books that they share with their children (van Kleeck, 2003). For the very young children between one and three, books are only attractive if book reading includes more than just sounding out text. Parents make books accessible by skipping difficult parts, adapting text to the child's level, creating new stories, and the like. It is our impression (untested as yet) that young children's active participation and learning strongly depend on the parental ability to bridge the discrepancy between the child's world and the world of the book through careful choice of pictorial images and language. Young children need social support to stay attentive, in discovering exciting parts of a page, and to under-stand pictures. Infants' responses gain significance as denotative symbols through responding to the book together with the mother.

When reading to very young children, adults seem to emphasize main-taining the communicative relationship over teaching infants by pointing at the pictures and evoking referencing behaviors. For instance, in a study with 11- to 14-month-old infants (Bus & van IJzendoorn, 1997), it appeared that mothers did not make attempts to elicit referencing from the child when their infants had not yet started to use (proto) symbols spontane-ously. Responses by mothers were negatively correlated with children's act-ing upon books (i.e., banging on the book, hitting pages, touching pictures, reaching at the book, grasping the book, and random pointing). Mothers extended their infants' referencing behavior by pointing to the pictures and by evoking responses ("caress the baa-lamb") after the chil-dren showed referencing behavior. Pointing and evoking responses from their children were positively correlated with the child's responding (rs were .38 and .34, respectively) and referencing (rs were .47 and .35, respec-tively). In other words, adult expansion of children's referencing behavior is a consequence of children's level of responding and is not—as was sug-gested by Ninio and Bruner (1976)—present from an early age.

To bridge the gap between the book and the child, and to engage a young reader in the world of the book, the adult (e.g., mother, father, care-giver, or grandparent) has to become both "reader" (of the original written text) and "creator" (of the story as actually told). It is of the utmost impor-tance that adults capitalize on intimate knowledge of their child's personal world; on familiar and meaningful settings, possessions, and sensations; and on the language with which these are associated (Jones, 1996). It is therefore to be expected that caregivers will "read" the pictorial contents of an illustrated story and its accompanying text more idiosyncratically as children are younger and/or less experienced. Jones's (1996) ethno-graphic study shows that caregivers are more successful in engaging infant readers in books when they find cues that give pleasure and that narrow the gap between book and child. More successful adults identify a large number of pictorial details, their visual content and linguistic coding both carrying a high emotional charge for the infant reader. Adults create a story not of the hero but of their own child. A disproportionate amount of adult speech time may be devoted to details of the pictures that often have little to do with the printed version of the story. The adult may adapt the story to include pictorial details more salient to the child. In this way, the illustrations give pleasure, but not necessarily because they have anything to do with the ongoing action of the story as written.

Research has revealed examples of caregivers altering the text during book reading to make it more attractive to the child (e.g., Martin and

Reutzel, 1999). The following observation illustrates how this emphasis often had the effect of driving the "official version" of the story into the background. For instance, in one study we (Bus and Sulzby, unpublished data) observed a mother reading *Sam Vole and His Brothers* (Waddell and Firth, 1992). She started reading the text to her 28-month-old child but when she noticed that the child became more interested in a picture of a bumblebee (not mentioned in the text) she let him make up his own story about a bumblebee. The child asked, "What's that?" and, "What is he (means Sam) looking at?" When mom explained that it is a bumblebee, the child concluded that Sam sees a bumblebee. Mother and child then discussed that Sam might be frightened. The bumblebee was not part of the written story, but it was part of the child's story. Thematically, the discussions beyond the written story may reflect intimately the child's current real-life interest. As such these "moments of time out" seem to be highly motivating and engaging to the child.

These and other results of our studies clearly point to the conclusion that caregiver–preschooler book reading is a profoundly social process, embedded in the affective relationship. In line with these findings it is our conviction that we need family literacy programs that support caregivers scaffolding their child's motivations and understandings, and in dealing with their distractions or negative responses. Programs focusing on the intimacy of sharing books may help adults to change their reading habits in order to foster their children's enjoyment and engagement in book reading. Simultaneously, improving the interactive book reading practices may be equally important to building trusting and close relationships, and may strengthen the emotional bond between a caregiver and a child.

DIFFERENCES ACROSS CULTURES

This form of scaffolding may be culture-specific and may not be generalized across cultures (Serpell, 1997). Culturally disparate groups may differ in educational beliefs that result in different ways of responding to and supporting their children (Serpell, Baker, and Sonnenschein, 2005). For instance, when for adults themselves reading is not a source of pleasure and entertainment, activities such as book reading may not be firmly embedded in family practices and routines, and parents may not know how to engage children in reading sessions.

With a group of 30 Dutch indigenous mothers with low education, De Groot and Bus (1995) tested the hypothesis that the mothers' own interest in reading for enjoyment is a decisive factor for opportunities of their babies and toddlers to become involved with books. In addition to their views on book reading to young children, we tested the mothers' familiarity with the domain of reading. We asked the mothers to recognize authors or magazine titles from checklists that contained plausible foils similar to lists used by Stanovich and colleagues (e.g., Cunningham and Stanovich, 1990). The results of this study strongly supported the hypothesis that when reading as a source of enjoyment was less important for the parent personally, parents did not view book reading as a source of pleasure and learning for their babies and toddlers. Mothers who agreed more with statements in favor of starting early to share books with children were those who themselves were more familiar with authors and magazine titles (*r*s were .56 and.68, respectively).

From the interviews, we concluded that most of the immigrant parents did not doubt the importance of book reading but that they doubt the value of reading to infants and very young children. In addition to 30 Dutch indigenous mothers, De Groot and Bus (1995) interviewed 20 Dutch immigrant mothers about reading to young children soon after their baby's birth. We asked the mothers originating from Morocco (North Africa), Turkey (Europe), or Surinam (South America) to choose from two contrasting statements, for instance: "My caregiver read to me" versus "I cannot remember being read to as a child." Most immigrant mothers (88%) agreed with the statement that book reading is an important preparation for school. Furthermore, 80% agreed with the statement that children learn from book reading and 95% with the statement that children who are read to will become better readers at school age (95%). However, these mothers did not agree with statements emphasizing that an early start is desirable: Only 25% of the parents agreed that book reading to infants or toddlers is worthwhile, while 35% believed that book-reading routines give a boost to babies' and toddlers' reading development. Thus a first step must be to convey in ways meaningful to parents and other caregivers with similar views the importance to later academic success of book reading with infants and toddlers.

In a study involving four-year-old Turkish-Dutch and Surinamese-Dutch parents with little reading experience, we noticed that parents, who themselves rarely read stories, have problems clarifying the language and the story by being interactive when reading aloud (Bus, Leseman, and Keultjes, 2000). These parents offered considerable less help to their 48-month-old child than similarly low-educated Dutch parents. For example, in the story Alice's friends bring her a stray dog that they have found on the street. Dutch parents try to explain with questions and comments why the friends brought the dog to Alice. It is not explicitly stated in the text but from all sorts of information it can be deduced that they would really like Alice to have some company during the long days that she has to be at home because she is ill.

The Turkish and Surinamese parents provide this sort of explanation much less frequently during reading the story and restrict themselves mostly to just reading the text out loud. These parents do not do much to increase the pleasure derived from the story. Storybook reading might not be a "pleasurable" experience for them because they are anxious about their reading, or they may think that they are not "doing it right." Another explanation might be that the Turkish- and Surinamese-Dutch parents have much more difficulty in seeing how complex the plot actually is of what is apparently a simple story and in noticing where children need help to follow the story and the language. We suspect that this is related to the reading experience of the parents themselves. Functional reading played a similar role in the families but in comparison to Dutch families the Surinamese-Dutch and Turkish-Dutch families involved in this study rarely read for pleasure.

Based on these results we may question whether the provision of books to families and the encouragement to read together actually will produce meaningful conversations around text in homes and cultures in which reading is not intrinsically embedded in the parents' daily activities and entertainment. When parents are not used to reading storybooks and reading might not be a "pleasurable" experience for them, they may need permanent support in scaffolding interactions.

MULTIMEDIA STORIES

Until recently we introduced young children to the world of reading only by means of fictional literature. Today's children become literate in an environment that also includes multimedia stories on TV, Internet sites, videotapes, and DVDs. According to an American survey in the census of 2000 under more than 1,000 parents (Rideout, Vandewater, and Wartella, 2003), children in the age range of zero to six watch television 1–2 hours a day whereas they spend only about half an hour per day reading. In less educated families TV and DVD take an even more prominent place in the reality of 3- to 5-year-olds: 3.5 hours on weekdays soar to 6 hours a day in the weekend (Zeijl, Crone, Wiefferink, Keuzekamp, and Reijneveld, 2005). By contrast, this group of children spends less than 15 minutes a day on (print) book reading with adults. Expectations are that the share of multimedia stories in young children's activities will increase even further during the coming decennial, probably even at a higher rate than up till now.

In line with the finding that interest in stories emerges from social interaction with an adult we observed that three-year-olds from low-educated families lapsed into passive viewing when they watched Maisy stories with additional filmic representations, music, and sounds. On the other hand, multimedia storybooks on the computer may have the potential to serve as "electronic scaffolding" that supports children's comprehension of fictional literature (Verhallen, Bus, & de Jong, 2006). Smith (2001), for instance, describes how her son James (2- to 3-year-old during the study) often responded directly to the computer screen. For instance, reading *The Tortoise and The Hare*, he clicked eight times on the hare thus revealing a hypertext ("Hey I was supposed to win") and he answered talking directly to the hare on the computer screen ("Well, he already winned") and not to his mother.

Now that screen media takes an increasingly prominent place in children's daily experiences, we became interested in effects of viewing multimedia stories when this is alternated with interactive book reading sessions. *Miffi, Maisy,* and *Musti,* all popular book series for the very young and originally available only as picture storybooks, are broadcasted by Dutch educational television and are also on sale as DVDs (which are often cheaper than the original print books). A unique result of a first experiment with three-year-olds is that the demand for repetition—an important condition especially for children at risk—is satisfied not only when the same story is read repeatedly to them but also when they hear a story in different formats—a common situation nowadays (Bus, Verhallen, & de Jong, in press). In half of the cases we alternated the static and multimedia version of the story, whereas the other half encountered the story supported only by static pictures.

We also found support for the hypothesis that alternation of print book reading sessions with viewing multimedia stories has added value because the multimedia images stimulate children's text comprehension. A unique result of this project was that the new processing tools have advantages that seem to compensate for a high percentage of unknown words. Rather than detracting from the story text, the extra nonverbal information sources seem to expose children to an additional set of processing tools, which, in combination with oral text, contributes to their ability to comprehend text. Probably because children hold verbal and nonverbal representations in working memory at the same time, they are able to build referential connections between seeing how the water flows away through a hole in the bath and the text telling that the bath leaks. As a result, alternation of reading the static story with viewing a multimedia version of the same story produced higher scores on questions about the stories' core vocabulary than did the static condition alone, a result that matches previous findings with five-year-olds (Verhallen et al. 2006). In this study involving Moroccan and Turkish preschoolers we found that children learned about seven new words in the multimedia situation (12–14% of words we suspected children would not know), twice as many as the average amount they learned with static pictures (three or four new words). There is no evidence that the film effects and the sounds distract attention from the spoken text so that the effects of multimedia stories lag behind the effects of reading aloud on the basis of only static images.

In other words, there is evidence that young children can profit from multimedia stories available on Internet sites, TV, and DVD on condition that encounters with multimedia stories are alternated with adult-led book reading sessions in which adults raise the children's interest in the stories and support story comprehension with questions. Alternating media may add to young children's urgent need for repetition and may improve their poor linguistic skills.

DESIRABLE INTERVENTIONS IN PEP GROUPS

PEP (Pre- and early-school Education Program) programs are intended to call a halt to the depressing cycle of poor environments creating poor school performance, by enriching the environment of children with activities and social interaction that strengthen oral and written language development. It is assumed that in the pre- and early-school phase the chances of compensating for deficits that arise in this phase are the most favorable. Reading aloud regularly, an activity that closely matches the interests of toddlers and preschoolers provides—according to the research—a strong impulse to both oral and written language development. About 8% of the differences in reading proficiency are connected to reading aloud (Bus, van IJzendoorn, & Pellegrini, 1995). In comparison to other interventions this has to be classified as a potentially considerable effect.

Social interaction around books seems to be an extremely effective way to stimulate the reading development of PEP pupils. Reading aloud has been proven to be a method for stimulating vocabulary and text comprehension. Both the frequency with which books are read aloud as well as the quality of books probably plays a decisive role. In most PEP programs reading aloud is indeed part of the program but we do not have the impression that this component is given more emphasis than, for example, ad hoc training of vocabulary during play. More can certainly be expected from reading aloud: Vocabulary is repeatedly offered in a rich context. Multimedia picture story books on DVD or Internet sites would seem to be a promising addition to reading aloud but are not yet part of the PEP programs.

However, reading aloud is not a simple task when children have no experience with books. If the content of picture books is difficult to access for toddlers and preschoolers, then reading aloud requires a lot of preparation by play-group leaders and teachers (van Kleef & Tomesen, 2002). When we recently listened in on a group of nonnative toddlers we noticed how few children were able to complete sentences that were repeated again and again in the story, despite having heard the story at least five times. The play-group leaders tried hard enough. They did not use words in a roundabout fashion to explain events but tried with pointing and cardboard cutout figures to explain the events. They tried to elicit responses from the children but most children in the group of twelve sat silently without showing engagement or interest. Afterwards one of the play-group leaders told us that she did not read to the children every day because it required a lot of effort. It may be more profitable to advocate individual adult-child book reading sessions in which the play-group leader creates an intimate atmosphere for sharing a story with individual children.

New materials such as multimedia stories may trigger new opportunities for social interaction about stories. For the near future we can imagine that we can make the most of the availability of new media by having play-group leaders read stories to children that can be watched on television at home or on Internet sites to which schools provide access. Stimulating parents to log their child in to Internet sites seems within easier reach than stimulating low-literate parents to create a daily book-reading routine. Note that this suggestion is at odds with teachers' and other caregivers' common strategies. They intuitively seem to prefer reading (print) books to children above children watching multimedia stories on the computer because they attribute negative outcomes to the computer (Robinson and Mackey, 2003). Multimedia are considered as "an easy medium" that hampers active involvement and learning, contrary to print books.

On average children learn about 14 new words per week. If children would hear two books four times, it may make a considerable contribution to the weekly portion of new words that are to be learned, quite apart from other effects of being read to on story comprehension and knowledge of reading conventions. This development would represent a considerable gain for PEP children but is still a long way short of what high-achieving children learn each week. On the basis of test results it is estimated that 17-year-olds in preuniversity education have a vocabulary of about 80,000 words. Assuming that these words have been learned in approximately 15 years that would mean that children are able to learn about 15 words per day. An estimate of the number of hours that would be needed to provide children from families with little language input with sufficient experience of spoken and written language in order to make the same progression each week clearly demonstrates how extensive interventions would have to be to give them equal preparatory educational opportunities. Reading aloud, even if it happens four times per week should be a minimum requirement for PEP programs.

SUMMARY AND CONCLUSIONS

We found support for the assumption that interest in books emerges from early forms of interaction in which adults "share" with rather than "communicate" messages; such learning depends on the adults' ability to create a close and intimate atmosphere in which to share books together. While young children may not be interested in a particular story, they can enjoy the intimacy of situations like book reading (Bus, 2001, 2003). Adults sensitive to their very young children's needs respond by "sharing" rather than "communicating" messages or eliciting referencing behaviors with *what* and *who* questions. Caregivers point at pictures and evoke responses, thereby stimulating children's vocabulary, but they apply such strategies sparsely when the children are not very interested in the topic of the story. We doubt, therefore, the appropriateness of the assumption that the effects of book reading depend on adults placing demands on very young children for active participation in the beginning stages of sharing books (e.g., Storch and Whitehurst, 2002). The bottom-line of our findings is that provoking young children's interest in books in the early stages of reading development strongly depends on the quality of the social interactions and caregiver–child emotional relationship. Picture books offer a rich context for new vocabulary but also for story comprehension and knowledge of reading conventions, all precursors of later literacy. New media add new dimensions to picture books which according to our recent findings support the development of story comprehension and vocabulary especially in groups who have deficits and little experience with books. We therefore conclude that the role of new media should be given more attention especially as these alternative forms of processing stories are less biased towards practices in families of disadvantaged children.

REFERENCES

Bus, A. G. (2001). Early book reading in the family: A route to literacy. In S. Neuman & D. Dickinson (Eds.), *Handbook on Research in Early Literacy* (pp.179–191). New York: Guilford Publications.

Bus, A. G. (2003). Social-emotional requisites for learning to read. In S. Stahl, A. van Kleeck, & E. Bauer (Eds.), *Book sharing in families* (p. 3–16). Hillsdale, NJ: Erlbaum.

Bus, A. G., Leseman, P. P. M., & Keultjes, P. (2000). Joint book reading across cultures: A comparison of Surinam-Dutch, Turkish-Dutch, and Dutch parent–child dyads. *Journal of Literacy Research, 32,* 53–76.

Bus, A. G., & van IJzendoorn, M. H. (1997). Affective dimension of mother–infant picture book reading. *Journal of School Psychology, 35,* 47–60.

Bus, A. G., van IJzendoorn, M. H., & Pellegrini, A. D. (1995). Storybook reading makes for success in learning to read. A meta-analysis on intergenerational transmission of literacy. *Review of Educational Research, 65,* 1–21.

Bus, A. G., Verhallen, M. J. A. J., & de Jong, M. T. (in press). How multimedia stories contribute to early literacy. In A. G. Bus & S. B. Neuman (Eds.), *Multimedia and literacy development: New approaches to storybook reading.* New York: Taylor & Francis.

Cunningham, A. E., & Stanovich, K. E. (1990). Tracking the unique effects of print exposure in children: Associations with vocabulary, general knowledge, and spelling. *Journal of Educational Psychology, 83,* 264–274.

De Groot, I. M., & Bus, A. G. (1995). *Boekenpret voor baby's. Ervaringen met het opgroeiboek* [Book-fun for babies. Final report on a project to stimulate emergent literacy]. Leiden/The Hague: Leiden University/Sardes.

Dickinson, D. K., McCabe, A., Anastasopoulos, L., Peisner-Feinberg, E. S., & Poe, M. D. (2003). The comprehensive language approach to early literacy: The interrelationships among vocabulary, phonological sensitivity, and print knowledge among preschool-age children. *Journal of Educational Psychology, 95,* 465–481.

Hart, B., & Risley, T. R. (2003). The early catastrophe. The 30 million word gap by age 3. *American Educator, 27*(1), 4–9.

Jones, R. (1996). *Emerging patterns of literacy. A multi-disciplinary perspective.* London: Routledge.

Martin, L. E., & Reutzel, D. R. (1999). Sharing books: Examining how and why mothers deviate from the print. *Reading Research and Instruction, 39,* 39–70.

Ninio, A., & Bruner, J. S. (1976). The achievement and antecedents of labeling. *Journal of Child Language, 5,* 1–15.

Rideout, V. J., Vandewater, E. A., & Wartella, E. A.(2003). *Zero to six. Electronic media in the lives of infants, toddlers, and preschoolers.* A Kaiser Family Foundation Report.

Robinson, M., & Mackey, M. (2003). Film and television. In N. Hall, J. Larson, & J. Marsh Eds), *Handbook of early literacy* (pp. 126–142). London: Sage.

Scarborough, H. S., & Dobrich, W. (1994). On the efficacy of reading to preschoolers. *Developmental Review, 14,* 245–260.

Sénéchal, M., & LeFevre, J.-A. (2002). Parental involvement in the development of children's reading skills: A five-year longitudinal study. *Child Development, 73,* 445–460.

Serpell, R. (1997). Literacy connections between school and home: How should we evaluate them? *Journal of Literacy Research, 29,* 587–616.

Serpell, R., Baker, L., & Sonnenschein, S. (2005). *Becoming literate in the city. The Baltimore early childhood project.* Cambridge: Cambridge University Press.

Smith, C. R. (2001). Click and turn the page: An exploration of multiple storybook literacy. *Reading Research Quarterly, 36,* 152–183.

Storch, S. A., & Whitehurst, G. J. (2002). Oral language and code-related precursors to reading: Evidence from a longitudinal structural model. *Developmental Psychology, 38,* 934–947.

Sulzby, E. (1985). Children's emergent reading of favorite storybooks. A developmental study. *Reading Research Quarterly, 20,* 458–479.

Teale, W. H., & Sulzby, E. (1986). *Emergent literacy. Writing and reading.* Norwood, NJ: Ablex.

van Kleeck, A. (2003). Research on book sharing: Another critical look. In A. van Kleeck, S. A. Stahl, & E. B. Bauer (Eds.), *On reading books to children. Parents and teachers* (pp. 271–320). Mahwah, NJ: Lawrence Erlbaum.

van Kleeck, A. Alexander, E. I., Vigil, A., & Templeton, D. E. (1996). Verbally modeling thinking for infants: Middle-class mothers' presentation of information structures during book sharing. *Journal of Research in Childhood Education, 10,* 101–113.

van Kleef, M., & Tomesen, M. (2002). *Stimulerende lees—en schrijfactiviteiten in de onderbouw. Prototypen voor het creeren van interactieve leessituaties en het ontlokken van (nieuw) schrijfgedrag* [Stimulating reading—and writing activities in the lower primary class. Prototypes for the creation of interactive reading situations and the eliciting of (new) writing behavior]. Nijmegen: Expertisecentrum Nederlands.

Verhallen, M. J. A. J., Bus, A. G., & de Jong, M. T. (2006). The promise of multimedia stories for kindergarten children at risk. *Journal of Educational Psychology, 98,* 410–419.

Waddell, M., & Firth, B. (1992). *Sam Vole and his brothers.* Cambridge, MA: Candlewick Press.

Zeijl, E., Crone, M., Wiefferink, K., Keuzekamp, S., & Reijneveld, M. (2005). *Kinderen in Nederland.* Den Haag: SCP-publicatie 2005/4.

CHAPTER 12

IF YOU'RE NOT LIKE ME, CAN WE PLAY?

Peer Groups in Preschool

Carollee Howes and Linda Lee

When we think of preschool we often picture children playing together—pretending, running, or making "cakes" in the sandbox. A rich historic and contemporary research literature suggests that early pretend play with peer play is linked to competent social development (Fantuzzo, Sekino, & Cohen, 2004; Howes & Matheson, 1992; Rubin, Bukowski, & Parker, 1998) as well as other areas of development including early literacy and cognitive development (Kavanagh, 2006). In this chapter we are concerned with who plays with whom; who gets to play and who does not; how play groups and playing are organized in preschool classrooms. Our particular focus is on classrooms in which children do not share an ethnic/racial heritage and/or home language and on children who are different in socially stigmatized ways not play styles.

Contemporary Perspectives on Social Learning in Early Childhood Education, pages 259–277
Copyright © 2007 by Information Age Publishing
All rights of reproduction in any form reserved.

FOR TODDLERS AND PRESCHOOLERS
PLAYING AND EXCLUDING CHILDREN GO TOGETHER

Toddler and preschool age children could be considered very sophisticated in their peer interaction. They can develop complex games and pretend play involving turn taking, action reversals, scripts, and roles (Howes
& Lee, 2006). On the other hand, much of the sophistication of the peer
interaction of toddlers and preschoolers is dependent on the size and composition of the peer group. With too many players or with too few players
familiar with the game or script, the interaction quickly breaks down
(Howes, 1988). To sustain play children must find ways to protect their play
space by excluding children. Hence, the familiar phrase, "You're not my
friend, you can't play" (Corsaro, 1981; Paley, 1992).

If children do not get to play because other children tell them, "You
can't play," or because their own anxious behavior with peers keeps them
from trying to play, they lose opportunities to learn how to play. Only with
multiple opportunities to engage with peers do young children begin to
understand how to engage in prosocial and complex play with peers
(Rubin, Burgess, Dwyer, & Hastings, 2003); as well as how to resolve conflicts (Bakeman & Brownlee, 1982; Chen, Fein, Killen, & Tam, 2001; Fonzi,
Schneider, Tani, & Tomada, 1997; Hay, 1982). Young children who do not
play with others are at risk for not learning how to play.

A particular concern about children who do not play with others at
young ages is that they may develop patterns of aggression and conflict
with peers. Conflict and aggression within peer groups is particularly significant because of the longitudinal consequences of such interactive styles.
In one longitudinal study, toddler peer interaction style and content predicted third grade relations with peers (Howes & Phillipsen, 1998). While
examining the child and environmental influences on aggression is a topic
beyond the scope of this chapter there are some recent studies of peer
interaction in preschool that raise concerns about very young children's
experiences with conflict and aggression in peer groups. Preschool children classified as aggressive in one study of a Head Start classroom only
played with a few children, and in general had difficulty establishing play
contacts and friendships (Snyder, Horsch, & Childs, 1997). At the first
observation point aggressive and nonaggressive children tended to form
friendships with children similar to themselves in aggression. In this study
the more that aggressive children played with aggressive peers at the first
time point, the more aggressive they were observed and rated three
months later.

A second recent study found that when preschoolers are in conflict, for
example over who is going to be the mother and who is going to be the
baby, or whose turn is it to have the swing, children tended to engage in

nonaggressive conflict strategies unless one of the children involved in the conflict engaged in physical aggression (Thornberg, 2006). In other words turn-taking on the swing without hitting or pulling usually happened more or less smoothly. If physical aggression was introduced into the conflict then the partner tended to be aggressive as well. To continue the swing example, if a child who wanted a turn on the swing yanked on the feet of the swinger, the swinger would be more likely to hit than if the same child yelled, "I really want the swing and you have had it for too long!" This research suggests that everyday conflicts between very young children can become aggressive all too quickly.

Finally, a three year longitudinal study, beginning in toddlerhood, found that early aggressive behavior reduced children's likelihood of being the target of prosocial behavior (Persson, 2005). Thus children who begin their peer group experiences with aggression became less likely to be the recipients of overtures that could have resulted in more productive play.

THEORETICAL FRAMEWORK

If children must exclude because not everyone can play; who gets to play? To address this question we used a theoretical framework that integrates constructs of cultural community drawn from Rogoff (2003) with constructs drawn from attachment theory and applied to preschool context (Howes & Ritchie, 2002). We use this theoretical framework because the preschool experience for children of color, from low-income families, or the children of immigrants must be understood through the lens of both developmental psychology and of the larger society that discriminates against these children (Johnson et al., 2003; Ramsey, 2006).

Cultural Communities

A cultural community is a grouping of people who share goals, beliefs, everyday practices around how to engage with others and often a home language and/or racial or ethnic identity (Rogoff, 2003). We assume that in order to understand children's social and emotional development, including the development of interpersonal relationships with peers, researchers must examine both the cultural communities that form the context for the interaction of children with others and the nature of interpersonal interactions between children and others. When we examine peer interaction in peer groups composed of children from diverse backgrounds we need to consider two cultural community contexts. The first context concerns the experiences and the "taken for granted" ways of interacting and thinking that children bring to a peer group from their home cultural communities. The second context is the cultural community that adult and child participants form in the preschool classroom. That is, the everyday ways of playing together and forming relationships, and the implicit and explicit rules for behavior, for example, boys can (or can not) play with dolls and dress-up clothes in the housekeeping corner or, as Paley describes, who can say (or not) "you can't play" (Paley, 1992).

Home-Based Cultural Communities Brought to the Classroom

When the peer group includes children from diverse cultural communities, children enter the group with diverse interaction styles. Everyday practices, that is, ways that adults in the community expect and sometime insist children to behave, shape children's social interaction styles. For example, within Linda's home community of Taiwanese families, parents expect toddler-age children to identify the adults in the extended families with the appropriate kinship terms (e.g., aunts from the father's side of the family are termed differently than ones from the mother's side of the family). So in extended family gatherings parents are focused on instilling respect within kinship relationships between older and younger generations and less on the kind of play that might develop between cousins.

In contrast, the parents in recent Mexican immigrant families that Carollee has been studying, while also concerned with children recognizing kinship and kinship terms, focus on instilling ideas of sibling/cousin caregiving during extended family gatherings, and therefore expect the older children to entertain the younger children (Howes & Wishard, 2004). We could imagine that the children in these different cultural communities therefore would have different expectations and repertoires of behaviors for peer interaction if they were part of the same diverse peer group.

Children not only bring interaction styles derived from cultural communities into the classroom, they bring, as well, ideas about engaging with people different than themselves. Within families there is great variation in young children's exposure to adults and other children who are different in ethnicity/race and language heritage. Some children live in neighborhoods with diverse race, ethnic, and language heritages and from a very early age play with neighbors quite different from themselves. Other children begin child care programs that include many different families and as early as infancy experience peers and their parents who speak different languages and have different styles of engagement. Still other children live in homogeneous neighborhoods with parents who only socialize with people like themselves.

These variations in children's experiences within families influence children's responses to and understanding of racial/ethnic differences (Ramsey, 1996; Ramsey, 2006). There are as well differences among families in their ideas about others different from themselves and whether these differences are to be appreciated, hated, feared, or be the basis for discrimination (Hamburg & Hamburg, 2004). And of course children learn inside of families whether difference is valued or feared and hated.

Therefore children bring to preschool classrooms not only different ways of engaging with others but different ideas about diversity. Preschool age children are probably not able to articulate these differences, but they can and do act them out in their behavior. Since not playing together at preschools means exclusion, being different may become the basis for exclusion. If children who are different are welcomed to play with others, their ability to develop competent interaction with peers is enhanced. If children who are different are not allowed to play, excluded from play, and then fail to learn how to play cooperatively, they, of course, only increase their undesirability as play partners.

Adults, as well as children, differ in their acceptance of others who are different in race/ethnicity and home language. Teachers are powerful authority figures who can foster or inhibit positive relationships among children within a classroom (Hamburg & Hamburg, 2004; Schofield, 1995). While most of the work in this area has been conducted with school age children, we suspect these findings would especially apply to young children. For toddler and preschool age children, teachers are especially powerful because they act as both teachers and mothers (Howes, 1999). In one of the few studies conducted on young children, Sanders (2005) found that teacher's racial attitudes predicted cross-ethnic peer play in preschool classrooms composed of diverse mixes of African-American and Latino(a) children.

If children and teachers come from diverse cultural communities and, particularly, if the differences are mirrored by dominant/minority culture discrimination and racism, the children may fare better in classrooms when there are teachers who share the children's cultural communities (Baker, 1999; Howes & Ritchie, 2002; Johnson et al., 2003). In one of our recent studies in very diverse low income child care settings in a city marked by heightened racial and ethnic conflict, we found that children who had conflictual interactions with teachers different from them in racial/ethnic heritage as they entered child care had not achieved positive relationships with these teachers even after six months in the classroom (Howes & Shiver, 2006). If, as we will suggest below, we assume that having a positive teacher–child relationship to use as secure base in forming relationships and developing play with peers is important, then these findings are disturbing.

Cultural Communities Formed in the Classroom

In working with the construct of cultural community it is important to recognize that each individual can and most likely does participate in more than one cultural community (Rogoff, 2003). While the participants, teachers and children, in any given classroom come from several or only one home cultural community, by engaging with others within the classroom, they participate in a classroom cultural community. So teachers and children simultaneously participate in both cultural communities. Classrooms have common everyday practices: Where do you start your day? Sitting in your place on the rug for morning circle or having breakfast with a favorite teacher, your brother, and your cousin? If you disrupt the morning circle do you loose minutes from outside playtime, have to sit in a teacher's lap, or go to the time-out chair? And as we alluded to earlier, can you say you can't play and to whom?

FEELING SAFE ENOUGH TO ENTER INTO THE WORLD OF PEERS

Working within an attachment perspective we assume that classroom cultural communities differ in children's feeling of trust and safety within the classroom (Howes & Ritchie, 2002). Therefore in integrating a cultural communities perspective with an attachment perspective it is important to examine common everyday practices that help children feel sufficiently safe to explore the world of peer relations. Our previous work has identified four types of everyday classroom practices that help or hinder children from feeling safe enough to engage with peers: (a) attachment relationships with caregivers; (b) how teachers help children as they join the classroom; (c) the social and emotional climate of the classroom; and (d) the time to play.

Relationships With Caregivers

There is extensive literature on attachment relationships between children and their teachers that exceeds the scope of this chapter (Howes, 1999). To briefly summarize, children form attachment relationships with their teachers that are independent of parental attachment quality, the antecedents of attachment quality are similar for teachers and parents, and teachers who are rated as more sensitive in their interactions with children are associated with more secure attachment scores (Howes, 1999). Most importantly for our argument, children with more secure attachments to teachers are concurrently and longitudinally more socially competent with peers even when controlling for parental attachment quality. (Howes, 1999; Mitchell-Copeland, Denham, & DeMulder, 1997; Pianta, Hamre, & Stuhlman, 2002).

We sometimes incorrectly assume that children who form more secure relationships with teachers are more competent with peers because a positive relationship is generalized or that sociable children form good relationships with all people. Working within attachment theory we assume that children who form secure teacher–child relationships have more competent peer relations because they use the teacher as a secure base. When a child trusts a caregiving adult to be positive, loving, and warm then that child can use the adult as a base for exploration and mastery (Grossman, Grossman, & Zimmerman, 1999). Mastering peer relationships, particularly mastering competent cooperative play with peers, is easier when the child can explore and experiment with peers while making forays back to a trusted adult. If children feel valued and supported by a teacher, then they can try out what happens if they, for example, invite a potential friend to play, pretend to be a scary monster, or stand their ground in the face of bullying. If children do not trust the teacher to value and support them, then it is all too easy to pick a fight, refuse to let someone play, or hide from a bully.

Entering the Peer Group

Having adults as secure bases for exploring the peer group take on added importance when children enter new peer groups. When children are new to peer groups they neither know the games or the players, and thus may be at risk for exclusion from or withdrawing from already formed play groups (Feldbaum, Christenson, & O'Neal, 1980; Fox & Field, 1989). As we have discussed, children who are excluded or who anxiously withdraw from peers miss opportunities to play with others and to develop social interaction and relationships skills with peers. So the time period when children enter new (to them) classrooms becomes an important stage setting time for the development of peer relations. In early studies of children entering preschool (Feldbaum et al., 1980; Fox & Field, 1989) children appeared to rely on adults during the transition to preschool. Typically children would spend most of the first two weeks in a new setting close to the adults and then begin playing with peers.

From an attachment perspective we would not expect children to be attached to new teachers with only two weeks of interaction. Most studies of attachment to teachers have assumed that at least two months must pass before the quality of relationships with teachers can be assessed (Howes, 1999). There is a bit of evidence, however, that children who enter new classroom settings are from the first day assessing whom, among the adults in the setting, can be trusted. In one small scale intensive study children who successfully made attachment bids to new teachers in the first few days within a new classroom[1] were assessed as having positive attachments with these teachers two months later (Howes & Oldham, 2001).

The story is different, from this attachment perspective, for children with previous maladaptive relationship histories. These children, who have not had experiences with trusting adults and secure base behaviors, are less likely to look for adults who can be trusted and more likely to antagonize teachers and peers as they enter the classroom (Howes & Ritchie, 2002). The entry period is extremely important for these children. Encountering an adult who behaves in a warm and trustworthy manner can help such a child begin relationships with these new peers in a more positive manner (Howes & Ritchie, 2002).

Social-Emotional Climate Created for Playing With Peers

The social-emotional climate of the classroom is the third area where everyday practices within the classroom can enhance or impede the development of competent relationships with peers. Although there is an extensive literature describing the interactions of teachers and children and classroom management strategies (see Pianta et al., 2002 for a review of this literature), only recently has attention turned to the general climate that is created within the classroom from the interactions of participants.

Several recent large scale observational studies of classrooms for young children identified two dimensions of classroom climate: instructional support and social-emotional support (Hamre & Pianta, 2005; La Paro, Pianta, Hamre, & Stuhlman, 2002; NICHD ECCRN, 2002; Pianta et al., 2005). Classrooms that score high on the measure of social-emotional climate are pleasant places where there are conversations, spontaneous laughter, and enjoyment expressed as children and teachers engage in various activities and interactions. Teachers are warm and sensitive to all of the children; they are emotionally and physically involved with the children's activities, and they rarely are intrusive, angry, or annoyed. In these classrooms there are clear, but flexible rules and expectations for classroom routines. Children tend to follow these rules so that teachers' rarely have to employ control techniques. In contrast, classrooms with negative climates are characteristically filled with relational as well as physical aggression among children and hostile conflictual interactions between children and teachers. Children in these classrooms have few options for activities. Interactions and activities are adult-driven and most often based on behavioral management of out-of-control children.

Classrooms with positive emotional climates are associated with positive teacher–child relationships (Howes, 2000; Howes & Ritchie, 2002). Children in classrooms with high scores for positive-emotional climate are likely to construct positive relationships with teachers. But beyond the secure base that positive teacher–child relationships provide, a positive emotional climate appears to facilitate peer relationship development by providing rules for engagement that promote prosocial rather than hostile peer interactions. In one longitudinal study children who experienced positive emotional climates as three-year-olds were also likely to have positive peer relationships as second graders (Howes, 2000). If it is difficult for young children to construct play sequences when they are just developing the capacity to do so, it is even more difficult to do so when they are interrupted by conflict occurring around them.

Positive social-emotional climates also can facilitate positive peer relationships in newly formed peer groups. In our recent study of children entering preschool, the social-emotional climate of the classrooms was very negative (Howes & Shiver, 2006). In most large-scale studies of preschool classrooms, climate scores are on the average fairly positive, above the median of the scale (see for example Pianta et al., 2005). In this study however, average social-emotional climate scores were near the negative end of the scale. As such, children in these classrooms were challenged to create relationships and complex play within these newly formed peer groups (Howes, Sanders, & Lee, 2005).

Time and Permission to Play

Creating peer play requires teachers to create an environment that values play. Children need physical space to play, materials that encourage pretend (Sutterby & Frost, 2006), and teachers who do not redirect them from playing back to work. Although the National Association for the Education of Young Children statements on practice (Bredekamp & Copple, 1997) and on program standards (National Association for the Education of Young Children, 2005) explicitly endorse providing opportunities for children to develop complex play with peers, the current academic accountability climate of early childhood (Kagan & Carroll, 2004) can impede their implementation. As teachers are pressured and expected to teach preacademic content, early shared understandings about the importance of time, materials, and spaces for enhancing peer play seem to fade into the background. In our own work we have seen the amount of time children engage in complex pretend play decrease over the 20 years we have been observing in local programs (Howes & Wishard, 2004). This decrease is consistent with anecdotal reports that programs are providing relatively little unstructured time for children to play.

PEER GROUP ORGANIZATION

Children in preschools construct a social organization we call the peer group. While, as we have discussed, adults influence the quality of the social interaction within the peer group, it is the children who form friendships, play groups, and construct hierarchies of popular, rejected, and neglected social status. In this section of the paper we will first provide an elaborated description of the development of these social groupings, describe what we know about the influence of ethnicity, race, and home language on the construction of classroom peer groups, and speculate on how classroom practices may lead to inclusion and exclusion of children who are different.

Friendship Formation

All children have friends but not every peer interaction results in friendship. Some children are able to "hit it off" and become friends, while others never pass the stage of acquaintanceship. Beginning in infancy, friendships are relationships based on mutual support, affection, and companionship. The question of how particular children become friends while others do not continues to intrigue developmental psychologists. One simple explanation for friendship formation is the similarity hypothesis, which postulates that children like others who are similar and dislike others who are not similar. Descriptions of young children and their friends suggest that friends are similar in many attributes, such as sex, race, academic achievement, and socioeconomic status (Kupersmidt, Burchinal, & Patterson, 1995). Can similarity hypothesis explain young children's tendency to prefer same-ethnic friends? Is the statement, "If you are not like me, you can't be my friend," really true? The similarity hypothesis has been challenged and dismissed on several grounds.

First, the correlational nature of most studies on similarity hypothesis renders it difficult to determine whether similarity is a predictor or a product of friendships. It is likely that through frequent mutual socialization, friends become more similar overtime. If this is the case, similarity is a product rather than a determinant of friendship. Second, it is difficult to tease out similarity from proximity. Many children attend preschool with only children of their own ethnic, racial, or language heritage. As a consequence, similarity in race among friends is likely to be a reflection of proximity rather than actual preference or friendship selection criteria. This is especially the case for children who live in racially segregated neighborhoods and who are too young to initiate their own contacts, and are therefore limited to social environment prescribed by their parents. The similarity hypothesis appears too simple an explanation to account for the complex process of friendship formation. After all, not all children of the same age, gender, and ethnicity become friends. It is more likely the case that similarity concerns initial phase of attraction and not later phase of friendship (Aboud & Mendelson, 1996). Friendship is more than just interpersonal attraction; it encompasses mutual support, affection, and companionship. These qualities of friendship require more than being similar on physical attributes or demographic characteristics. In a classic study, Gottman (1983) audiotaped play conversations of 18 dyads of unacquainted children ages 3 to 9 during play sessions and examined the friendship formation processes. Findings suggest that a progression toward friendship consists of the following social processes: communication clarity and connectedness, information exchange, exploration of similarities and differences, establishment of common-ground activities, resolution of conflict, positive reciprocity, and self-disclosure.

Moreover, Parker's experimental study of friendships formation (Parker & Seal, 1996) provides additional support for the predictive power of these conversational processes. In his study, a "surrogate" child (a 2-foot-tall, extraterrestrial-like doll) named "Panduit" was introduced to a group of 4- to 5-year olds and was manipulated to be either a skilled or unskilled communicator using Gottman's findings. As expected, children who interacted with skilled Panduit were significantly more likely to hit it off than children who interacted with unskilled Panduit.

Friendship Formation of Children Who Do Not Share an Ethnic/Racial Heritage and/or Home Language

Except the two studies cited above, there is a lack of research attention on the process or specific behavioral mechanisms underlying young children's friendship formation. Even less is known about friendship formation of young children who do not share an ethnic/racial heritage and/or home language in preschool. It is unclear whether the process of cross-ethnic friendship formation is different than or similar to that of same-ethnic friendship formation. In a study of elementary school-age children, Aboud and colleagues (2003) found that the quality of children's cross-ethnic friendships, such as loyalty, help, and emotional security, does not differ significantly from that of same-ethnic friendships.

Though there are no differences in friendship qualities, young children who do not share an ethnic/racial heritage may confront additional challenges and obstacles in friendship formation. Some challenges specific to friendship formation may include gaining access to peer groups and mastering coordinating interactional styles.

From the theoretical perspective of the present paper, children enter preschool with interaction practices derived from their families and cultural communities. As we alluded to earlier, different cultural communities have different interactional practices. Much of the sophistication of the peer interaction of preschoolers is dependent on shared understandings of how to interact. It is important to note that peer interaction is conceptually different from friendship formation. As we defined earlier, relationships with friends are more intense and intimate than ones with peers. Young children behave differently toward friends than nonfriends; for example, they engage in more complex play with friends and are more likely to stay close with one another after conflicts (Hartup, Laursen, Stewart, & Eastenson, 1988; Howes, 1996). In essence, friendship formation entails moving beyond peer interaction and becoming more involved and invested in one another. However, if children who lack peers of the same ethnic/racial heritage are denied access into play groups or discriminated against based on dissimilar interactional practices or demographic characteristics, their chance to interact with peers and then to form friendships is more limited.

This is not to suggest that children of ethnic/racial minorities in the classroom do not have friends. On the contrary, in two studies of young children in an ethnically diverse school, we found that children were able to form and maintain cross-ethnic friendships (Howes & Wu, 1990; Lee, Howes, & Chamberlain, 2006). Nevertheless, what we do not know at this point is whether the process of friendship formation for children who do and do not share an ethnic/racial heritage and/or home language is similar.

The issue gets more complicated when we think about the within-group variation of children who do share an ethnic/racial heritage. Children with the same ethnic, racial, or home language label are not a homogeneous group; they come from cultural communities that vary in historical background, socioeconomic class, cultural beliefs, practices, and values. Thus, it would be a mistake to study ethnicity/race as a category without situating it in the context of other personal characteristics and social situations. Ethnic minority children as a group are confronted with racism, prejudice, and segregation in the United States which can exert both direct and indirect influences on children's developmental competencies (Garcia Coll et al., 1996). But children's direct experiences of these practices vary. In studying ethnic minority children, it is important to keep in mind both their experiences as a unique individual as well as member of ethnic minority.

Friendships do not exist in a vacuum. They are embedded in multiple contexts, such as classroom, school, and neighborhood. Likewise, the four types of classroom practices identified in the first section of the chapter can also promote friendships among children who do not share ethnic/racial heritage. Several researchers assert that without additional support and encouragement, mere exposure to cross-ethnic peers may not be sufficient for cross-ethnic friendships to develop or sustain (Allport, 1954; Hewstone & Brown, 1986). One documented source of support for children's cross-ethnic interactions comes from the classroom. Hallinan and Teixeira (1987) reported that when classrooms are organized by ability grouping, White students were less likely to choose Black peers as best friends.

Moreover, one can reasonably speculate that when teachers are active advocates of diversity, students are less likely to hold prejudiced attitudes against cross-ethnic peers or to exclude others based on ethnicity/race. Studies show that it is only when teachers depict assigned groups of peers with different attributes (e.g., skin color, hair-type, T-shirt color) as varying in status that in-group favoritism (assigning positive judgments or rewards for members of one's own group) and out-group derogation emerges (Bigler, Brown, & Markell, 2001). These studies highlight the important role that teachers and social-emotional climate of the classroom play in shaping children's cross-ethnic friendships.

Play Groups

Children's friendships develop within the context of their larger social network of playmates. While preschool children are most likely to play with friends, play groups are composed of children who like to play together but may not be friends. Playing, for young children, involves sharing the meanings of games, "Let's play fire engine," and knowing how to engage the other as a social partner (Howes & Wishard, 2004).

There are well-documented sequences for the development of complexity of interaction with peers (Howes & Lee, 2006). While these sequences depend in part on cognitive and communicative development, even toddler-age children can engage in complex peer play if they play in environments that permit and foster such play (Howes & Matheson, 1992; Howes & Wishard, 2004).

Play Groups of Children Who Do Not Share an Ethnic/Racial Heritage and/or Home Language

There is some evidence that, like friends, children as young as preschoolers tend to select playmates who are of the same race (Fishbein & Imai, 1993). Different interactional practices and/or home language may disrupt the flow and complexity of play between children who do not share a language or an ethnic/racial heritage. In one of our recent studies of toddlers and preschoolers (Howes et al., 2005), we found that children who lacked a shared ethnic heritage and home language peer within peer groups appeared to be struggling more than other children with peer interaction six months after entry into the peer group. In particular, children who lacked a same ethnic peer engaged in more rated physical aggression with peers than children who had same ethnic peers in the classroom. This finding is alarming given the literature on aggression and its negative consequences on children's peer interactions and relations.

However, in this study children had just entered a new peer group. As we have reviewed, children who enter new peer groups often rely on adults to assist them in the transition. The children in this study were the same ones we discussed earlier who had particularly negative social and emotional classroom climates (Howes & Shiver, 2006). Moreover in this classroom, all teachers and children were unlikely to construct positive attachment relationships and this was particularly so for children who did not share an ethnic/racial heritage with their teacher (Howes & Shiver, 2006). Therefore, not only did these children not have peers like them, but they were also in classroom communities with practices that hindered rather than enhanced the development of positive peer relations in general. This study illustrates the importance of considering practices from both home cultural communities and practices within classroom cultural communities as we attempt to understand peer groups.

IMPLICATIONS AND INTERVENTIONS

Thus far we have suggested that both home practices brought into the classroom and the everyday practices of classrooms influence the development of peer group organization as young children create peer groups organized around friendships and play groups. We found some evidence that friendships and play groups are organized around shared race, ethnicity, and home language; that in some cases children who are different may be excluded from play and friendship; and that the consequences of exclusion may be maladaptive peer relations. However these conclusions are more based in speculation than certainty. In contrast, we can say with a great deal of certainty that young children initially play with and become friends with cross-sex peers and then, before they leave the preschool years, play and become friends with predominantly same-sex peers. And although there is considerable data and as well much speculation about the relation between these developmental trends that lead to sex-segregation and sexism, children are amazingly resistant to attempts to reverse these trends (Howes & Ritchie, 2002; Ramsey, 2006).

Sometimes the field of early childhood would like to believe that young children are protected from societal bias, that children play with and make friends with children like and not like themselves without regard for difference. But as this review has suggested, classrooms are porous, ideas about status and discrimination do find their way into the classroom. Organized attempts to intervene in the processes of exclusion based on difference are scant, most interventions into classroom and peer group organization and dynamics begin with grade school children (Hamburg & Hamburg, 2004).

One promising approach to prejudice and discrimination reduction that may be useful with preschool age children is cooperative interaction (Fishbein, 2002). Cooperative interaction involves asking children to work or talk together on a project that consists of positive goal interdependence. This approach has been shown to increase opposite-sex friendship choices and decrease racial/ethnic prejudice toward classmates among grade school children. The effectiveness of this approach on preschool children's attitudes and behaviors warrants further research. There are multicultural educational programs for young children (see Ramsey, 2006 for a comprehensive review of these programs) and we assume that such programs would sensitize young children to the hurt feelings implicit in being excluded for being different.

What the field of early childhood does have is NAEYC's Anti-Bias Curriculum (Derman-Sparks, 1989). This curriculum teaches children to recognize and act against bias in a developmentally appropriate manner. Although there are few formal evaluations of the implementation and effects of the Anti-Bias curriculum (Perkins & Mebert, 2005), and none that we could find that examined peer relations, the curriculum does give teachers a place to begin. We hope that this chapter encourages teachers of young children to think about how young children engage with peers who do and do not share their ethnic/racial heritage or home language and encourages researchers to extend their research programs into diverse classrooms to understand the processes that surround who can play with whom. As the school population in the United States has become increasingly diverse, issues related to cross-ethnic peer relations are no longer concerns of solely a few geographical areas in the United States. Further understanding of peer group organization and dynamics, especially its relation to ethnic/racial composition of the classroom, will not only promote school policies that improve children's social relationships but also have implications for cross-ethnic relations of the society at large.

NOTES

1. Being successful meant that the child asked for comfort and the teacher responded in a sensitive manner.

REFERENCES

Aboud, F. E., & Mendelson, M. J. (1996). Determinants of friendship selection and quality: Developmental perspectives. In W. M. Bukowski, A. F. Newcomb, & W. W. Hartup (Eds.), *The company they keep* (pp. 87–112). New York: Cambridge.

Aboud, F. E., Mendelson, M. J., & Purdy, K. T. (2003). Cross-race peer relations and friendship quality. *International Journal of Behavioral Development, 27,* 165–173.

Allport, G. W. (1954). *The nature of prejudice.* Cambridge, MA: Addison-Wesley.

Bakeman, R., & Brownlee, J. (1982). Social rules governing object conflicts in toddlers and preschoolers. In K. Rubin & H. Ross (Eds.), *Peer relationships and social skills in childhood.* NY: Springer-Verlag.

Baker, J. A. (1999). Teacher–student interaction in urban at-risk classrooms: Differential behavior, relationship quality, and student satisfaction with school. *Elementary School Journal, 100,* 57–70.

Bigler, R. S., Brown, C. S., & Markell, M. (2001). When groups are not created equal: Effects of group status on the formation of intergroup attitudes in children. *Child Development, 72,* 1151–1162.

Bredekamp, S., & Copple, C. (Eds.). (1997). *Developmentally appropriate practice in early childhood programs* (Rev. ed.). Washington, DC: National Association for the Education of Young Children.

Chen, D. W., Fein, G. G., Killen, M., & Tam, H.-P. (2001). Peer conflicts of preschool children: Issues, resolution, incidence, and age-related patterns. *Early Education and Development, 12,* 523–544.

Corsaro, W. A. (1981). Friendship in the nursery school: Social organization in a peer environment. In S. R. Asher & J. M. Gottman (Eds.), *The development of children's friendships* (pp. 207–241). Cambridge: Cambridge University Press.

Derman-Sparks, L. (1989). *Anti-bias curriculum: Tools for empowering young children.* Washington, DC: National Association for the Education of Young Children.

Fantuzzo, J., Sekino, Y., & Cohen, H. L. (2004). An examination of the contribution of interactive peer play to salient classroom competencies for urban Head Start children. *Psychology in the Schools, 41,* 323- 336.

Feldbaum, C., Christenson, T., & O'Neal, E. (1980). An observational study of the assimilation of the newcomer to the preschool. *Child Development, 51,* 497–507.

Fishbein, H. D. (2002). *Peer prejudice and discrimination.* Mahwah, NJ: Erlbaum.

Fishbein, H. D., & Imai, S. (1993). Preschoolers select playmates on the basis of gender and race. *Journal of Applied Developmental Psychology, 14,* 303–316.

Fonzi, A., Schneider, B. H., Tani, F., & Tomada, G. (1997). Predicting children's friendship status from their dyadic interaction in structured situations of potential conflict. *Child Development, 68,* 496–506.

Fox, N. A., & Field, T. M. (1989). Individual differences in preschool entry behavior. *Journal of Applied Developmental Psychology, 10*, 527–540.

Garcia Coll, C., Lamberty, G., Jenkins, R., McAdoo, H. P., Cunic, K., Wasik, B., et al. (1996). An integrative model for the study of developmental competencies in minority children. *Child Development, 67*, 1891–1914.

Gottman, J. (1983). How children become friends. *Monographs of the Society for Research in Child Development, 48*(3), 1–86.

Grossman, K. E., Grossman, K., & Zimmerman, P. (1999). A wider view of attachment and exploration: Stability and change during the years of immaturity. In J.Cassidy & P. Shaver (Eds.), *Handbook of attachment: Theory research and clinical implication* (pp. 760–786). New York: Guilford.

Hamburg, D. A., & Hamburg, B. A. (2004). *Learning to live together.* New York: Oxford University Press.

Hamre, B., & Pianta, R. C. (2005). Can instructional and emotional support in the first grade classroom make a difference for children at risk for school failure? *Child Development, 76*, 949–967.

Hartup, W., Laursen, B., Stewart, M. I., & Eastenson, A. (1988). Conflict and the friendship relations of young children. *Child Development, 59*, 1590–1600.

Hay, D. R. H. (1982). The social nature of early conflict. *Child Development, 53*, 105–113.

Hewstone, M., & Brown, R. (1986). Contact is not enough: An intergroup perspective on the "contact hypothesis." In M. Hewstone & R. Brown (Eds.), *Contact and conflict in intergroup encounters. Social psychology and society* (pp. 1–44). Cambridge, MA: Basil Blackwell.

Howes, C. (1988). Peer interaction of young children. *Monographs of the Society for Research in Child Development, 53*(1), 1–92.

Howes, C. (1996). The earliest friendships. In W. M. Bukowski, A. F. Newcomb, & W. W. Hartup (Eds.), *The company they keep friendships in childhood and adolescence.* (pp. 66–86). New York: Cambridge.

Howes, C. (1999). Attachment relationships in the context of multiple caregivers. In J. Cassidy & P. R. Shaver (Eds.), *Handbook of attachment theory and research* (pp. 671–687). New York: Gilford.

Howes, C. (2000). Social-emotional classroom climate in child care, child–teacher relationships, and children's second grade peer relations. *Social Development, 9*, 191–204.

Howes, C., & Lee, L. (2006). Peer relations in young children. In L. Balter & C. S. Tamis-LeMonde (Eds.), *Child psychology: A handbook of contemporary issues.* New York: Taylor & Francis.

Howes, C., & Matheson, C. C. (1992). Sequences in the development of competent play with peers social and social pretend play. *Developmental Psychology, 28*, 961–974.

Howes, C., & Oldham, E. (2001). Processes in the formation of attachment relationships with new caregivers. In A. Goncu & E. Klein (Eds.), *Children in play, story and school* (pp. 267–287). Greenwood, NY: Greenwood.

Howes, C., & Phillipsen, L. C. (1998). Continuity in children's relations with peers. *Social Development, 7*, 340–349.

Howes, C., & Ritchie, S. (2002). *A matter of trust: Connecting teachers and learners in the early childhood classroom.* New York: Teachers College Press.

Howes, C., Sanders, K., & Lee, L. (2005). *Can we play?* Paper presented at the Biannual Conference of the Society for Research in Child Development, Atlanta, GA.

Howes, C., & Shiver, E. M. (2006). New child-caregiver attachment relationships: Entering child care when the caregiver is and is not an ethnic match. *Social Development, 15,* 343–360.

Howes, C., & Wishard, A. G. (2004). Revisiting sharing meaning: Looking through the lens of culture and linking shared pretend play through proto narrative development to emergent literacy. In E. Zigler, D. G. Singer, & S. J. Bishop-Josef (Eds.), *Children's play: The roots of literacy* (pp. 143–158). Washington, D.C.: Zero to Three.

Howes, C., & Wu, F. (1990). Peer interactions and friendships in an ethnically diverse school setting. *Child Development, 61, 537–541.*

Johnson, D. J., Jaeger, E., Randolph, S. M., Cauce, A. M., Ward, J., & NICHD ECCRN. (2003). Studying the effects of early child care experiences on the development of children of color in the united states: Towards a more inclusive research agenda. *Child Development, 74,* 1227–1244.

Kagan, S. L., & Carroll, J. (2004). *Alignment in early care and education: A pilot study.* New York: National Center for Children and Families, Teachers College, Columbia University.

Kavanagh, R. D. (2006). Pretend play. In B. Spodek & O. Saracho (Eds.), *Handbook of research on the education of young children* (pp. 269–278). Mahwah, NJ: Lawrence Erlbaum Associates.

Kupersmidt, J. B., Burchinal, M., & Patterson, C. J. (1995). Developmental patterns of childhood peer relations as predictors or externalizing behavior problems. *Development and Psychopathology, 7,* 825–843.

La Paro, K. M., Pianta, R. C., Hamre, B., & Stuhlman, M. (2002). *Classroom assessment scoring system (class) pre-k version.* Charlottesville, VA: University of Virginia.

Lee, L., Howes, C., & Chamberlain, B. (2006). *Ethnic heterogeneity of social networks and cross-ethnic friendships of elementary school boys and girls.* Los Angeles: University of California at Los Angeles.

Mitchell-Copeland, J., Denham, S., & DeMulder, E. (1997). Q-sort assessment of child–teacher attachment relationships and social competence in the preschool. *Early Education and Development, 8,* 27–39.

National Association for the Education of Young Children. (2005). *Early childhood performance standards and accreditation criteria.* Available at: www.naeyc.org/academy.

NICHD ECCRN. (2002). The relation of global first grade environment to structural classroom features, teacher, and student behaviors. *Early Elementary School Journal, 102,* 367–387.

Paley, V. G. (1992). *You can't say, you can't play.* Cambridge: Harvard University Press.

Parker, J. G. (1986). Becoming friends: Conversational skills for friendship formation in young children. In J. M. Gottman & J. G. Parker (Eds.), *Conversations of friends* (pp. 103–138). New York: Cambridge.

Parker, J. G., & Seal, J. (1996). Forming, losing, renewing, and replacing friendships applying temporal parameters to the assessment of children's friendship. *Child Development, 67*, 2248–2268.

Perkins, D. M., & Mebert, C. (2005). Efficacy of multicultural education for preschool children. *Journal of Cross-Cultural Psychology, 36*, 497–512.

Persson, G. E. B. (2005). Young children's prosocial and aggressive behaviors and their experiences of being targeted for similar behaviors by peers. *Social Development, 14*, 206–228.

Pianta, R., Hamre, B., & Stuhlman, M. (Eds.). (2002). *Relationships between teachers and children* (Vol. 7). New York: Wiley.

Pianta, R., Howes, C., Burchinal, M., Bryant, D., Clifford, R., Early, D., et al. (2005). Features of pre-kindergarten programs, classrooms, and teachers: Do they predict observed classroom quality and child-teacher interactions? *Applied Developmental Science, 9*, 144–159.

Ramsey, P. G. (1996). Preschool children's entry attempts. *Journal of Applied Developmental Psychology, 17*, 135–150.

Ramsey, P. G. (2006). Early childhood multicultural education. In B. Spodek & O. Saracho (Eds.), *Handbook of research on the education of young children* (2nd ed., pp. 279–301). Mahwah, NJ: Lawrence Elbaum and Associates.

Rogoff, B. (2003). *The cultural nature of human development.* New York: Oxford University Press.

Rubin, K. H., Bukowski, W., & Parker, J. G. (1998). Peer interactions, relationships, and groups. In N. Eisenberg (Ed.), *Social, emotional, and personality development* (5th ed., Vol. 3, pp. 619–700). New York: Wiley.

Rubin, K. H., Burgess, K. B., Dwyer, K. M., & Hastings, P. P. (2003). Predicting preschoolers' externalizing behaviors from toddler temperament, conflict, and maternal negativity. *Developmental Psychology, 39*, 164–176.

Sanders, K. (2005). *Early race socialization of African American and Latino children in child care.* Los Angeles, CA: University of California at Los Angeles.

Schofield, J. (1995). Promoting positive intergroup dynamics in school settings. In W. D. Hawley & A. W. Jackson (Eds.), *Towards a common destiny: Improving race and ethnic relations in America* (pp. 257–289). San Francisco: Jossey-Bass.

Snyder, J., Horsch, E., & Childs, J. (1997). Peer relationships of young children: Affliative choices and the shaping of aggressive behavior. *Journal of Clinical Child Psychology, 26*, 145–156.

Sutterby, J. A., & Frost, J. (2006). Creating play environments for early childhood: Indoors and out. In B. Spodek & O. Saracho (Eds.), *Handbook of research on the education of young children* (pp. 305–322). Mahwah, NJ: Erlbaum.

Thornberg, R. (2006). The situated nature of preschool children's conflict strategies. *Educational Psychology, 26*, 109–112.

CHAPTER 13

SOCIAL LIFE OF
YOUNG CHILDREN

Co-construction of Shared Meanings and Togetherness, Humor, and Conflicts in Child Care Centers

Elly Singer and Dorian de Haan

INTRODUCTION

Doenja (2;5)[1], a Moroccan girl, has just entered the multicultural play group in the Netherlands. During free play she has chosen the home corner. There are many children who want to play with the stove and cooking utensils. Doenja gets totally caught up in defending her territory against these "intruders." She looks angry, yells "no," "don't," and succeeds in defending her territory, has owned the cooking utensils, but hardly plays with the other children. A week later, we see Doenja again during free play, now in a different social situation. Doenja has chosen to play with glue, paper, and scissors. She sits next to Hind (3;6), also a Moroccan girl. Doenja glues a piece of paper, but she is most interested in Hind. She looks at her, and when Hind makes a funny face, she immediately takes her chance to make contact. Doenja laughs at Hind, imitates her funny face and laughs brightly when

Contemporary Perspectives on Social Learning in Early Childhood Education, pages 279–302
Copyright © 2007 by Information Age Publishing
279

Hind imitates her. Then they start to make and imitate each others nonsense words; a mix of Dutch and Moroccan words and sounds (pattojaaaaaaaa, pattojpattojpattoja). (Singer & de Haan, 2006)

Within a week Doenja has experienced different social situations with peers and has showed diverse strategies to deal with them. In her study of children's experiences on starting day care, Dally (2003) analyzes how 2-year-olds learn the basic rules of the peer group by trial and error in peer relations, and with help of the teacher. They learn rules about ownership, such as, "If I try and take an object from someone, they may/will take it back." They learn about the rules related to power: "It is easier to get what you want if the other claimant is younger, and/or in the absence of a teacher." And they learn moral rules related to fairness or being generous towards other children. Besides learning rules, young children develop skills to communicate, negotiate, and solve problems with peers. Doenja, for instance, may have learned that you don't make friends when you are only focused on defending and ownership of objects, and that imitation is an effective tool to make contact.

In this chapter we will review research on early social and moral learning in interaction with peers in child care centers. We will discuss how young children make contact and create togetherness; how they make fun and jokes together, and how they deal with peer conflicts and co-construct social and moral rules. Finally we will shortly discuss the educational consequences, how teachers can support social life in the peer group.

THEORETICAL APPROACHES

Teachers of young children used to be taught that infants and toddlers do not form peer relations, and that they cannot share and enter into joint play (Howes & Ritchie, 2002). Until the '80s these ideas were confirmed in mainstream psychology (Schaffer, 1984; Verba, 1994). Peer relations of children under 4 years old were considered to be rare, short-lived, and often aggressive. But this opinion was hardly based on research. Since the '70s, the increase of day care facilities for babies and toddlers in western countries has led to a growing body of observation studies of peer relations of young children in natural and laboratory situations. These studies have radically changed our views of social skills and the importance of secure peer relationships in early childhood. Teachers have to understand how infants and toddlers co-construct a shared reality and shared rules, and how they can foster positive peer relationships. From the perspective of the children, the best thing in day care centers is playing with other children (Hännikäinen, 1999). Therefore, positive peer relationships are seen as an important characteristic of high quality early childhood education and care.

Studies of interactions between 0- to 4-year-old children and their teachers often have an ethnographic and explorative character. The focus is on diverse aspects of peer interactions and teacher behavior with regard to: togetherness and belonging (Brennan, 2005; Hännikäinen, 1999); level of joint play (Brenner & Mueller, 1982; Camaioni, Baumgartner, & Peruchini, 1991; Göncü, 1993); communication of young children (Blum-Kulka & Snow, 2004; Rayna & Baudelot, 1999; Verba, 1994); imitation (Eckerman & Didow, 1996; Meltzoff, 2002); pretend play (Howes, Unger, & Matheson, 1992); conflict behavior and reconciliation (Shantz, 1987; Verbeek, Hartup, & Collins, 2000); humor (Loizou, 2005; Burt & Sugawara, 1988); and social and moral rules (Dalli, 2003; Killen & Nucci, 1995).

There are two dominant theoretical approaches of the study of peer interactions. From the attachment theoretical approach, the quality of the teacher–child relationship is put in the center, and the effects of the teacher–child relationship on peer interactions is studied (Howes & Ritchie, 2002; Howes & James, 2002). These studies are built on a theoretical model for teacher–caregivers relationships with children similar to that found in mother–child relationships. The focus is on how teachers can foster secure attachment relationships with (individual) children within group settings. This research points out that children's relationships with teachers are emotionally significant and affect how children develop, what they learn and how they interact with peers (Bowman, Donovan, & Burns, 2001).

The second dominant theoretical approach is based on socioconstructivist assumptions, and often puts the child–child interactions in the center; how they co-construct a shared reality and how teachers can support processes of co-construction. Inspired by Piaget, the child is conceptualized as an active learner and constructor of (sensomotor) schemes and structures (Verba, 1994); Vygotskian theory is the background of studies of co-construction of shared meanings in the social context, appropriation of cultural tools, and the role of the teacher (Brennan, 2005; Singer & de Haan, 2006). Teaching and learning of young children is conceptualized as a collaborative and co-constructed process. In this chapter we will mainly focus on studies based on a *socioconstructivist* approach. The term socioconstructivist is broadly used for studies that share some basic theoretical assumptions. We will shortly discuss three theoretical assumptions that are formative in the studies of peer relations in this chapter.

Socioconstructivist Assumptions

The Child Is an Active Learner
Piaget, Vygotsky, and current socioconstructivist psychologists assume that the urge actively to adapt to the environment is basic to human devel-

opment (Fischer, Shaver, & Carnochan, 1990; van Emde, Biringer, Clyman, & Oppenheim, 1991; Piaget, 1967; Vygotsky, 1978). From the start, the infant explores the environment, seeking what is new in order to make it familiar. Confronted with the environment, there is a basic motive to "get it right." This process of achieving balance, or equilibrium, leads children to develop new, adaptive psychological structures (Piaget, 1967). At a subjective level, this means that children as well as adults need to experience their own actions as logical and sound. This assumption of the child as active learner has inspired studies of young children's actions, skills, and tools to explore and to communicate (see for instance Verba, 1994; Oliveira & Rossetti-Ferreira, 1996). Moreover, many studies are focused on reconstructing the logic of young children's activities from their own perspective. Piaget's interviews with young children about their behavior in a range of experiments are outstanding examples of this focus on children's argumentation to understand underlying cognitive structures. An important key to understand young children's logic is the concept of "logic-in-action" (Singer, 2002). As Piaget stated, infants and toddlers mostly think at a sensorimotor level; they learn by doing, observing, touching, exploring. Vygotsky's theory (1978, 1987), extended by others (Rogoff, 1990; Wertsch, 1985), stresses the developmental transition from interpsychological to intrapsychological functioning. Children's learning and development takes place through guidance provided by caretakers or a more experienced peer who monitor and support the child. Imitation and appropriation are seen as processes of active reconstruction by the child in relationships with important others.

The Child Is a Relational Being

For young children, the environment is first and foremost a social environment. They are focused on understanding their social world. This is probably related to another basic motive, to maintain social relationships, and their need to bond (Bowlby, 1982; van Emde et al., 1991; de Waal, 2000). Infants come into the world preadapted for initiating, maintaining, and terminating human interactions (Schaffer, 1984). By 3 months of age, infants and their caregivers are jointly experiencing pleasure in simple face-to-face interactions. Within this familiar frame of joint play, infants learn to "read" their mother's faces and they develop particular procedures for monitoring their caregiver's emotional availability. From 10 to 12 months, most infants engage in social referencing. They use their caregiver's emotional expressions as a guide to how they are expected to feel and act in a particular situation. The assumption of the human being as a relational being—which is shared by most influential theoretical approaches nowadays (Bowlby, 1982; Stern, 2002; Løkken, 2000)—has inspired many researchers to study verbal and nonverbal communication of young children with adults and peers. With regard to peer relationships, the functional and behavioral differences in child–child relationships and adult–child relationships are analyzed. The relative equality of partners with respect to competence and social power in peer interactions allows processes of co-construction to emerge that differ from those characteristic in adult–child interaction (Verba, 1994).

Unity of Actions and Social, Emotional, and Cognitive Processes

Socioconstructivist psychologists assume that thoughts, affects, and (social) behavior form an indivisible whole in human behavior. In line with Vygotsky and Piaget they emphasize that all our activities, including our thinking, are motivated (Piaget, 1967; Vygotsky, 1987); and that all our emotions and moral affects suppose cognitive processes to signal that important interests are at stake (Frijda, 1986). They try to overcome the dichotomy within traditional developmental psychology of studying cognitive development and socialemotional development as separate domains. This requires new theoretical concepts. Fischer at al. (1990), for instance, use the concept of *script* to refer to the socially embedded knowledge of children as to how to act, feel, and express their emotions in specific situations. Another example is the concept of *cognitive-affective structures*, by which is meant complex synthesizing structures integrating cognition (in the form of appraisals, expectations, and beliefs) with motivation (in the form of interests, goals, moral commitments, and emotional action tendencies), affect (in the shape of physiological arousal and sensory and bodily feeling), and actions (in the form of motor responses and social procedures and methods for acting (Singer, 2002). We prefer the concept of cognitive-affective structures, because structure directly refers to the self-evident frames in which a person observes, feels, and acts (i.e., to their "inner logic").

These new conceptualizations of the relationships between cognition, motivation, and (social) activities lead to new insights into the development of a self. The theory of the early development of the moral self by van Emde and colleagues (1991) is an example of this approach. Van Emde et al. stress that the cognitive-affective structures of infants are sensorimotor in nature. According to them these structures are stored as procedural knowledge of the infant's most emotionally engaging experience with their caregivers. They argue that the co-construction of procedural knowledge (how to act) is crucial for the development of a moral self in infants and a sense of belonging to a parent, family, and cultural group. As a result of face-to-face turn-taking behavior with caregivers, infants learn rules for reciprocity—for give and take—together with the powerful motive for using these rules—"together" is so pleasurable. The authors argue that acting according to this procedural knowledge is a basic form of morality, long before the child is able to verbalize moral rules. "All systems of morality have a sense of reciprocity at their centre with a version of the Golden Rule: 'Do unto others as you would have them do unto you'" (van Emde et al., 1991, p. 261). Because of shared regularities, infants know how they can influence their caregivers; this gives them their first sense of control and agency. Later on, shared procedures, for consolation for instance, are put to use by the toddler as tools for self-regulation of his or her emotions. One might think here of children who imitate with their teddy bear the rituals of consolation they have constructed with their caregiver.

These insights are also very important in the child–child relationships, as we will show in the next paragraphs in which we will discuss three aspects of peer relationships of young children: co-construction of shared meanings and togetherness, humour, and conflicts.

CO-CONSTRUCTING SHARED
MEANINGS AND TOGETHERNESS

Young children show interest into each other from an early age. "From at least as early as 2 months of age they touch one another, make noises to draw one's attention, stare avidly at an age mate, and smile" (Shonkoff & Phillips, 2000, p. 166). Often such initiations are returned in kind by the other child, thereby demonstrating the existence of social interest (Vandell, Wilson, & Buchanan, 1980). For instance Merel and Bram in a Dutch day care center:

> Merel (0;5) has a play object in her hand, but is more interested in Bram (0;5) who lies next to her on the play mat. She touches his arm, smiles, but Bram is more interested in Merel's play object. Merel holds on in trying to catch Bram's attention. She lightly touches his hand and face. Then Bram looks at her, and Merel and Bram produce shining smiles to each other. (Singer & de Haan, 2006)

Children as young as Merel and Bram are able to make contact and to respond to initiatives of a peer. Simple series of interactions can be observed from the age of 8 or 9 months old, like rolling a ball to each other, exchange of objects, and mutual imitation. In current studies interactions between infants like Merel and Bram in the example above, are interpreted as revealing intentional acts that display understanding of other children's feelings (Løkken, 2000; Musatti & Panni, 1981; Rayna & Baudelot, 1999).

Without doubt caregivers are the most important sources of security in the life of young children. But young children in day care centers spend increasingly more time with peers. In Swiss day care centres Simoni (2004) found that, during free play, infants from 9 to 25 month old spend 39% of the time playing alone, 31% of the time involved with peers but without direct interactions (for instance parallel play), and 29% in direct interaction. In a Dutch study of 2- and 3-years-old children during free play comparable percentages are found: 43% alone, 34% parallel play, and 23% in direct interaction (Krijnen, 2006). These children play most of the time without direct contact with their teachers; only 22% of the time they interacted with their teacher (Pollé, 2006). Viernickel (2000) found that 90.7% of all interactions of 2-years-old children during free play was with peers. Kontos (1999) shows that, although the teacher spends 70% of her time involved with children, she is relatively rarely involved from the perspective of the individual child. Sometimes teachers help to sustain the interactions between young children by participating in their play (Kontos, 1999). But most of the time young children succeed in making sense of each others actions and utterances on their own (Verba, 1994).

These observations of peer interactions of children younger than 4 years old strongly contradict the earlier opinions that peer interactions at that age are diffuse and fragmented; a view that has not disappeared completely (Rubin, Bukowski, & Parker, 1998). These negative opinions of peer interactions of young children are probably related to the assumptions about "joint play." Two-year-olds don't have a plan, or don't discuss story lines and roles before they start playing. They develop the story line and often several story lines at the same time, during their play—logic-in-action. For instance Oliveira and Rossetti-Fereira (1996) show how two girls of 21 and 23 months follow different story lines during their joint play that sometimes conflict and sometimes converge. In their play you can see, among other things, fragments of a birthday singing ritual, a combing-and-washing-the-baby-routine, and the game of building up a pile of blocks and knocking it over. In the most dramatic part of this joint-play episode, Vania uses various strategies trying to involve Telma in the role of baby-to-be-taken-care-of. Vania acts as a mother in a very expressive way.

> Vania looks at Telma, smiles to persuade her and touches her in a gentle way. But she also assumes an authoritarian postural attitude, trying to force Telma into submission, and is quick to reconcile the ensuing disagreement to prevent any escalation. Telma initially remains more passive, but later on she tries to escape from the script proposed by Vania by introducing a new script of her own. At the moment of crisis, both girls look at the researcher. Telma is almost crying and seems to ask for help, while Vania produces a kind of vague smile. The researcher refrains from intervening. After a few seconds Vania gives way and for a while complies with Telma's proposal to play with the blocks. (pp. 198)

The joint play of Vania and Telma has the character of a collage and has many fragments that are unconnected. So it depends on the observers' norms and concepts how to evaluate their play—as an example of young children's lack of skills to play together, or as an example of their improvisation talent and involvement in social contact. According to Løkken (2000), the value of peer interaction studies is that the ways in which toddlers socialize are more easily recognizable, "to be valued as fully worthy social 'style,' meaningful to the children, although different and possibly appearing to be meaningless from an adult point of view" (p. 538).

Reciprocal Imitation

Although children from the age of 18 months old often use simple verbal utterances to communicate with peers—"no," "that," "ohh"—they mostly rely on nonverbal tools. They use mime, gestures, body language. A central role play is the use of reciprocal imitation: one child imitates the other and the other goes on with the imitation, or brings in new elements that lead to new series of reciprocal imitation (Camaioni et al., 1991; Rayna & Baudelot, 1999; Völkel, 2002). Most interactions of young children contain elements of imitation. By deliberatively inviting the other child to imitate, young children are able to accomplish long series of interactions.

> Jouri (2;2) puts his head between the wall and the closet, and yells, "Ohhhh!" He pulls his head back, looks at Emma (2;3). Emma does not react. Jouri puts his head again between the wall and closet, and yells again, "Ohhhh!", looks at Emma again. Now Emma reacts. She bows herself in the direction of the wall and closet, and calls, "Ohhhh"! Jouri immediately repeats his game and he laughs while he is yelling, "Ohhhh!" Then Emma changes the game. She starts clapping on the wall with both her hands, looks smiling at Jouri, but still imitates his call, "Ohhhh!" Jouri takes over Emma's new game, and a new series of interactive imitation evolve. (Singer & de Haan, 2006)

Reciprocal imitation suggests not only that a given child is socially interested in a peer to the point at which he or she is willing to copy that peer's behavior, but also that the child is aware of the peer's interest in him or her and aware of being imitated. Mutual imitation, which increases rapidly during the second year, appears to lay the basis for later emerging cooperative play, for instance pretend play (Howes, 1992; Stambak & Sinclair, 1993). See Figure 14.1 for an overview of levels of intersubjectivity and joint play in 0- to 4-years-old children.

Children's imitation is not just the copying of movements of other people, but a reflection and interpretation of the meaning of actions witnessed (Lindahl & Pramling Samuelsson, 2002). Young children use imitation as a creative tool to activate the interaction of a peer, to confirm one's wishes, and to respond to. Hanna and Meltzoff (1993) describe how infants more

1. *Simple contact:* smiling, touching, and making noises, staring at each other. From the age of 3 or 4 months (Vandell, Wilson, & Buchanan, 1980; Völkel, 2002).

2. *Simple series of interactions,* for instance exchange of objects; give and take games. From the age of 8 or 9 months (Brenner & Mueller, 1982).

3. *Simple imitation.* Child 1 imitates child 2, and child 2 is aware of that imitative behavior. So they create shared meanings. From the age of 9 months (Rayna & Baudelot, 1999; Völkel, 2002).

4. *Reciprocal imitation.* Both children imitate each other to co-construct a shared game and meanings. From the age of 9 months (Brenner & Mueller, 1982; Camaioni, Baumgartner & Perucchini, 1991).

5. *Parallel play.* Children play nearby each other with the same sort of objects. From the age of 9 months (Parten, 1932).

6. *Complementary interactions related to objects.* Child 1 adds to the activity of child 2, for instance by giving a block to help with the building of a tower. Complementary interactions increase towards the end of the second year of life (Camaioni, Baumgartner, & Perucchini, 1991; Verba, 1994).

7. *Associative play.* Children play parallel with episodes of reciprocal imitation and complementary interactions. Associative play becomes more frequent during the second year of life (Parten, 1932).

8. *Reciprocal interactions.* Growing awareness of peer's needs and interests. More frequent turn-taking when children play together from the age of 20–24 months, but few responses are related to prior topic. Peers respond contingently to each other from the age of 29 months (Eckerman & Didow, 1996; Howes, Unger, & Matheson, 1992).

9. *Early forms of joint symbolic play* from the age of 21 months. Playing the same script without integration from 25 months; cooperative play with complementary roles from 31 months. Reciprocal interactions, symbolic play and cooperative play increases during the third year of life (Howes, Unger, & Matheson, 1992; Camaioni, Baumgartner, & Perucchini, 1991; Stambak & Sinclair, 1993).

10. *Advanced and sustained forms of symbolic play* from the age of four years.

Figure 13.1.   Levels of intersubjectivity and joint play (0–4 year olds).

often imitate children of their own age than adults. Imitation for children is a natural way to communicate with peers.

Several psychologists consider imitation as central to the development of social understanding in early childhood. According to Piaget (1967), imitation fits into the general framework of the sensorimotor adaptation. He describes, for instance, how young children learn the game of marbles, first by imitating older children without understanding the rules and assimilating the observed new behavior in the old schema; they move the marbles without focusing on the "pot." Only later on do they accommodate the old schema to the new behavioral model, and follow the rules of winning and fair play (Piaget, 1932).

Meltzoff (2002) theorizes that early imitation reflects an understanding that the other is "like me" and relates imitation with early moral development. Reciprocity at first occurs in action, through imitation. Without an imitative mind, we might not develop this moral mind. This insight into the importance of imitation for the moral development is also confirmed by the studies of Forman, Aksan, and Kochanska (2004). Responsive imitation reflects a relationship in which shared values are likely to develop over time.

In short, imitation plays an important role in sensorimotor learning and communication in peer interactions in early childhood, and is a good example of the intrinsic relationships between cognitive, social, and affective processes in young children's functioning.

Emotional Dramatic Recurrent Activities and Routines

According to Thyssen (2003), early recurrent imitative activities often are "emotional, dramatic activities." In running together, jumping, falling on the couch, climbing up the slide and gliding down, taking an object and running away to be chased, and so on, children capture each other's ideas. Thyssen (2003) gives an example in the following episode.

> Mia (18 months) follows Victor into a room where you may tumble in mattresses and pillows. They crawl around in Duplo bricks and then let themselves fall down into a beanbag chair. Victor then sits down in the chair. Mia lies down on her stomach. A game begins. Victor touches Mia carefully on her back. She raises her head, looks at him, and then turns her head again. Victor laughs delightedly. They repeat the sequence in a quickly rising tempo. Victor laughing more and more. Finally, Mia tumbles down from the chair. She climbs up onto the chair again. They sit side by side. Then Victor takes hold of Mia and they tumble into each other, laughing. (p. 593)

The simple structure of the joint play of toddlers makes the meaning of the game easily clear to all participants, and is therefore easy to repeat (Vandell & Mueller, 1980). Within this simple structure, the children are understood to elaborate a common theme, and cultivating their play into "routines" (Corsaro, 1997). Most of these routines are nonverbal. An example is the "little chair routine" of Italian toddlers described by Corsaro (1997), in which every morning the little chairs were pushed by the children into the middle of the room, put in line to move upon them, jump, or letting themselves fall down in different ways. This routine was an authentic creation of the children without adult initiates. Because of the simple structure, a large number of children could participate with a fairly wide range of communicative and motor skills.

A fine example of recurrent activities in the form of music making is giving by Løkken (2000): A playful "glee concert" performed by seven toddlers in a Norwegian day care center, with no adult "conductor" present. In Løkken's words:

> What happened during 11 minutes of "making music" was the children improvising their own and very special version of well-known songs, rhymes, and play usually performed in this setting. Additionally, the children constructed playful "conversations" on the spot, among other things in the form of a "Mama-choir." Musically the sequence may be viewed as a "symphony," as experiencing "melting together of simultaneously jingling sounds." (p.536)

According to Løkken this sharing of the other's flux of experiences results in the experience of the "We" which is at the foundation of all possible communication. Probably, the repeated activities and co-constructed procedural knowledge lays the foundation of shared cognitive-affective structure. As van Emde et al. (1991) already stated, emotional experiences are remembered as procedural, sensorimotor, knowledge in early childhood.

Humor and Laughter

As we have seen in our examples, succeeding in making contact often evokes a bright smile as in the case of Merel and Bram, or delighted laughter in the case of Mia and Victor. In studies of peer interactions of young children, researchers often mention the children's joy and laughter in joint play. Humor seems to be an important tool for young children to feel and construct togetherness, as well as to feel agency of the self and to test limits and boundaries in social relationships (Loizou, 2005). This becomes clear when we look at when and why children laugh and smile. During free play of 2- and 3-years-old children in Dutch child care centers, the children seldom laughed or smiled when playing alone; only in 4% in the humorous episodes that were collected. So laughing and smiling seems predominant behavior in social situations in young children. They most often laughed during physical play, such as running and jumping, and during pretend play (Bartholomeus, 2006; see also Løkken, 2000). Loizou (2005) found in her study of children between 15 and 30 months old in a day care center on Cyprus two broad reasons why young children laugh. Firstly, the children tend to laugh about the unexpected and incongruence. She calls this the *theory of the absurd.* This theory explains the joy because the events are a mismatch from the children's world and do not fit their existing schemata (e.g., funny gestures, sounds or words, incongruous actions, and incongruous use of objects). Laughing about the incongruity of an event is also found in other studies (see Bartholomeus, 2006; Burt & Sagawara, 1988; McGhee & Chapman, 1980). An example of a funny gesture is:

> Katie and Akiko are at the table. Katie drops something on the floor and says, "Oh my!" using her hand to touch her head and smiles. Akiko looks at her, smiles and repeats, "Oh my!" Katie and the caregiver look at Akiko and laugh. Akiko goes on to repeat the action. She vocalizes and uses her hand to touch her face and head, laughs out loud looking at Katie and the caregiver. (Loizou, 2005, p. 48)

Burt & Sagawara (1988) present the following example of incongruous labeling of objects and event in 2- to 3-year-old children: "While nibbling cookies around the snack table, Trina presents her chewed cookie and says, "See my shoe," then laughs, children laugh and continue to exchange information" (p. 18).

Secondly, the children tend to laugh when they violate the expectations of the caregiver. Loizou (2005) calls this the "empowerment theory." This kind of humor arises most often in the caregiver–child relationship, and sometimes with several children who are "naughty." At an early age challenging adult authority starts to be a source of humor and laughter (Burt & Sagawara, 1988). Corsaro (1997) gives several examples of pleasure and excitement related to power and control over the authority of the teachers, for instance during the "little chairs" routine that we mentioned earlier. When the children start jumping down from the chairs and pretending to fall, sometimes a child hurt him/herself. In the case someone is hurt a "little bit," they hesitate to ask help from adults, but console each other. They know the teachers' ambivalence towards the game because of safety reasons. But they love the excitement and adventure.

In the study of free play in the Dutch day care centers we did not find laughter because of violating the teacher's rules; neither did we find laughter to tease or hurt another child (Bartholomeus, 2006). But a third reason for laughter was found that closely related to the recurrent activities during joint play. Children not only laugh because of an incongruity, but also because of a congruency; that is, when something fits into their expectations. Good examples are peek-a-boo and pretending to fall. Maybe the children laugh because the fulfilling of a prophecy leads to a feeling of agency and empowerment in young children.

Verbal Means to Co-Construct Togetherness

When language comes in children's life, reciprocal imitation and recurrent activities remain important tools to share their world. From then on, their nonverbal co-acting sequences alternate with verbal chants, which may last huge periods of time as Dunn (1988, p. 112) shows for a child of 24 months who plays a forty minute *"loola loola loola"* chanting-laughing-prancing game with an older child. The "glee concert" that we earlier quoted from Løkken (2000), is also a good example. Children's sensitivity to the playful potential of the sounds of language can be seen in the *"pat-tojaaaaaaaa, pattojpattojpattoja"* imitation and variation of Doenja and Hind in the introductory vignette of this chapter, which was only a small part of a long rhythmic verse. But not only sounds, also words, phrases, and whole sentences become tools to co-construct togetherness for toddlers and pre-schoolers (de Haan & Singer, 2003). In the analysis of peer talk of two dyads, Katz (2004) found a 65 percentage of repetition utterances during a painting episode. She, too, emphasizes the function of this kind of imita-tion "to establish copresence, joint attention, and shared or agreed-upon knowledge that cemented the dyad" (p. 341).

De Haan and Singer (2001) have applied the taxonomy of Brown & Levinson (1987) to explain the choice of strategies which adults use when they wish to satisfy their desire for freedom of action and at the same time want to maintain good relationships. For the "desire of relationship," the model distinguishes three dimensions: (a) the expression of "common ground" in attitudes and knowledge, (b) the expression of cooperation, and (c) the fulfilling of the needs and desires of the other. With regard to the first dimension, the expression of common ground, de Haan & Singer (2001) also found that imitation is a powerful tool of children to communi-cate their membership of the same in-group. Other ways to express com-mon ground is the use of nicknames, jokes and "dirty words," and especially the explicit labeling of sameness like Randa's (2;7): "We're all eating together," or the use of, "me too," as in conversations like those of Bob (2;10) and Cas (3;2):

> Bob: I'm a monkey.
> Cas: I'm a monkey too.
> Bob: You're a monkey too. . .

Further, young children often explicitly label or refer to the friendship, as the following example shows.

> Cas (3;5): You're my friend, aren't you?
> Emma (2;8): Yes.
> Cas: And Bob is my friend too.
> Emma: I'm, I'm, I'm Leanne's friend too.

Relating to the second dimension, the expression of cooperation, chil-dren may communicate common desires and goals in offering something to the other, or when they promise something. Another way to index unity in play is the use of language forms like *let's*, and the pronoun *we* as in the example in which Cas steps up to Bob:

> Bob: Stepping together!
> Cas: Yaa.
> Bob: We'll do it like this!

Relational talk is further to be seen in proposals to cooperate to play "would you like...", in which the child inquires for the other child's wants and in the verbalization of play continuity. In pretend play in particular, in which children co-construct a shared "reality," their use of connectives, lexical cohesive devices, and parallelism in constructions sustain each others' contribution.

Finally, regarding the third dimension, the fulfilling of the needs and desires of the other, children offer help, express compassion "What happened to Noortje?", and comfort other children. Sometimes they express social understanding, as in an example of Cas (3;1), who offers a back seat on his tricycle to a moody Vera, "You may sit here!" Children may also support another child in conflict and repair the relationship afterwards (Verbeek et al., 2000).

In using this relational talk, children may co-construct particular relational styles. Katz (2004) shows that relational styles are not a matter of personal traits of an individual child, but the results of dyadic interactions. She shows how Elisabeth (2;10) varies her style in playing with Elena (2;9) or with Nina (2;9). Elisabeth and Elena co-construct a "narrative style" in their joint play, full of descriptions of what they are going to do or are doing, explicitly bringing in topics and, by continuing them, reinforcing their intersubjectivity. Together they build up a narration of their actions. However, with Nina, Elisabeth makes a humorous game out of their conversations. Phonological inventiveness, rhyming "puzzle, fuzzle," invention of nonsense words, violation of semantic categories in silly talk like, "Would you like to eat some paint?" Dramatic enactment of strong emotions, high pitched voices, laughter, and a ritualized use of asking silly questions make up the "humor style" of these young girls. Both dyads often use repetition, but in different ways: Elisabeth and Elena's repetition is the basis for further improvisation and elaboration of their narrative, while Elisabeth and Nina's repetition is the focus of joke exchange:

> Nina: [yells] Would you like some veeda?
> Adult: Some veeda?
> Elizabeth: [laughing] Would you like some geeda?
> Nina: [laughing] Would you like some geeda?
> Elisabeth: [laughing] Would you like some feeda?"
> (Katz, 2004, p. 342)

CONFLICTS, RECONCILIATION, AND
CO-CONSTRUCTING SOCIAL AND MORAL RULES

Social life in child care groups also causes conflicts in young children. Many of those toddlers who are frequently involved in conflicts with peers are the most socially outgoing (Rubin et al., 1998). In an extensive review, Shantz (1987) mentions young children playing in groups have a median number of 5 to 8 conflicts per hour. Most of these conflicts have a short duration, with a mean of 24 seconds; the majority of conflicts of 2- to 5-years-old children entailed only five turns. Kinoshita, Saito, & Matsunaga (1993) found that 3-year-olds had a number of encounters with an offensive action of a child but no resistance of the other and 22% of their conflicts were simple one or two-turn conflicts. Singer and de Haan (2006) even found that 43% of the conflicts of 2- and 3-year-old children in day care were one- or two-turn conflicts with an offensive action of one child and hardly any resistance of the other. Full-blown quarrels and aggressive acts that hurt the opponent are relatively rare (Verba, 1994). Singer and de Haan (2006) found a mean of one crisis per hour in Dutch day care centers during free play; that is, a conflict in which children show negative emotions like anger or sadness.

Recently, researchers are focused on the social functions of conflicts and on reconciliation during and after conflicts. For instance, de Waal and his colleagues propose a relationships model in which individuals are studied from the perspective of their social embeddings (de Waal, 2000; Aurelli & de Waal, 2000). According to them, the expression of aggressive behavior is constrained by a need to maintain beneficial relationships. Members of nonhuman and human groups have histories of interaction and expected shared futures. De Waal and his colleagues found that nonhuman primates and children engage in acts of "reconciliation" after a conflict. Wherever social relationships are valued, one can expect the full complement of checks and balances. Dunn (1988) has also pointed to a relationship model to account for the development of social understanding. Social development would start from the child's interest in and responsiveness to the other; the literature of the preceding paragraphs provides ample evidence for this view. With development, the children become aware of the tension between their own agency and the desires of the other; and they learn to deal with conflicting wants of self-concern and relationship with others. Butovskaya, Verbeek, Lungberg, and Lunardini (2000) have investigated the relationship hypothesis with regard to peace-making strategies of young children. It was hypothesized, that friends would be more inclined to engage in post-conflict peace making than children who were only acquaintances, since friends have a close relationship worth protecting. However, both groups of children showed comparable behavior, which leads the authors to suggest that, next to relationships, interactions as such do matter to young children, simply because the continuation of playing together is most attractive. In fact, the finding that playing together after a conflict occurs significantly more often when children played together before the conflict than when they played alone, is one of the most stable results of conflict studies (Shantz 1987; Laursen & Hartup 1989; Singer & de Haan 2006).

Maintaining the Relationship and Reconciliation

What do young children do to restore the interaction with their play-mates? Forms of reconciliation, expressed in invitations to play, body contacts, offers of objects, self-ridicule, and verbal apologies, all serve to enhance tolerance (Verbeek et al., 2000). Smiling, ignoring, and giving in are also very common strategies to prevent the escalation of a conflict (Singer, 2002; Singer & de Haan, 2006). Children under 4 years old predominantly rely on nonverbal means. But from their second year, they begin to use justifications as one of the more adaptive strategies of verbal conflict resolution. Eisenberg and Garvey (1981) show that most 3- to 5-year-olds do not accept a bare "no" opposition, and that conflicts in which children just insist and repeat their positions ("Yes!," "No!," "Yes!," "No!") lead to longer adversative episodes, and are the least successful in resolving the conflict. However, insistence is most used in this age group of 3- to 5-year-olds—they make up 40% of the strategies used. Killen and Turiel, (1991), analyzing conflicts of 3-year-olds, show that many of their conflicts ended without active resolutions; in a setting without teachers, 60% of the conflicts ended by topic dropping. Eisenberg & Garvey (1981) found that the use of adaptive strategies like countering moves and compromises, was frequently successful. An important finding is, that the children respond in a similar way to the strategies of their opponent—they often imitate the other child's behavior, by taking words, phrases, and entire utterances. This is found for adversative behavior, but also holds for the adaptive strategies. However, only 12% of all strategies were countering moves and compromises. The 2- and 3-year-old Dutch, Antillean-Dutch, and Moroccan-Dutch children in the study of Singer & de Haan (2006) also used adaptive strategies to a limited extent, in 9% of their conflicts these were nonverbal strategies, and also in 9%, verbal strategies (e.g., offering objects, making a game out of the conflict, proposing alternatives and compromises). There were no differences between the 2- and 3-year-olds in the frequency of adaptive behavior, although the strategies used and the linguistic expression of the older children was more sophisticated (de Haan & Singer, submitted). The use of these strategies may be already rather advanced at this age of 3 years. For instance:

> Otto (3;10) wants to play with the fire engine of Jim (2;0), he starts off with a proposal, "I am a fireman too!" And when Otto refuses, he says, "Can we be two fireman?" Then, during a ten minute interaction, in which Jim persists in his refusal, Jim changes from snatching to asking, "Can I go one round?", from tempting by laying his arm around Otto's neck to demanding, and from just looking appealingly to calling upon an engagement, "Together, YES?!" (Singer & de Haan, 2006)

Kinoshita et al. (1993) analyzed the strategies of young children in Japanese kindergarten at different ages, from 3;7 to 6;3 years, in more detail. They show how in the course of development, termination of the conflict without consent decreases with age. Percentages of the use of adaptive strategies (opinion sharing, explanation, use of rules, and compromise) increase from 27% when the children were 3 years old, to 31% when they were 4, and 63% at the age of 5 years. The authors emphasize the growth of verbal abilities and interaction skills, and suggest that participation in kindergarten provides a facilitative context in this respect: They show how the 3-year-olds make a progress from 13% of using adaptive strategies when they just have entered kindergarten in the beginning of the summer, to 29% in the autumn, and 37% in the winter.

Types of Conflicts, Social Rules, and the Teacher's Role

This latter finding brings us to the question about the educational implications. There is a firm consensus about the view that conflicts may be conductive in learning the social and moral rules of the environment (Piaget, 1967; Vygotsky, 1978; Killen & Nucci, 1995). In day care and (pre)school, children encounter a continuous flow of moments which confront them with conflicting wants and interests, and urge them to make social choices. These moments may be learning moments in becoming a social and moral person. However, the pedagogical context seems crucial in creating learning opportunities. The 27% of (verbal) adaptive strategies among the 3-year-old Japanese kindergarten children in the study of Kinoshita et al. seems considerably high, compared with the 9% verbal strategies in Singer & de Haan's (2006) study and the 12% in the study of Eisenberg & Garvey (1981). Peacemaking may be culture specific, but there may also be differences on the local level of the (pre)school. Killen and Turiel (1991), for instance, show significant differences between three preschools. Therefore, it may be supposed that teachers may influence children's social development, and may provide a context to learn social and moral rules.

The most frequent types of conflicts in day care are object disputes, physical encounters or irritations, entry disputes, and arguments about ideas (Shantz, 1987; Singer & de Haan, 2006). It may be worthwhile to investigate the effects of a pedagogy explicitly directed to the appropriation of the different rules related to these conflicts. For instance, in object disputes, children may learn to cope with the contrary rules of "share your belongings" and "respect another's possession," and they may learn social skills like not to snatch, taking turns, and playing together. In physical encounters, children may learn the basic moral rule of "don't hurt one another," and they have to find out the boundaries between respect for "another's physical domain," and "valuing physical intimacy." The social skills of not to intrude and to touch only when the other child agrees are very difficult for young children. Pim (3;8), for instance, hardly can understand why the other children don't like to join in his rough and tumble play. Because of his need of physical contact and his impulsivity, he repeatedly falls into minor conflicts and is frequently turned down. In entry or territorial conflicts, the opposing rules to "respect another's social domain" and the rule to "be generous and to share with newcomers" are central. Garvey (1984) pointed at three "don'ts" for successful entry: "Don't ask questions for information," "don't mention yourself or show your feelings about the group or its activity," and "don't disagree or criticize the proceedings" (p. 164). Corsaro (1997) found a number of successful play-entry strategies, reflecting the social skill to focus on the other child's frame of reference and participation structure. A funny act may also do wonders.

> Walid (3;8) fails in his first attempt in which he takes a wagon within the territory of Rahul (3;8) and Daan (3;10). Then he watches a while and laughs, and takes another wagon in saying, "This is a good one, eh? He suits into this house, look! He suits in this!" Daan responds, "Yes that's funny!" and the three boys continue playing together. (Singer & de Haan, 2006, p. 106)

Arguments about opposing ideas bring children to learn the rule to attend to another's ideational domain. Opposing ideas may be seen in all kinds of play. The most advanced form in the social domain is pretend play. To act in concert, children have to be able to coordinate their pretend acts and extend each others' contributions into a narrative (see Figure 14.1). Each turn is a move of potential accommodation or opposition. In the following example two 3-year-old girls accommodate to each other's ideas. Suzanne (3;4) knows how to use language to make sure of Sarah-Noor's cooperation, by repeating Sarah-Noor's utterances, using the tag questions, "eh?", and a mitigating "almost" in the final turn. Sarah-Noor

tries to influence the plot, and uses markers like "well" and "or so," to miti-
gate her attempts. They play that they are traveling:

Sarah-Noor: Yes, we almost are there.
    Suzanne: We almost are there already. We almost have to get off. We
             have to get off. We have to get off now.
Sarah-Noor: We are there!
    Suzanne: No, we are not yet there. We go túúút into the air. We go
             into the air once more. We are not yet there eh?
Sarah-Noor: We are almost there.
    Suzanne: We are almost there.
Sarah-Noor: Are we there?
    Suzanne: No, we are not yet there. Almost. We are there. We are
             there already.
             (Singer & de Haan, 2006, p. 110)

Suzanne and Sarah-Noor are expert players. They know how to interweave their concern for relationship with the complex requisites of pretend play. Younger children do not yet cooperate in this advanced way
(Howes et al., 1992).

Children often develop positive strategies. However, of course they may
also develop negative strategies. Jordan, Cowan, & Roberts (1995) have
shown that children who master the rule not to use physical power, may
adopt more covert alternative strategies to occupy space but which are not
liable to the teacher's disapproval. These strategies are already there in the
preschool, but in kindergarten the children develop them to a considerable sophisticated level.

Therefore, the teacher's role is crucial in creating a context in which
children learn (to co-construct) positive social rules. In a meta-analysis of
studies of the quality of caregiver–child attachments in day care group settings, Ahnert, Pinquart, & Lamb, 2006) found that group related sensitivity
of the teachers predicts children's attachment security better than the
teacher's sensitivity towards the individual child. This study underscores
the importance of studying the influence of the specific ecological characteristics of the teacher–child relationships in group settings. In this respect,
studies of enhancing a sense of belonging and security in group settings
are illuminative. As we discussed before, shared procedural knowledge is
crucial for the development of a sense of belonging between individuals.
But recursive interactions are also basic in the creation of group affiliation.
They motivate to participate in the group (Brennan, 2005; Hännikäinen,
1999). Social rules, rituals, and routines make the world predictable and
safe, and central values are communicated at a concrete level of action

(Butovskaya et al., 2000; Corsaro, 1997); for instance, rituals for consoling a hurt child or for keeping in touch with a sick playmate or teacher.

The emphasis on rituals and routines, however, should not blind us for pitfalls. Routines that are mainly based on institutional rules can make children feel powerless or obstinate, and hinders the development of a sense of agency of the child (Jones & Reynolds, 1992; Hakkarainen, 1991). Strict application of rules has a negative effect on the children's willingness to obey (Singer & Hännikäinen, 2000), and on the group climate and children's sense of security (Jones & Reynolds, 1992). Transgression of the rules is for young children a chance to experience agency, and to get personal attention of the teacher (Brennan, 2005). Humor between peers is often based on mild transgressions of the teachers' rules (Corsaro, 1997). So the teachers have to balance between room for exploration and transgressions, and providing the security of recurrent activities at group level.

CONCLUSIONS

Research of peer interaction has shown that young children are already able social beings. Their curiosity in others and their desire of communication provide them with a strong force for achieving basic social capabilities. Young children appear to be agents in creating togetherness, and they do that with their own ways of acting and talking.

Although the family context, with parents and siblings, is a rich resource to learn social and moral rules, today, day-care centers increasingly become an important environment for young children. Here, they become real little citizens in their interaction with teachers and peers. Their day-to-day conflicts teach them about ownership, inclusion and exclusion processes, respect for the physical and psychological territories, and the ideational world of others. In short, day care centers are the first public places for many children to learn about living in a democracy.

Evidence of quantitative and ethnographic research makes it clear that the focus on good relations between children is of utmost importance in group settings. The teachers' role is central, in furnishing a well-considered pedagogical structure and a favorable atmosphere to foster positive relationships. Whereas the children may find out the rules of social life themselves in experiencing that other children may have different interests, the teacher has to support their growing awareness of moral standards. Balancing between being sensitive to children's agency and mediating the social and moral rules of culture seems to be the most fruitful approach.

NOTE

1.   The child's age is stated in years and months in brackets.

REFERENCES

Ahnert, L., Pinquart, M., & Lamb, M. E. (2006). Security of children's relationships with nonparental care providers: A meta-analysis. *Child Development, 77*(3), 664–679.

Aurelli, F., & Waal F. B. M. de (Eds.). (2000). *Natural Conflict Resolution.* Berkeley: University of California Press.

Bartholomeus, D. (2006). *Peuters in Nederlandse kinderdagverblijven en humor* [Toddlers in Dutch day care centers and humor]. Unpublished master's thesis, University Utrecht, Netherlands.

Blum-Kulka, S., & Snow, C. E. (2004). Introduction: The potential of peer talk. *Discourse Studies, 6,* 291–306.

Bowlby, J. (1982). *Attachment and loss: Vol. 1. Attachment.* London: Hogarth.

Bowman, B., Donovan, M., & Burns, S. (2001). *Eager to learn: Educating our preschoolers.* Washington, DC: National Academy Press.

Brennan, M. A. (2005). *"They just want to be with us." Young children: Learning to live the culture. A post-Vygotskian analysis of young children's enculturation into a childcare setting.* Unpublished doctoral dissertation, Victoria University of Wellington, New Zealand.

Brenner, J., & Mueller, E. (1982). Shared meaning in boy toddlers' peer relations. *Child Development, 53,* 380–391.

Brown, P., & Levinson, S. C. (1987). *Politeness. Some universals in language usage.* Cambridge: Cambridge University press.

Burt, L. M., & Sugawara, A. I. (1988). Children's humor: Implications for teaching. *Early Child development and Care, 37,* 13–25.

Butovskaya, M., Verbeek, P., Ljungberg, T., & Lunardini, A. (2000). A multicultural view of peacemaking among young children. In F. Aurelli and F. B. M. de Waal (Eds.), *Natural Conflict Resolution* (pp. 243–258). Berkeley: University of California Press.

Camaioni, L., Baumgartner, E., & Perucchini, P. (1991). Content and structure in toddlers' social competence with peers from 12 to 36 months of age. *Early Child Development and care, 67,* 17–27.

Corsaro, W. (1997) *The sociology of childhood.* Thousand Oaks, CA: Pine Froge Press.

Dalli, C. (2003). Learning in the social environment: Cameos from young children's experiences of starting childcare. Transitions. *European Early Childhood Research Monograph. Series No. 1,* 87–98.

Dunn, J. (1988). *The beginnings of social understanding.* Oxford, UK & Cambridge USA: Blackwell.

Eckerman, C. O., & Didow, S. M. (1996). Nonverbal imitation and toddler's mastery of verbal means of achieving coordinated action. *Developmental Psychology, 32,* 141–152.

Eisenberg, A. R., & Garvey C. (1981). Children's use of verbal strategies in resolving conflicts. *Discourse Processes*, 4, 149–170.

Emde, R. N. van, Biringer, Z., Clyman, R. B., & Oppenheim, D. (1991) The moral self of infancy: Affective core and procedural knowledge. *Developmental Review*, 11, 251–270.

Fischer, K. W., Shaver, P. R., & Carnochan, P. (1990) How emotions develop and how they organize development. *Cognition and Emotion*, 4, 81–127.

Forman, D. R., Aksan, N., & Kochanska, G. (2004). Toddler's responsive imitation predicts preschool-age conscience. *Psychological Science*, 15, 699–704.

Frijda, N. H. (1986). *The emotions*. Cambridge: Cambridge University Press.

Garvey, C. (1984). *Children's talk*. Cambridge, MA: Harvard University Press.

Göncü, A. (1993). Development of intersubjectivity in the dyadic play of preschoolers. *Early Childhood Research Quarterly*, 8, 99–116.

Haan, D. de, & Singer, E. (2001) Young children's language of togetherness, *International Journal of Early Years Education*, 9, 117–124.

Haan, D. de, & Singer, E. (2003). "Use your words." The teacher's role in the transition from nonverbal to verbal strategies of conflict resolution. *Journal of Early Childhood Research*, 1, 95–109.

Haan, D. de, & Singer, E. (2006). *Verbal resolutions strategies of children in multi-ethnic day care centers*. Manuscript submitted for publication.

Hakkarainen, P. (1991) Joint construction of the object of educational work in kindergarten. *The Quaterly Newsletter of the Laboratory of Comparative Human Cognition*, 13, 80–97.

Hanna, E., & Meltzoff, A. N. (1993). Peer imitation by toddlers in laboratory, home, and day-care contexts: Implication for social learning and memory. *Developmental Psychology*, 29, 701–710.

Hännikäinen, M. (1999). Togetherness. A manifestation of early day care life. *Early Child Development and Care*, 151, 19–28.

Howes, C. (1992). *The collaborative construction of pretend*. Albany: State University of New York Press.

Howes, C., & James, J. (2002). Children's social development within the socialisation context of childcare and early childhood education. In P. K. Smith & C. H. Hart (Eds.), *Blackwell handbook of childhood social development* (pp. 137–155). Oxford, UK: Blackwell.

Howes, C., & Ritchie, S. (2002). A matter of trust. Connecting teachers and learners in the early childhood classroom. New York: Teachers College Press.

Howes, C., Unger, O., & Matheson, C. C. (1992). *The collaborative construction of pretend*. Albany: State University of New York Press.

Jones, E., & Reynolds, G. (1992) *The play's the thing. Teachers' roles in children's play* New York: Teachers College Press.

Jordan, E., Cowan, A., & Roberts, J. (1995). Knowing the rules: Discursive strategies in young children's power struggles. *Early Childhood Research Quarterly*, 10, 339–358.

Katz, J. R. (2004). Building peer relationships in talk: Toddlers' peer conversations in childcare. *Discourse Studies*, 6, 3, 329–346.

Killen, N., & Nucci, L. P. (1995) Morality, autonomy, and social conflict. In M. Killen and D. Hart (Eds.), *Morality in everyday life. Developmental perspectives* (pp. 52–85). Cambridge: Cambridge University Press.

Killen, M., & Turiel, E. (1991). Conflict resolution in preschool social interactions. *Early Education and Development 2*(3), 240–255.

Kinoshita, Y., Saito, K., & Matsunaga, A. (1993). Developmental changes in antecedents and outcomes of peer conflict among preschool children: A longitudinal study. *Japanese Psychological Research, 35*(2) 57–69.

Kontos, S. (1999). Preschool teachers' talk, roles, and activity settings during free play. *Early Childhood Research Quarterly, 14*, 363–382.

Krijnen, E. A. M. (2006). *Peuters in Nederlandse kinderdagverblijven. Een observatiestudie naar de invloed van sekse en leeftijd tijdens vrij spel* [Toddlers in Dutch day care centers. An observational study of the influence of sex and age during free play]. Unpublished Master's tehsis, Utrecht University, The Netherlands.

Laursen, B., & Hartup, W. W. (1989). The dynamics of preschool children's conflicts. *Merrill-Palmer Quarterly, 35*(3) 281–297.

Lindahl, M., & Pramling Samuelsson, I. (2002). Imitation and variation: Reflections on toddlers' strategies for learning. *Scandinavian Journal of Educational research, 46*, 25–45.

Loizou, E. (2005). Infant humor: The theory of the absurd and the empowerment theory. *International Journal of Early Years Education, 13*, 43–53.

Løkken, G. (2000). Tracing the social style of toddler peers. *Scandinavian Journal of educational Research, 44*, 163–177.

McGhee, P. E., & Chapman, A. (Eds.). (1980). *Children's humor.* New York: Wiley.

Meltzoff, A. N. (2002). Imitation as a mechanism of social cognition: Origins of empathy, theory of mind, and the representation of action. In U. Goswani (Ed.), *Blackwell handbook of childhood cognitive development* (pp. 6–25). Malden, MA: Blackwell Publishing.

Musatti, T., & Panni, S. (1981). Social behavior and interaction among daycare toddlers. *Early Child Development and Care, 7*, 5–25.

Oliveira, Z. M. R., & Rossett-Ferreira, M. C. (1996). Understanding the co-constructive nature of human development: Role coordination in early peer interaction. In J. Valsiner & H.H. Voss (Eds.), *The structure of learning processes* (pp. 177–204). Norwood NJ: Ablex.

Piaget, J. (1932). *The moral judgment of the child.* Glencoe, IL: Free Press.

Piaget, J. (1967). *Six Psychological Studies.* New York: Vintage.

Pollé, M. A. B. (2006). *Peuters in Nederlandse kinderdagverblijven. De rol van de leidsters tijdens vrij spel* [Toddlers in Dutch day care centers. The teacher's role during free play]. Unpublished master's thesis, University Utrecht, The Netherlands.

Rayna, S., & Baudelot, O. (1999). Peer relationships and cognitive growth during the first year of life: Educational implications. In H. Vejleskov (Ed.), *Interaction and quality. Report of the CIDREE collaborative project on early childhood education* (pp. 1–9). Dundee: CIDREE.

Rogoff, B. (1990). *Apprenticeship in thinking: Cognitive development in social context.* New York: Oxford University Press.

Rubin, K. H., Bukowski, W., & Parker, J. G. (1998). Peer interactions, relationships, and groups. In I. E. Sigel and K. A. Renninger (Eds.), *Handbook of psychology. Vol. 4: Child psychology in practice* (pp. 619–700). New York: Wiley.

Schaffer, H. R. (1984). *The child's entry into a social world.* London: Academic Press.

Shantz, C. U. (1987). Conflicts between children. *Child Development, 58,* 283–305.

Shonkoff, J. P., & Phillips, D. A. (Eds.). (2000). *From neurons to neighborhoods. The science of early childhood development.* Washington, DC: National Academy Press.

Simoni, H. (2004). Kleinkinder im Kontakt mit andern Kindern und mit Erwachsenen [Infants' interactions with peers and adults]. In *undKinder. Klein Kompetent, 23* (pp.31–44). Zürich: Maria Meierhofer-Institut für das Kind.

Singer, E. (2002). The logic of young children's (non)verbal behaviour. *European Early Childhood Education Association, 10,* 55–66.

Singer, E., & Haan, D. de (2006). *Kijken kijken kijken. Over samenspelen, botsen en verzoenen bij jonge kinderen* [Watch and see. Joint play, conflicts, and reconciliation in young children]. Utrecht: SWP.

Singer, E., & Hännikäinen, M. (2002).The Teacher's Role in Territorial Conflicts of 2- to 3-Year-old Children. *Journal of Research in Childhood education, 17,* 5–18.

Stambak, M., & Sinclair, H. (Eds.). (1993). *Pretend play among 3-year-olds.* Hillsdale NJ: Erlbaum.

Stern, D. N. (2002). *The first relationship. Infant and mother.* Cambridge: Harvard University press.

Thyssen, S. (2003). Child culture, play and child development. *Early Child Development and Care, 173,* 589–612.

Vandell, D. L., & Mueller, E. C. (1980). Peer play and friendships during the first two years. In H. C. Foot, A. J. Chapman, & J. R. Smith (Eds.), *Friendship and social relations in children* (pp. 181–208). London: Wiley.

Vandell, D. L., Wilson, K. S., & Buchanan, N. R. (1980). Peer interaction in the first year of life. *Child Development, 51,* 481–488.

Verba, M. (1994).The beginnings of peer collaboration in peer interaction. *Human Development, 37,* 125–139.

Verbeek, P., Hartup, W. W., & Collins, W. A. (2000). Conflict management in children and adolescents. In F. Aurell and F. B. M. de Waal (Eds.), *Natural Conflict Resolution* (pp. 34–53). Berkeley: University of California Press.

Viernickel, S. (2000). *Spiel, Streit, gemeinsamkeit* [Play, conflicts, and togetherness]. Landau: Verlag Empirische Pädagogik.

Völkel, P. (2002). Geteilte Bedeutung—Soziale Konstruction. In H. J. Laewen and B. Andres (Eds.), *Bildung und Erziehung in der frühen Kindheit* (pp. 159–207). Weinheim: Belz.

Vygotsky, L. S. (1978). *Mind in society. The development of higher psychological processes* Cambridge, MA: Harvard University Press.

Vygotsky, L. S. (1987). Thinking and speech. In R. W. Rieber, A. S. Carton, and J. S. Bruner (Eds.), *The collected works of L. S. Vygotsky, Vol. 1. Problems of general psychology* (pp. 39–285) New York: Plenum Press..

Waal, F. de (2000). Primates. A natural heritage of conflict resolution, *Science, 289,* 586–590.

Wertsch, J. V. (1985). *Vygotsky and the formation of the mind.* Cambridge, MA: Harvard University Press.

CHAPTER 14

SOCIAL LEARNING AS THE BASIS FOR EARLY CHILDHOOD EDUCATION

Olivia N. Saracho and Bernard Spodek

INTRODUCTION

Social learning relates to the acquisition of elements of social competence. Children are initially socialized into the family as they develop relationships with family members. They learn their roles and functions within the family as a member of that social group. The interactions within the family help to integrate the behavior and thought processes that lead to effective interpersonal relations.

Studies in social competence have focused on situation-specific behavioral repertoires (e.g., actions and behaviors that build friendships), interpersonal problem solving, role taking, and verbal self-direction and impulse control. Social competence is crucial in early childhood. As enrollment in early childhood programs has increased, young children spend a large portion of their days in groups within centers and schools.

Since the beginning of the 19th century young children's social competence has been emphasized in early childhood education programs. For example, early childhood education pioneers, like Robert Owen, Friedrich

Contemporary Perspectives on Social Learning in Early Childhood Education, pages 303–310
Copyright © 2007 by Information Age Publishing

Froebel, and Maria Montessori and education leaders such as John Dewey have emphasized the importance of young children becoming contributing members of democratic society. Several early educators and feminists (e.g., Harriet Johnson, Caroline Pratt, Elizabeth Irwin, and Lucy Sprague Mitchell) were influenced by John Dewey and created early childhood programs that were concerned with social learning and were consistent with contemporary constructivist theory. Dewey believed that children could be taught to become accomplished thinkers and rational contributors to a democratic society by helping them to actively explore their experiences in their social world. Programs were developed that reflected adult society, with children seeking information, integrating that information into concepts, and communicating these concepts in a variety of ways using a variety of media, including language. While a variety of hands-on teaching material were important to such teaching, the role of the teacher in creating a curriculum that was meaningful to the children and that was constructed with the children was central (Cuffaro, 1995).

Young children have the energy, curiosity, and imagination to act and interact within their environment. Being self-centered, however, they have a narrow and unilateral perspective of that environment. They live with their family, play with their peer group, decide how they will relate to others, how to spend their free time, whom to play with, which books to read, and even how to spend money. Young children learn about the larger social world through television and other media, travel, family, and friends. But they often lack the conceptual base to integrate the new knowledge from these experiences into what they already know about the immediate social environment. They also lack the skills to consider other perspectives in solving problems or to expect consequences from their behavior (National Council for the Social Studies, 1984).

Young children exhibit a variety of patterns of social organization. Regardless of their unique behavioral characteristics and their own unique personalities, they organize themselves over time into coherent clusters. Young children's development influences the organization of their social groups (e.g., the development of social, regulatory, communication skills). Understanding their social systems is very complex. Even in contexts such as the classrooms or playgrounds, where researchers collect detailed, systematic, and continuous data on social interactions, it is difficult interpreting the dynamics of social interactions. Researchers have developed observational coding procedures to gather data on children's social behaviors and their peer interactions. They have combined these procedures with methodologies to analyze the depth of the children's peer socialization processes. The results of these studies have reflected the social organization of the classroom and school and indicated the patterns and the processes that underlie these dynamics (Martin, Fabes, Hanish, & Hollenstein, 2005).

Young children develop their attitudes and values toward society at an early age usually outside the school setting. In the *Position Statement on Developmentally Appropriate Practice in Early Childhood Programs Serving Children from Birth through Age 8,* the National Association for the Education of Young Children (Copple & Bredekamp, 1997; National Council for the Social Studies, 1988) summarizes the literature on the developmental characteristics of children.

- *5-year-olds* need experiences for their cognitive, physical, emotional, and social development. Their interest in the community and the world outside their own can be used to extend their experiences beyond the children's self, home, and family.
- *6-year-olds* have the ability to use their verbal skills, to learn games with rules, and to learn concepts and problem-solving skills. Since they are active learners, they need hands-on experiences that give them the opportunity to test their ideas.
- *7-year-olds* have the ability to reason, listen to others, and share.
- *8-year-olds* integrate their extraordinary curiosity and their incremented social interest. They learn about people all over the world.
- *9-year-olds* tend to be self-conscious and like to work in groups rather than by themselves. Since they function at a concrete level, they can be provided with authentic experiences of society and social institutions like those in social studies.
- *10-year-olds* tend to experience changes in their body and accelerated growth spurts, which prompts frustration and anger. Usually 10-year-olds are curious and exited about settings and problems in the news. They are interested in the events that led to such problems, their location, and their causal factors. At this age level, they possess the social studies skills and can use them in these situations.
- *9- and 10-year-olds* have developed their racial and ethnic prejudices, which are very difficult to modify. Children need to learn about other cultures and holiday celebrations including families, music, shelter, customs, beliefs, and other commons of all cultures.
- *11-year-olds* are experiencing a transition period between childhood and adolescence. They are required to make many decisions. Although they are sociable, they need opportunities to communicate their feelings and opinions. Eleven-year-olds are not able to understand issues from the perspective of a whole society, although they need to respond to analytical questions about history, society, and social, and political behavior, which emerge in their social studies learning.

While the descriptions of these characteristics are simplistic, they suggest that social learning is a critical component of the early childhood education curriculum. In social studies, young children gain knowledge and are introduced to a range of opinions, which develops, affirms, and reviews their beliefs. They learn to reason and develop a sense of ethics and moral courage. These can help children become aware of the nature of social justice and begin to learn ways to create a more just society; helping to eliminate discrimination within our society (Derman-Sparks, 1987). They also learn to effectively engage in groups and learn to interact with both their peers and adults. The school setting becomes the young child's laboratory for social learning and learning about the social world. Social learning develops young children's emotional and practical competence. It offers them the means to help them overcome hierarchical, linear behavioristic learning, and enhances their democratic development.

Hein (1991) believes that theories of learning and knowledge are integrated in constructivism. He applies constructivist learning theory to both social learning theory and epistemology. Hein justifies this belief that social learning is the way individuals learn the nature of knowledge, an idea that reflects Dewey's view. He believes that social learning should focus on the learners' thinking about learning rather than on the subject or lesson that is being taught. He also believes that social learning depends on the meaning attributed to the experience that the learner or community of learners construct.

It is a personal and social construction of meaning of the bewildering and unorganized range of perceptions that are presented to them. Therefore, meaning is constructed for young children, situations are structured for them, and learning situations are provided to transmit our thoughts concerning the meaning of experience. Hein uses visitors' attitudes toward museum guided tours as an example of the persisting strain. Visitors have expressed that they often avoid guided tours at all costs. Tour guides interpret, move, and select the visitors' knowledge and learning. This example is similar to the teachers' instruction who present the world through their views and the way they want young children to construct their own world, becoming more than an intellectual way to guide the children's social learning. Hein suggested the following principles of learning derived from constructivist theory to help children to construct meaning:

1. Children are engaged in the learning process. They use their sensory information to construct meaning.
2. Children are involved in the learning process where they construct meaning and systems of meaning. For example, when children learn the chronological dates of a series of historical events, they also learn

the meaning of a chronology. Each meaning that the children construct helps them give meaning to a similar pattern.

3. Children learn using hands-on experiences, but the construction of
meaning requires an intellectual process.

4. Children use language in the learning process, which may require
that children learn in their dominant language.

5. Children learn in a social environment. They closely relate to others
(e.g., peers, teachers, family members). Children learn through interactions. Thus, the social facets of learning includes conversations,
interactions with others, and practical applications of knowledge.

6. Children learn best in a natural context rather than by accumulating
isolated facts and theories that are abstract and irrelevant from their
lives. Children learn based on prior knowledge, beliefs, prejudices,
and fears. This principle suggests that learning involves an active and
a social process.

7. Children use their prior knowledge as a basis for assimilating new
knowledge. Their prior knowledge provides children with the structure to integrate new knowledge.

8. Children revisit ideas, test them, try them, and use them over a
period of time.

9. Children need motivation to learn and understand new ideas and
knowledge.

Hein's principles of learning reflect the concept that children need to
be active in their learning process. They learn through hands-on experiences but they also have to think about what they do, which also contribute
to their intellectual development. His constructivist learning paradigm
promotes the children's cognitive development, because they actively build
their knowledge about their world. For example, in social studies children
learn skills to be able to read maps and globes. Lucy Sprague Mitchell
(1967) believed that preschool and elementary school children need to be
presented with geographic learning. Children would go on field trips collecting information that they could later use to make interpretations. She
used maps as a symbol system to teach about geography. Children learned
to read maps and to create maps, coming to understand such concepts as
location, distance, and direction as they compared their representations to
the real entities.

The National Council for the Social Studies (1988) recommends that
children learn, understand, and use locational and directional terms,
which can only be learned by actually engaging in activities where they
locate and follow directions. In social studies, children also develop abilities to learn, to make decisions, and to develop as competent, self-directed

citizens, which are shared with communication skills (e.g., writing and speaking), research skills (e.g., collecting, organizing, and interpreting data), thinking skills (e.g., hypothesizing, comparing, drawing inferences), decision-making skills (e.g., considering alternatives and consequences), interpersonal skills (e.g., understanding the others' points of view, accepting responsibility, and dealing with conflict), and reading skills (e.g., reading pictures, books, maps, charts, and graphs).

Social studies can easily be taught in early childhood classrooms, because young children's experiences in early childhood education are actually those learned in social studies. Everyday they learn (a) new social skills, (b) a new understanding of socialization levels, and (c) a new awareness of issues that relate to their experiences with families, groups, schools, communities, nations, and cultures. During the early childhood years, young children develop essential social skills, attitudes, and dispositions, which affect their social behaviors and attitudes through adulthood. They learn that they need to respect everybody and learn the social skills (e.g., collaboration, cooperation, interpersonal problem solving) to succeed in a democratic society (McLean & Moyer, 1996).

Programs for 4-year-old and 5-year-old children have been developed to teach interpersonal skills by designing alternative social strategies to solve given problems and by motivating them to think of the consequences of their actions. The National Council for the Social Studies (1984) organized the social studies content for young children around 10 large themes including:

- Culture
- Time Continuity and Change
- People, Places, and Environments
- Individual Development and Identity
- Individuals, Groups, and Institutions
- Power, Authority, and Governance
- Production, Distribution, and Consumption
- Science, Technology, and Society
- Global Connections
- Civic Ideals and Practices

The National Council for the Social Studies (1984) suggest that the content be selected based on the children's interests. In addition, the development of the theme should be based on the young children's previous experiences, developmental stages, and skills. For instance, time continuity and change for 4-year-old children might consist of a study of grandparents; whereas global connections for 8-year-old children might consist of e-mail correspondence with Australian children. The concepts drawn from the 10 themes can use inquiry-based processes to promote young children's curiosity, problem-solving skills, and knowledge of investigation. They can also motivate young children to solve classroom and school issues as well as learn about the neighborhood and community problems to understand and develop civic pride.

Social studies need to focus on self-development in a social context that includes children, teachers, caregivers, neighborhoods, and families. Personal interactions help young children understand the social world of their classroom, child care program, school, and community. For each age group—infant, toddler, preschool, and primary—social interactions develop the children's learning of their social world. Their everyday experiences modify their perceptions of themselves (such as who they are in the social world). As early as 2 years of age, the young children's experiences affect their character, which is an individual's approach to ethical issues. Ethical issues consist of decisions about honesty, fairness, courtesy, and respect for others. Toddlers in child care settings learn that they should not take a piece of banana from a friend's plate; rather they need to take pieces from the serving platter. Preschoolers share responsibility in keeping the classroom tidy and running smoothly.

Young children become knowledgeable about skills that they need both for everyday life and as a prerequisite for future learning. Their approach to the physical world is direct. They test their ideas about physical things by touching, listening, or viewing. Young children have direct contact with people and directly observe their behavior, but only the *meaning* of that behavior that is important. The outcomes of social behavior and the context in which that behavior occurs are more available. Young children need to learn to understand themselves, the world around them, and their relationship to it. They learn about themselves through feedback from the outside world when they test their powers on the physical and social worlds. They become aware of the different social contexts and attempt to understand them by defining the boundaries between themselves and their surrounding world (Spodek & Saracho, 1994).

REFERENCES

Copple, C., & Bredekamp, S. (1997). *Developmentally appropriate practice in early childhood programs.* Washington, DC: National Association for the Education of Young Children.

Derman-Sparks, L. (1987). *The anti-bias curriculum: Tools for empowering young children.* Washington, DC: National Association for the Education of Young Children.

Hein, G. E. (1991). *Constructivist learning theory.* San Francisco, CA: Institute for Inquiry Exploratorium. Retrieved November 3, 2006, from http://www.exploratorium.edu/ifi/resources/constructivistlearning.html.

Martin, C. L., Fabes, R. A., Hanish, L. D., & Hollenstein, T. (2005). Social dynamics in the preschool. *Developmental Review, 25*(3–4), 299–327.

McLean, S. V., & Moyer, J. E. (1996). Perspectives: Social studies as child's play: Social development in early childhood. *Social Studies and the Young Learner, 9*(1), 27–29.

National Council for the Social Studies. (1984). In search of a scope and sequence for social studies. *Social Education, 48,* 376–85.

National Council for the Social Studies. (1988). *Social studies for early childhood and elementary school children preparing for the 21st century.* A Report from NCSS Task Force on Early Childhood/Elementary Social Studies. Retrieved November 3, 2006, from http://www.socialstudies.org/positions/elementary/.

Spodek, B., & Saracho, O. N. (1994). *Right from the start.* Boston: Alyn and Bacon.

ABOUT THE CONTRIBUTORS

Kimberly D. Bronz is an early career research scientist and clinician at OSLC. She graduated from the University of Oregon with a doctoral degree in school psychology. Dr. Bronz's research interests include the effects of early childhood maltreatment on long-term development and the development of evidence-based interventions to ameliorate the effects of trauma. Dr. Bronz is also interested in the process of improving school functioning for at-risk populations of children by promoting the development of executive functioning, early literacy skills, and socioemotional development. Currently, Dr. Bronz is the clinical director of two clinical treatment programs including the KITS Program, and the Multidimensional Treatment Foster Care Program for Preschoolers (MTFC-P), an evidence-based treatment program serving preschool-age children in foster care.

Adriana Bus is a professor of learning problems and impairments at the Department of Education and Child Studies, Leiden University, the Netherlands. Dr. Bus published research in the areas of parent–child book reading, young children's writing development, relationship between multimedia stories and literacy development, and phonemic awareness.

Claire E. Cameron is a 2007 Ph.D. candidate in the Combined Program in Education and Psychology at the University of Michigan, Ann Arbor. Her research centers on the development of self-regulation in the early school years. Projects have included the design of observational assessments to study executive function, behavioral self-regulation, and delay of gratification, natural experiments to disentangle effects of schooling on these skills, as well as classroom observational work to discover the techniques and activities teachers use to help young children learn to control, plan, and direct their behavior in educational contexts.

Contemporary Perspectives on Social Learning in Early Childhood Education, pages 311–317
Copyright © 2007 by Information Age Publishing
311

Kimberly Dadisman is the Director of Intervention Research at the Center for Developmental Science at UNC-CH. She completed her Ph.D. in Educational Psychology at the University of Wisconsin-Madison. Her research has centered on identifying factors that contribute to participation in out-of-school settings, evaluations of students' experiences while attending after-school programs, and the role of after-school environments and extra-curricular activities on adolescent development.

Dorian de Haan is associate professor at the School of Education of the Inholland University, and at The University Utrecht, Department of Developmental Psychology. Her primary research interest is the language acquisition of children in relation to their social environment, in particular, day care and school. She is published in international journals such as *Journal of Child Language, Language in Society, International Journal of Early Years Education, Journal of Early Childhood Research,* and *European Early Childhood Education Research Journal,* and is (co)author of *Deep Dutch, towards an Operationalization of School Language* (dissertation) and *Women's Language, Socialization and Self-Image.*

Maria T. de Jong is associate professor of learning problems and impairments at the Department of Education and Child Studies, Leiden University, The Netherlands. She studies how new media (writing programs or books on CD-ROM or DVD) affect early literacy. She participates in studies that include children of different age, cultural background, and language proficiency.

Stacy DeZutter has been a teacher of children's theatre and creative dramatics for over seventeen years. Currently, Stacy is completing her Ph.D. in Education at Washington University in St. Louis, with specializations in the learning sciences and the social contexts of cognitive development. Stacy's research interests include creativity, improvisation, distributed cognition, and cultural models of teaching and learning.

Thomas W. Farmer is an Associate Professor of Special Education in the College of Education at the Pennsylvania State University and he is also the Director of the National Research Center on Rural Education Support. His work focuses on children's social development and the development of classroom social contexts that promote children's academic achievement and growth.

Gary Fertig is an Associate Professor in the School of Teacher Education at the University of Northern Colorado in Greeley, Colorado, where he also serves as coordinator for the Master of Arts in Teaching program in elementary education. Gary is a former elementary school teacher who has taught social studies to children at all grade levels and currently teaches social studies methods to preservice teachers in elementary education at UNC. He has authored numerous journal articles linking theory and research in education to best classroom practices for social studies educators at the elementary level and collaborates with teachers in partner schools to conduct action research dedicated to curriculum development in the social studies.

Philip A. Fisher is a research scientist at OSLC and a senior scientist at the Center for Research to Practice. He received his Ph.D. in clinical psychology from the University of Oregon in 1993. Dr. Fisher is interested in prevention research in the early years of life, on the effects of early stress on the developing brain, and on the plasticity of neural systems in response to environmental interventions. He is also involved in family-based prevention activities in American Indian communities. Dr. Fisher is a licensed clinical psychologist. He serves on a number of national advisory groups, including a NIDA workgroup of Native American researchers and scholars and a National Institutes of Health study section that evaluates proposals for community-based interventions. He is the principal investigator on the KITS Program efficacy trial.

Kathleen Cranley Gallagher is an Assistant Professor of Early Childhood, Families, and Literacy in the School of Education at the University of North Carolina at Chapel Hill. She worked with young children and families for 15 years, teaching and administering programs in early intervention, preschool, and kindergarten settings. Her research focuses on children's development in the context of social relationships, with the goal of improving circumstances for children who may struggle in school and social environments.

Cynthia V. Heywood is a clinician and research associate at OSLC. She is currently pursuing a Ph.D. in school psychology at the University of Oregon and collaborates in research with the Oregon Resiliency Project. Ms. Heywood's research interests include risk prevention and the development and implementation of evidence-based intervention for young children and their families particularly related to high-risk populations and children who have experienced trauma and maltreatment. Ms. Heywood is currently supervising the implementation of the play group component of the KITS Program and provides therapeutic services for children in the Multidimensional Treatment Foster Care Program for Preschoolers (MTFC-P), an evidence-based treatment program serving preschool-age children in foster care.

Carollee Howes received her Ph.D. from Boston University, completing post doctoral work at Harvard University. Since 1981 she has been a faculty member in the UCLA Department of Education where she teaches in the Applied Developmental Ph.D. Program. Her research focuses on the social and emotional development of young children.

Laura Huss is a graduate student in the School of Education at the University of North Carolina at Chapel Hill.

Bryan Hutchins is a graduate student in the School of Education at the University of North Carolina at Chapel Hill.

Abigail M. Jewkes is Assistant Professor of Early Childhood Education at Saginaw Valley State University, where she teaches undergraduate and graduate courses in assessment, literacy, and action research. Dr. Jewkes directed a NICHD and NSF-funded longitudinal investigation of children's learning in multiple contexts from preschool through the early elementary grades and conducts classroom-based research involving mixed methodologies. Her current research examines the influence of preschool on children's language, literacy, numeracy, and self-regulation development, and other interests include assessment, school readiness, and gender and cross-cultural differences in early development. Dr. Jewkes is an author of *The Ounce Scale*, an observation-based infant-toddler assessment.

Kurt Kowalski received his Ph.D. in early childhood education from Arizona State University where he studied child development and research methods. He is currently an associate professor in the Department of Educational Psychology and Counseling at California State University, San Bernardino. His research interests include the development of social identity and intergroup behavior in children, teacher beliefs, and early education.

Linda Lee is completing her Ph.D. at the University of California at Los Angeles. She is a National Head Start Scholar. Her research focuses in peer relations among children of immigrants.

Megan M. McClelland is an assistant professor in Human Development and Family Sciences at Oregon State University. She received her Ph.D. in Developmental Psychology from Loyola University, Chicago in 2002. Her research focuses on children's learning-related skills and the developmental pathways through which behavioral self-regulation and social-emotional competence influence academic and school success. She is also interested in intervention research for children at-risk for social and academic problems in preschool and elementary school.

Frederick J. Morrison is a developmental psychologist whose current research focuses on the nature and sources of literacy acquisition in children during the transition to school. His current work examines the impact of child, family, and schooling factors in shaping children's growth and in contributing to early problems in school. In one series of studies he is examining the impact of schooling by using a "natural experiment" (school cutoff) in which children who just make vs. miss the cutoff for school entry are compared on growth of a variety of skills important for school success. In another project, he is a co-investigator on the NICHD Study of Early Child Care and Youth Development. This national study has been following over 1,000 children since birth in 10 different sites around the nation, focusing on the impact of different contexts (family, child care, school) on children's psychological growth.

Amy Murray is a graduate student in Human Development & Family Sciences at Oregon State University. She is a former preschool teacher and her research focuses on how parenting and child temperament influence aspects of children's social-emotional competence.

Toby L. Parcel is Dean of the College of Humanities and Social Sciences and Professor of Sociology at North Carolina State University. Her interests are in the areas of work and family effects on child social and academic outcomes, and comparative studies of work and family issues. With Mikaela Dufur she is studying the relative effects of capital at home and capital at school on child achievement and social adjustment, and with Lori Ann Campbell she is studying the effects of family and parental work characteristics on children's home environments, child achievement, and child behavior problems in the United States and Great Britain.

Katherine C. Pears is a research scientist at the Oregon Social Learning Center (OSLC). She graduated from the University of Oregon with a doctoral degree in clinical psychology. Dr. Pears' research interests broadly include examining a number of predictors of later behavioral and social problems in early childhood with the goal of using this information to develop preventive interventions. More specifically, she is interested in the development of children's understanding of the emotions and intentions of others and how this is affected by parenting and children's early experiences and how, in turn, children's social and emotional understanding affect the development of later problem behaviors. Additionally, Dr. Pears is interested in the effects of maltreatment on children's development and on outcomes into adolescence and adulthood, and how these effects might be ameliorated by interventions. She is the coinvestigator on the Kids in Transition to School (KITS) Program efficacy trial.

Olivia N. Saracho is a professor of education in the Department of Curriculum and Instruction at the University of Maryland. Her areas of scholarship include family literacy, cognitive style, play, and teaching, and teacher education in early childhood education. She is widely published in the field of early childhood education. Olivia N. Saracho is coeditor, with Bernard Spodek, of the *Handbook of Research on the Education of Young Children,* 2nd ed. (2006, Erlbaum). They are also coeditors of the *Contemporary Perspectives in Early Childhood Education* series (Information Age).

Elly Singer is associate professor at the University Utrecht, Department of Developmental Psychology; and at the University of Amsterdam, Department of Education. Her work includes historical studies of early childhood education and care, and of the construction of "the child" in western countries (*Child-Care and the Psychology of Development,* Routledge); and theoretical and empirical studies of social, emotional, and moral development of children in child care centers and at school. She publishes in international journals like *Human Development, Early Child Development and Care, Theory and Psychology,* and *Childhood.* She was involved in international and national committees on quality day care. Recently she is leading the project Dutch National Curriculum to construct a shared pedagogical framework for child care centers for young children.

Bernard Spodek is Professor Emeritus of Early Childhood Education at the University of Illinois at Urbana-Champaign where he has taught since 1965. He received his doctorate in early childhood education from Teachers College, Columbia University, then joined the faculty of the University of Wisconsin-Milwaukee. He has also taught nursery, kindergarten, and elementary classes in New York City. His research and scholarly interests are in the areas of curriculum, teaching, and teacher education in early childhood education. Dr. Spodek has lectured extensively in the United States, Australia, Canada, China, England, Greece, Hong Kong, Israel, Japan, Korea, Mexico, Portugal, and Taiwan. From 1976 to 1978 he was President of the *National Association for the Education of Young Children,* and from 1981 through 1983 he chaired the Early Education and Child Development Special Interest Group of the American Educational Research Association. Currently, he is president of the *Pacific Early Childhood Educational Research Association (PECERA).* He is widely published in the field of early childhood education. Bernard Spodek is coeditor, with Olivia N. Saracho, of the *Handbook of Research on the Education of Young Children,* 2nd ed. (2006, Erlbaum). They are also coeditors of the *Contemporary Perspectives in Early Childhood Education* series (Information Age).

Angela M. Tomlin completed a doctorate in clinical psychology at the University of Wisconsin-Milwaukee, with research and clinical interests in multigenerational families, attachment, and the development of very young children. As the Coordinator of Psychology for the Riley Child Development Center LEND Program, she is involved in many teaching and clinical activities. Dr. Tomlin earned the designation Distinguished Infant Mental Health Mentor through the Michigan Association for Infant Mental Health in 2005. She is a founding member and current chair person for the Indiana Association for Infant and Toddler Mental Health. Dr. Tomlin is a frequent trainer for the Indiana Department of Education, Head Start, Healthy Families, First Steps (Indiana's Part C program) and many child care programs. She recently cowrote and presented material on trauma in young children in foster care for community mental health centers, foster care providers, and child protection workers through a project with the Indiana Department of Mental Health and Addiction.

Marinus van IJzendoorn is a professor of child and family studies at the Department of Education and Child Studies, Leiden University, The Netherlands. His research focuses on attachment across the life-span, and he was involved in several meta-analyses on topics in attachment and (emergent)literacy.

Shannon B. Wanless is a doctoral candidate in Human Development & Family Sciences at Oregon State University. She has a Masters of Arts in Early Childhood Education from the University of Michigan and is a former Head Start teacher. Her research focuses on the role of teachers and parents in children's development of social and literacy skills before they begin kindergarten. Shannon is conducting research in Taiwan with funding from a Fulbright Predoctoral Fellowship to clarify the nature of learning-related skills in Taiwanese preschoolers, and the roles of teachers and parents in the development of these skills.

Printed in the United States
82119LV00001B/34-36